# IMMOR TALES

## SEX AND HORROR CINEMA IN EUROPE 1956-1984

C000246654

CATHAL TOHILL and PETE TOMBS

TITAN BOOKS

**IMMORAL TALES: SEX AND HORROR CINEMA IN EUROPE 1956-1984**
ISBN 1 85286 661 6

Published by
Titan Books Ltd
42-44 Dolben Street
London SE1 0UP

First Titan edition October 1995
10 9 8 7 6 5 4 3 2 1

*Immoral Tales* copyright © 1995 by Cathal Tohill and Pete Tombs. First published in 1994 by Primitive Press. The authors have asserted their rights under the Copyright, Designs and Patents Act 1988 to be identified as the authors of this work.

Designed and typeset by Chris Brennan.
Cover designed by Chris Teather.

British Library Cataloguing-in-Publication Data. A catalogue record for this book is available from the British Library.

For a complete list of all Titan's publications, please send a large stamped addressed envelope to Titan Books Mail Order, 42-44 Dolben Street, London SE1 0UP. Please quote reference IT on both envelopes.

## ACKNOWLEDGEMENTS

The authors would like to give special thanks for their help and advice to: Jean Rollin, Jesús Franco, José Bénazéraf, José Ramón Larraz, Carlos Aguilar, Howard Vernon and Simon Birrell.

Thanks are also due to the following: Alain Robbe-Grillet, Sam Selsky, Lionel Wallmann, Jack Taylor, Tony Crawley, Nigel Wingrove (Redemption Films), Lina Romay, Mark Ashworth, Daniel J. White, Marc Morris, Tim Greaves, François Choquet, Alicia Iglesias, Antonio Mayans, Perla Cristal, Juan Amalbert, Elaine Graham, Gérard Dôle, Darren Ross, Adrian Smith, León Klimovsky, Amando de Ossorio, Karl-Heinz Mannchen, Paul Naschy, Michel Pagel and Charlotte Mordin.

Stills and illustrations are from the authors' own collections and: Jean Rollin, Mark Ashworth, Tony Crawley, BFI Stills, Posters & Designs, Charles Peltz, Juan Amalbert, José Ramon Larraz and Paul-Hervé Mathis.

Acknowledgements are due to the following companies: 14 luglio cinematografica; AIP; Ambrosiana cinematografica; Ancla Century; Aquila; Arca; Arcadeie-Madeleine; Argos; Atlas; Blackwater; Cannon Productions; CCC; Cetelci; CFF; Champs Elysées Production; Cinéma Plus; Constantin; Conti-film; Dino de Laurentis cinematografica; Edicomic; Editori del Grifo; Elite Film; Emmepi cinematografica; Essay Films; Eurociné; Fenix; Films & co; Films du chesne; Films du Griffon; Films E.G.E.; Finition; Fleuve noir; Galatea; Golden Films; Gondola Film; Hesperia; HiFi Stereo 70; Hispaniola; Impex; J.E. Films; Jörg Buttgereit; José Frade; Julia Film; Le terrain vague; Lea Film; Les Films ABC; Les Films Univers; Lisa; Manacoa; MBS cinematografica; MCA Universal; MGM; Morgana; National cinematografica; Nero Film; Nordia; Penta; Phoenix cinematografica; Plata; Productions René Château; Profilmes; R.P.A.; Rapid Films; Redemption Films; Rodiacines; Sam Selsky; Showking; Telecine; Titanus; Towers of London; Trinacra; Triton; TV13; UFA; Unité un; Vox Film; Wanguard Film; Welp; Whodunit Productions.

The front cover image shows Marianne Morris from *Vampyres* and is reproduced courtesy of Brian Smedley-Aston.

The back cover images are from *Les démoniaques* (top); *Night of the Sorceress*; poster from *Fascination*.

The authors and publishers apologise for any omissions and will undertake to make any appropriate changes in future editions of the book.

Printed and bound in Great Britain by Hillman Printers (Frome) Ltd, Frome, Somerset.

# Contents

Note: Most films are dated by the year of their release. Foreign films are listed under their original language release titles with the most common English language title following in brackets in bold type. Any further mention of the title will then be under the English language title. Exceptions to this rule are where the film is better known under its foreign language title (ie **Le frisson des vampires** rather than **Sex and the Vampire**). Where no accepted English language title could be found the film is mentioned under its original release title with an appropriate English translation following in brackets in normal type. Further mention of the film will then be under its original release title.

The following abbreviations have been used: Be for Belgium; Cz for Czechoslovakia; De for Denmark; Fr for France; GB for Great Britain; Ger for Germany; It for Italy; Pol for Poland; Sp for Spain; US for U.S.A.; Liech for Liechtenstein; Switz for Switzerland; Can for Canada, Port for Portugal. Dir for directed by; Sc for script written by; Co dir for Co-directed by.

# Introduction

'I urge you: learn how to look at "bad" films, they are so often sublime.'
Ado Kyrou, *Le Surréalisme au Cinéma*

During the 1960's and 70's, the European horror film went totally crazy. It began to go kinky—creating a new type of cinema that blended eroticism and terror. This heady fusion was highly successful, causing a tidal wave of celluloid weirdness that was destined to look even more shocking and irrational when it hit countries like England and the U.S.A.

The erotic horror boom lasted until the mid-seventies, when the arrival of hardcore films like **Deep Throat** and **The Devil in Miss Jones** made the sex-horror combination seem obsolete. As a result of these changes, many Continental low budget horror directors were forced to move sideways into the skin-flick market, where they turned out even weirder and wilder films in order to compete with the explicit attractions of porno.

The films they made were filled with outrageous scenarios and strange fantasy, drawing heavily on the same kooky material that had helped make their earlier horrors so potent. Inside Europe, audiences lapped up the weird thrills that these movies offered, causing them to become even wilder. Many of them were just too way out for overseas consumption. Too hot-blooded and intense for England and the U.S.A. Unlike earlier, sexy, European films they couldn't be marketed as art. They were too strange and disreputable for that. As a result, many of them ended up mangled by the censor, with key scenes left lying on the cutting room floor. Today many of these obscure films have resurfaced, uncut, on video, making the whole knotty area ripe for reassessment.

Over the past few years, a diverse bunch of people have made tentative steps towards mapping out this dangerous cinematic terrain: from horror fans to academics, they've all played their part. *Immoral Tales* goes one step further, providing in-depth profiles of the prime movers and combining this with a detailed historical approach. For the first time it's possible to stand back, make sense of the whole wild and woolly area, and see the logic behind these offbeat creations.

The cinematic roots of this strange phenomenon can be traced back to what the French call the 'fantastique'. If it's 'fantastique' it has to be erotic, way out and fabulous. Linear narrative and logic are always ignored in a 'fantastique' film. The pictorial, the excessive and the irrational are the privileged factors. If it does have a structure, it's the structure of a crazy dream. A dream full of potent, frightening and sometimes inexplicable images. With logic and rationality out of the way, the repressed takes the centre stage, and it's hardly surprising that the other guiding factor inside the 'fantastique' film is its predilection towards the erotic.

All the people who were prime movers on the Euro sex-horror scene were film fans. They grew up during the heyday of the early motion picture. Films such as Louis Feuillade's **Fantômas** series from the early 1910's and Fritz Lang's **Metropolis** were a major part of their cinematic diet. Many of the films they saw and loved are now forgotten. Yet their legacy lives on, revamped and reworked inside their humble sex and horror movies.

The influence of the 'fantastique' is an important one, but there were others. The evolution of the erotic horror film and its bastard offspring, the bawdy, European sex flick were influenced by the changes that happened in European low budget film-making during the 1960's and 70's. Our opening chapters document these vital developments, showing how the whole wild phenomenon grew and mutated inside Spain, Germany, Italy, France and England. This erotic revolution was also influenced by older cultural movements, drawing power from surrealism, romanticism, and the decadent tradition, as well as early 20th century pulp-literature, filmed serials, creaky horror-movies and sexy comic strips. The European horror film was unique in this respect: filmmakers had a grab-bag of high weirdness they could plunder for inspiration. What's interesting is the different way each of them was inspired by the same source material, picking up on elements that resonated with their own tastes, using them in different ways to fuel their strange sojourns into new territory.

Because of this, these bizarre flicks defy simple pigeon-holing. They're too lowbrow to be considered arty, but too intelligent and personal to be described simply as Euro-trash. They're a curious hybrid, milking the dynamism of popular literature and comic books, combining it with the perverse romanticism of real Art.

Early 'fantastique' films were more surreal than sexy, the drive towards eroticism was restrained by fear of censorship. It wasn't until the late 1950's and early 60's that sex came into the foreground as a staple element. This process

◄ (Facing page)
**The Night Evelyn Came Out of the Grave** (1971)

happened in stages. Georges Franju's **Eyes Without a Face** (1959) was a major catalyst, with its mixture of poetry, surgery and unspeakable emotions. Other similar films quickly followed —**The Head** (1959) and Jess Franco's **Awful Dr. Orlof** (1961) were the two most important. Cheaper, more irrational and pulpy than **Eyes Without a Face**, each of them played up the erotic horror aspect .... after that, the floodgates opened.

As the sixties progressed, the shackles of censorship began to break down. Mainstream films moved towards nudity and sexual suggestion, reflecting some of the breakthroughs that were happening in the bargain basement of popular cinema. Low budget film-makers were more daring than their high profile counterparts— they had to be in order to survive. Compared to the U.S. and U.K. scene, the developments in Europe were wild and untamed. The framework of the '*fantastique*' offered more opportunity for them to go sexy, get perverse and turn bizarre.

Like the surrealists, European horror directors hoped to liberate man's latent eroticism, and many of them were drawn to the low budget arena because of the freedom it seemed to offer. Inside the horror film they had a certain amount of leeway. They could indulge themselves, film things that tickled their fancy—provided they had enough nudity and strangeness to pull in the punters. In the 1960's censorship loosened, erotic license increased, and horror films became even hotter. It was during this period that the boundaries between sex and horror became blurred.

By the mid seventies the sex-horror boom was over, and low budget filmmakers were forced to move into sexploitation and porno films. This didn't mean they had to drop the horror or the kinky erotic stuff. Many of them simply reworked these elements, using them inside a more sex orientated framework. This crisscrossing of boundaries, is one of the reasons why this area hasn't been tackled properly until now. Most critics take a simple genre approach to the subject, concentrating on the horror films, while ignoring the sex flicks, and vice versa. By looking at both areas, it's easier to make sense of the whole thing, pick out who the most interesting filmmakers are, see how each of them is different—and find out what they have in common.

The main chapters focus on six filmmakers: Jess Franco, Jean Rollin, José Larraz, José Bénazéraf, Walerian Borowczyk and Alain Robbe-Grillet. The first three moved from horror into sexploitation. Bénazéraf, Borowczyk and Robbe-Grillet are not known as horror film makers, yet they're kindred spirits to Franco, Rollin and Larraz. They're all cultured mavericks. They were all influenced by the '*fantastique*', and they all dip freely into high art and vibrant, popular culture. Each of them makes movies that reflect their own personality and interests. What's remarkable about them is that they all plug into the same wide range of influences, using them to create six different types of erotic cinema.

Of the six, Franco is the most prolific. He's lived life on the run, constantly moving, constantly filming. His films are like jazz improvisations. When he's on form, they can be hot and inspiring, if he's uninterested they can be depressing and lacklustre, but most of his films contain at least one high octane scene where he cooks with both burners. These sequences are priceless, and have a spark of derailed genius about them. Some of José Larraz's output comes close to this, mainly because of its intensity. Larraz's work is more mysterious. His sexy horrors are less adventurous, more contemplative. His style is more painterly than Franco's, yet it's still passionate and fiery.

At first glance, Jean Rollin's films would seem to lack the intense emotionalism that's a hallmark of both Franco and Larraz. Yet he too deals in heightened sensations. His films are eerie and ethereal. Watching a Rollin movie is like visiting a Gothic abbey or wandering round an ancient but well kept cemetery: after a while it begins to affect you, suggesting all sorts of moods and emotions. Rollin's horror movies are poignant and personal, filled with the images and themes that fascinate him. Some people find them slow-moving, yet that's part of their charm. They look back to a romantic, doom laden past, filled with displaced vampires and uncanny beauty. Like Larraz, Rollin is attracted to mysterious situations, places and people. His best films have a bleached out intensity, a unique mood all of their own.

Borowczyk, Bénazéraf and Robbe-Grillet also make personal movies that are commercially successful because they contain sexual imagery. Each has his own way of working. Borowczyk draws on his background as an animator and painter. He makes films packed with images of old erotic implements and naughty drawings that add depth and humour to his quirky, sexy scenarios. These artifacts carry a potent charge, taking his films into mythic territory, posing questions and revealing the unstoppable nature of man's eroticism.

▲ **Mill of the Stone Women** (1960)

Borowczyk's films are stylish and highly crafted. José Bénazéraf, on the other hand, makes classy but gutsy sex films. His approach lies somewhere in between Borowczyk and Franco—he makes his movies quickly, he likes to have fun, but he still wants them to look good. His films attack and undermine conventional values; he's drawn to the erotic because of his rebellious nature, and it's this quality that makes him a blood brother to the other five directors.

Robbe-Grillet is regarded as the most intellectual European erotic film-maker. Yet Franco, Rollin, Bénazéraf and Borowczyk are also intellectuals in their own way. Robbe-Grillet's films are colder, they're more distant and cerebral. His output lacks the others' gut vitality, using pulp imagery and art in a more clinical way. Like Rollin, his films are influenced by serials, old pulps and high art, elements he handles with scientific precision, negating their mesmerising effect with his cool, dispassionate approach. He's the ultimate modernist.

These six filmmakers represent a major strand in Continental low budget filmmaking. There are others, many of whom appear in short entries in the appendix. Their sensibilities are slightly different, less concerned with pushing the boundaries of good taste and unleashing the sexual imagination by using the *'fantastique'* as a launching pad into the unknown.

*Immoral Tales* is more than just a kaleidoscopic tour of this incredible area. It's a celebration of a bygone era. A period when European mavericks threw caution to the wind and filmed unfettered fantasy. These erotic experiments are still a benchmark of the permissible—their potent reveries easily surpassing the realism of pornography.

Get ready for the weirdest film trip ever. Say goodbye to the ordinary—let your imagination soar.

EYE

# Dreamers & Decadents

Two of the most enduring of all horror myths began in dreams: Bram Stoker's *Dracula* and Mary Shelley's *Frankenstein*. The history of horror is the history of making dreams real. Of taking seriously the figments and fancies of our imaginations. To understand the hold that the fantastic has over us we must understand the sensibility that tells us our dreams are important.

Towards the end of the 18th century, in the middle of what historians call 'the Age of Reason', a re-orientation took place in both the visual and the verbal arts. In contrast to the accepted Classical styles of the day, value began to be placed on the power of the imagination to transform the commonplace. The drawings of Venetian artists Tiepolo and Piranesi showed fantastic scenes of witches and gruesome rites and Goya produced some of the most macabre work of his career. In describing his series of prints called *Los caprichos* he wrote: 'Fantasy abandoned by reason produces impossible monsters; united with it, she is the mother of its arts and origin of its marvels.'

This was the period when writers began to rediscover the old folk tales and traditions that had kept up a vibrant life of their own, isolated from the official court culture. It became important to include 'atmosphere' as a component of fiction. Dark woods and ruined castles were valued for the sense of mystery and wonder they could provoke.

In the imagination at least, the primacy of reason had been overthrown. Now what was important was how deep and powerful and affecting the products of that imagination could become. New sensations were sought after, and the old moral order was seen as a restriction to the all important search for the new. Outlaws were valued for the imagined freedoms they represented. The cult of 'genius' was born.

Byron, the archetypical Romantic hero, wrote 'The great object of life is sensation, to feel that we exist, even though in pain.' He lived a life of such accelerated physical and emotional excess that when he died, aged 36, post-mortem surgery showed him to have the body of an old man. The myth of the Byronic hero has become such a cliché of romantic fiction, it's hard to believe that Byron in fact created it himself from a synthesis of many elements current at the time. Foremost among his models were the Gothic novels and 'tales of terror' so popular during the late 18th and early 19th century.

Matthew Gregory Lewis's *The Monk* and Charles Maturin's *Melmoth the Wanderer* both tell the story of men seduced by evil and, ultimately, destroyed by it. Unlike the hero of Goethe's earlier *Faust*, which has a superficially similar theme, their ultimate aim is not the discovery of truths about themselves or the universe but, in a Byronic sense, the search for sensation. To become, as Melmoth explained, 'amateurs in suffering'.

◀ (Facing page) **Eyes Without a Face** (1959)

◀ Witchcraft and the
▲ grotesque in the art of Goya

◀ Illustration from 19th century 'Penny Dreadful'

Gaston Leroux's ▲
*La poupée sanglante*
(Top) *The Monk* ▲

This is the important difference between the doomed heroes of the Gothics and the unfortunate heroines of earlier novels such as Richardson's *Clarissa*. There, the tragedies that befall the poor wronged heiress are all in spite of her and not brought about by her own actions. In contrast Ambrosio, the Monk, willingly renounces his vows and denies his God for a taste of the alluring flesh of the seductive Matilda—in reality the devil in disguise. He knows that hell and damnation await him—but he doesn't care. He can't resist the lure of the forbidden, the joy of sensation.

The Marquis de Sade, who seems to have suffered in real life most of the misfortunes of these earlier fictional characters, forged the first link between the doomed heroines and fatal heroes of the Romantic period. And he did so by expressing a philosophy that turned the moral order of the day on its head. Quite simply, he showed that not only is vice rewarded and virtue punished, but more—this is an expression of the real nature of the world. More exactly—by doing 'evil' we are following the true dictates of a nature that is in its essence evil. His greatest frustration was that no act man could do would ever match up to the evils of nature.

By extension, true perversity is the desire to do 'good' in the world and, oddly enough, the Marquis seems to have been a reasonably benevolent sort becoming, briefly, a hero of the French revolution, raised to the post of Judge.

In his enormous novels *Justine, Juliette* and *The 120 Days of Sodom*, he catalogues all the perversions and cruelties that a fertile imagination and long periods of enforced idleness allowed him to come up with. These he intersperses with philosophical dialogues on the nature of the universe, and concludes that freedom will only come when man rises up and murders the God that he has created.

The influence of de Sade was wide, but often unacknowledged. He became a sort of talisman, a mark of honour for many of the writers of the mid to late 19th century—the so-called 'decadents'. In France, following the collapse of Napoleon's dreams of Empire and the rise of the practical middle class of merchants and traders, the artistic elite felt themselves cut off from society, useless, unwanted and lost in their dreams of a better past. They seized on anything that would challenge the small-minded morality of their times.

To them de Sade represented the highest example of man's search for truth in sensation—

outside the moral order. He showed that we could become gods by killing God. Swinburne wrote of de Sade: 'He, indeed, fatalist or not, saw to the bottom of Gods and men.'

If the outlaw aristocrat was the archetypal figure of the Romantics, then the fatal woman, destroyer of men, was the obsession of the decadents. Swinburne wrote of Dolores 'Lady of pain', and Baudelaire: 'I even love, O beast implacable, The coldness which makes you more beautiful!'

They saw her as the sphinx, as the Medusa, but above all as the vampire. Through adoration of the cold, impossibly distant and cruel woman the decadents would be led on a voyage into the furthest hinterlands of the imagination. And there was no escape. Mirbeau, in *The Torture Garden*, describes how, when the hero tells his lover Clara, that he wants to kill her to get his release, she offers up her throat to him and says "So, kill me, my sweet. I would love to be killed by you, dear heart."

Considering the contrast between the doomed, Byronic hero—seeker after new and dangerous experiences—and the cool, implacable gaze of **the sphinx-like 'vampire woman' shows the** essential difference between the earlier romantics and the decadents. The decadents were essentially passive. The prevailing mood of the decadent sensibility is one of languid contemplation—at best—or morbid stagnation at its worst extreme.

So the ultimate expression of the decadent mood is found in the huge popularity towards the end of the nineteenth century of the idea of the androgyne. This marriage in one form of the male and female was the final denial of any notion of physical or spiritual progress, and even found its political expression in the works **of the amazing 'Sar' Péladan.**

This school of 'frenetic' decadence sounded echoes in England, Spain and Italy, with each nation imparting its own particular flavour to the theme. In Italy the derivative, myth-inspired work of Gabriele d'Annunzio had a baroque and florid poetry; in Spain, through writers like Ramón del Valle-Inclán, there was a more robustly erotic tinge, with a Goyaesque feel for the grotesque and a profound sense of the 'joy' of sinning; English writers like Swinburne brought a cruelty and coldness of feeling to the theme.

As the end of the century approached, the notion that things were falling apart, that there were no certainties, took a firm hold on the imagination. This generation of the 1890's became even more profoundly seekers after sensation. They were satirised in song as:

*'Pretty boys, witty boys, too, too, too*
*Lazy to fight stagnation,*
*Haughty boys, naughty boys, all we do*
*Is to pursue sensation.'*

The decadent influence on the more popular forms of literature was subtle but unmistakable. It was most apparent in horror stories and serials. In the States, *The King in Yellow* by Robert Chambers, in Britain M.P. Shiel's *The Purple Cloud*, and in France the overheated melodramas of Gustave Lerouge (*The War of the Vampires*) and Gaston Leroux, were all profoundly marked by the influence of the decadents.

The almost mystical figure of the arch-criminal Chéri-Bibi, who featured in five of Gaston Leroux's novels, is a clear example of the new type of popular hero. Obviously he has affinities to other fictional super-criminals, such as Fantômas, but his origins and the astonishing amorality of his actions place him on a special rung. He's a loner, capable even of stealing another man's skin off his living body if it suits his plans. But still he carries within him a great sadness, always remaining true to the idealised figure of his childhood love, Cecily. He's the perfect illustration of Dostoevsky's dictum that 'the man with Sodom in his soul does not renounce the ideal of the Madonna, and in the bottom of his heart he may still be on fire, sincerely on fire, with longing for the beautiful ideal, just as in the days of his youthful innocence.'

Cinema, which had started as a sideshow novelty attraction, was beginning to take itself seriously at about this point. Looking for respectability it sought literary models, gravitating towards the big, naturalistic writings of the Zolas and the Dickenses and the biblical and historical episodes, well enough known by the majority of its audience not to need too much verbal explanation.

The dream-like quality of cinema was exploited all too rarely in those early days. **The Cabinet of Dr. Caligari**, **Nosferatu** and **Warning Shadows** are obvious examples of films that do attempt to deal with the dark subconscious, but they are largely the exceptions that prove the rule. Too often the feeling is, as Buñuel said of Fritz Lang's **Metropolis**, that there are two films—the one of magnificent, inspiring images, the other of leaden, dull, obvious ideas.

The novels and themes of the decadents were not found to be suitable subjects for adaption in the early days of cinema—at least not for 'serious' films. Only von Stroheim struggled—to the detriment of his career—to present the decadent sensibility on film. On the other hand, frenetic crime novels—in France, the *Fantômas* books of Souvestre and Allain and, in the US, the Fu Manchu stories of Sax Rohmer, found a ready road into the cinema, where they quickly established a whole range of stock characters and situations. It's from these films that we derive the mad doctors, arch-criminals, femme fatales and bland heroes that have come to haunt popular cinema down the years. There's no mistaking the sheen of a decadent sensibility in the trappings of so many of these characters—particularly the villains.

In the 1890's, the self-styled decadent artists and writers had searched for, and found, echoes of their own obsessions in such predecessors as Bosch and Arcimboldo. In a similar fashion the surrealists of the 1920's found much to admire in Poe and de Sade, but also closer to hand—in works such as the *Fantômas* books and the films made from them.

Louis Feuillade, artistic director of the French Gaumont company, was one of the first producers to exploit the public's attraction to these diabolical antiheroes. He made five Fantômas films between 1913 and 1914. Although they used series characters they were not really 'serials' in the Hollywood sense of the word, each hour long film being complete in itself. The films were quickly and cheaply made, and Feuillade was something of a genius in overcoming his budgetary limitations through astute use of lighting effects and ready-made sets.

An easy distinction can be made between the American serials, also popular on the continent at the time, and the Feuillade variety in that, rather than having a blonde-haired victim as heroine (**Perils of Pauline** etc.), Feuillade's **Les vampires** (1915 successor to the Fantômas series) had a dark-haired villainess (Irma Vep—an anagram of Vampire).

The ten episodes of **Les vampires** that appeared between 1915 and 1916 were even more successful than the Fantômas films. Again, the productions were put together in an incredibly short time, often without a script in the conventional sense. Stories made up on the spot, using real locations around the Gaumont studios, were the order of the day. As Roy Armes puts it: 'It is the improvisation and incoherence which gives **Les vampires** its power. Continually we are confronted by moments of total incongruity...unexpected deaths and resurrections, sudden car chases or rooftop pursuits, secret panels and catacombs.'

▼ **Nosferatu** (1921)

Fantômas towers over Paris ▼

Feuillade made a trip to Spain just before the outbreak of war and shot several scenes that he planned to use as local colour in a film he was working on. The commencement of hostilities put paid to the idea, but he liked the footage so much that he decided to use it in **Les vampires**. He inserted it into the narrative quite arbitrarily, framing it like a dream sequence, creating a moment of total incongruity, charged with poetry. Years later, this kind of cinematic collage would become common in the commercial underground of European cinema. Jess Franco's films abound in such moments. From **Golden Horn**, through **The Castle of Fu Manchu** and **The Fall of the House of Usher**, he practises exactly that kind of pick and mix filmmaking that Feuillade invented so unselfconsciously.

Much of the audience's fascination for Fantômas and the films that followed in his wake was fuelled by the exploits of the Bonnot gang of anarchist criminals. French newspapers were filled with stories about them.[1] But the unconscious appeal of the serials was more to do with the mood of the times. The cheap and quickly made films with their lack of continuity, their frantic and constant movement, reflected the way people experienced life, as the old order passed away and Europe moved towards uncertainty and chaos.

André Breton, founder of the surrealist movement, wrote of **Les vampires** that they reflected: 'the reality of this century. Beyond fashion. Beyond taste.' That reality is beautifully expressed at the end of the opening chapter—called 'The Genius of Crime'—of the very first Fantômas book. There had been talk around the dinner table at the Château of Beaulieu concerning the almost mythical exploits of the arch-villain. Later, young Charles Rambert wakes in the middle of the night, unaware that his hostess, the Marquise de Langrune, is being horribly murdered by Fantômas at that very moment. 'Was he dreaming or had he really awakened? He did not know. And still, still he was conscious of Fantômas—of mystery—of Fantômas.'

Perhaps Feuillade was too successful in expressing this uncertain mood. A series of anarchist inspired strikes led to **Les vampires** being banned by the French authorities for two months, and Feuillade's subsequent films—**Judex** and its successors—were considerably calmer and more conventionally structured.

The films' use of everyday locations in the streets and suburbs of Paris added to their sense of danger. As the audience left the cinemas and walked those very streets through which the masked heroes had stalked, there was always the feeling that there, around the next corner, they might stumble on the corpse of one of Fantômas's victims, or see the flapping tail end of his cloak as he disappeared down a dark alleyway. In fact, the actors who played parts in the serials were sometimes recognised in cafés and bars and huge arguments would break out between their defenders and detractors. For the first time, but not the last, the press also took sides, accusing the film-makers of stirring up dangerous emotions, of corrupting public morals with their diet of cheap thrills and violent tales.

This influence of 'place' is enormously important in explaining the appeal of the Fantômas serials and their successors: the way a mundane location, transfigured by the spirit of mystery imparted to it by a fictional story, can inspire its own peculiar poetry and set of associations. This can move the plot on from having to make the logical connections that traditional, so-called '19th century', narrative demands into a much freer and richer territory. Pulp fiction has, for a long time, taken advantage of this 'poetry of the particular', which was also cleverly exploited by Alain Robbe-Grillet in *House of Assignation* and *Project for a Revolution in New York*. Perhaps it goes back as far as Poe and his *Murders in the rue Morgue*, or Eugene Sue's *Mysteries of Paris*. Whatever the derivation, the strain runs deep. Gothic novels used a mythic version of Germany and later Italy. In the nineteenth century it was Russia, and for many European popular writers in the early twentieth century, England—specifically London—became a focus for the imagination. Jean Ray, for example, with his stories of Harry Dickson—'le Sherlock Holmes américain'—all set in a peculiarly distorted French version of England, with titles like *The Haunted House of Fulham Road*, or *The Treasure of Streatham Manor*. In this context it's significant that filmmakers as diverse as Alain Resnais, Walerian Borowczyk and Jean Rollin have all expressed a desire to film the Dickson stories.

It's still the case that many French and Italian comics, particularly those that deal with crime or horror, are set against the background of a mythic England, reminiscent of the Hammer films that often inspired them.

Another major influence—and one that was to decisively affect the post war European film industry—were the novels of the English crime writer Edgar Wallace. He began writing in 1905, at the height of the period of uncertainty that also influenced the works of Feuillade and Gaston Leroux. ' Such is the insanity of the age that I do not doubt for one moment the success of my venture', he wrote; having decided that his formula would be 'crime and blood and three murders the chapter.'

There was a German vogue for Wallace's books as far back as the 1920's, but it was thirty years before the long series of films based on them began. Originally made in black and white, and inspired by the same romanticised/stylised view of London's foggy back streets and gruesome crimes that fuelled the stories of Jean Ray, the Wallace films were immensely popular. Their cinematic antecedents may have been the films of Fritz Lang (**Mabuse** and **M**, in particular), but their use of grand guignol horror and lurking sense of sexual and moral tension puts them immediately in the same camp as the Gaston Leroux books and Feuillade serials of the pre World War One period.

Echoes from the Wallace films abound, not only in the Italian *'gialli'*[2] series that they directly inspired, but in very many of Jess Franco's early films....the bumbling police inspectors, the obscure revenge plots, even the names of characters.

The success of the series, not only in Germany but in Spain and Italy, led to a vogue for similar spin-off productions that continues to haunt the Euro film industry. Most of them are secret agent and superhero films. The French **OSS 117** and the Spanish/Italian **Superargo** are typical examples. But thanks to Edgar Wallace, horror films, and even sex films, run in series on the Continent.

▲ Poster for Feuillades **Les vampires** (1915)

◄ Karloff and Lugosi. **The Black Cat** (1934)

Obermusikmeister
Potsdam
10000 Mk.
Wer ist d
Seit Montag, dem 11. Juni ds.
Der Schüler Kurt Klawitzky und
gewesen Müllerstr.
Aus verschiedene
ähnlichen
Jahres

By the end of the 1950's, there was a distinct air of pent up momentum. After the war there had been an enormous influx of American product into Europe. Some of this was down to the very real presence of American troops in the area, but very often it was in response to a hunger from the public for something they had been denied for too long. And it wasn't just movies, it was books and comics as well. Soon a feeling grew up amongst the Masters of the new Europe that this foreign trash was having a bad effect on the minds and morals of their youth. In France, Italy and Germany there were moves to ban much of the imported US material and thereby stimulate the growth of indigenous forms.

Naturally, in the shadow of the great Holocaust that had swept through Europe only a dozen or so years earlier, straight horror films were not the order of the day. The Edgar Wallace films, in many ways quaintly old-fashioned, pointed the way. But what was needed was some method of reinvesting the old myths with new power.

All the important ingredients were already in the pot, along with the essence of the Gothic tradition and the lingering taste of the Naughty Nineties: the fatal hero, the cruel vampire woman, the frenzied worship of excess, the morbid desire for contemplation rather than action. All it needed was something to bring the mixture to the boil, to thicken the soup. Then, in 1959—right at the end of the decade, a French film-maker imbued with the surrealist tradition, in love with the serials of Feuillade and drenched in the American cinema, made a film that was to take all these elements and combine them in a way that made them all seem fresh. And in so doing was to set the agenda for the next decade with a mixture of sex, cinema and surgery that set the horror world on its ear.

◀ (Facing page) M
◀ A typical Edgar Wallace mystery

---

[1] They also inspired contemporary comic strips like Louis Forton's *La bande des pieds nickelés*. The continuing fascination for this bunch is shown by the 1978 French hardcore film **Les aventures des queues nickelées**—The Adventures of the Nickel-Plated Cocks.

[2] It means 'yellow.' A series of thrillers were published in yellow covers and so crime and murder films based on them were given the same name. Agatha Christie, Fredric Brown and Cornell Woolrich were all 'yellows' in Italy.

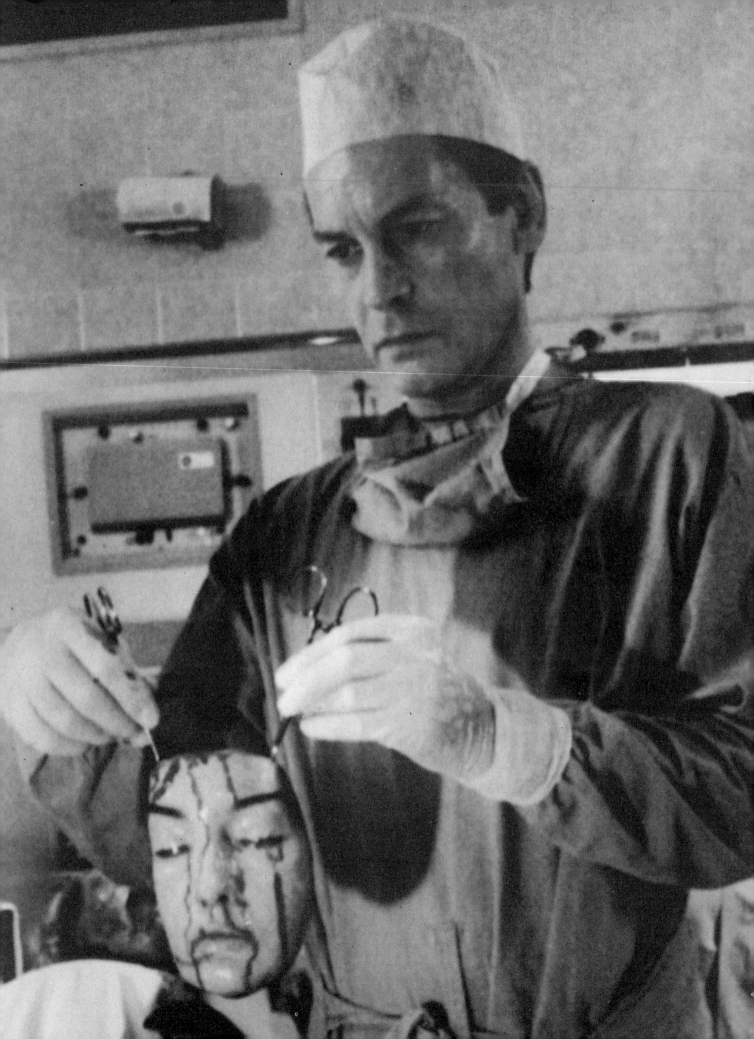

# Sex, Cinema & Surgery

'There is in the act of love a close similarity to torture or to a surgical operation' Baudelaire

None of the elements that went into the construction of Georges Franju's **Les yeux sans visage (Eyes Without a Face**; 1959) were entirely original. There had been mad—or obsessed—scientists in the cinema before; the notion of the faithful assistant who procures fresh victims was already a staple of the horror film; even the idea of skin grafts and surgery were reasonably familiar to horror fans.

But Franju, along with screenwriters Boileau and Narcejac—who went on to write **Vertigo**—took each of these ingredients and concentrated them, twisting them in the process to make the whole composition somehow askew and dangerous.

To understand fully the impact that **Eyes Without a Face** had on the popular audience as well as the critics, it's necessary to look briefly at the history of the horror film in the preceding decades.

During the early days of the silent cinema, horror themes had been used from time to time but usually as novelty items. Frequently the denouement was a rational one, with the ghosts or vampires turning out to be fakes, as in **The Ghost Breaker** (1922). Only occasionally were genuinely supernatural themes incorporated into the stories. It was in Germany, with the expressionist influenced **Nosferatu** (1921), **Der Golem** (1920) and Fritz Lang's **Der müde Tod** (1921) that the Gothic spirit of the 18th and 19th century tales of terror were used with any degree of genuine commitment.

Along with **Häxen** (1922) and **Seven Footprints to Satan** (1929) by the Danish director Christensen, these films were real attempts to deal with the fantastic and the strange by utilising the cinema's ability to show an audience its own dreams and fears. In America the dominant attitude was still one of parody or outright comedy, as in films like **The Gorilla** (1927) and the original **Cat and the Canary** (1927). Many of these were based on successful stage shows, and even the first serious attempts at *Dracula* and *Frankenstein* were based on plays rather than the original source novels.

It was not until the 1930's that horror became a recognisable genre in the cinema. A German emigré, Carl Laemmle, was the first horror specialist to emerge in the US, and by the end of the decade the main requirements and themes of classic horror had emerged. As displayed in Browning's **Dracula** (1931) and Whale's **The Bride of Frankenstein** (1935), the American model had largely abandoned the expressionist experiments of the 1920's, and stock characters and situations were quick to emerge. As an anonymous newspaper reviewer put it, in a passage quoted by John Brosnan: `Although UFA and other foreign companies revel in weird camera work, such as we saw in **The Cabinet of Dr. Caligari** and **Variety**, American audiences demand realism in their stories, and in their photography at least apparent realism. Therefore while European special effects men go in for bizarre shots, their American counterparts have only one endeavour: to make every trick shot look as realistic as possible.'

▲ **The Cat and the Canary** (1927)

◄ (Facing page) Helmut Berger in Franco's updating of **Les yeux sans visage**, **Faceless** (1988)

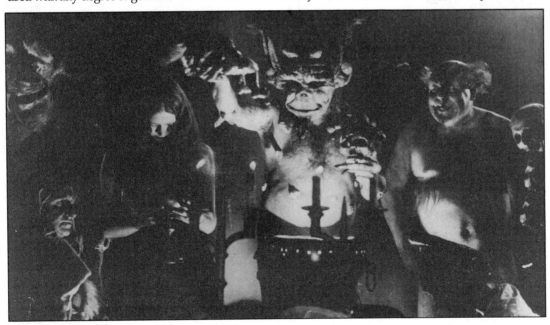

◄ Santanic Rites From **Häxen** (1922)

Actors such as Bela Lugosi and Boris Karloff were the crowd pullers, and the impact and direction of the films was derived more from the grand guignol of stage models than from the grotesqueries and frenzy of the Gothic novels. Mad doctors and obsessed scientists were popular items, giving the actors full licence for demonic grimaces and portentous utterances. Beautiful women—actresses or showgirls—were the objects of their obsessions and, as in the often filmed story of Jekyll and Hyde, the villains had two distinct sides to their nature. They would appear to the world like benign geniuses, curing the sick or making great discoveries, but down in the basement of their souls—and often literally in their basements—something terrible would lurk.

Occasional gems would emerge—**The Most Dangerous Game** (1932), for example, or **Mad Love** (1935), but by the beginning of the 1940's there was the unmistakable sense of a treadmill being pounded. Series characters—Dracula, Frankenstein (now totally identified with the monster) and the Wolf Man would be thrown together into unlikely combinations or would pop up in cameo roles in films featuring popular comedians of the time. The Ritz Brothers, Abbott and Costello and The East Side Kids all made 'horror' films that generally reused the old Cat and the Canary, haunted house type plots that had been around since the silent days.

There seemed to be a lack of genuine commitment in the American horror film, a feeling, perhaps, that the shiver of real terror was not something to be sought for its own sake, let alone manufactured in earnest.

By the late 1940's, the horror film had largely ceased to be of interest to the major motion picture companies in the US. It was left to the smaller independent 'B' producers like PRC, Monogram and Republic to capitalise on the public's continuing appetite for them. It was from these studios, too, that the long running serials emerged, where at least traces of the delirium and surreal energy of the old Gothics and turn-of-the-century romances survived. Radio, the most popular form of electronic entertainment in these pre-TV times, was also plundered for plots and characters with the I **Love a Mystery** and **Inner Sanctum** series.

An interesting throwback to the mood and spirit of the decadent nineties was provided by many episodes of Universal's series of Sherlock Holmes films, starring Basil Rathbone as Holmes and Nigel Bruce as Watson. **The Pearl of Death** and **The Scarlet Claw** (both 1944) are two particularly chilling episodes; the latter featuring a series of spectacularly gruesome 'slasher' murders that certainly prefigure films like **Blood and Black Lace** (1964) and **Blue Eyes of the Broken Doll** (1973). **Sherlock Holmes and the Spiderwoman** introduced the superb Gale Sondergaard as the eponymous spider woman, who was then teamed with Rondo Hatton, the villainous 'Hoxton Creeper' from **Pearl of Death**, in **The Spiderwoman Strikes Back**, a non-Holmes second feature full of shivery moments filmed in luminous black and white.

Val Lewton, a literate and unworldly figure of a kind rare in commercial cinema, made a series of 9 low budget but imaginative horror and terror films during the 1940s (and 2 non-horror films). These were notable for their restraint rather than any sensational elements—which Lewton himself disapproved of. Full of atmosphere and a kind of sad poetry, they are something of a detour in the history of the horror film. Although they were successful enough at the time they were soon forgotten, until a belated revival began in the 1970's, largely as a reaction to the excessive nature and literalism of much of the horror fare produced in the post-**Exorcist** period.

Dark, expressionistic elements resurfaced in main features towards the end of the 1940's in the crime melodramas and film noirs that became the key-note films of the post war period. But it was the emerging science fiction genre that soon became the staple diet of the sensationally inclined popular film. Only in Mexico, with its strong folk traditions and genuine sense of the ever-present past, were truly unselfconscious and effective horror films made. But these had little if any effect on the mainstream of mass commercial cinema. Made for a largely illiterate and critically unsophisticated audience, they remain isolated but powerful indications of the potentiality of the medium.

The first horror films had been main features, aimed at a large audience. The sequels they produced created their own genre—'the horror movie'—which, like action films, thrillers and westerns were increasingly aimed at smaller, 'specialist' audiences. This, combined with the action of censors, particularly in Great Britain, effectively drove horror films underground. However, as Barrie Patterson points out in *The Seal of Dracula*, they were not forgotten: 'opposed by the prosperous and enjoyed by the less affluent, in whose neighbourhood theatres they continued to circulate....As with most censorship the effect was the reverse of the intention...For some people such films remained

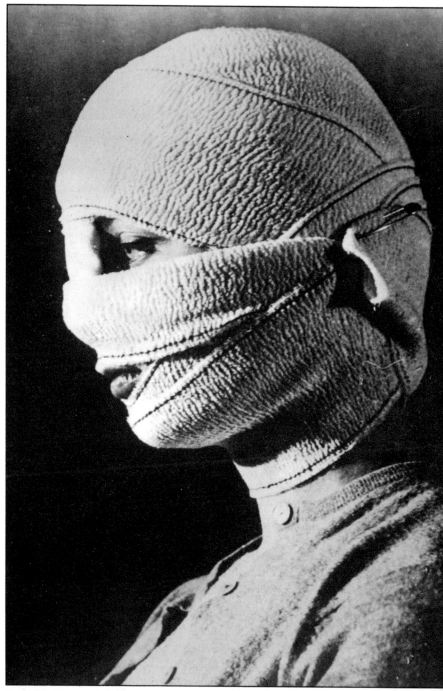

the ultimate entertainment experience of their lives. This fact was to shape the form of a new and less innocent group of films.'

The growing popularity of television was also a factor here. In 1957 Universal sold off much of their back catalogue of the 1930's and 40's for syndication to US TV stations. Many of the old 'classic' horror films began to be shown as late night programme fillers or in special horror slots. They were enormously popular with the new young audience, and also revived the older generation's fondness for the Karloff's and Lugosi's of their youth.

▲ **Eyes Without a Face** (1959)

◄ (Facing page) Boris Karloff in **The Mask of Fu Manchu** (1932)

Belgian Poster for ▲
**I vampiri** (1956)

Subtly at first, but soon unmistakably, the commercial horror film began to come back to life. In England, Hammer, who had been churning out cheap B films for years, began their successful horror cycle with **The Curse of Frankenstein** in 1957. In Germany at the very end of the 1950's two isolated examples of horror surfaced in the semi-surreal **The Head** and **Horror of Spider Island**. But predating all of these was Riccardo Freda's **I vampiri** (**The Devil's Commandment**; 1956) from Italy, a country not previously known for its horror tradition.

Riccardo Freda, like his contemporary Mario Bava, trained as an artist. His involvement in the Italian cinema began when he was called in to help with some set construction. This closely parallels the experience of Bava's father, whose first job in the movies involved the manufacturing of some sets for an early Italian epic. Bava himself vividly recalled later in his life the first scene that his father had worked on—the gates of a great tomb, filmed in the early morning mists.

Freda's cinematic models were all American—Raoul Walsh, Howard Hawks and so on. He found nothing to sympathise with in the neo-realist films of the day. "Perpetually anchored in sordid human misery", he called them. He brought to his films a real sense of the picturesque and a deep love for the traditions of narrative cinema: American cinema as seen from a European perspective. His early films were historical epics. Although shot on shoestring budgets they exhibit a lush pictorialism and warm sense of eroticism.

In 1956 Freda began work on the first real Italian horror film—certainly the first Italian vampire film—**I vampiri**.

This reworking of the Elizabeth Bathory legend set in contemporary Paris is often, incorrectly, described as having been influenced by the success of the Hammer films—**Dracula** and

The Monsters meet at the ▶
**House of Frankenstein**

**The Curse of Frankenstein**. As Freda began work on his film a good year before Terence Fisher's **Frankenstein** this would seem unlikely. Moreover, the style, approach and spirit of Freda is a world away from the cool, rational and linear approach of Fisher. Freda's background was in the fine arts, painting and sculpture. His approach to film was to cram the screen with lush detail, to create a world of languid and seductive promise. Fisher, whose long apprenticeship in film began as an editor, takes a much more measured and formal approach. The Manicheistic view that he brings to horror is radically different from that of Freda, who presents a one-dimensional but truly 'Sadean' viewpoint, in which the universe dances to the tune of his demonic protagonists, whether they be the necrophiliac Dr. Hichcock (**The Terror of Doctor Hichcock**;1962) or the beauty-obsessed Julien Du Grand (**I vampiri**; 1956)

Freda's film was not a success. Ironically, it was overshadowed by Fisher's first two Hammer horrors, leading to the practice, among Italian directors, of signing their films with English sounding pseudonyms, to convince the audience that they were about to see a film made by an American or English company. However, to compare the two styles is to see laid bare all the differences between the English models and their Continental rivals.

It lies not only in the profoundly conservative good/evil dualism of Fisher, or in the coolness of his visual style when compared with the passion and delirium of the Continental tradition, but even more in the Europeans' abandonment of dramatic logic for so called 'cinematic' logic. This is the basis of much of the criticism aimed at these films, and is related to what Alfred Hitchcock called the 'ice-box effect'. That's to say, that moment when a spectator gets home after seeing a film, goes to the ice box to get a

beer and then says "Hey, wait a minute!" And suddenly the whole structure of the film collapses in his mind's eye—he has seen the fatal flaw in its dramatic logic.

Hitchcock spent a long time trying to get around this difficulty, with his famous 'MacGuffin', and through judicious use of cinematic point-of-view. Freda, Bava et al solved the problem by simply ignoring it, or by creating circular, unsolvable plots that spiral out of control in the mind of the over-analytical viewer. The most common solution, however—and it doesn't sound like a solution at all—was to repeat the same simple plot trick in film after film until, finally, the notion of salvation through plot or resolution of the puzzle becomes a meaningless one. Plots come to consist of what Alain Robbe-Grillet, in a literary context, called 'generators'. That's to say they are launching off points for both audience and film-maker into a shared world of wonder, terror and spectacle.

This is obviously related to, but very different from, the notion of 'atmosphere' that English and American film-makers *could* understand—even if they seemed to have lost the ability to create it after the end of the 1940's.

What these 'generators' do is to open doors for the spectator into the visual structure of the films. Common reference points give the audience a sense of familiarity and free the film-maker from the need to logically underscore each plot-point. In horror terms, a film-maker like Erle C. Kenton, with his **House of Dracula/House of Frankenstein** double for Universal in the mid forties, understood the principle well. By the late fifties it seems to have been largely forgotten in the English and American film world.

Its application to European popular cinema was to create a series of visual and dramatic building blocks, around which the various stories—spy films, horror films, sex melodramas and so on could be constructed. Each would have its own points of reference, although with time these might be combined to produce a more complex structure. Variations would evolve that drew on and adapted the audience's familiarity with and expectations of the key scenes, situations—even characters—that comprised the raw material of the film-watching experience.

It's possible to trace, in a simple way, the evolution of some of these forms. For example, in the series of zombie films that grew out of the success in Italy of George Romero's Living Dead films. These became combined with already existing currents, filtered through peplums, European westerns and the so-called 'mondo' films, to create a whole new genre, that drew on documentary images of a war-ravaged Europe and a sense of a decaying colonial past, to create a very European—and specifically Italian—form: the Cannibal Movie. Another example would be the crop of Nazi films, initially inspired by the success of **Night Porter** (1973). The powerful and disturbing undercurrents stirred up by the 'generators' of this particular series became quickly out of control. A final mating with the zombie film created a third sub-genre—that of the 'Nazi-zombie' film.[1]

The inherently 'European' nature of the images and generated experiences of these films is powerfully demonstrated by the fact that it was these very genres that led to the later 'video nasty' scare in the UK. Shocked and ill-informed arbiters of the public good seemed to see this rash of appalling and dangerous movies springing ready-made out of the fevered minds of a bunch of sick subversives. There was no attempt to place them in a cultural or historical context. Because that context was entirely alien to the minds that set out to judge the films.

Why such a narrative method should have evolved in European cinema is a complex question. European culture is certainly more visually

▼ French admat for **Blood and Black Lace** (1964)

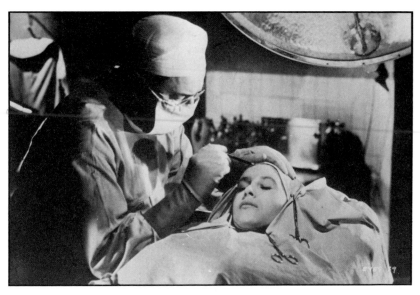

(This page and opposite) ▲
**Eyes Without a Face** ▶

oriented. Perhaps the standard of literacy was lower; maybe the influence of the iconic and religious paintings of European churches was a factor. Why, for example, has the comic book evolved into the sophisticated 'adult' form that it has in Italy, France and Spain? Perhaps the preponderance of badly-dubbed American movies led the audience to concentrate more on the visual logic of the films than on the verbal logic of the plot. There's no simple answer, but the difference is there for anyone to see.

The commercial dominance of the American product, however, was inescapable. Such that, by the end of the 1950's, when a European film-maker set out to make a horror film the sources he drew on—the 'generators'—would naturally be American ones; there was no European horror cinema.

But ...there was! The European horror cinema *was* the American horror film. The authors and architects of its original successes were largely French and German emigrés, and its heart beat, its life-blood—although now very weak and thin—were the frenzied Gothics, the languid decadents and the superheroes and criminals of the silent serials and their literary counterparts.

And, just as the British censors were unable to understand the cultural climate that created the 'video nasty', the European film-maker was uninterested in the strain of New World rationalism and 'ice-box effect' realism that the horror film had acquired in its long journey between continents. So he simply ignored it. In the process restoring the morbid desire to 'look', the Sadean delight in spectacles of cruelty, and the whole refined and sophisticated visual integrity that had been missing for 20 years. It was as though Pandora's Box had been opened

up again. The ruined castle in the forest, the Stregas and Vampires that threatened the lonely traveller, archetypal fears turned into fairy tales; in fact, the whole Gothic treasure trove that the Romantics had dug up all those years before. Now it was being dusted off and brought once more into the light of the full moon.

All of these elements had a bearing on the genesis of **Eyes Without a Face**. But Franju also brought his own approach, rooted in the surrealist tradition (itself an outgrowth of the 1890's decadent movement), and wove this so seamlessly into the story that, while the European audience watching **Eyes...** might be reminded of earlier films, such as **The Face Behind the Mask** (1941), they would also recognise the common roots of both.

It's worth remarking here on the special relationship between a horror film and its audience; the subtlety of which is often overlooked by the vast body of critics and commentators. Horror film fans make great demands on the makers of their entertainments, but they also bring a lot to the films. The relationship is a very lively and often self-conscious one. The audience likes to play games with the films. Initially it's a game of "show me your worst, I can take it", but it's also a game of searching for particular signs and symbols. For example, knowing that the spooky music means something horrible is about to happen and being disappointed when it doesn't...but also delighted; because it means that the film is playing with you, leading you along. And of course you know—because, after all, this is a *horror* film—that something horrible *will* happen. And now, just when you least expect it. Consider, for example, the way an audience follows the subtle variations on the vampire myth through the many permutations of a long series like the Hammer Draculas. The suspension of disbelief that the audience brings to each successive film is not shattered by new revelations of the vampire's power to rebirth itself. The horror audience expects something new, surprising and slightly ridiculous. As long as its trust is not betrayed, it will follow wherever the film may lead.

Often, of course, the films fail to live up to the expectations of the audience and the lurid promise of the trailers and garish posters that seduced them into the cinemas. But then, as memories of the actual film fade and its lingering images merge in the filmgoers' minds with other films and with their initial expectations, they recreate a new film in their imagination— far closer to the ideal of their unrealised expectations. This is what Ado Kyrou meant when he wrote, in *Le Surréalisme au Cinéma*, about 'the cinema that could be', and of the possibilities that it offered for a 'collective dream', composed of the banal images projected onto the screen and the fantasies of the audience as they watched them. Horror cinema presents this possibility more strongly than any other form.

In Franju's hands, the images suggested by the screenplay of **Eyes Without a Face** were woven into an allusive, poetic whole so that they seemed to acquire a life of their own, over and above the story that was developing through them. This takes us back to Buñuel's words about **Metropolis**. But now, 33 years on, and with the safety net of an audience's expectations and genre conventions to refer to, Franju had the freedom to play with that expectation and twist those conventions to produce an entirely new and unexpected type of film that yet was, paradoxically, exactly what the audience wanted. And in doing so he created one of the standards by which the whole genre was to be judged, and set in motion a whole new set of 'key' images for subsequent film-makers to borrow from, refer to, twist and subvert in their own way, exactly as he had done with his source material.

Franju tells how he met the film's producer, Jules Borkon, and was told that he was to make a horror film—but one that would not give Borkon problems with either the censor or the church. Borkon became more specific—he did not want any animals to be cut up because this would upset the English; not too much blood, as this would make the film unsuitable for a young audience; and there could be no mad doctors as this would upset the Germans, who would see references to the experiments of the concentration camps.

Franju says that, far from abandoning the project at this juncture, he welcomed these strictures. He found that they freed his creativity rather than limiting it. They gave him ideas....subversive ideas. He realised that the doctor in the film—Genessier—should not be a classic demented genius, but a normal man who does extraordinary things. That, he says, is what gives us the frisson of fear and makes us believe in the events of the film.

Next, he decided to use as co-adaptors the writers Boileau and Narcejac, because their talent was to see things always from the victim's point of view and not, as was traditional in the crime story, from the detective's or criminal's perspective.

And finally, the victim in **Eyes Without a Face** was to be Christine Genessier, the doctor's disfigured daughter. She was to move through the film like an almost silent, expressionless (because of her wax mask), and totally unearthly creature, around whom all these terrible things happen. In fact she is very much like one of the coldly beautiful and ethereal female figures in the paintings of the Belgian surrealist Paul Delvaux, whose work has so profoundly influenced both Alain Robbe-Grillet and Jean Rollin.

Christine Genessier becomes the emotional centre of the film. She helps us escape from the sordidness and horror of the events that surround her, not into unreality but into a new reality.

**Eyes Without a Face** was a widely seen and influential film. Its combination of unflinching gruesomeness, bizarre poetry and pulp imagery was picked up by a host of imitators. Some only exploited its more obvious and easily borrowed elements. But there were others who saw, in its revitalisation of the sadean and decadent tradition, renewed possibilities for their own excursions into the murky world of European horror. Meanwhile, as horror crept back into mainstream movies, another element was emerging from the margins of the film business. With the dawning of the 1960's, sex was reappearing on cinema screens. Once again, it was in Europe that the trend began.

---

[1] Particularly in France—**Zombies' Lake, Oasis of the Living Dead** and **Devil's Story**.

filmax
PRESENTA

ALDO MACCIONE
EN "EL MONSTRUO"

# FRANKENSTEIN
## A LA ITALIANA

con
GIANRICO TEDESCHI • NINETTO DAVOLI • JENNY TAMBURI • ANNA MAZZAMAURO
LORENZA GUERRIERI
dirigida por
ARMANDO CRISPINO TELECOLOR
producida por
FILIBERTO BANDINI

# The European Experience

For a good 200 years now, mainland Europe has been a fascinating and dangerous place for the English—ever since the sons of 18th century squires embarked on their Grand Tours, bringing back all sorts of odd ideas to their country estates. Then it was things Italian that were all the rage. Later, when the ideas of the dangerous decadents began to filter across the Channel from Paris, France became the byword for all things strange, exotic and immoral.

Foreign travel broadened horizons. It also led to a taste for the forbidden. In the nineteenth century, travellers would bring back nudie postcards culled from vendors in the back streets of Paris. In the 1950's and 60's Swedish films were the first to bring unashamed female nudity to the popular screen, while the street-front brothels of Hamburg and Amsterdam displayed an attitude to sex that the English hadn't even dared dream about.

One often used to read, twenty or so years ago, of films that were made in two versions. Hammer films, it was alleged, would include a bit of softcore groping for the domestic audience, while the Euro version would have full frontal nudity and orgy scenes. There was even talk of a third version, with added blood and gore, made for the Far East. This is a rumour that refuses to die, fuelled, in the first place, by Continental publicity photos of scenes absent from the English prints.

Nowadays it's denied that these versions were ever made. And, given the conservative nature of film production and pre-censorship that existed then, the stories are probably just a lively myth. But that's the whole point. It was something people wanted to believe; something that reinforced their view of the naughty world beyond Calais.

Envious, suspicious, fearful and in the end, perhaps, relieved that there was a good solid stretch of water separating us from the rest of them, the English film-going public was quite satisfied with the fare presented them by the people who knew what was best.

Or were they...?

For a brief period, during its 'swinging' heyday, London enjoyed some sort of a reputation as a sin-seeker's paradise. How this could happen in a town where the bars shut at eleven and the last train home is at midnight is a mystery. But, on the Continent the image took firm hold.

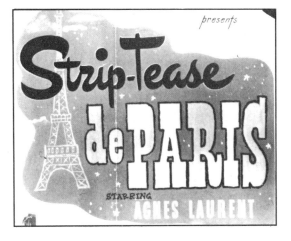

◀ (Facing page)
**Frankenstein, Italian Style** (1976)

European filmmakers exploited the idea of swinging London in a swathe of celluloid, from Antonioni's **Blow Up** (1966) to a whole series of the German Edgar Wallace films.[1] Mostly set around Soho—which seemed to stretch from the docks of the East End to Portobello Road—these films used key images such as the illuminated billboards of Piccadilly Circus or the tower of Big Ben to show that they were 'really' shot in London. British producers soon climbed onto the bandwagon and this was the heyday of the Great British X. *'Shot on location in London, England'* was the essential end-credit.

A film like **Night After Night After Night** (1969) is a classic example, with its seedy setting of Soho strip clubs, dirty bookshops and dreary suburban streets.

"Overcome it," says the psychopathic Judge—in secret a leather-clad killer of prostitutes—to his pornography-reading clerk. "Overcome it, or it will destroy you." That night, dressed in black, he creeps out into the London streets to seek another victim. Later, in his secret den, he fondles a pink bra pinned up over a huge photo of a pair of breasts.

The permissive, Swinging Sixties were in full sway by the time films like this jumped up to exploit the new freedoms. But there have always been people who want something stronger than the everyday fare that their local picture palace provides. Today, video fills that gap. In the 1960's and early 70's it was places like the Jacey cinema chain.

With a history that stretches back to the drab days of the early 1950's, the Jacey specialised in imported American and Continental films, always with the X certificate prominently displayed, and normally with a grossly overstating title—often nothing to do with the original film.[2] Frequently so hacked about by the censor that they would have to be shown in triple bills to

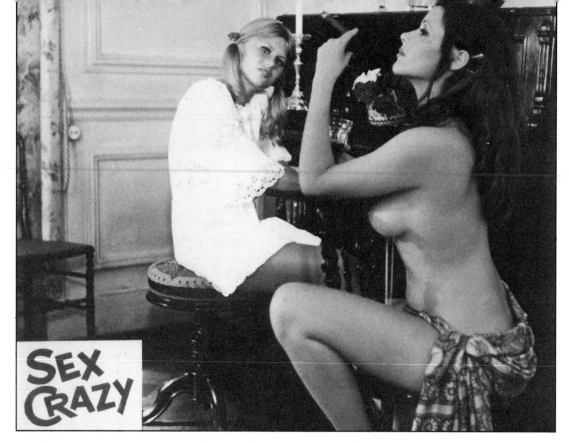

Rollin favourite Joëlle Cœur ▶ puffs it up in **Tango de la perversion** (1974)

**SEX CRAZY**

produce a decent programme length, these films became the classic fare of the dirty raincoat brigade. The Jacey's position, in the heart of Soho, gave it that magic naughty ambience essential to the complete experience of immersing oneself in sleaze.

It was in the Jacey, and its successors the Royal in Charing Cross Road, the Centa Piccadilly and the various Classics that the films of Jess Franco, Jean Rollin and the countless other French, German and Italian makers of what came to be called 'adult' films had their UK premieres. No full appreciation of their work can ignore the flavour imparted to them by the shady, twilight world of flea-pit cinema, where a film of painfully personal longing like Franco's **Les avaleuses** (in its 59 minute cut UK version as **The Bare Breasted Countess**) would be shown alongside an unashamed piece of commercial trash like **Unfaithful Wives** to an audience entirely blind to the merits of either. An audience whose only common factor was their fitful search for something 'forbidden', something dangerous—something 'European'.

The early seventies in London were, in fact, something of a golden age for the energetic consumer of what's now lovingly called 'trash cinema'. The above mentioned Jaceys and Classics led the way but there followed the Continental in Tottenham Court Road, The Biograph in Victoria (all seats 20 pence, when

£1.00 was the West End average!), and numerous local versions such as the Clapton Kenninghall and the Tollmer.

Few of these showed first-run, big releases but serendipitous discoveries were rife. A typical double bill—from the Hendon Classic in August 1972—coupled **The Queer and the Erotic**, a late flowering of the Mondo genre from Marcello Avallone, with **The Road To Corinth** —a rare Chabrol from 1967.

Then there were the late night showings. From the same week in 1972, the Stamford Hill Odeon had **Horror of Party Beach** and **Curse of the Living Corpse**—a Del Tenney double bill, no less. While the Classic in Charing Cross Road had a vampire all nighter, with two Bava's and Giorgio Ferroni's now rarely seen **Night of the Devils**.

Finally there were the clubs. With no 'artistic' pretensions, these existed solely for the purpose of showing uncut dirty movies, mostly American. In the wake of **Deep Throat** (1972) there was a huge and growing market for hardcore, catered to by the likes of Cineclub 24 at 24 Tottenham Court Road and the Compton in Old Compton Street. There you could see **Blow the Man Down**, which promised 'You will behold the most provocative and perverse acts of lesbianism, rape and guttural (sic) degeneration...Includes the story of Melissa, the virgin drugged with the 20th Century aphrodisiac LSD and wantonly raped by three lesbians.'

Even the radical London Film Maker's Co-op

got in on the act with a showing of the vintage hardcore flick **Madame Butterfly**; advertised as 'one of the dirtiest, horniest and funniest movies ever made. Includes two Japanese girls sucking a British naval officer's enormous cock, while frigging themselves off at the same time, no holds-barred group bang-ups.' This was presented in a double bill with Irma and Ed Summer's Happening film **Nitch**, 'another wallop of dirt that really packed them in last time.'

What was happening in London was no more than a reflection of the wider picture. All across the world there was an opening out of the arts, a new liberalism. Youth had come to the fore in the late 1960's, now there was a harvesting of the seeds that had been sown then. The American, Jim Haynes, who had founded Edinburgh's Traverse Theatre in 1960 and later opened the London Arts Lab, published *Suck*— 'That first European sexpaper'—from a base in Amsterdam in 1969. The following year he organised The Wet Dream Film Festival, the first international platform for out-and-out sex films. A judging panel, that included Germaine Greer and underground playwright Heathcote Williams, gave the first prize to **A Summer Day**, a film that featured the animal antics of Denmark's Bodil Jensen. Haynes explained: 'What most people don't understand...is that we are not concerned with the pornographic aspects primarily, but with the libertarian concept. It is an attack on paternalism because it asks why people can't see any image they want.' In the same spirit **Deep Throat** was promoted as an 'artistic' film, becoming something of a *cause célèbre* for the chattering classes of the time.

This was symptomatic of a new explicitness in the visual arts generally. The underground and exploitation film-makers led the way, looking for loopholes in the law and riding in on the back of constitutional guarantees of 'freedom of expression.' Pretty soon, audiences demanded more. What had previously been suggested was now to be shown and the commercial cinema followed suit. Drug-taking, for example, could be featured as a casual fact and not just examined as a social problem (**Woodstock**). Wife swapping became the subject of big budget comedies (**Bob and Carol and Ted and Alice**). Russ Meyer, a director previously known for his sexually explicit and idiosyncratic comedies, was hired by 20th Century Fox and given his biggest ever budget for **Beyond the Valley of the Dolls**.

One of the roots of this new cinematic openness was the rise of international film festivals during the early 1950's. Cannes, Venice and Berlin may have been the big ones, but pretty soon any smallish resort town with hotels to fill and conference facilities to promote was in the running for its very own festival. It was at these bashes that the cream, and the dross, of world cinema was shown. Japanese and Swedish films, with their more upfront or bizarre attitudes to sex, were eye openers to many of the overseas buyers attending these new market places. As their acquisitions could be sold as 'art'—particularly if they had managed to pick up a prize or two—they enjoyed a much wider distribution and greater respect than the exploitation films that had preceded them, which had probably been just as explicit.

Male and female nudity had long been an accepted part of Swedish cinema, along with an often glum willingness to examine contemporary social and sexual problems. But there was little of the steamy decadence and downright kinkiness that characterised the output of some other European countries. In fact, as one moves towards the hot South, very different attitudes emerge. Perhaps the Swedes were so open about sex because it wasn't really that important to them. For the Italians, however, it was a whole different ball game....

---

[1] Not to be confused with the b&w programmers from Merton Park Studios.

[2] For example—**Le grand ceremonial**, based on a highly regarded play by Arrabal, became **The Weird Weirdo**, and Max Pécas's **Luxure** became **A Clockwork Nympho**.

▼ A surprise discovery for Carlo Giuffre in **Bella ricca lieve difetto fisica cerca anima gemella** (1973)

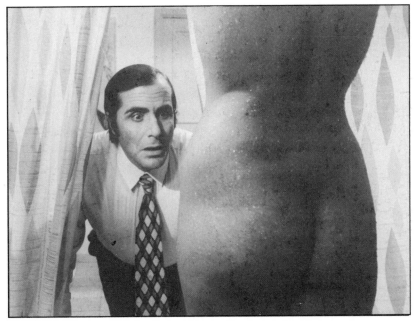

# Italian Style

## THE ITALIAN FILM INDUSTRY

The Italian film industry is one of the oldest and largest in Europe. From the beginning it has been spectacular, larger than life—a modern day version of the ancient Roman circuses, with blood, passion and spectacle. In the silent days film-makers like Mario Caserini and Giovanni Pastrone turned out huge historical epics, often based on famous literary properties—like **Quo vadis** (1912) and **La caduta di Troia** (The Fall of Troy; 1913). Cinema was a prestigious enterprise in those days. For Pastrone's **Cabiria** (1914), the famous poet Gabriele d'Annunzio was roped in to write the title cards. One of his inventions was the hero Maciste, who later went on to star in a whole series of films based on his exploits. In fact, one of the trademarks of the Italian industry—then and now—was its propensity to remake popular items. **The Last Days of Pompeii** had 4 remakes by 1926 and was remade as late as 1959.

Violence and sex were an integral part of these spectacles, with the figure of the eternal 'femme fatale' acting often as a centre-point for the unfolding of the dramatic action.

The dangerous female, who causes desire in men—provoking and destroying them, but in the process being herself destroyed... this image is common to a lot of Italian art. It's there in the operas of Puccini, in the books and stories of D'Annunzio and in the paintings of Capuletti. You'll find it in all the popular genres of Italian cinema from the mythological, through Neo-realism[1] and most obviously in violent *gialli* thrillers like Mario Bava's **Blood and Black Lace** (1964) and Dario Argento's **Tenebrae** (1982).

In her book *Passion and Defiance*, Mira Liehm traces the beginnings of the concept of the Movie Star to this eternal and equivocal sense of doomed beauty. And when one thinks of the Italian film it's nearly always of its female stars: Gina Lollobrigida, Sophia Loren, Claudia Cardinale and the many lesser lights: Silva Koscina, Rosalba Neri, Marisa Mell; earthy and ethereal at the same time, passionate and defiant. Even the 'Paper Women', the stars of the popular comic strips,[2] like Guido Crepax's *Valentina*, Magnus's *Satanik* and Angiolini's *Isabelle* had to suffer for their beauty.

The other eternal strand of the Italian film is the comic stereotype, familiar from the old days of the Commedia dell'arte and the stories of

Boccaccio: the bumbling fool, the cuckolded husband, the lustful priest. During the Fascist period that began with the rise of Mussolini in the late 1920's and lasted until his ignominious death in 1945, it was this comedic strand that came to the fore. Smoothed out and combined with a notion of aesthetics drawn from the sophisticated American comedies of the 1930's, this became the so-called 'white telephone' genre of Italian cinema.

This notion of gloss, of style above content, was put into sharp contrast by the self-styled Neo-Realists of the immediate post-war period. Drawing again from American models—the hard-boiled world of James Cain, the earthiness of Steinbeck and Erskine Caldwell—the Neo-Realists put sex back into the movies. Giuseppe de Santis's **Bitter Rice** (1949) was a huge international success, not only on account of its poignant and timely story, but above all for the figure of Silvana Mangano, skirt tucked into her knickers, full-breasted, big-lipped and openly sexual.

The Government of the New Republic was not impressed. They began to introduce laws to control the burgeoning industry, which was only just recovering from the devastation of the war years. Films were denied export licences if it was felt that they were 'slandering Italy abroad'. Even the Left got in on the act, commenting that 'breasts and legs cannot contribute to an analysis of the problems of poverty'.

As in other European countries in this post-war period, there was a move to control the vast influx of American films. Taxes were imposed on foreign films and compulsory programming

▲ (Top) Sex symbol Sylvana Mangano confronts Yorick

◄ (Facing page) Barbara Steele unmoved by **Terror Creatures From Beyond the Grave** (1966)

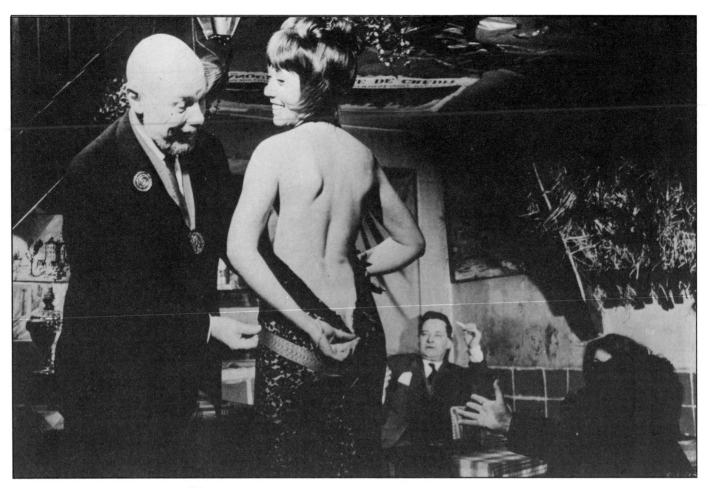

**Mondo Cane** (1962) ▲
showed life with the lid off.
**This Shocking World**
(1964) went one better

of Italian films for 80 days per year in every cinema were introduced. This had the twofold effect of reviving the local industry but also of attracting outside producers to this lucrative new market. Further incentive was provided by the unfreezing of pre-war foreign earnings for their use in local productions. The studios of Cinecittà in Rome, which Mussolini had opened, were found to be ideal and soon the city was being described as 'Hollywood on the Tiber.'

During the fifties, Italy was very much 'in'. The movies led the way, but soon Italian fashions, art and furniture followed. Italian style was the latest thing. Every English town had an Espresso bar and every spotty young Romeo had a Vespa. *"Ciao"* was everyone's way of saying goodbye and **Arrivederci Roma** made people nostalgic for a place they'd probably only heard about in the history books. *La Dolce Vita* was here.

The lure of the good life and the prospect of undemanding and constant employment drew a host of foreign stars to the walls of Cinecittà. Some, like Farley Granger, Jack Palance and Arthur Kennedy, were former matinee idols whose stars were on the wane in Hollywood. Others—like Lex Barker and Steve Reeves—made their names in the

new industry and became bona fide box office draws on the Continent.

During the late 1950's and into the 60's, under the sheltering umbrella of the big men of the Italian industry—Carlo Ponti, Dino de Laurentis and Alberto Grimaldi—the little cinema of low budget productions and high exploitation values thrived. The Historical/Mythological film made a comeback.[3] Alessandro Blasetti's **Fabiola** (1947), a remake of a 1917 production, showed the way. By 1965 there had been over 170 films featuring Hercules, Ursus, Maciste and Samson, including one featuring all four of them—**The Invincibles**. Although full of quintessentially Italian stereotypes, these films were widely exported, contributing massively to the image of Italy as a sun-drenched, fun-loving and sexy place.

Every bit as Italian as these 'sword and sandal' films were the hundreds of westerns that followed in the wake of Leone's **A Fistful of Dollars** (1964). Even the notion of borrowing an American form such as the western was a long established local custom, as the 'white telephone' and neo-realist films had shown.

In all these films sex and violence were major components. Whether it was the glistening bodies and pulchritudinous breasts (both male and female) of the superhero films, or the rape and revenge plots of the westerns, there was no getting away from it.

Stripped of its foreign influences, the Italian taste for classy sex and violence gave rise to two totally home-grown genres—the 'Mondo', and the 'Sexy'. These semi-documentaries took the local taste for the weird and wonderful to absurd limits, presided over by a tongue in cheek moralising commentary. This form of spectacular film-show has its roots in the same Roman *circenses* that underpinned the epics of the silent days. The Italians, as Mira Liehm points out, 'love to pass moral judgments in life as well as in art'. The Mondo films, with their pseudo verité display of venality, lust and plain stupidity drawn from all over the world, gave this audience just what they wanted: the chance to gawp, shake their heads in disbelief and tut disapprovingly at it all, whilst queuing round the block for the next episode.

Jacopetti's **Mondo cane** (Dog World; 1961) is probably the most famous of them all. Not only was the film widely exported, but it spawned a hit tune (*More*) and a direct sequel (**Mondo cane 2**; 1963) as well as creating a worldwide genre that continues to repel and fascinate, with titles like **Mondo Hollywood**, **Mondo Bizarre**, **Mondo erotico** and **Mondo inferno** being followed today by the likes of **Shocking Asia 1** and **2** and the **Faces of Death** series.

The 'Sexy' films were more short-lived than the Mondo form, of which they were a close relative. Elio Bartelli's **Sexy Girls** of 1960 was an early contender, but 1962 and '63 were the boom years, with **Sexy proibitissimo**, **Sexy nudo**, **Sexy a Tahiti**, **Sexy magico**, **Africa sexy**, **Super sexy 64** and **Sexy show** among many others. There was even a comedy 'sexy'—**Toto sexy**, starring the famous Italian comedy actor Toto, whose career included many such loose parodies of popular genres.

The Sexy films, like the Mondo films, were essentially documentary clips strung together, with a pompous commentary on the sound track. Originally consisting of night club and striptease numbers, they grew to include a wide variety of spectacles from around the world, chosen to typify the 'sexy' character of the countries they passed through.

But it was not only peplums, westerns and mondo films that proliferated. Swashbuckling costume dramas (**The Black Pirate**, **The Prisoner of the Iron Mask**, **Mask of the Musketeers**), horror films (**The Embalmer**, **Black Sabbath**,

Nightmare Castle), science fiction films (**The Wild, Wild Planet**, **2+5 Mission Hydra**, **Planet of the Vampires**) and spy films (**Agent OS14: Operation Poker**, **Agente Sigma 3**, **Spy in your Eye** etc.) all poured forth from the fertile spring of the Italian movie industry. Many of these were co-produced with other European countries, mostly Spain. Until the late 1960's, when the Government there decided to clamp down on the rash of cheap deals, the Spanish film industry was practically an outpost of Cinecittà.

Some of these films from the 1960's now stand as bona fide classics. Films like Mario Bava's **Black Sunday** and Riccardo Freda's **Terror of Doctor Hichcock**, both starring English actress Barbara Steele are often featured in horror critics 'best of...' lists. But there were other, lesser known, films that in their cheap and cheesy way exemplify the attitudes of the industry better than any number of classics. For example 1965's **Bloody Pit of Horror** (*See review section at the end of this chapter*).

A crossover between many of these genres was provided by the host of films based on comic book heroes and heroines of the 1960's. These mixed thrills and kills in equal measure with large splashes of low grade sci-fi. Weird machines and diabolical devices abound in these quick and colourful productions. Mario Bava's **Diabolik** (1968) is probably the most famous but it was not the first. Umberto Lenzi's **Kriminal** (1967) led the way, with its sequel **I 4 budas di Kriminal** (Kriminal's Four Buddhas) following in 1968. **Mister X** and **Satanik**, both directed by Piero Vivarelli, were camp and colourful, as was Ruggero Deodato's 1969 **Zenabel**. In the same

▲ Spanish poster for Mario Bava's **The Evil Eye** (1964)

▼ A sacrifice to Moloch in **Hercules Challenge** (1963)

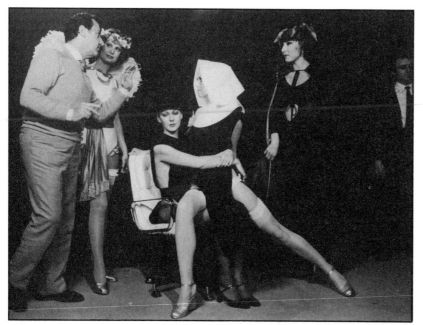

Nuns are fun in Alberto ▲
Sordi's **Il commune
senso del pudore** (1976)

historical vein as the latter was Bruno Corbucci's best film **Isabella** (1969). The strain continued well into the 1970's with Corrado Farina's **Baba Yaga** (1973), a version of one of Guido Crepax's *Valentina* stories, and as late as 1979 the optimistic Alberto Martino gave us **The Puma Man (L'uomo puma)**.

The 1960's also saw a huge rise in sexy comedies, with titles like **Sex Can Be Difficult**, **And Woman Created Man**, **Casanova 70** and **Divorce, Italian Style**. Directors like Pasquale Festa Campanile and Mario Monicelli specialised in this area, but many more—Lucio Fulci, Roberto Montero, Camillo Mastrocinque and Sergio Corbucci, for example—churned out these production line numbers with the same facility that they brought to westerns, horror films and, later, gory thrillers. As always in the Italian industry a hit film, either from Italy or from abroad, would spawn a host of unofficial sequels and outright copies.

This constant milking of successful genres, although a long standing practice of the Italian industry, spiralled almost out of control during the 1960's. Unlike nearly every other European country, this was not directly a result of TV. In fact TV set ownership actually declined for a while during this period. The truth of it was that the Italian audience were enormous consumers of cinema. The average Italian went to the movies almost once a month and so there was a huge need for new product to keep them happy. This is why there were so many Spanish co-productions. They were cheap and could be turned out in record time to cash in on any new trends. Paradoxically, this fevered activity never

Karin Schubert as sexy ▶
night nurse in **La
dotoressa sotto il
lenzuolo** (1976)

seemed to result in full coffers. Almost every week there came announcements of a new funding crisis. Much of this was down to the crucial 'north-south divide' of the country that caused a constant search for a 'universal' subject that would attract the widest possible audience from across the board.

The sophisticated and industrialised North, where the impact of television was first felt, has a very different set of preoccupations and standards from the more rural South—where the majority of less demanding filmgoers live. Consequently anything that attracted an audience in either part of the country would be reproduced in almost indecent haste to cash in on the demand before it dried up. Following the huge local success of Pasolini's **Decameron**, his 1971 film of **The Canterbury Tales** was being imitated in anticipation of its expected success even *before* it had been released. Unfortunately somebody didn't do their homework properly, and several of the resulting films laboured under the misapprehension that Canterbury was the author of the tales in question, which lead to some strange titlings, as well as peculiar hybrids like **The Sexbury Tales** (1971), **The Lusty Wives of Canterbury** (1972) and **The Other Canterbury Tales** (1972).

The sexual content of Italian films, which is also found in the 'adult comics' and now in the hardcore photonovels, featuring the likes of Gabriel Pontello, seems contradictory in a country with such a powerful moral watchdog as the Catholic

Les films du PALAIS ROYEL    et SOFRABIS présentent

KARIN SCHUBERT dans

# LA TOUBIB
# AUX COURS DU SOIR
## DES COURS TRÈS PARTICULIERS...

avec ORCHIDEA DE SANTIS et avec ALVARO VITALI · ELIGIO ZAMARA · ELY GALLEANI
et avec GASTONE PESCUCCI et GIGI BALLISTA

church. However, things are not as straightforward as they seem. Since the war censorship in Italy had consisted largely of 'protecting the public morals'. The Constitution of 1947 had enshrined in law the 'free expression and diffusion of ideas'—which, by extension, included films. However, this did not guarantee a freedom from prosecution under the articles of the Penal Code which forbade the distribution of obscene material. Magistrates had the right to seize individual films, either on their own initiative or following a complaint from an individual citizen.

In 1962 the law was reformed, bringing films under the control of the Minister of Tourism and Public Performances. A commission could then decide to limit viewing to 18 and above or 14 and above—or to ban films completely if they were thought to constitute 'an offence to public morals'. **Blow Out (La grande bouffe)** and **Empire of the Senses**, for example, were banned outright. The new law also limited the power of magistrates to seize individual films. This could now only be done following the first showing of the film. In theory this meant that if exhibitors were careful to premiere films in more liberal districts they should subsequently be able to show them anywhere.

However, in classic Italian style, the local legal system showed itself to be a thing of hot air and much confusion. Magistrates simply chose to ignore the new law and went ahead blithely seizing and destroying films as the whim took them. **Last Tango in Paris** was famously banned and all prints destroyed. Radical groups arranged the showing of a scratchy super-8 copy to try to break the ban. Other victims of this farce included Pasolini's **Salo**, **Salon Kitty** and, incredibly, the sexy Belgian animation **Tarzoon—The Shame of the Jungle** !

There is no immunity to prosecution for films judged 'obscene', and legal action can be taken against distributors, exhibitors and even directors of banned films. So Italian producers have become masters of compromise on issues of censorship. For commercial reasons they are always vying with each other to bring out films that are just that little bit more daring than their rival's previous release. They get away with it in some areas—gore scenes in horror films, for example; but in others—where politics is combined with sex—they get slapped down and are forced to retreat.

Needless to say, the church has not been slow to get in on the act. As early as the 1940's the Catholic Film Centre's magazine *La Rivista del Cinematografo* began to publish lists of films 'forbidden to all believers', as well as a list of

directors whose work was considered dangerous. Interestingly, Luis Buñuel and Jess Franco were once named together as the two *most* dangerous film-makers for Catholics.

The situation has never been resolved in Italy and as late as 1991, following a huge campaign from religious and women's groups, there were moves to institute a 'seal of approval' system whereby only films judged to be of artistic merit would be exempt from prosecution and eligible for state financing. But even the notion of what constitutes art is open to abuse. In 1974 Alain Robbe-Grillet was taken to court in Italy for his film **Glissements progressifs du plaisir**. The Magistrate had decided that the film was obscene because it "didn't make sense", and therefore could not be defended as a work of art.

During the 1970's the shape of the industry began to change. The ownership of film companies began to pass into fewer hands. Big business got involved. Furthermore, some of the names of the sixties had decided that Italy was too small for them and had uprooted for pastures new—in other words, Hollywood and the global market. And for the first time

▲ (Above left) **Diabolik** (1968)

▲ (Top) Comic-Strip capers with the irrepressible **Mr.X** (1968)

▲ (Bottom right) The deadly **Baba Yaga** (1973)

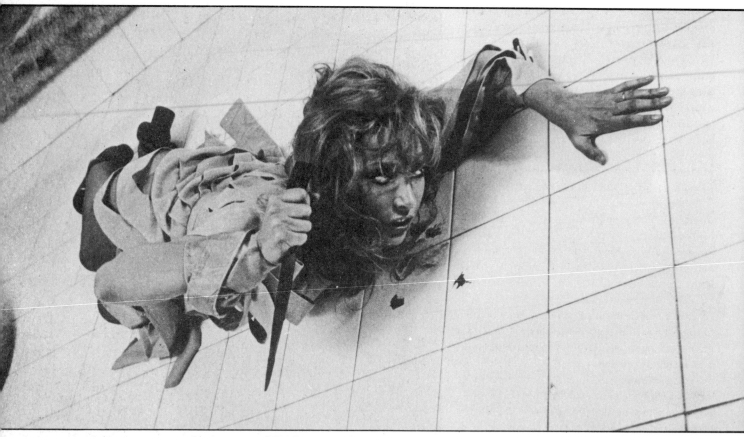

The Night Evelyn ▲
Came Out of the
Grave

the impact of TV began to be felt, drawing audiences away from the cinemas.

A hint of desperation crept into the industry and some of the wildest and most notorious films were made. Sequel followed success at an increasingly frantic pace. The international acclaim given to Pasolini's erotic trilogy **Decameron**, **Canterbury Tales** and **Arabian Nights**, gave birth to a rash of similar titles— **Decameron 2**, **Forbidden Decameron**, **Last Decameron**, **Decameroticus**, **Hot Nights of Decameron** and **Decameron's Sexy Kittens** amongst many others.[5] Some of these films were actually based on Boccaccio's stories, but many of them just used the name as a convenient marketing tool.

Pasolini attempted to stop the rot with his outrageous **Salo—The 120 Days of Sodom** (1975), but only succeeded in stopping himself; he was found dead in mysterious circumstances after finishing the film—which was then banned outright.[6]

Even less salubrious were the host of films that followed in the wake of Liliana Cavani's **Night Porter** (1974). An essentially worthy examination of the power games played by an ex-Nazi and his former victim, it opened the floodgates to films like **SS Experiment Camp**, **Red Nights of the Gestapo**, **Gestapo's Last**

A Blade In The Dark ▶
(1983)

(Facing Page) Magda ▶
Konopka as gun toting
Femme Fatale in
**Top Secret** (1966)

**Orgy** and **Deported Women of the SS Special Section**. There has been little attempt to rehabilitate this particular genre, but within the context of the Italian movie experience they do make perfect sense.

But the decline continued. Things were already grinding to a halt in the early eighties. By the end of the decade, with the growth of multi-channel television, video and a huge proliferation of porn mags that mixed sex with horror and beyond, the

**Immoral Tales**

steam seemed to have well and truly gone from the once vibrant engine of the Italian popular cinema. Even big name directors like Fellini and Tinto Brass found it difficult to get projects off the ground and turned to TV or the theatre. Films like **Blood and Black Lace**, **Django** and **Salon Kitty** were a thing of the past. A popular cinema needs an audience to support it. The Italian audience had simply moved on somewhere else.

---

[1] Sylvana in **Bitter Rice**, for example

[2] *Fumetti*

[3] They soon became known as Peplums from the short tunic that many of the characters wore. The phrase 'Sword and Sandal' was also coined.

[4] A 1953 film supervised by Neo-Realist veteran Cesare Zavattini—**Love in the City (Amore in città)**, which was a collection of six, semi-documentary segments showing different aspects of contemporary morals, pointed the way; but the most immediate precursor was Alessandro Blasetti's **European Nights (Europa di notte)**. The commentary for this 1959 effort was written by Jacopetti, whose training as a journalist and documentary maker stood him in good stead in his later career.

[5] These films even ripped each other off. 1972's **Decameron proibiti (Forbidden Decameron)** soon spawned **Decameron proibitissimo (Sexy Sinners)**—in Italian the title means 'Most Forbidden Decameron'.

[6] He was killed by a young boy, whom he was allegedly trying to proposition. However, in recent years persistent rumours of a political conspiracy have thrown new light on the case. Probably, the true story will never be known.

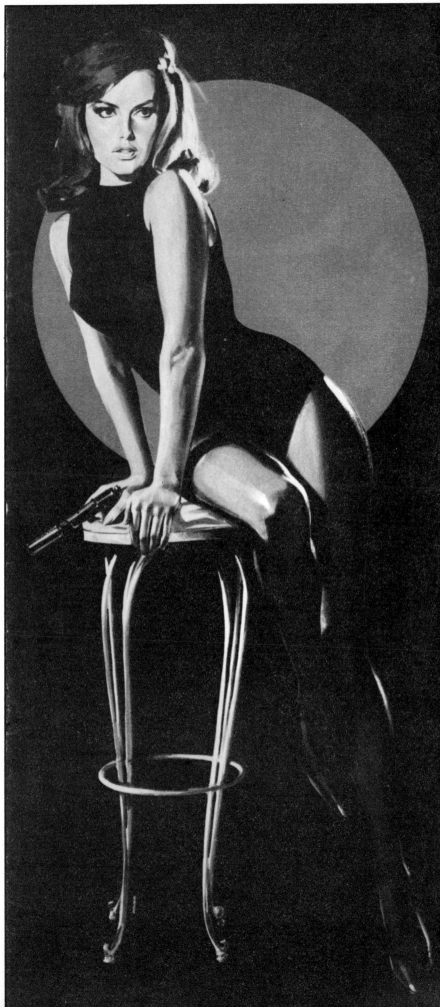

DANY
CARREL
PIERRE
BRICE

DANS

LE MOULIN des SUPPLICES

AVEC SCILLA GABEL et WOLFGANG PREISS

Une Réalisation de GEORGES FERRONI — INTERDIT AU MOINS DE 13 A

# Film Reviews

## ▶ THE MILL OF THE STONE WOMEN/ DROPS OF BLOOD
### (Il Mulino delle donne di pietra)

*With Piere Brice, Wolfgang Preiss, Scilla Gabel, Dany Carel, Robert Boehme. Directed by Giorgo Ferroni. Italy/France, 1960. 95 minutes*

A mist sweeps in over the flat Dutch landscape. A dark windmill is silhouetted against the cold winter sky. A man stands by the banks of a canal and rings a small bell to summon the ferry .

"The mill of the stone women," the boatman tells him. "It's beyond the cemetery at Weese."

Hans has come to the mill to study its most famous feature—a strange carousel, constructed in the last century out of the statues of famous murderesses and other notorious women from history.

As he approaches the mill from out of the late afternoon mists he hears the sound of a piano. Scales and snatches of tunes, like someone practising. But as soon as the stern faced housekeeper lets him inside, the music abruptly stops. While he waits to see the carousel's proprietor, Professor Wahl, Hans glances around. From behind a heavy, embroidered curtain a small dog appears and then, for only the briefest of instants, the face of a beautiful young woman, distorted suddenly into a mask of terror. Hans hears a horrible wail of pain, but before he can say anything the housekeeper ushers him into the professor's study, locking the door behind him

Totally disoriented, Hans wanders into the wood-lined chamber beneath the mill. He finds himself in front of a small stage. Curtains part and, to the accompaniment of a jaunty but bittersweet fairground waltz, the carousel comes to life. One by one the horribly life-like, but strangely grotesque, figures parade before him. He watches, transfixed.

**The Mill of the Stone Women** is a film of astonishing beauty and terror, told in an intense, at times hallucinatory style. In the process of solving the mystery of the mill and its bizarre inhabitants, Hans lives through several lifetimes of experience in only a few short days—and eventually comes to doubt even his own sanity. The unique setting of the film, its gorgeous but subdued colours—like a painting by Rembrandt—and the meticulously

worked out plot, all contribute to what is generally acknowledged as one of the masterpieces of 1960's horror cinema.

The atmosphere of turn-of-the-century Holland is beautifully captured through minute attention to period detail. Everything looks old and lived in. You can almost smell the ancient dust of the mill, almost taste the flagons of ale in the tavern and feel the damp air of the canal in your lungs. Dutch and Lowland fantasy has a very particular flavour that is hard to define, but is somehow a combination of the ethereal and the earthy. A result, perhaps, of the long tradition of seafaring and merchant trading of the area. Many different races passed through the ports of Holland and Belgium, bringing stories as well as ancient artifacts. The wide open skies, contrasted with the twisty, cobbled back alleys of the old towns, gives the people who live there a very particular outlook on life, composed equally of French rationalism, German mysticism and English stoicism. Few films have even tried to capture it. **Daughters of Darkness** (1971) comes close, with possibly **The Fourth Man** (1984) as an honest contender. Generally it's a literary tradition, with writers like Thomas Owen and Jean Ray being its foremost exponents. Not surprisingly, **The Mill of the Stone Women** is derived from a literary source: *Flemish Tales* by Peter van Weigen.

The director and co-writer of the film, Giorgio Ferroni, was better known, under the name of Calvin Jackson Padget, as a director of westerns during the spaghetti boom of the mid sixties. In the course of a long career he made only two other films that even begin to approach the quality of **Mill of the Stone Women**. **The Bacchantes** was made in the same year as his masterpiece, 1960. Twelve years later he came up with **Night of the Devils**. Generally written

▲ Panels from **Drops of Blood** photo novel

off as a pale imitation of the Wurdalak episode of Mario Bava's **Black Sabbath, Night of the Devils** is actually a pretty good horror film, with a great shock opening and several effectively gory scenes.

One of the minor features of **Mill of the Stone Women**, although it's cut out of most release prints, is a brief flash of nudity from heroine Dany Carel. This makes it probably the first 'nudie' horror film, a couple of years before Franco's **Awful Doctor Orlof**, which shares a similar 'mad doctor' story line.

## ▶BLOODY PIT OF HORROR
(Il boia scarlatto)

*With Mickey Hargitay, Louise Barrett, Massimo Pupillo. Directed by Massimo Pupillo (Max Hunter on American prints). Written by Roberto Natale. Italy/U.S.A, 1965. 80 minutes.*

While the ads promised 'A Hair-Raising Orgy of Sadism', the reality was a little different. **Bloody Pit of Horror** is an enticing little oddity that's like a Continental picto-novel in places, and a comic strip in others. The opening scenes are overblown and demented; they reveal the cackling, ranting psychosis of the Crimson Executioner, a deranged dude who slakes his lust, egotism and hatred in vile, pernicious torture. Despite this he has his own sense of style and his red pointy skullcap, snazzy tights, broad belt, black mask and huge medallion are pretty fetching.

The main story takes place over 300 years later; a group of fun-loving models, photographers and a writer chance upon the castle where the Crimson Executioner popped his clogs. Its new owner is Travis Anderson (Mickey Hargitay), a man whose growing strangeness and narcissism have caused him to retreat from the world. His kinship with the demented outlook of the Crimson Executioner is strong, and the arrival of these sex crazed guys and girls is the final factor that helps him flip his wig.

When they start to use his dungeons and torture devices as props in their pix, Travis goes over the edge and becomes that nasty madman—the Crimson Executioner. After this the film turns into a visual comic strip, the only things missing are speech bubbles and captions.

One incredible scene features a girl trapped in a huge spider web. Another sequence has Travis going AWOL in a room full of captive lovelies, branding, stretching and getting vindictive with their bodies. His out-to-lunch behaviour is too daft to be described as bona fide sadism, he reels around in an infantile frenzy, giving these outrageous sections more than a hint of pulp fantasy.

**Bloody Pit of Horror** is an uneven film, one that veers from comic-strip dementia to inconsequential noodling and back again. This deflates the crazy venom of the torture scenes, turning the film on its head, pushing it into a strange realm where kitsch meets the cyclical delirium of the Marquis de Sade.

## ▶GOLIATH AND THE VAMPIRES
(Maciste contro il vampiro)

*With Gordon Scott, Gianna Maria Canale, Leonora Ruffo, Jacques Sernas. Directed by Giacomo Gentilomo. Written by Duccio Tessari and Sergio Corbucci. Italy, 1962. 92 minutes.*

Maciste (Goliath only in the English versions), is out ploughing the fields and saving children from sea monsters when his village is attacked by pirates. All the women, including Maciste's fiancée Cora, are carried off to Salmanak, from where no-one has ever returned alive. Maciste sets off to rescue them.

On board the pirates' ship, the older women are weeded out and thrown overboard. The leader of the pirates drains the blood from the arms of the survivors to feed to a strange spirit who lurks in the hold of the ship, surrounded by swirling mists.

Maciste arrives in Salmanak where sadistic entertainments both horrify and fascinate the locals while the king, in thrall to the evil spirit Kobrak, is entertained by exotic dancing girls provided by his mistress, Astra—herself a slave to Kobrak.

At the local slave market Maciste battles with a small army of guards and is only saved by the surprise intervention of the magician, Kurtik.

Maciste rescues Cora, and they set off for home across a barren desert. On their way they are overtaken by a sandstorm and find themselves in a mysterious cavern. It is the domain of their friend Kurtik and his army of 'blue men.' Maciste, Kurtik and the blue men set out for the lair of Kobrak but are waylaid in a burning forest by the evil spirit and his army of faceless robots. Many adventures are in store for Maciste and his friends before they can overthrow the evil Kobrak and set the people of Salmanak free.....

**Goliath and the Vampires** is one of the liveliest and most inventive of all peplums. In the special *Cine Zine Zone* issue devoted to Gordon Scott, Pierre Charles describes it as 'one of the four or five masterpieces of the genre'. Much of the credit for its special flavour is down to the script by Duccio Tessari, writer and director of **The Sons of Thunder** and numerous other gems of Italian cinema. Sergio Corbucci, of **Django** fame, was also involved, not only co-scripting but directing many sequences as well.

The inventiveness of the film never flags. Scene after scene brings new surprises and new twists on old themes. Of particular note is the use of the character of Maciste, who is a long way from the fascist superman created by d'Annunzio. Here he's a democrat, putting his strength to the cause of the people and not too proud to dirty his hands with manual work. Again, good and evil are shown as choices that characters make, rather than as archetypal qualities that are somehow fixed.

One of the factors that marks out **Goliath and the Vampires** is its level of violence. In the UK it was released with an X certificate—suitable only for the over 16's. The sacking of Maciste's village is shown with particular force, and there are numerous other strong scenes: the bloodletting on board ship; the game in which a whipped man is forced to climb a greasy pole mounted on a spiked board; the trap full of giant scorpions. But perhaps the most delirious scene has Maciste imprisoned in a deep pit. Kobrak's faceless robots lower a giant bell over the mouth of the pit and relentlessly beat it with hammers in an attempt to drive Maciste mad.

Contrasted with these shock scenes are the many lighter moments—familiar from other peplums but here handled with a great sureness of touch. The costumes and settings are always a feature in Italian films from the early 1960's, and no less so here. And there are two dance numbers that are among the best in the genre. The night club sequence, with wonderfully anachronistic music, is a particular standout.

There was a brief vogue for horror peplums in the early 1960's. Mario Bava's **Hercules in the Centre of the Earth**, Riccardo Freda's **Maciste in Hell** and Giorgio Ferroni's **Hercules Challenge** date from the same period. Later versions of the myth became even more exotic, with Hercules journeying to South America **(Hercules Against the Sons of the Sun)**, fighting werewolves **(Hercules, Prisoner of Evil)** and discovering a strange race of rock-men **(Hercules Against the Moonmen)**. Eventually, as with all the great genres of Italian popular cinema, the muscle-men sagas ran out of steam

and the creative talent involved in them moved on to pastures new: mostly westerns, horror pictures and sexy comedies. During the 1970's the theme was briefly revived with **Hercules in New York**, starring a young Arnold Schwarzenegger, and again in the 1980's with Lou (The Incredible Hulk) Ferrigno as **Hercules**.

▲ The ultimate challenge: Goliath vs Goliath in **Goliath and the Vampires** (1962)

**NEKROMANTIK**

JOHN WATERS

# Germans on Top

## THE GERMAN FILM INDUSTRY

In *The Haunted Screen*, Lotte Eisner writes about the 'weird pleasure the Germans take in evoking horror', and puts it down to their 'excessive and very Germanic desire to submit to discipline, together with a certain proneness to sadism'. All of which combined to make the early German cinema the natural birthplace of the horror film.

The local industry had achieved a high degree of technical and artistic sophistication by the time sound arrived in 1929. Masterpieces like **Der Golem** (1914), **The Cabinet of Dr. Caligari** (1919) and **Nosferatu** (1922) paved the way for the likes of **M** (1931), **Vampyr** (1931) and **Death and the Maiden** (1936).

This particularly German form of mythic cinema, full of dark shadows and moody sets, influenced by the expressionist painters and writers, was exported fully grown to America in the mid 1930's following the rise to power of Hitler and the emigration of many of the German cinemas leading lights. It was quickly absorbed into the soon-to-emerge genre of the 'horror movie'.

Back in Germany, cinema came under the control of Hitler's brilliant Propaganda Minister, Goebbels, who understood very well the power of film. Mixed in with the light comedies and 'Mountain' films that extolled the virtues of a healthy lifestyle, were a host of films like **Jüd Süss** and **Die Ewige Jüde** (both 1940)—anti-Jewish pieces—and **Dorf im rotem Sturm** (1935)—anti-communist melodrama.

After the war, Germany was split into two countries. Most of the film production facilities—including the UFA studios—were in the Russian controlled East. The Allies, who controlled the West, had other priorities than rebuilding the local film industry. In the hands of a few individually licensed producers it quickly became a low-budget, fast buck business, turning out comedies, musical revues and nostalgic films about the good old days. These films, called Heimat (Homeland) films were very reminiscent of the pre-war Mountain films so dear to Hitler's heart. Films like **Schwarzwaldmädel** (Black Forest Girl;1950) and **Grün ist die Heide** (Green is the Heath; 1952) were full of pretty, picture postcard views, rosy cheeked maidens and a general nostalgia for a rural past

that had never really existed in the first place. Like the Mountain films, they showed dim traces of the old Germanic sense of mysticism that had inspired Fritz Lang and Murnau. Unfortunately, with all the darker elements squeezed out in the wash, that mysticism looked suspiciously like sentimentality.

Lots of war films were made, too, that tried to excuse themselves by showing the Nazi High Command as sexually and morally corrupt—with orgies included to prove it. Films like **The Devil's General (Des Teufels General)** and **The Last Ten Days (Der Letzte Akt)**, both from 1955, started a genre that was later picked up by Italian producers for their belated 'Nazi-sex' cycle in the mid seventies.

An attempt was made in 1951 to draw international attention to the industry with the founding of the Berlin Film Festival. The Film Evaluation Office was set up to select 'worthy' projects which would be entitled to state benefits and tax shelters. But even so, few German films of the fifties made it out of the country. They were noticeably parochial and made no attempt to compete with the Hollywood product that still ruled the screens.

One of the strengths of the German film industry was its female stars. They were also its most exportable products. Pre-war there had been Marlene Dietrich, Pola Negri and Louise Brooks. After the war it was Hildegard Kneff, Maria Schell and Vera Molnar. These women always had a smoky, exotic quality that appealed more to 'mature' tastes. What the tone of the times demanded was someone young and lusty.

In 1955, Arca studios advertised for a young actress to take the lead in a jungle film they were planning, **Liane, Jungle Goddess (Liane, das Mädchen aus der Urwald;** 1956). Basically the story was the same as Edgar Rice Burroughs' *Tarzan*, with the crucial difference that the hero was a young *woman* from a formerly privileged background. 11,800 hopefuls applied for the part and Marion Michael, a 17 year old amateur athlete, was chosen. The film was a huge success and led to a sequel, **Liane, the White Slave (Liane, die weisse Sklavin;** 1957). The escapist plot was an obvious attraction to the post war German audience, but probably no less of an attraction than the sight of young Ms Michael, swinging from the vines clad only in a tiny loincloth, or bathing *'au naturel'* in forest pools. The film was widely imitated. Subsequent Euro jungle films are as likely to have **Liane** as their inspiration than the Tarzan originals from which she sprang. Jess Franco's **El tesoro de la diosa**

▲ Drugs, nudity and angst. **Opium** (1919), one of Conrad Veidt's first films

◀ (Facing page) **Nekromantik.** Hard gore from Germany

Sybil Danning carries all ▲
before her in **Hercules**
(1983)

**blanca** (1983) is a virtual remake of the first **Liane** film, with another German actress, Katia Bienert, in the starring role.

Ms Michael's youth made her a natural for promotion as the ultimate in teen sex idols ('The German Brigitte Bardot'). She was soon followed by Elke Sommer, Laya Raki, Karin Dor and Nadja Tiller and, in the 1960's and 70's, Terry Torday, Uschi Glas, Andrea Rau and Elizabeth Volkmann. Films were tailored to exploit this feminine charm. **Caverns of Vice**, from 1959, was about a team of dancing girls involved in white slavery and diamond smuggling in Turkey. A 1961 film—**German Starlets (Deutschland—deiner Sternchen)** claimed to tell the sordid, behind-the-scenes story of these star-struck teens.

The life span of most of these starlets was limited. But two of them, at least, did go on to greater things. Barbara Valentin was the daughter of a set designer. She was discovered, in the classic fashion, by producer Wolf C. Hartwig in the canteen of a Munich film studio. Her first film, **You Belong to Me**, was a standard romance, but in 1959 came two extraordinary horror outings, again produced by Hartwig, **The Head (Die Nackte und der Satan)** and **The Horror of Spider Island (Ein Toter hing im Netz)**.[1] More softcore sex films, thrillers and comedies followed and then, in 1973, she began to work with the German cinema's new *'wunderkind'*, Rainer Werner Fassbinder. **Fear Eats the Soul** showed that she could really act and from then on her career entered a different plane.

Barbara Valentin had a broad appeal. In many ways she was like our own dear Diana Dors. As she got older and played more character parts she lost her youthful audience, but gained a whole new set of admirers. Like DD she even became a gay icon.[2]

Sybil Danning's career began in the early seventies, in sex comedies like **Loves of a French Pussycat** and **Passion Pill Swingers**. As the German sex film boom waned, she moved into the international market just as the success of **Star Wars** was creating a new boom—in high tech, fantasy adventures. Sybil Danning soon came to specialise in the sort of roles where her main weapons were a ray gun in her hand and her ample bosoms, spilling over the top of an armoured breastplate. **Battle Beyond the Stars** (1980), **Hercules** (1983), and **The Warrior Queen** (1985) made her the sort of star that teenage boys like to pin on their walls.

Teacher knows best in ▶
**Teenager-Report** (1973)

Since the departure of much of its creative talent to the US in the 1930's, the German industry

had been very much a producer's ball game. It was only from the late 1960's that young directors began to attract an international following and demand the kind of autonomy that the French New Wave had been granted. But it was a precarious business. Many producers came and went throughout the 1950's and 60's. The complexity of dealing with the co-production finance necessary for success, the fast turnaround of talent and the low profit margins saw something like 120 companies rise and fall. The survivors included Wolf C. Hartwig (Rapid Films), Artur Brauner (CCC), and Horst Wendlandt (Rialto), all of whom operated very much within the confines of popular cinema, finding out what the public wanted and giving them more of it.

German cinema has a special peculiarity in the idea of *'autorenfilm'*. From the beginning, films have been seen literally as filmed books. It's the author and the screenplay that are important, while the director is a technician, judged on the basis of his faithfulness to the written word. Producers have an ingrained notion that the film of a successful book, classic or pulp, will have a guaranteed audience; while the State compounds the problem by assessing funding for films on the basis of screenplays. This has led to some popular works being filmed many times.[3] This over-reliance on the screenplay made much of the home grown product too talky to be exportable.

During the 1950's and 60's, producers in search of potential material went back to their bookshelves. Perhaps recalling the success of the **Liane** films and the Tarzan books on which they had been based, they scouted around for other series books in the same low-brow popular vein. Amongst many others they came up with the westerns of Karl May, the secret agent stories featuring Jerry Cotton, and the crime books of Edgar Wallace

**Immoral Tales**

Horst Wendlandt of Rialto Films was the man responsible for the Edgar Wallace series. With 32 titles between 1959 and 1972 and earnings of more than 140 million marks, it's one the greatest success stories of the whole German film industry. In fact, there's a good case to be made for the Wallace films as being one of the few places where the old pre-war German cinematic talent for dark shadows, strange camera angles and gruesome violence was allowed to flourish.[4]

The middle-aged profile of the people involved in the production of the Wallace films, as well as their literary roots in 1920's England, accounts for their quaintly old-fashioned feel. Later, when they began to include 'swinging sixties' references, this resulted in an hilarious tabloid approach that also infected the Italian *gialli* they inspired.

When they ran out of Edgar Wallace originals to plunder, German producers turned either to the stories of his son, Bryan Edgar Wallace, created their own lookalike Wallace-copies (**Der Teppich des Grauens**—**The Carpet of Horror**;1962) or rediscovered such venerable old hacks as Francis Durbridge (**Piccadilly, Null Uhr 12**—**Piccadilly, Zero Hour 12**; 1963). Home grown antiheroes, like Fritz Lang's Dr. Mabuse, were dragged out of retirement and dusted off. Later on, characters like Fu Manchu were thrown into the pot. Many of these films shared stars, producers and directors, giving them a real cottage industry feel.

One of the first of Wendlandt's rivals to try to cash in on his success was Artur Brauner. He was an emigre Pole who had set up shop right after the war in Berlin, opening his Central Cinema Company (CCC) studios in an abandoned factory near Spandau jail.

Wendlandt had threatened an earlier rival, Kurt Ulrich, with legal action over his 1960 film **The Avenger**, claiming a copyright on the Wallace name, which was such an important trade mark for the success of the films. Brauner took the wily step of basing his first Wallace film—**The Secret of the Black Trunk** (1962) on a book by the great man's son, thereby avoiding the legal traps but still retaining that all important name on the credits. Wendlandt retaliated by stepping up production and then moving into colour. In a sense he won the battle but lost the war, as the series became increasingly routine after the mid sixties. Brauner shifted into Euro coproductions, with a similar but more flamboyant series of thrillers, starting with Dario Argento's **Bird With the Crystal Plumage** (1970) and then several Franco films—again loosely based on stories by Bryan Edgar Wallace (**Death Packs a Suitcase** and **The Devil Came from Akasava**).

Brauner's strength was his studio, which he hired out to many smaller independent producers. Almost every postwar film shot in Berlin was made in Brauner's studios, and it was still going strong up to the late 1960's. His weakness was that he didn't bother to establish strong contacts with the nascent TV industry, as his rivals in Munich and Hamburg had done. When the film business hit a financial crisis, Brauner's isolation spelled trouble for him.

As the impact of television began to make itself felt, the search for an audience became even more intense. The depths of popular taste were plumbed with a series of rural comedy films such as **The Lausbuben Tales** and pop-music films (schlagerfilme). Sex films proliferated. The semi documentary **The Girl Rosemarie (Rosemarie)** and **Love Now, Pay Later (Die Wahrheit über Rosemarie)** had been big successes in the late 1950's, with their tabloid type exposé of the seedy underbelly of German big business life. One of the foremost producers of this type of film was Wolf C. Hartwig, a man who would change forever the face of German cinema.

Hartwig began with a documentary, **Five Minutes Past Twelve (Bis Fünf nach Zwölf**; 1953), that dealt with the private life of Hitler and Eva Braun. The film ran into severe difficulties with the censor but it was a big success. So was Hartwig's next film, **Lukrezia Borgia**, a costume drama that featured a bare-breasted orgy scene. Towards the end of the fifties Hartwig produced two delirious horror films, **The Head (Die Nackte und der Satan**; 1959)

▲ Jess Franco's **Tesora de la diosa blanca** (1983)

▲ (Above left) Marion Michael as **Liane, Jungle Goddess** (1957)

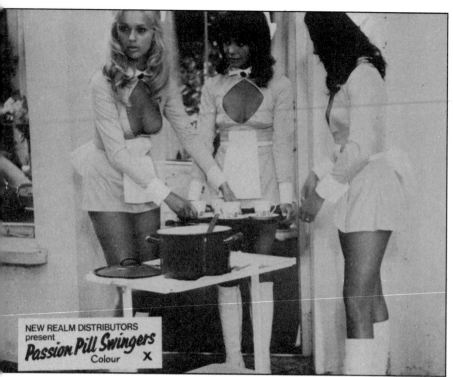

NEW REALM DISTRIBUTORS present *Passion Pill Swingers* Colour X

Before **Hercules**, Sybil ▲
Danning was one of those
**Passion Pill Swingers**
(1972)

Conrad Veidt shows why ▼
he was **Different from
the Others** (1919)

and **The Horror of Spider Island (Ein Toter Hing im Netz**; 1959) both of which featured Barbara Valentin.

However, Hartwig's lasting claim to fame—or infamy—came with his 1970 production of Ernst Hofbauer's pseudo-documentary study of the sex-life of German teens, **Schülmädchen-Report (Confessions of a Sixth Form Girl)**. Based on Gunther Hunold's book of the same title, the film was a huge success, drawing over seven million viewers worldwide. With a total of 13 titles in all and international viewing figures of over 100 million, the Schoolgirl Reports eventually outstripped even the Edgar Wallace films to become Germany's highest earning cinematic exports.

The formula was established pretty much with the first title. Short sections, each one illustrating a particular sexual situation or problem, intercut with real-life interviews—the whole thing framed by a story that linked the episodes in some arbitrary fashion. The ostensible purpose was to show to parents what their offspring were up to and, supposedly, to start some kind of dialogue between the generations. Teen pregnancy, rape, lesbianism and drugs were all featured at various times during the series.

Having found his metier Hartwig exploited it ruthlessly, as well as turning out a whole grab bag of similar films: **Urlaubsreport (Swedish Love Games**; 1971), **Krankenschwestern-Report (Nurses on the Job**; 1972) and **Erotik im Berüf (Sex in the Office**; 1971).

Basically, Hartwig was reviving an old German cinematic genre—the *'sexualaufklärung'* (sexual enlightenment) film, that rose very quickly to prominence after the end of the First World War. For a couple of years, from 1918-19, censorship was abolished, and a flood of sexually explicit films hit the screens. Titles like **Vow of Chastity (Gelubde der Keuschheit)**, **Hyenas of Lust (Hyänen der Lust)** and **Opium** were soon pulling in the punters as never before.

The pioneer of this movement had been the producer and director Richard Oswald,[5] whose career included comedies (**Unheimliche Geschichten**; 1932), horror films (**Nachgestalten**), and thrillers (**Der Hund von Baskerville**;1915). But his real fame began with **Es Werde Licht** (Let There be Light) in 1918, a film about the dangers of Syphilis, starring the wild girl of Berlin cabaret, Anita Berber. Audiences flocked to see it, and Oswald followed this success with **Cocaine**, **Figures of the Night** and **Prostitution 1** and **2** over the next two years.

His most daring film was 1919's **Anders als die Andern** (Different From the Others) which featured Conrad Veidt in his debut starring role and was the first open study of homosexuality. To deflect the censor's wrath, and to add authority to the film, Oswald employed the talents of the famous sexologist Dr. Magnus Hirschfeld as a sort of Master of Ceremonies. This format was later copied by American films like **Reefer Madness** (1936), **Marijuana: Weed With Roots in Hell** (1936) and Ed Wood's astonishing **Glen or Glenda** (1953).

Hartwig was not the first post-war producer to see the possibilities of this particular genre. In 1967 Eric Bender's film **Helga** had been an enormous success. This earnest sex-education film was followed by several sequels (**Michael and Helga**; **Helga and the Men**; and even **Little Helga**) and a spate of 'Dr.' type films. Often they were produced by medics (or pseudo-medics, as with the famous series starring Dr. Oswald Kölle), and had titles like **The Wonder of Love**, **Love is a Parlour Game** and **Your Wife—The Unknown Creature**.[6] The format for them was pretty much the same as with the later Schoolgirl Reports; a didactic look at the techniques and problems of sex for man and wife, introduced by a series of comfortingly bland medical experts. The respectability conferred by the presence of a Doctor or two permitted the inclusion of sex scenes that probably would not have been allowed in a straight drama.

The attraction of these films for a sensation hungry audience is obvious. But there were other reasons for their post-war popularity.

Their style and format supported a particularly German source of security, in its preoccupation with order, hygiene and authority. And there was also the feeling, very much current at the time, of a need to educate the new generation and clear the guilt of the past; sex was as good a place to start as any.

From the late sixties and well into the seventies this type of film and its bastard offspring—the sexy comedy—dominated, to the extent that many middle class people just stopped going to the cinema; they came to believe that cinema meant sex-films. **Porno-Baby** from 1969 was typical, being a sensational story about a wife swapping club. **Teenager Report** from 1973 was a version of the schoolgirl series and there were burlesque comedies too—**Otto und die Nackte Welle** (Otto and the Nudist Craze;1968) combined the old Heimat genre with the sex comedy in its story of a Naturist and a sex-film maker.[7] 1973's **Tanzstunden-Report (Techniques of Love)** plumbed new depths—it was about the sexual shenanigans that go on during dancing lessons! **Prostitution Heute (Prostitution Today;** 1970) was another semi-documentary on a subject of eternal interest, and soon the Schoolgirl Reports had turned into **Hausfrau** (Housewife) Reports. Perhaps the high point of it all was 1970's **Wunderland der Liebe—der Grosse Deutsche Sexreport (Wonderland of Love)** which was a barefaced celebration of Germany as the new paradise of sexual freedom.

Many directors, such as Ernst Hofbauer, Alois Brummer, Franz Antel, Walter Boos and Franz Marischka came to specialise in these films, working endless variations on the Lederhosen/Air-hostess/Ski-instructor models that were the staples of the genre. The probable nadir was reached by a trio of 'Yodelling and Sex' films that came out during 1974. **Yodelling in your Underpants, Yodelling Makes your Lederhosen Itch(There's no Sex Like Snow Sex)** and **Yodelling is No Sin** were the titles. The last was actually written and directed by Ulli Lommel, former Fassbinder collaborator.[8]

Today it's the camp and kitschy window dressing that gives these films their appeal. Terrible seventies' fashions abound, along with lava lamps, Jason King posters and garish wallpaper, all served up to a soundtrack of strident MOR choogling and jaunty Europop. But at the time they struck a deep chord in many countries and the films were widely exported, to France and the UK, in many ways inspiring the home-grown exploitation industries to produce their own versions.

During the early part of the sixties, following the so-called Oberhausen Manifesto[9] in 1962, some young film-makers did try to make an impact on the German scene. People like Peter Schamoni and Bernhard Wicki began to deal with contemporary issues in a way that was a recognisable reaction against what they called 'Grandpa's cinema'. Yet even here their attempts to deal with sex amongst the young middle classes (**Quartet in Bed** and **Supergirl**) generated their own series ripoffs. Some good films did come out of this new young cinema. Peter Fleischmann's **Hunting Scenes From Lower Bavaria** (1969) is a savage indictment of backwoods mentality, with a homosexual man being hunted down and killed by a gang of 'normals'; and his **Dorothea's Revenge** (1974) makes pointed use of its scenes of sex and sadism.

But generally, audiences weren't seduced by the message films of the post Oberhausen generation. One of the results of this indifference was the emergence of a large and well organised underground film scene. Cut off completely from State funding and official distribution channels, a host of radical film-makers simply went their own way, ploughing their own marginal furrow with all the usual German diligence and single mindedness. Occasionally they would come out of hiding to stage 'Happenings' and disrupt official film festivals, but to most filmgoers they remained invisible. It was only much later, in the 1980's that films like Jörg Buttgereit's **Hot Love**, and **Nekromantik** emerged from their under-

◄ Doing the laundry.
**Give 'Em an Inch**
**(Hausfrauen Report 3;**
1972)

ground fastness to herald the arrival of a tentative new wave of 'Sauerkraut Shock' cinema.

At one time Germany had one of the biggest film-going audiences in the world. But, with the introduction of colour TV in the early sixties and the lack of young talent in the film industry, audiences began to dwindle. There were 8,000 cinemas in Germany in 1965; by 1968 this had shrunk to 3,000. Many producers and distributors went broke. The few that did survive had to become involved in co-productions with Spain, Italy or France to stay afloat. Stuck between the devil of commercialism and the deep blue sea of state approval and funding much of the new talent drifted off to the lucrative pastures of TV productions, particularly following the Film/Fernsehen Abkommen [10] of 1974.

This was also the year that hardcore sex films were legalised, slowing down the production of the softcore Report-type films, but leading to an increase in more minority appeal specialist films, often featuring bondage and sadomasochism. From the late seventies onward, this became the new growth market and directors like Hans Billian, who had formerly specialised in pop-music films and softcore comedies, now began to turn out hardcore films with equal facility. Billian's contributions include four versions of the famous novel *Josefine Mutzenbacher*, about the sexual escapades of a 19th century Viennese prostitute. [11] Hartwig, on the other hand, in com-

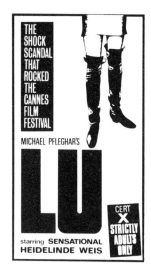

pany with many other softcore producers, went into more mainstream territory, with Peckinpah's **Cross of Iron** and later into the horror field with **Die Säge des Todes (Bloody Moon**; 1981) directed by Jess Franco.

Technically there had been no censorship in Germany since 1949. The law guaranteeing freedom of expression explicitly states that. However, the industry has set up a self-controlling body that classifies films with an age limit, as in many European countries. Adult designated films are restricted to venues where alcohol is sold—effectively marginalised. And the films are still subject to arbitrary seizure by local magistrates. This happened recently with Jorg Buttgereit's **Nekromantik 2**—one of the main contenders in the new German mini-boom of explicit horror that rose out of the old underground scene. Then it is up to the producers and distributors to defend a destruction order placed on the print by demonstrating that the film is not obscene. An expensive and time consuming process.

The German film business today, as in every European country, is largely an annexe of the huge TV industry. Hollywood dominates the screens as never before. Some German films do make it out of the country. Recently, **The Boat** and **The Never Ending Story**, both directed by Wolfgang Petersen, had some international success. Inevitably, Petersen soon became another Hollywood-bound exile. For years German producers have been churning out serious, message-laden epics that still trade on the fifty year old post-war sense of guilt. Even comedies, like the recent **Schtonk!**, dealing with the fake Hitler diaries, have a touch of the post-war blues about them. Now, with the reunification of the country causing another burst of cinematic angst, it seems unlikely that Germany will ever go back to what it once was—the producer of the biggest pile of celluloid trash in the history of cinema.

---

[1] See Review Section at end of chapter.

[2] Freddy Mercury was a worshipper at the Valentin shrine and Fassbinder asked her to marry him. He said she reminded him of his mother. "But, of course," he pointed out, "We'll have to share the bed with my boyfriend". Politely, Barbara declined the offer, reflecting that even genius has its limits.

[3] A popular novel in the 'Heimat' genre, *Schloss Hubertus (Hubertus Castle)* by Ludwig Ganghofer was filmed three times—in 1934, 1954 and 1973—and was a hit each time round. From the other end of the spectrum, *Alraune*, by the notorious Hans Heinz Ewers, was filmed an incredible five times (1918—twice, 1928, 1930 and 1952), making it something of a German horror classic. Ewers' notoriety stems largely from his friendship with Hitler and his authorship of the Nazi anthem—*The Horst Wessel Song*. His other literary efforts are often overlooked. In fact he was a unique and powerful writer, obsessed with blood and strange rituals. *Alraune* tells the story of the scientist Ten Brinken, who decides to create the perfect woman by impregnating a Berlin prostitute with the semen of a hanged murderer. The resulting creation, Alraune, is the ultimate, soulless femme fatale.

[4] There was not a lot of young talent about on the creative side in those days and the chosen director for the first Wallace adaption—**The Fellowship of the Frog (Der Frosch mit der Maske;** 1959)—Harald Reinl, although born in 1908 had not made his first solo film until 1949. He had started in the business before the second world war as assistant to Arnold Fanck and Hitler's favourite film-maker, Leni Riefenstahl.

After the war, Reinl turned his hand to a wide variety of popular genres, included War films(**U-47, Kapitänleutnant Priess;** 1958), sports films (**Bergkristal;** 1949) and comedies (**Kloster-jäger;** 1953). But it was the Wallace films that gave him a chance to show his true colours. Later, in 1967, he directed one of the few out-and-out German horror films, **The Blood Demon**. When Reinl went off to work on the Karl May westerns his successor on the Wallace films, Alfred Vohrer, brought a similar Gothic feel to his work. His 1961 film, **The Dead Eyes of London** was probably the first real 'horror' film of the post-war German cinema.

◀ **The Green Archer** (1961). A typical Edgar Wallace thriller from Germany

[5] Father of **Outer Limits** stalwart Gerd Oswald.

[6] These films were produced by Arca Studios, originators of the **Liane** series.

[7] Played by England's Harrison Marks.

[8] And director of the arty horror film **Tenderness of the Wolves.**

[9] Oberhausen was the location of the foremost German festival for short films.

[10] Film and Television Agreement.

[11] **Josefine Mutzenbacher—Wie sie wirklich war; Die Beichte der Josefine Mutzenbacher; Das Tagebuch der Josefine Mutzenbacher** and a softcore version of the last called **Die heissen Nächte der Josefine Mutzenbacher.**

**Illustrierte Film-Bühne**

VEREINIGT MIT Illustr. Film-Kurier

Nr. 5249

# EIN TOTER HING IM NETZ

# Film Reviews

## ▶ HORROR OF SPIDER ISLAND/ IT'S HOT IN PARADISE
(Ein Toter hing im Netz)

*With Barbara Valentin, Alex d'Arcy, Helga Frank. Directed and written by Fritz Boettger. West Germany/Austria, 1959. 82 minutes*

When it was released in Paris in February 1961, **The Horror of Spider Island** was immediately slammed by the Office Catholique du Cinéma. More than 30 years down the pike there are very few people who'd be upset by its innocent mixture of flesh and horror. **Spider Island** is an infantile fantasy, where mundane reality is overthrown by the exotic and the deliciously fabulous.

French critic Ado Kyrou was the first to pick up on its subtle charms, describing it as 'one of the peaks of the genre (of erotic terror). Here the fantastic and the soft porn unite in an absence of scenery, building or mise-en-scene and the result is to leave us with unforgettable images. Involuntarily **The Horror of Spider Island** is a Dadaist film.'

Kyrou's analysis of this low budget gem is timeless and remarkably astute. He explains how it works differently from films that use a logical or linear narrative. **Spider Island** is a succession of erotic and tenderly macabre moments that culminate in 'a Tahitian party' where 6 curvy gals go pagan in order to attract the only two men on the island. This harmless, delightful male fantasy sequence filled with 'sexy dances, erotic configurations, bared breasts and flowers in the navel' results in a cat-fight and one of the girls' breasts being tantalisingly exposed.

The idyllic revel is rudely interrupted when their manager, Gary, returns. He's been transformed into a spider man monster, a deranged man-beast who proceeds to attacks the woman he loves. As Kyrou puts it 'the man who is dormant in every monster wakes up. He steps back. It will be his end, since all the survivors, armed with illuminating psychoanalytical torches, give chase and push him towards the providential quicksand.' Like King Kong, the ghoulish spider man dies because of love—it was beauty who really killed the beast.

**The Horror of Spider Island** starts off in Hollywood, home of female pulchritude, with Gary (Alex d'Arcy) holding auditions in a kitsch office to the sounds of strip'n'jive jazz. He's looking for girls who can twirl energetically, long legged babes who know how to provide an all-important flash of taut hose, suspenders and cotton panties. He selects eight of Hollywood's finest. One of them is Babs (Barbara Valentin), a bona fide expert at adjusting her clothing, knowing exactly when to innocently reveal a hint of plump thigh offset with tasty undergarments. The first section of the film milks these sizzling glimpses for all they are worth, using these little sensual pings to effortlessly provide momentum.

Gary plans to take the girls to Singapore, but en route their plane crashes, leaving the group adrift on a life raft in the middle of the ocean. Luck, however, is with them and they find a tropical island, complete with shelter and spring water. The dishevelled gals teeter around the island on 2 ½ inch high heels and chance upon a scientist's hut which has 'a body in a web. It is an old man who is hanging from thick, badly interweaved lines in the hope of creating a spider web'. Kyrou also notes 'a large spider, as Lautréamont would say, glances at the girls, and ends up biting their manager. This bite transforms him into a spider man, obsessed by only one thought, how to suck the girlies dry. Terror mounts. One girl dies, then another.'

◀ (Facing page) Five girls, one spider man. **Horror of Spider Island** (1959)

**Horror of Spider Island** starts off like a saucy nudie cutie, with daring flashes of raised skirt. When the action hits the island there's even more of these little erotic incidents. The girls peel off in response to the tropical heat and, because there's eight of them, the innocently naughty permutations seem delightfully endless. All of the girls are healthy and curvaceous, each of them has a different personality and hairdo. They spend most of the film, dressing and undressing, alluring men, fighting over them and delivering dialogue like "hello big boy" with carefree aplomb.

These tiny moments do more than just fuel the film's momentum. They create an air of delicious fantasy, with each one adding more and more to the mixture. When the spider appears and bites Gary, the film slips further into this exquisite realm. The spider man adds a macabre, romantic flavour. He hides in hollow tree trunks and lurks behind trees and bushes. When the girls are near him he tries to reach out and grab them. Sometimes he kills them. More often than not his efforts come across as lovelorn and confused. In one memorable scene he tries to grasp one of the girls from behind. He tenderly clutches at her chiffon scarf. She steps forward to freedom; he seems inept, rendered harmless by a whiff of perfume.

**Horror of Spider Island** has plenty of these remarkable scenes. By combining sex and horror the film creates new possibilities. For surrealists such as Ado Kyrou, this blending of genres was like collage, it opened up new opportunities and helped liberate the creative imagination. This method was something that other film-makers including Franco and Rollin used to good effect later during the 1960's and 70's.

## ▶ THE BLOOD DEMON
(Die Schlangengrube und das Pendel)

*With Lex Barker, Karin Dor, Christopher Lee. Directed by Harald Reinl. Written by Manfred Koehler. West Germany, 1967. 85 minutes.*

"I have the blood of 12 virgins—you shall be the thirteenth," says Count Regula (Christopher Lee), gazing matter-of-factly at his buxom prisoner, Karin Dor. Regula has returned from the grave after thirty five long years. His black eyes are filled with ice cool determination. He looks pretty good for a guy who had a spiked metal mask mashed into his face before he was pulled apart by a team of four horses. Death doesn't hold much sting for this supernatural villain.

Regula has plans for eternal life, he also wants to revenge himself on the two families that executed him many moons ago. In true demonic style he manages to combine them both, and lures Karin Dor and Lex Barker to his eerie castle. To get there they have to travel through a misty forest filled with hanging corpses. This sequence is one of the high points of the film. Hands stick out of trees and pale bodies lie on thick branches. The whole tableau is beautiful and chilling.

When Dor and Barker arrive at Regula's 'bloody castle' it's clear they have entered a world where ordinary rules just don't apply. The castle walls are covered with spectacular murals—the scenes they depict are straight out the hell-worlds of Heironymous Bosch. Regula's dungeon is filled with secret passages, has armour that moves and also contains twelve virgins strapped into torture devices and skewered by implements of doom.

His victims seem helpless against his fiendish power, they're blown by unnatural winds onto shaky ledges or popped into torture rooms on his slightest whim. This uncertainty, coupled with the incredible decor, gives the film a surreal edge. Unfortunately the ghoulish atmosphere these scenes provide isn't sustained throughout, nevertheless it still contains some highly potent moments and is well worth investigating.

Karin Dor, the 13th virgin ▼
**Blood Demon** (1967)

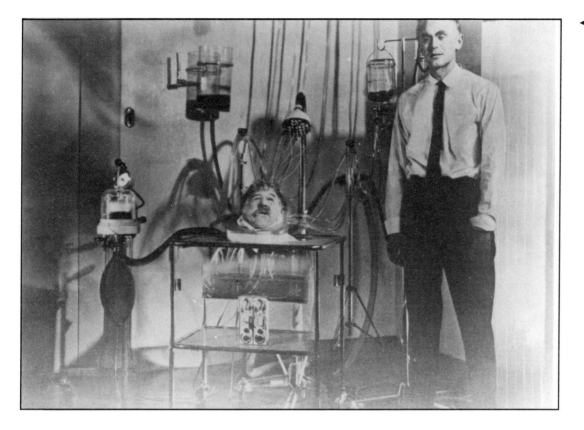

## ▶ THE HEAD
### (Die Nackte und der Satan)

*With Horst Frank, Michel Simon, Christine Maybach, Karin Kernke. Directed and written by Victor Trivias. West Germany,1959. 92 minutes*

This demented epic totally revolutionised the severed head sub-genre, but more importantly it must also have been an influence on Franco's **Diabolical Dr Z** (1965). Both films have an intense, claustrophobic edge and feature similar preoccupations and style. Architecture is very important in each of them with spiralling staircases and large stone buildings providing echo-ridden surroundings in which unsavoury dramas unfold.

**The Head** is a dark brooding film, and much of the action, lighting and character motivation harks back to the early days of German expressionism. This is what gives the film its deep rooted power. The menacing blackness is broken up by irregular patches of light and the characters emerge unnervingly from the shadows. Branches of trees often fill the screen like tentacles—the world seems unsavoury and unsafe.

Such is the environment the mysterious Dr Ood comes to ... and pretty soon he's decapitating bodies left, right and centre. He keeps the head of a famous scientist wired up in the basement and transplants the head of a beautiful but deformed

girl onto the body of a voluptuous dancer. His crazed genius gives him the power to breathe life into his overblown desires. Luckily his grisly obsessions are put to an end, but not before he has disposed of or physically altered half of the cast.

**The Head** is a real shocker, not just because of the trail of mutilated corpses or the eerie quality of the photography. It's a whammer with a genuine taste of the macabre—this is mainly due to Ood(Horst Frank) and his supernatural determination and desire. He helps give the film its unstoppable drive.

Director Victor Trivias had previously worked in Hollywood as a director/writer/producer and **The Head** was his last film. Which was unfortunate, as it's well put together with plenty of unusual touches and outlandish ideas.

Emmanuelle

エマニエル夫人

Immoral Tales

# French Undressing

## THE FRENCH FILM INDUSTRY

In France, the softcore sexploitation film had reached a high degree of gloss and sophistication by the beginning of the 1970's. Directors like Vadim (**Barbarella**), and Bénazéraf (**L'éternité pour nous**; **Frustration**) had created an indigenous industry that reached its peak in 1974 with the release of **Emmanuelle**. The film was astonishingly successful—to date, the highest grossing French film of all time. In the same year the intellectual avant-garde moved into the lucrative area of the erotic, in the persons of Walerian Borowczyk (**Immoral Tales**) and Alain Robbe-Grillet (**Glissements progressifs du plaisir**).

Hardcore sex scenes had begun to appear in French cinemas a couple of years earlier, but only in a clandestine, underground form. In Marseilles, with its large shifting population of immigrant workers and sailors, local distributors had begun to cut short hardcore segments into otherwise 'soft' films to attract an audience. At the Cannes festival the following year, films were offered to potential buyers with a whole series of optional 'inserts' that they could choose from to spice up the final product. Soon French producers were making films to order, pushing things as far as was legally allowed. Both Jess Franco and Jean Rollin were early producers of these *'chop suey'* pornos. Many of the actors and actresses who featured in the additional scenes were later to become bona fide stars of the homegrown porno industry.

The following year, things began to move quickly. The new Giscardien government had made great play of their intention to liberalise the arts and do away with censorship. Their mettle was soon tested by the opening in Paris, in April 1975, of the first genuinely 'hardcore' film to be commercially shown in cinemas there. It was Alex de Renzy's famous **History of the Blue Movie** and it was a sensational success, with over 207,000 tickets sold that year. Soon the first home grown hardcore, Jean-François Davy's **Exhibition,** opened to packed houses. Well over half a million people went to see it .

Due to a combination of the liberal laws and a long history of sexual openness in the French commercial cinema, films like **Emmanuelle**, **Exhibition** and the later **Story of O** were backed

by large distributors and shown in mainstream cinemas. **Exhibition**, for example, had the might of UGC behind it, while **Les jouisseuses (Unfaithful Wives)** was distributed by Gaumont, and broke records in many of their houses. The big cinemas in the Champs Élysées, right in the heart of Paris, would openly show hardcore films. They were mixed in with and advertised alongside mainstream, general audience fare such as **The Sting** or **Jaws**. The contrast was especially vivid during the holiday period; few of the big companies put out their major product in the summer months and distributors of adult films took advantage of this, shipping their works in June, July and August to maximise viewer interest.

Soon the river had turned into a flood. It seemed as though the whole of the French film industry was about to be possessed by the demon of sex. Even small cinemas in out of the way provincial towns were showing openly hardcore films after midnight or on special matinées. While the specialist cinemas that might have shown horror films, spaghetti westerns or kung fu had almost all gone over to an exclusive diet of sex. The number of films in distribution that could bear the label 'pornographic' rocketed in a very few years. In a two week period in 1972 only six films showing in Paris could be classed as broadly 'adult'; by 1975 in the same two week period this had risen to an astonishing 75.

Several of the producers and directors involved in this phenomenon were renegades from the fantasy and horror cinema—a genre that has never had an easy ride in France. This group included old hands like Jess Franco and Jean Rollin, but also Francis Leroi, Claude

"You bring out the beast in me!" **La bonzesse** (1973)

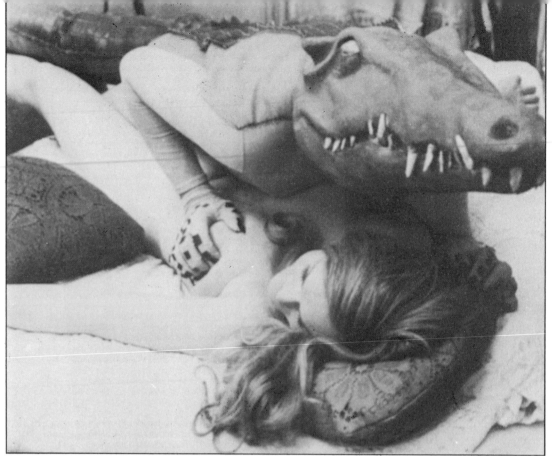

Mulot and Jean-François Davy—all of whom would become leading lights in the hardcore area. [1] Michel Lemoine, who had worked as an actor in horror films for many years, including a stint with Franco (**Necronomicon, Kiss Me, Monster**), and former *Midi-Minuit Fantastique* alumnus Michael Caen were also enthusiasts. In January of 1975, at the Avoriaz Festival of Horror and Science Fiction films, eyebrows had been raised by the programming of the hardcore comedy **Flesh Gordon** and the awarding of a prize to Borowczyk's **La bête**. And it was with a fantasy subject, pushed to the point of parody, that Mulot and Leroi gave the French sex film industry its first hardcore classic, **Pussy Talk (Le sexe qui parle)**. [2]

1975 was the Year of Woman. It was also the year of sex. Culminating in the First (and last) Festival of Pornographic Films in Paris. It was organised by Michel Lemoine, who solemnly handed out the awards (Golden Willys) to homegrown stars like Claudine Beccarie and to US product like Jim Buckley's **S.O.S.** Seven years on from the *'événements'* of May 1968 there were now a new set of events for the press to get excited about. Everywhere there was talk of liberation—but sexual, this time, not political. Even though there were plenty with memories long enough to say that they were the same thing. The political had become the personal. And the personal meant sex.

Almost overnight, magazines sprang up to exploit and celebrate the new permissiveness. Titles like *Absolu* and *Sexpol* were the sophisticated end of the spectrum, while *Sex Stars System*, *Sex Hebdo* and *Ciné Girl* catered for the less respectable sectors of the market. There was much talk of 'The Pornocrats', this new breed of young, iconoclastic film-makers who suddenly seemed to have everything going for them. Leroi and Davy were its leading lights but it was a broad definition that also included actresses like Beatrice Harnois and Sylvia Bourdon and actors like Richard Allan (nick-named 'Concrete Cock') and Thierry de Brem. If Bénazéraf and Borowczyk were its *eminences grises*, it also included well-respected critics like Noël Simsolo and 'straight' film-makers like Paul Vecchiali.

Naturally, this phenomenon did not pass without comment. From the Right the complaint was the familiar one of "moral decline"; from the Left it was the equally familiar protest about "exploitation". There was also a fear, from some of the more moderate elements in the industry, that French cinema was in danger of going the way of the German industry a few years earlier. There, towards the end of the 1960's, a flood of sex films combined with the rise of TV drove the middle class, middle of the road audience away and nearly destroyed the film business.

An unprecedented French press campaign soon led to official intervention. In October 1976 the so-called 'X Law'—actually a finance bill—was passed by the legislature. The law was designed not to ban sex films—something that would have been contrary to the expressed philosophy of the State—but to limit their growth.

To this end, official support was withdrawn from makers of sex-films. France has always had an enviable system whereby a producer can receive an advance of the estimated box-office takings. Soon rigid definitions of what constituted a 'quality' or artistic film were introduced to deny this assistance to sex films. More insidiously, a tax was to be levied against the takings of sex films which would then be put back into the production of films of 'artistic merit' as decided by the state. Finally, the actual distribution of X films was to be severely limited by only allowing them to be shown in specially designated cinemas, where advertising would be reduced to a minimum: no pictures on the posters, no photographs outside the cinemas. All that remained to attract the viewer would be the title. It was during this period that the names of French sex films became more and more outrageous.

Effectively, the first X law drove the sex film into a semi-clandestine underground, the commercial underground, from where it has never really escaped. The days of big-budget, prestige productions were soon over. A top-rate porno at the time would cost about 800,000 francs—a cheap one, 80,000; by contrast an average budget for a commercial film was about 2,000,000 francs.

In their ghetto, invisible to the mainstream critics, all kinds of scams were indulged in by the producers and distributors of sex-films. Old films were rereleased with new titles; outtakes or sequences from existing films would be edited together to create a 'new' film; even some old non-porno films would be released with added hardcore scenes. An English softcore film, **Groupie Girl**, directed by Derek Ford, was released in 1973 with added sex scenes, under the title of **Les demi-sels de la perversion** (The Pimps of Perversion); a year later, as things hotted up, it was released *again* with even harder additions as **Les affamées du mâle** (Man-hungry Women), credited to Derek Fred. But perhaps the saddest instance of this ploy was the addition of hardcore scenes into Terence Fisher's old-fashioned SF movie **Night of the Big Heat**! There was even a practice of reintroducing cut sequences into 18-only films after they had been certificated, turning them back into pornos. The assumption being that the licensing authorities would never actually go to

see the films once they had been passed. A variation on this scam was the tacking of credit sequences and certification 'visa' numbers from old softcore films onto the beginning of hardcores. In this way they could be shown and advertised outside the specialist circuit, and so get a much wider audience. Francis Mischkind of Alpha France—one of the veterans of the French hardcore industry—says that there was a veritable growth market in second hand visas at the time.

But in spite of these and many more tricks, the industry drifted into a perpetual twilight. There were many who mourned its passing. Not least the directors, actors and technicians who had seen the dramatic rise of porno providing lucrative employment for years to come. They, above all others, were aware of the telling fact that cinema attendance in France had fallen from a high of 276 million in 1964 to 176 million by 1973. Only porno had drawn the crowds back to the cinemas. Now they were drifting away again.

As though things were not already bad enough, in 1981 the Minister of Culture, having observed the shady goings on in the lower depths of the industry for some years, decided to come down hard on all transgressors. Laws were now to be rigorously enforced and loopholes closed. Many companies went out of business. Then, a couple of years later, video came onto the scene, completely killing off the small, specialist cinemas. At the end of 1976

◀ **What a Performer** (1975)

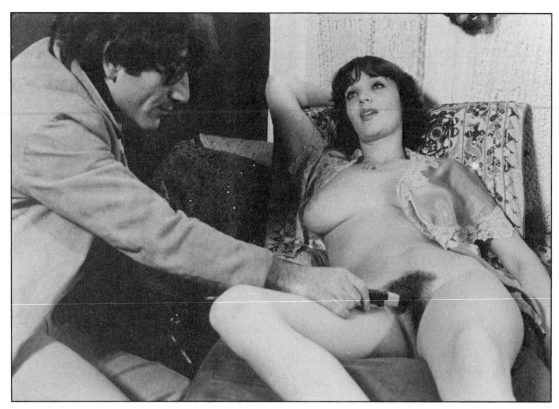

there were 160 Paris cinemas licensed to show X-designated films. By the beginning of 1990 this number had fallen to 25. In 1985 the famous Midi-Minuit ³ closed its doors for the last time. It was the end of an era.

The sex film industry in France today, if it can be graced with the name at all, is only a shadow of its former self. The notion that young directors had in the early 1970's, of carving out a career for themselves through the ranks of the X film is a thing of the distant past. As is the idea that sex films are part of some general 'post-68' political wave. Things have turned full circle and now the sex film has gone back to its furtive beginnings and its audience of 'dirty old men and spotty adolescents'. Gone are the days when the bare breasts of Sylvie Meyer (on the poster for **La bonzesse**) confronted Giscard d'Estaing as he walked along the Champs Élysées to the Tomb of the Unknown Soldier.

The industry is now resolutely ghettoised. Some film-makers still specialise in X productions and there are a couple of agencies who provide the rare (very rare) homegrown talent to star in them. Most of the product is now shot direct to video, with a derisory budget, around 20,000 francs on average, and a one or two day shooting schedule. Video producers and distributors such as Marc Dorcel specialise in this field and the films are sold on cassette or shown in special video booths in the sex shops of Pigalle and Clichy.

The idea that there is a universal audience for porn has also vanished. Most product today is rigidly categorised into 'specialist' classes—films for lovers of big tits, anal sex or S&M etc. Video shops rank them accordingly to save their customers the trouble of having to browse in search of their particular predilection.

Recently there has been talk of a revival of porno in France. The TV channel Canal Plus shows hardcore films late at night to an audience who were either too young or too embarrassed to have seen them the first time round. Some of the old guard, such as Francis Mischkind, feel that now, with the levelling out that the small screen performs, hardcore may at last be seen for what it is—just another part of the film industry, with its good and its bad product like any other genre. But secretly he knows that the days when a director like Clouzot, maker of classics such as **Les diaboliques** and **Wages of Fear**, would come to him fired up with enthusiasm to make a hardcore film are probably gone forever.

---

¹ It was in fact the problems he encountered with his film version of Kurt Steiner's dark thriller **Le seuil du vide** (Threshold of the Void) in 1971 that led Davy to become his own producer. A road which eventually brought him to **Exhibition** in 1975.

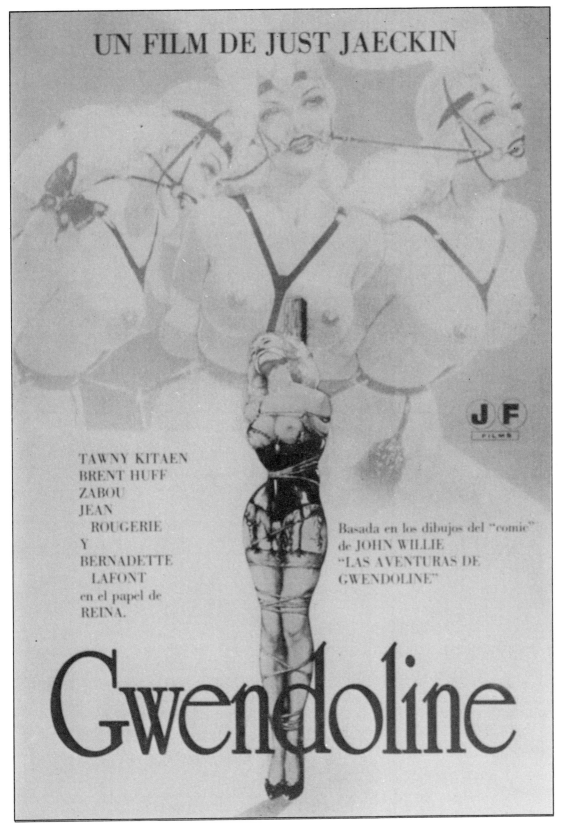

UN FILM DE JUST JAECKIN

TAWNY KITAEN
BRENT HUFF
ZABOU
JEAN
    ROUGERIE
Y
BERNADETTE
LAFONT
en el papel de
REINA.

Basada en los dibujos del "comic"
de JOHN WILLIE
"LAS AVENTURAS DE
GWENDOLINE"

JF FILMS

# Gwendoline

◄ Spanish press book for
Just Jaeckin's
**Gwendoline** (1984),
based on the famous John
Willie comic strip

[2] The film also featured Jean-Lou Philippe, star and co-writer of Jean Rollin's **Lèvres de sang**.

[3] The Midi-Minuit, along with Le Colorado, Le Styx, Le Scarlett and Le Mexico were all Paris cinemas that showed horror films, westerns, Italian epics and sexy thrillers. When hardcore came in they all started showing that instead. Le Brady is now the only small Paris cinema that regularly shows old horror films.

# SPERMULA

*Certaines femmes vampires*
*ne se nourrissent pas de sang.*

FILM AND C° présente   DAYLE HADDON   dans **SPERMULA**   avec   UDO KIER

FRANÇOIS DUNOYER · JOCELYNE BOISSEAU et GEORGES GERET

GINETTE LECLERC · ISABELLE MERCANTON · SUZANNAH DJIAN · ANGELA Mc DONALD · RADIAH FRYE · SYLVIE MEYER et PIERAL

un film écrit et réalisé par CHARLES MATTON · Directeur de la photo JEAN-JACQUES FLORI · Musique de JOSÉ BARTEL · Édition Musicale GRENADINE MUSIC

INTERDIT AUX MOINS DE 18 ANS   distribuée par WEA FILIPACCHI · C'est une Production FILM AND C° France   Distribution PARAFRANCE

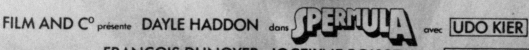

# Film Reviews

▶**SPERMULA**

*With Dale Haddon, Udo Kier, Georges Geret, Ginette Leclerc. Directed and written by Charles Matton. France, 1976. 110 minutes*

The film begins with a few lines of explanation. During the 1930's, in America, there was a sect composed of rich and eccentric libertines. They rejected any idea of love, considered artistic creation as a form of evil and tried to find in total sexual freedom the ecstasy of pure being. Following a conference that they called in New York in 1937, all members of the sect disappeared. Years later a journalist tracked them down to a secret location in the forests of South America. He too was never heard of again.

*'This film is the story of some of their daughters.'*

From out of a mist a huge flying boat wings its way through the nighttime sky. Inside, resplendent in art deco gowns and perfect make-up, Spermula and her cohorts are on their way back to 'civilisation.' Their mission....? To bring their message of peace and freedom to a world gone mad. Their method....? To 'spermulise' men. That is, to draw off the sexual essence that causes aggression, acquisitiveness and jealousy.

The women communicate by means of telepathy, a power that they also use to entice people into their circle. They take up residence in a huge mansion, whose neighbours include the town's mayor, his unhappy and abused wife, his venal, social climbing assistant and a fat and frustrated widow who has incestuous designs on her lazy son.

Gradually Spermula and co. draw together the strands of the plot that finally ends in a huge orgy in which everyone gets what they want—or, at least, what they deserve.

Unfortunately, the women become corrupted by this contact with the outside world and their beautiful leader, Spermula, falls in love with a young artist and sacrifices her immortality for a night of passion with him.

**Spermula** is a beautiful and enigmatic film, full of glossy and apparently meaningless images, that nevertheless haunt the mind long after the film has finished. It should come as no surprise to learn that its writer and director, Charles Matton, trained as a painter and sculptor. He also worked for many years as a fashion photographer and illustrator for magazines like *Lui* under the pseudonym of Pascalini. The art direction of **Spermula** is by him, as are the many strange models of landscapes and human figures that float in and out of the frame.

**Spermula** is not an easy film to assess. It creates its own rules and demands that we enter into the world it presents to us. All sense of continuity is fractured by Matton's eccentric editing, in which events seem to take place in an almost random sequence. On the soundtrack, the fantasies and memories of the women combine with their telepathic communications to each other, giving a strange sense of alienation to the on-screen events.

Despite its title, there is actually little explicit sex in **Spermula**. The name brings to mind the heroines of Italian adult comics of the 1970's—*Jacula, Uranella, Sybilla*—and the film shares their almost parodic, teasing sense of fun. The real delights of the film are visual rather than venal. The costumes, the lavish decor of Spermula's mansion and the luminous photography, with the light constantly playing on the glossy lips and shiny satin gowns of the women, are a testament to Matton's exquisite sense of style.

**Spermula** could have been a classic. Unfortunately, it appeared in cinemas in France at just that time when the so called 'X law' was coming down hard on anything that looked remotely like a sex film. Matton's previous feature—**L'italien des roses**, from 1972—had earned him good notices and he looked like being a contender. The debâcle surrounding **Spermula** effectively finished off his career. Now the film is best appreciated as the high point of the French erotic cinema of the mid-seventies, and a requiem to that whole period.

"Fancy directing a sex ▲
flick?" **La Goulve** (1972)

## ▶EROTIC WITCHCRAFT
(La Goulve)

*With Hervé Hendrickx, César Torres, Maïka Simon,
Marie-Ange Saint-Clair, Anne Varèse. Directed by
Mario Mercier and Bepi Fontana. Written by Mario
Mercier. France, 1972.*

Raymond tells us his story. How his father killed
himself and his wife and how he came to live
with Monsieur Alex, a sorcerer, who taught him
all the secrets he knew. Including the secret of
the Goulve—an ancient goddess imbued with
the power of snakes.

An outcast in the small mountain village
where he lives, Raymond decides to use his
knowledge of magic to win over Agnes, a local
girl on whom he has designs. But Monsieur
Alex had warned him that the power of the
Goulve must not be abused, and soon Raymond
must face the consequences when the goddess
takes her terrifying revenge.

There are two types of film that linger on in the
mind of the viewer: the first are 'classic' films—
ones that use the traditional language of cinema
in a new and exciting way to tell a story that
moves or disturbs. The other sort—much rarer
—are films that seem to have sprung out of
nowhere, that seem to have no antecedents, creating their own grammar and going their own
way, regardless of our aesthetic or artistic preconceptions. **Erotic Witchcraft** is one such.

The lowness of the budget is obvious in every
shot of the film. There was no money for special
effects, and so the film makers resorted to the
oldest tricks in the book—probably reinventing
them as they went—shifting in and out of focus
to effect scene changes, using very obvious fil-
ters and distorting lenses, and lighting
nighttime scenes with searchlights (possibly
even car headlights). The cast are obvious amateurs and the costumes homemade. At one
point the camera pans along a row of witches,
posed to reveal their stockinged thighs. One of
the girls winks broadly into the lens. For some
inexplicable reason the effect is not to dissipate
the tension of the scene. It heightens it. We are
watching a home movie. But one made by someone with very serious intentions. Obsessive.
Someone who sees things that he is desperate to
show us. At any cost.

Watching **Erotic Witchcraft** is like having the
top of your skull taken off and blown into. It
shakes up your preconceptions about cinema
and what it is and should be. Finally you know
that you are seeing the world in a new way,
through eyes that have a different perspective
from the rest of us.

Most of the credit for this has to be put down
to the film's author and co-director, Mario
Mercier. He was originally a painter and sculptor, based in Nice in the South of France. The film
is set in the hot, mountainous regions nearby,
where ancient cults still survive into the present
day. Mercier worked as a nurse in a psychiatric

hospital and in a funeral parlour while he wrote the book that would make him notorious—*Jeanne's Journal*. Its publisher, Eric Losfeld, was prosecuted and Mercier's subsequent book, *Le Nécrophile*, was banned outright.

**Erotic Witchcraft** was produced and co-directed by exploitation specialist Bepi Fontana, whose Welp Films had released an erotic thriller called **Quai du désir** a couple of years earlier. Apparently Fontana reedited **Erotic Witchcraft** after it had been completed to make it more 'commercial.' A fact that probably accounts for some of its more incongruous moments. He should have let Mercier have his own way.

**Erotic Witchcraft** was a reasonable success, and a couple of years later Mercier, on his own this time, made **La papesse**. Again the subject of the film is witchcraft, but this time the fictional elements are kept to a minimum. The cast are mostly members of an existing sect and the 'Popesse' of the title is a genuine adept—Géziale. **La papesse** shows scenes of real possession, secret rites and initiations in a way that is both terrifying and fascinating. Too terrifying for the authorities at the time, who banned it. The Minister of Culture, Michel Guy, described the film as consisting of 'an uninterrupted succession of scenes of sadism, torture and violence'.

Other critics were equally harsh. *Écran*, reviewing the film on its release in 1975, cried 'Rollin, you are not alone!' describing Mercier, with misplaced irony, as 'a disciple of this Master in the creation of a pompous naiveté and a genuine French camp'. In fact Rollin did have several meetings with Mercier during the mid 1970's and their careers have followed similar paths since. Both have taken up writing as a substitute for film-making.

What they share is a rare ability to visualise those states of existence that are beyond the rational, beyond analysis. For that reason they, like any others who venture into similar terrain, will always run the risk of being not only misunderstood but openly ridiculed—unless they have the safety net of a big budget and 'artistic' pretensions to protect themselves with.

As Mario Mercier wrote: 'Death by silence is the fate of all who refuse to follow the safety of the well trodden paths.

'But whoever dies such a death can always place his hopes in resurrection.'

▲ Mario Mercier

GEMINI FILMS present *Erotic Witchcraft* COLOUR X

# Spanish Customs

## THE SPANISH FILM INDUSTRY

Spain, at the beginning of the 1950's, was a country culturally and politically divorced from the rest of Europe. Film censorship was rigid. Anything that dealt in a controversial way with sex, politics or religion was totally forbidden. Historical dramas about Spain's 'Golden Age', or religious films like Rafael Gil's **The Lady of Fatima**, were the staple fare. Young film-makers and film enthusiasts had little hope of seeing any of the ground-breaking foreign films that they read about in the press. This led to the formation of film-clubs in many of the larger towns, where subtitled imported films were shown to a specialist audience. A tentative new movement began to grow up around these clubs and the film reviews they published. Two of the most important figures of this Spanish new wave were Juan Antonio Bardem and Luis Garcia Berlanga. Films such as Berlanga's **Bienvenido Mr. Marshall (Welcome Mr. Marshall**; 1953), along with Bardem's **Comicos** (1954) and **Muerte de un ciclista (Death of a Cyclist**; 1955), were the first new Spanish films to have impact at festivals overseas.

But still Bardem was moved to write: 'Spanish cinema lives in a state of isolation. It is isolated not only from the world, but from our own reality.'

From the mid-1950's onwards things began to change. Throughout the decade there had been behind the scenes moves to readmit Spain to the international community, which culminated in 1959 with Eisenhower's visit to Madrid. As the barriers came down, new money from tourism and new ideas from outside began to make their influence felt. Imported Italian comedies introduced a more contemporary and provocative form of eroticism than had been seen in Spanish cinemas. Previously it was only in historical dramas or romantic tragedies that any notion of 'hot blood' had been allowed to creep in.

A new genre began to emerge, in the form of contemporary comedies set in holiday resorts up in the mountains or on the coast. With a cast of 'bright young things' and the trappings of an emerging consumer society—fashionable clothes, sports cars and pop-music—the New Spain began to make an appearance. Films like **Muchachas en vacaciones** (Girls on Holiday;1958) and **Une chica de Chicago** (A Chick From Chicago; 1958) were the first trickles of what would soon become a flood.

During the next decade things began to move even faster. This was the period of the 'Happy Sixties' (Los felices 60), when Spain became the new playground of Europe. **Bahia de Palma** (1962) with Elke Sommer, **La chica del autostop** (Hitch-hike Girl;1964) and **Las nenas del minimini** (Dolls in Mini-skirts) all showed the profound changes that the unstoppable juggernaut of tourism was bringing into the peninsula.

In 1962, the forty year old Manuel Fraga was appointed as Minister of Information and Tourism. He was a cautious liberal, and under his direction and that of the cinema supremo, José Garcia Escudero, the rigid system of censorship began to mellow slightly. New laws were brought in to help Spanish producers, quota systems were instituted to support home-grown product, and in 1967 a system of 'special theatres', largely derived from the model of the film clubs, allowed imported films to be shown under less rigid systems of control.

This was the Golden Age of Spanish cinema, with the rise of genre films and co-productions with other European countries. Samuel Bronsten's **King of Kings**, **El Cid** and **55 Days At Peking**,[1] had injected a new professionalism into the local industry. For the first time they found themselves working with American producers and directors. But, rather than attempt these huge scale productions, Spanish film-makers preferred to split the risk by sharing production costs with other European countries.

Exotic secret agent films were popular. These gave the chance to film across Europe in a wide variety of locations, milking the maximum benefit from the co-production deal. Their episodic nature also allowed the chance to squeeze in brief guest appearances by well known stars, who would them be prominently displayed on the posters and newspaper ad-mats. These films may have been inspired by the success of the Bond series, but they soon outstripped their models with exotic trappings and sheer deftness of plot.[2] **Operation Counterspy** (1965) and the **O77** series starring Ken Clark are typical of the product, of which Jess Franco's **Attack of the Robots** is probably the peak.

Westerns, comedy thrillers and even peplums were also grist to this energetic mill of popular cinema. A huge repertory company of actors—Helga Line, Diana Lorys, Mara Cruz, Antonio Casas, Ricardo Palacios, Fernando Sancho—and directors—León Klimovsky, Juan Bosch, José Luis Merino, Rafael Gil—existed to service the needs of this hungry machine. Some, like actor Antonio Casas and director Rafael Gil, had been

la cruz del diablo

◄ (Facing page) Blind dead Templars seek new victims, **Tombs of the Blind Dead** (1971)

**TONY KENDALL**
**HELGA LINE · SILVIA TORTOSA**

Two from Amando de ▲
Ossorio. **Lorelei's**
**Grasp** (1972)

around since the 1940's, others got their first breaks during this Golden Age.

There was a temporary setback at the end of the sixties. The government was concerned about the huge growth in cheap co-productions and tried to limit them by imposing higher minimum budgets. This was combined with a general tightening up of the political situation, resulting in the removal of Fraga and an attempt to return to the 'good old days' of the 1950's. The immensely popular film clubs also came under close scrutiny. But this move by the aging General Franco to reassert his influence was short lived. There was a limit to how much could be done, even by a dictator, to keep people in blissful ignorance. Audiences have an infinite need to be corrupted—or to test their incorruptibility by exposure to things that are bad for them.

In the early seventies, Spanish audiences became fascinated by reports of the 'forbidden' films being shown just across the border in France. Special trips were arranged to Biarritz and Perpignan to see films like **Last Tango in Paris** or **Decameron**. The canny French distributors were not slow to spot an advantage, and soon there were regular 'Spanish weeks' at the local cinemas, advertised in Spanish papers, with films shown in subtitled versions whenever possible.

Every weekend during 1973 and through 1974 a regular convoy of battered Seat cars would descend on these border towns, and for years it was impossible to get a hotel room in Perpignan on a Friday or Saturday night. In 1973 five new cinemas opened there and **Last Tango in Paris**, a particularly hot item at the time, was seen by more than 150,000 viewers in the town's cinemas. With a population of 200,000 this is an astonishing figure. The cinemas would open their doors at ten in the morning and show films right up until midnight. Often, keen Spaniards would catch three or four films in a weekend, before returning bleary eyed across the border, their pockets full of 'specialist' sex film magazines that the Spanish customs officers would duly confiscate.

Several Spanish films were made at the time that used these 'sleaze weekends' as subject matter. **Lo verde empieza en los Pireneos** (Smut Begins at the Pyrenees;1974) directed by Vicente Escriva was one of the best. These films usually featured a definite moral sting in their tail to assure local audiences that the world 'out there' was really a dangerous and unhappy place. It was much safer, was the message, to stay at home in Spain. Under this guise of moral edu-

cation things became much more explicit. Suddenly it was possible to show more than ever before of the behaviour and effects of the permissive society—sex, drugs, crime—so long as the moral lesson learned at the end of it was always that such things were not good.

**Odio mi cuerpo** (I Hate My Body;1973), directed by León Klimovsky, was a clever blending of genres, beginning with a brain transplant performed by an ex-Nazi doctor. The woman with a man's brain then comes up against the usual problems when she tries to get a job—the brain only knows how to do man's work for which her woman's body makes her ineligible. In desperation, she digs up the man's corpse and destroys it. The message of this one is obvious—woman, know your place.

From crime thrillers (**Aborto criminal**; Illegal Abortion) to comedies (**¿Doctor, me gustan las mujeres, es grave?**; Doctor, I like Women—is it Serious?), the vicarious thrill was served up as a cautionary tale. But probably the most fertile ground for salutary kicks was the horror film.

The Spanish horror film changed in the late sixties and early seventies. Not that there had been many Spanish horror films before then. Mostly they were dark thrillers concerning mad scientists or crazed killers with scarred faces[3]—rational films short on sinister psychology or sexual undercurrents. The only genuine horror films from the early sixties were Italian co-productions like **The Blancheville Monster** and **Crypt of Horror**. These were outgrowths of the current Italian horror boom, rather than part of any local tradition.

....and **Fangs of the**
**Living Dead** (1968) ▶

**Immoral Tales**

If there was a local tradition it was that of parody, and horror elements were used for laughs in several films of the period. As early as 1959 Franco's first feature—**Tenemos 18 años** (We Are Eighteen) had included a parody of straight horror as one element of its loose, episodic format. As did films like **Escala en hi-fi** (Moving Up to Hi-Fi; 1963) and, in particular, **Un vampiro para dos** (A Vampire for Two) from 1965, where a pair of Spanish guest workers are vampirised by their German employer. **Malenka** (**Fangs of the Living Dead**;1969) written and directed by Amando de Ossorio also has elements of comedy and parody in a film loosely inspired by Polanski's **Dance of the Vampires**.

But the first real Spanish horror film came in 1967, with **Frankenstein's Bloody Terror/Hell's Creatures**, written by and starring Paul Naschy in the first of his many appearances as the werewolf Waldemar Daninsky. The film was a big budget effort for the time, shot in 3D and 70mm widescreen. It had some local success and was distributed abroad—a rare event for any Spanish picture in those days. But the horror 'boom' really began with the success of **The House That Screamed (La residencia)** in 1969, and was consolidated by **Werewolf versus the Vampire Woman** the following year.

Then the floodgates opened, and for the next four years or so films appeared at the rate of one or two a month. Again they were mostly co-productions, usually with Italy, France and Germany—or combinations of all three. But there was always a definable Spanish tinge to the mixture, most marked when Spanish directors helmed the productions.

In lots of ways these films were a sublimation of the forbidden elements—sex, religion, politics—into horror forms. It doesn't take much imagination to find in the plots of the various 'Blind Dead' films of Amando de Ossorio, for example, a not too subtle reference to the notion of the old Spain of the Templars rising out of its grave to strike back at the decadent young. Lesbianism and other officially defined 'perversions' featured in many of these films. Although the prints shown in local cinemas were often milder than the export versions—particularly those directed at Italian or German audiences.

Several of the directors who would constitute the next new wave of Spanish cinema rose to prominence during this horror mini boom. Vicente Aranda made **The Blood-Spattered Bride (La novia ensangretada**; 1972), Eloy de La

▲ Mind games and psychological horror, **The Bell of Hell** (1973)

Iglesia made **Cannibal Man (La semana del asesino**; 1972), and one of the most interesting films of the period, **The Bell of Hell (La campana del infierno**; 1973) was begun by Claudio Guerin Hill. His accidental death during the shooting of the film robbed Spanish cinema of one its most promising talents. Interestingly, the film was finished by Bardem. Ten years later it was still the thing for young turks to cut their teeth on horror material as a way of breaking into the international market; for example Almodóvar's **Matador** (1986), and the much touted Bigas Luna with **Anguish (Angustia**; 1988).

Not all the directors who got their first break in this brief horror boom went on to greater things. Francisco Lara Polop, for example, whose **Murder Mansion** (1972) was a clever and spooky little thriller, went on to **Virilidad a la Española** (1975), a corny piece of old-fashioned macho. While Carlos Aured (**Horror Rises From the Tomb, Blue Eyes of the Broken Doll**) ended up in the eighties' porn ghetto with

**Apocalipsis sexual** (1982), which features such scenes as the blade of a flick knife being slid into Ajita Wilson's vagina.

Again there was a team of actors and actresses whose names are forever associated with this seventies' mini-boom; Helga Line, Patty Shepard, Maria Kosti, Barbara Rey and Teresa Gimpera for the women, Paul Naschy, Antonio Mayans, Julien Ugarte and Alberto Dalbes for the men.

Spanish horror was born out of commercial necessity. The Government had been clamping down on cheap co-productions. To recoup the costs of their bigger budgets, Spanish film-makers were being forced to find a formula that appealed to overseas markets. León Klimovsky, whose **Werewolf versus the Vampire Woman** was one of the first great successes of the boom, recalls that foreign distributors were not interested in Spanish films—but they were interested in horror films, no matter where they came from. So, initially, the films were a combination of elements drawn from the successful markets at which they were aimed—the **Psycho** style mad killer films from the US, for example, Hammer films, and the Italian Gothics of Bava and Margheriti—both of whom made films in Spain.

There was not really a Spanish literary tradition in horror to match the English and American forms and, for political as well as commercial reasons, the traditional folklore of the country was not considered a suitable model. But there is a Spanish flavour—almost Goyaesque—which is unmistakable in the best films of the period. They are cruder, more violent and visceral, with a definite flavour of the grotesque. Audiences are more often led to identify with the monsters than their victims. Paul Naschy's werewolf, for example, or his incarnation of Dracula in **Dracula's Virgin Lovers** (1973), are presented as sad, romantic characters whose monstrous natures are a source of pain to them. This is in marked contrast to the bloodlusting Count played by Christopher Lee in the Hammer versions of the myth.

Naschy himself was a great admirer of the traditional horror heroes, and in **The Howl of**

**Immoral Tales**

the Devil (**El aullido del diablo**; 1988) he set about impersonating a whole bunch of them—including his customary werewolf, but also Mr. Hyde, Quasimodo, Frankenstein's monster and the Phantom of the Opera. He was also drawn to traditional Spanish stories, and his script for the 1975 film **The Devil's Cross (La cruz del diablo)** draws heavily on the work of the 19th century Andalucian poet Gustavo Adolfo Becquer, who was also fascinated by ancient folk tales. **The Devil's Cross** tells of an English writer, Alfred Dawson, who begins to lose his grip on reality and sees the figments of his imagination come to haunt him through the figure of a strange and beautiful woman.[4] It's one of the most successful attempts to use Spanish models rather than imported horrors but it wasn't a commercial success. Spanish horror had passed its peak.

One of the factors that lead to the decline was the Government's clamping down on the practice of making double versions of films—with added sex and violence for export. This, combined with the post-**Exorcist** revival of horror in the American film industry, effectively put an end to the commercial appeal of the Spanish product. But there were even more important changes on the way.

General Franco died at the end of 1975. Many people, inside and outside Spain, expected a dramatic change in the status of the Arts, but in fact what began was a 'period of transition' that seemed to last almost ten years. Veteran Franco supporter Rafael Gil's 1980 film **...Y al terco año resucito** (And on the Third Year He Rose From the Dead) summed up a widespread mood. Ostensibly a comedy, the film tells how a mistake by a newspaper reporter puts into circulation the story that Franco has come back to life. The country is in turmoil. But for many people the reaction is one of relief, as they dig out their old uniforms and Nationalist flags and mass outside Franco's palace in Madrid, calling for him to lead them out of their confusion.

This period was given the name *'destape'* which means 'stripping off'. And that's pretty much what happened in the cinema. Lots of sexy, nudie type films were made. **Carry On** style comedies and cheap thrillers that showed abundant female flesh. In 1977 censorship was theoretically abolished in Spain. Out and out hardcore was still banned, though, and age limits for some types of films remained. More importantly, a new classification label 'S' was introduced. This was attached to films that were 'likely to damage the sensibility of the viewer'—in other words sex and horror films.

As the industry became more liberalised, there was a feeling among some Spanish filmmakers and producers that hardcore was soon to be legalised. Some of them began turning out films in double versions again—soft for the local market but with hardcore scenes added for export, and maybe also for the home market if things went the way they expected. Amongst these precursors of the later hardcore mini boom were Carlos Aured (who had begun as a director of horror films) with **Apocalipsis sexual**, Jaime Puig with **Bacanales romanas**—both starring Ajita Wilson—and two films by Jorge Gigo under the pseudonym of George Lewis, **Porno Girls** and **Trampa par una call girl** (Trap for a Call Girl). Jess Franco had also returned to Spain and made a whole series of 'S' designated films, to many of which hardcore scenes were added for export. Some of these films were co-produced with other European companies. Irwin Dietrich's Elite Company, for example, made a whole series of films about sex-crazed Swedes abroad in Ibiza (**6 sueces en Ibiza**, **Ibiza al desnudo** etc.).

The problem with the mainstream industry in this post-Franco period was that too many film-makers still seemed to be preoccupied with the past. Perhaps some of them were actually nostalgic for the embattled feeling of those years when they all had something to be

◀ The diabolical Paul Naschy, **Inquisición** (1976)

'against' and there was at least hope for the future. Now the future was here they didn't know what to do with it. It was only really with Almodóvar, who made his first feature in 1978, that films about the new, young Spain began to appear. As he said, "I never speak of Franco. I hardly acknowledge his existence. I start *after* Franco, and so there is no nostalgia or anything like that." A sort of turning point was reached in 1979 with Pilar Miró's film **El crimen de Cuenca**. The film was banned for its violent and unsympathetic portrayal of the revered Guardia Civil. Its director, one of the few women working in the Spanish industry, was threatened with imprisonment. Fortunately for Miró, a rebel band of Guardia Civil invaded the Spanish Parliament in 1981 and held the congress members up at gunpoint to protest about the moral decline of the nation.

The incident was shown on TV sets all over the world. A shocked audience reacted quickly against this resurgence of Francoism. Later that year Spain's first Socialist government was elected—with Pilar Miró appointed as Director General of Cinematography. She began to institute a policy of unconditional government support to films of 'artistic merit'. Financial backing, guaranteed distribution and advances of up to 65% of budget were promised to approved film-makers—to be selected by a Miró-appointed panel of film professionals. There were some rumblings of discontent. A few pointed out that this was just another form of censorship—a different sort of iron fist in a bright new velvet glove. But they were largely ignored.

By 1984 censorship had been abolished in Spain. The 'S' label was done away with and replaced with an 'X'. Specially licensed theatres were allowed to show these uncut hardcore films and a mini-boom began. The first 'official' Spanish hardcore film was Jess Franco's **Lilian, la virgen pervertida**. Originally planned as an S film, it was turned into an X on the eve of legalisation by the inclusion of hardcore shots. Over the next few years Franco made a series of hardcore films, mostly starring the Catalan actress Lina Romay (Rosa Maria Almirall). These films—**El chupete de Lulu**, **El ojete de Lulu** and **Las chupónas**,[5] for example—were often signed with pseudonyms and were made very quickly on extremely low budgets. Other directors involved in this short-lived boom included Ismael Gonzalez and Diego Figuero.

Unfortunately for the film-makers involved, works categorised as X were denied the government support given to art films and were heavily taxed—over 45% of gross receipts going to the State. More importantly, unlike the situation in France, the import of foreign films was not taxed heavily. Consequently it was cheaper to bring in films from abroad than to make them locally. Gradually the home-grown industry was driven underground. The films, if they were to be made at all, had to be produced very cheaply. Often they would be shot direct to video with two films being made at the same time, using the same sets and performers.

Soon the films began to follow a rigidly predictable formula. Mostly they were shot indoors, in one or two locations, and with a very small gallery of characters and dramatic situations. Increasingly, too, the Spanish audiences were demanding harder and harder sex-scenes and less and less talk. It was as though, having been starved of sleaze for such a long time, they were determined to gorge themselves on it. Obviously this situation was not good for anyone who had the slightest artistic pretensions about what they were doing. What use is a story or witty dialogue for an audience who only want an endless parade of organs in constant close-up?

Within a very few years the boom in Spain had turned to bust. Killed off by government restrictions and audience indifference. The proliferation of hardcore sex magazines and imported videos seemed to fill the gap, satisfying the public's appetite for formerly forbidden fruit.

Elsewhere, too, there was a feeling that the golden age was over. Too much freedom had

Torture scene from the ▼ banned **Crime of Cuenca** (1979), made by one of Spain's rare female directors, Pilar Miró

**Immoral Tales**

◄ The Almodóvar produced
**Mutant Action** (1993)

perhaps not been such a good thing. The porno boom had given many film-makers a chance to push the limits of the acceptable. But now they were stuck on a treadmill, turning out tedious repetitions of the tired sexual dance.

The video explosion of the early eighties certainly helped to kill off the small independent cinemas, and the post '84 AIDS scare began to give even sex itself a bad name. By the middle of the decade the liberal gravy train was well and truly derailed.

The career of Jess Franco is a perfect illustration of the ups and downs of the European film business. Of how it can nurture new talent, while at the same time frustrating any real ambitions. His story begins in Spain in the mid 1950's and touches on almost all aspects of commercial European filmmaking since then. Our next chapter looks in detail at the man, his movies and the many factors that went into making them the way they are.

---

[1] The Bronsten empire was set up as a clever way of using American film companies' earnings, that had been frozen after the war and could only be spent locally. This was also the case in Italy with many of the US co-productions made there from the early fifties onwards.

[2] The **Superargo** series, for example, has an ex wrestler with superpowers and his butler, a former Tibetan Lama, take on a variety of dastardly criminals, such as the mad scientist Diabolicus who is trying to take over the world by manufacturing gold.

[3] Films like **The Face of Terror (La cara del terror**;1962) and León Klimovsky's **Ella y el miedo** (Woman and Terror;1963) fit this bill with Jess Franco's **Awful Dr. Orlof (Gritos en la noche**;1961) as an obvious standout.

[4] The film was actually directed by an Englishman, John Gilling, although he had lived in Spain for some years. It was heavily promoted on the back of Gilling's reputation as a maker of Hammer films like **Plague of the Zombies**. There was some reaction against this upstart Englishman taking Spanish jobs—similar to the reception José Larraz, a Spaniard working in England, got over **Symptoms**. Both films suffered from the adverse publicity

[5] **Lulu's Lollipop, Lulu's Arsehole, The Suckers**

AUDIFILM
présente

PAUL NASCHY
GABY FUCHS
BARBARA CAPELL
et
PATY SHEPARD
dans

# LA FURIE DES VAMPIRES

mise en scène de
LEON KLIMOVSKI

une coproduction Plata
HI-FI STER

eastmancolor
interdit aux moins de 13 ans

突然、狂ったように子供たちが大人を襲う――
これはSFでも小説でもない
現実に起りうる恐怖だ!

供たちに一体何が起ったのか!?

マヌエル・ペレス■製作
〇ソ・イバネス・セルラドール■監督
J・J・プランス■原作
ルイス・ベニャフィエル■脚本
ホセ・ルイス・アルカイネ■撮影
ワルド・デ・ロス・リオス■音楽

フィアンダー◆プルネラ・ランサム
ル・ナルロス◆アントニオ・イランソ
ルイス・アリアス◆マリサ・ポルセル

WHO CAN KILL
A CHILD?

# The Labyrinth of Sex

## THE FILMS OF **JESUS FRANCO**

Inside a darkened room the naked body of a curvy chanteuse lies limply on a table. Her eyes gaze upwards glassily. Bandages swathe her face like a clinical yashmak. A suave, granite-jawed surgeon poises over her seductive cadaver, his knife balanced with professional aplomb. The air pings with perverted chemistry. He's cultured, tender but ghoulish. A thought flickers. Perhaps he's changed his plan? A moment passes and his hands slide gently over her upturned breasts. Cheesy organ music pours across the soundtrack. The surgeon begins to operate. In the corner his blind, disfigured henchman lapses into an eerie spasm. He hears, and twitches pallidly ...

The surgeon's name was Orlof, the girl on the slab was played by Mara Lasso. The guy who invented this twisted scenario, and eventually filmed it, was Jesús Franco. Released in 1962, **Gritos en la Noche (The Awful Dr. Orlof)** was a cinematic time bomb; it was morbid and erotic, a horror film that pulled no punches at all. Even today it still seems brazenly shocking. Before **Orlof**, horror films had opted for the poetic approach, playing down the sexual element, only hinting at the dark recesses of the human psyche. With **Orlof** sex sizzled into the foreground, changing the face of Euro horror for the next twenty years.

Nudity was still fairly taboo in 1962. For the censor, it was only acceptable if it was wholesome and educational—if it implied desire it was considered dirty and dangerous. The only legitimate outlets for skin on film were outdoor nudist camp films and carefree 'nudie cuties'. Naive, healthy and joyous, they were a far cry from the subterranean depths of **Orlof**.

In some ways the material of Franco's film was familiar—many of the dark motifs and visceral icons were plucked from the pulp fictions of Edgar Wallace, or were reworked staples of the popular horror film. In lesser hands the whole tale would have clanged dismally. Yet there was nothing old hat about this dank masterpiece, it pulsed with a new freshness, ransacking the annals of cinema with deviant vigour. Like a trumpet blast, **Orlof** seemed to herald the arrival of a major new talent. No one could deny its unhealthy attractions, and few film fans could

resist an approach that blended claustrophobic film noir, spooky horror and morbid sexuality.

If the visuals were potent, the soundtrack was just as exciting. Most films use music to emphasise the onscreen action and provide momentum for the film's trajectory. **Orlof** was different. Avant garde, crazed, easy listening added a range of moods to this dark shocker. During key scenes it offered a scattershot of emotions, some scary and psychotic, others sensual but sadistic. It was an aural triumph.

Great things don't happen by accident, especially in cinema. Film is a complex craft. You must master the basics and pay your dues if you want to produce a slice of inspired cinema that breaks the rules in an imaginative way.

**Orlof** looked like the work of a veteran, but in fact it was the first film made for the Continental market by the feisty Spaniard Jess Franco. Before this he had turned out films aimed squarely at a Spanish audience, doing his damnedest to work within the confines of the local film industry. When he made **Orlof** he was thirty one, still a young gun—yet the film packs a lifetime's knowledge of cinema and music into a fevered 88 minutes. On top of that it has the spark of daring, a quality that is found in all his films, even his most unsavoury epics.

There's something rigid and fossilised about the Spanish film industry. Filmmakers like Almodóvar, Buñuel and Franco aren't exactly the norm inside Spain. They're outsiders and wildmen, guys who have an unholy fascination with sex, excess, and the dreamlike potential of film. To these men, predictability means stagnation and death. Like Buñuel, Franco is a born rule

▼ Demon doctor Howard Vernon. **The Awful Dr. Orlof**

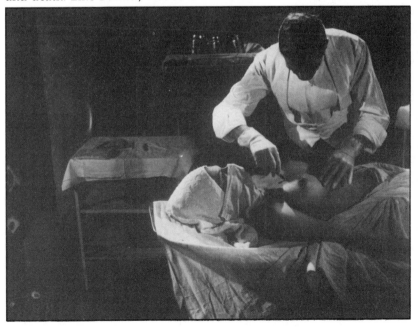

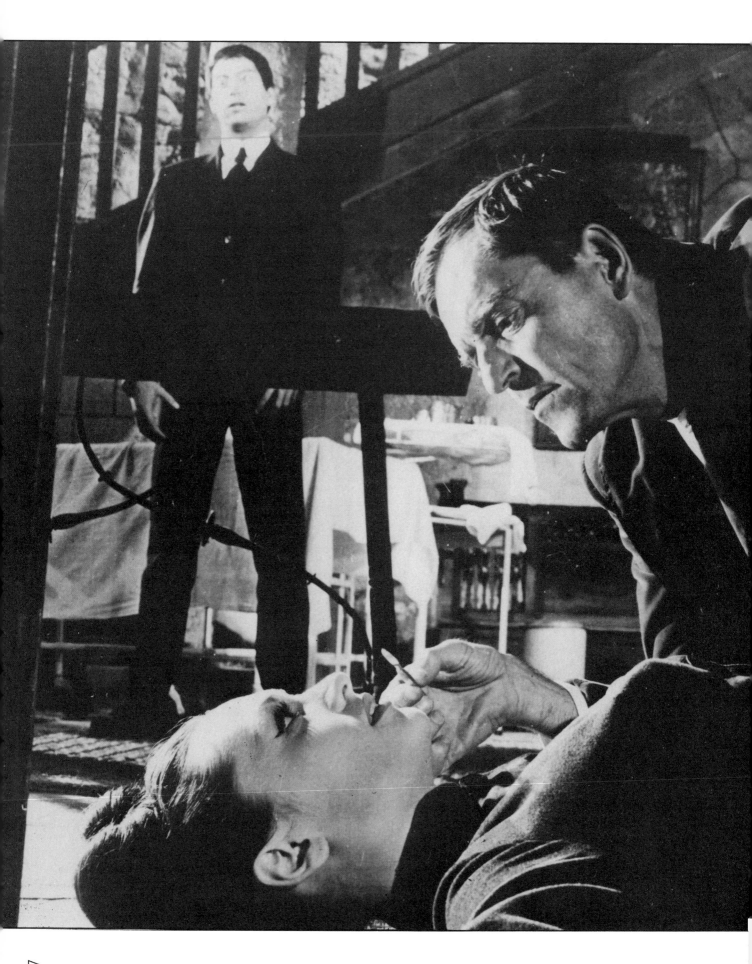

Immoral Tales

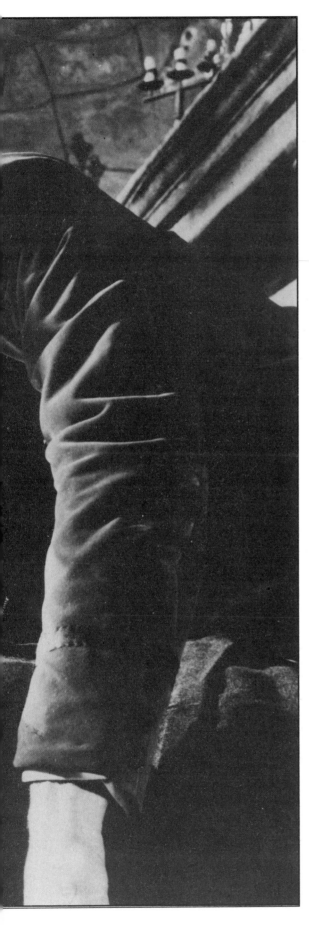

breaker, a man driven to make his own brand of sex soaked cinema, a maverick trailblazer who personifies the untapped potential of film. Inside the Spanish film industry strict conformity is the norm. To deviate from the traditional, inward-looking mode is asking for trouble. It takes a certain breed of person to ride roughshod over these pervasive restrictions. In some ways Almodóvar, Buñuel and Franco are creative bedfellows. Each follows a different trajectory, but they all curve inexorably towards sex. Of the three, Franco has followed its steamy siren-call further and longer, he's taken his flesh-filled interest to the very limits of human imagination.

There's only one thing more important than the sexual undertow in a Franco film, and that thing is jazz. Franco's films move to a jazz beat. They ebb and flow to some crazy musical rhythm that only he seems to understand. On the subject of jazz his enthusiasm is unquenchable, his knowledge encyclopaedic, his taste sure and heartfelt. If his obsession with film started early, his love of music goes back even further. His brother Enrique taught him the piano almost before he could speak, and he went on to pass piano exams at 15, progressing to harmony and musical theory. In his teens his taste for jazz erupted like a demon. Perhaps he liked its primitive undercurrents, its spontaneity and veneer of anarchy. Who knows? Whatever propelled him into the jazz arena kept him there, and his love for this creative high octane music also led him towards the hot sounds of mambo and salsa. As a teenager he played in various jazz bands and also worked out in local Latin outfits, blasting his trumpet to the body beat of mambo, equally at home soloing on trumpet and accordion, or providing an assertive backbeat on drums.

A love of jazz was generally considered essential for most post- and pre-World War Two Continental intellectuals, but bespectacled high-brows almost always avoided the crass, populist sounds of the mambo. Franco was different. He loved an assorted grab bag of music, relishing the giddy heights or depths that each brand could take him to. For him, cinema and music weren't different. Emotion was everything. Music touched a range of experiences, it didn't follow a straight line. Film was the same. So he set out to make films that had "a variety of timbres", or as he puts it "moved many strings."

Is music the food of lust for Franco? If it is, it competes with a passion for comics, architecture, art, literature and food itself. His love for gourmet cooking is well known: according to his actors,

▲ Spanish poster for **Dark Eyes of London** (1939), the early chiller that inspired Franco's **Awful Dr Orlof** (facing page)

**The Awful Dr. Orlof ▲**
(1962)

he'll film in a faraway region simply to sample its high rep cuisine. Good meals are as important to him as cinema and music.

Even by Continental standards Franco is a top notch chow hound. Howard Maurer, (husband of Dyanne Thorne, the infamous **Ilsa**) tells the weird gourmet tale of driving through Europe and dining at Franco's recommended munching spots with an itinerary so complex that it gave the exact time of day to ask for particular dishes. As friends of Franco they were given VIP treatment from one end of the Continent to the other. Suave Franco mainman Howard Vernon also talks about Franco's unerring knack of locating the finest food. "Within hours of arriving in any town he'll have located the best restaurant and probably be dining there."

Most people have one or two guiding passions, but Franco dips deeply into everything. He comes from a family of "super-intellectuals". His uncle Julian Marias is a famous philosopher, his brother Enrique a musicologist, and his nephews are respected writers, critics and film-makers. In many ways Franco is considered to be the black sheep of the family. His nephews sigh when they talk about "poor old uncle Jesús". His family feel uneasy about the wayward genius. They'd hoped he'd become a diplomat, but the young Franco had other ideas. He packed in his Law and Philosophy studies and went to film school, learning as much as he could about the technical side as well as acting. Undaunted and without money, he supported himself by writing pulp novels under various pseudonyms and spent the rest of his free time sitting in with local jazz bands and orchestras.

These youthful pulps were crazed, fantastic creations. Many of their plots and strange scenarios were later to provide inspiration for his films. He wrote over a hundred crime thrillers and horror stories and was paid around $20 per title. After two years he'd tired of Spanish film school, and enrolled in the I.D.H.E.C., the French Government's film school in Paris, to learn about direction. Paris also offered him the chance to soak up a host of cinematic delights. The film drought caused by the war was over, and French film buffs were catching up on an incredible potpourri of filmic gems—and so was Franco. French new wave directors like Godard, Truffaut and Chris Marker were regulars at the Cinémathèque. Franco came so often he was admitted free, and its mainman, Henri Langlois, even arranged some special screenings so that the Spaniard could bone up on some key titles he'd missed.

Even in the early fifties Franco was a culture hopper, at ease in any number of countries. Today he's fluent in at least six languages—something that comes in useful when you're slipping round Europe trying to clinch film deals. In many ways he's a man who knows no boundaries. His tastes in reading range from comics to more highbrow and literary pleasures. His knowledge of Spanish and World literature is complex and complete, his diversity and enthusiasm are awe inspiring. Add to these his freakishly fantastic memory and you have a truly unique creation.

His first films were soaked with this literary background. He could have pursued this wholesome and acceptable direction to become one of the acknowledged greats. But he didn't, and the reasons are complex and gnarled. Something deep inside propelled him on his wayward trail, forced him to follow his own demons and search out his own sort of cinema.

When he returned to Spain from Paris, Franco began to burrow his way into the Spanish film industry. With his talent for music and writing, enthusiasm for film, and mastery of the technical basics, he had quite a few options he could pursue.

During this period he worked with many of the so-called new wave of Spanish cinema, a mob of guys who produced films based on serious themes and literary works. With many of these men the visual sparkle of cinema was a secondary consideration, they preferred to follow the approach of the Italian neo-realist school. Franco was more iconoclastic and restless. Rather than slavishly copy one style or one approach, his head was filled with ideas, culled from cinema, comics, pulp literature, poetry, prose and spilling forth from his own fevered imagination. He loved the plastic aspects of cinema, its ability to create something strange, unheard of and new. Other Spanish film-makers were more interested in producing message films—messages they had to sneak past the hard-nosed political censor. Film was like jazz for Franco, if you tried to inject a message into it the spontaneity and uniqueness were long gone.

Franco's natural inclination was to make movies that spun some sort of crazy fiction. As a child his ability to create hair-raising tales and fabulous scenarios was remarkable, almost unstoppable. He would elaborate the most commonplace happening, turning it into something beautiful, fantastic, yet still believable. It's one of his great gifts. Yet, like all storytellers, he finds the act of weaving and creating is more important than the final result. Making the fiction is everything.

This ability to suggest new things from what looks like stale material is a rare talent. Filmmaker León Klimovsky says Franco was a real boon—he thought on his feet, came up with all sorts of comic scenes and provided the best material in the films they worked on together. Franco took dog tired plots and twisted them, giving them a certain hellbent zing. He spewed out good ideas like a fertile volcano.

Klimovsky wasn't the only one who found Franco stimulating to work with, and from 1954 to 1958 he helped out on a hefty number of films. He wrote music for six features, was assistant director on another 14, turned in some good acting performances and helped out with a mess of scripts. In 1957 he took the plunge and directed his first film, **Arbol de España**, a documentary about the humble Spanish olive produced for the Ministry of Industry. His next solo short was also a serious piece and won several awards; it was an appreciation of Pío Baroja—a poet Franco had first enjoyed when he was 7 years old. With two shorts to his name, a host of other credits and a growing critical reputation, the future looked pretty good. In many ways he seemed to be on his way to the top.

Multi-talented, feisty but humble. That's a good description of the young Franco. Although he'd crammed a lifetime's work into a few short years he still felt he wasn't ready to direct his first feature. So he focussed his attention on making more documentary shorts. In 1959 he finished **El destierro del Cid**. He also directed two other documentaries, more ambitious pro-

jects than the earlier shorts, but they were never completed because he ran out of money. The first unfinished piece, **Viaje al año 1000** (Journey to the Year 1000), was inspired by a philosophical essay written by his uncle Julian Marias, while the second, **La chanson de Roland**, was based on some verses of the mediaeval poem.

It was during the making of **La chanson de Roland** in Roncesvalles that Franco came up with a revolutionary idea. "It occurred to me that I could make a film without any storyline. It had to be shot with the basic equipment that I carried with me, that's a van, a small group of people and an electric generator ... Being an admirer of novelist Julio Camba I thought it would be possible to make a film about different subjects linked by a storyteller." This simple idea, full of possibilities, became the basis for his first full length feature **Tenemos 18 años** (We Are 18; 1959). Franco thought it would be "a revolution in cinematic narrative—but it was not." The film ran into censorship problems. A sequence with an escaped prisoner got the politically sensitive authorities hot under the collar and, although the film was a madcap comedy, it received the Spanish equivalent of an 'X' certificate. Distribution was restricted to selected parts of Spain. As Franco puts it, they did it "just to fuck me up, you know. They didn't like it from the political point of view." So even if the film *was* a revolution in narrative, only a few people got to see it.

As a first feature **Tenemos 18 años** was a bona fide whammer. Despite all sorts of technical problems, including the lack of good equipment, it was restless, effervescent, new wave and mercurial. Thirty five years on it's still a winner. The photography, by Eloy Mella, was pretty and kooky, shot at unusual times of day, with a palette that ranged from the supersaturated all the way through to twinkly oddball pastels. It

▲ An early acting role for Franco in Fernán Gómez's **Strange Voyage** (1964)

◄ More victims for **The Awful Dr. Orlof**

suited the crazy, jaunty story down to a tee.

Like many first films, **Tenemos** was a prototype of what would come later. The madcap story, about two gals, a watery-eyed guy and a yellow car, moves around like a demon on heat. Just when you think it's going to settle down and become tiresome, it transforms into a hotwired goofy concoction, a fifteen minute tour-de-force that's like some kind of monster-injected acid trip, milking every known horror element for carefree but cheesy laughs. For this sequence Franco threw away the rule book and gave lead actor Antonio Ozores the time of his life. Ozores picks up the girls in a carriage, Dracula style, then relates his hypnotic tale—how he stabbed his father, spread terror like Jack the Ripper, had his face acid-washed *à la* Phantom of the Opera, bongoed in the Congo, and eventually ended up as an aristocratic mish mash. It's an affectionate homage to the roots of horror, a hell for leather zap though 'B' movie terrain that pummels along lickety spit. This was something new, the sort of sequence that would make you gag on your popcorn.

For most directors the first feature is a leg up towards the big-time. For Franco, **Tenemos** was a mixed blessing. He'd tried out some of his goofy but inspired theories and revitalised the humble Spanish comedy, but had failed to get any serious attention. The film was buried by restricted distribution and he was back at square one, looking for another backer with some money.

When he made **Tenemos 18 años** he'd had some help from his friend, the respected director Luis Berlanga. After the censor had hammered the film this lifeline dried up, and Franco realised that if he was going to carry on it would have to be alone and regardless. Undaunted by the setbacks, and with very little money, he prepared his next feature, **Labios Rojos** (Red Lips; 1960). His theory about filmmaking then is the same as it is now—"Keep filming, keep moving forward and the money will come later."

The film had the same leading lady as **Tenemos 18 años**, the pretty, sparkly Isana Medel. Medel was Franco's girlfriend at the time, which solved one of his major problems—getting a good actress who'd work now and get paid later. He had met her a few years earlier when he was the manager of a production house in Madrid, and had hired her to play a part in a Fernán Gómez[1] comedy he'd written. Petite and perky, she was perfect in his first two features.

**Labios Rojos** was "made for nothing, from nothing." Midway through shooting, Franco found a backer with just enough money to finish the film. One of the people who saw it was Serge Newman, the man who would later produce the sizzling **Awful Dr. Orlof**.

Newman contacted Franco and they signed a three picture deal, starting with a musical, **La reina del Tabarín** (Queen of the Tabarin; 1960), which Franco took over after León Klimovsky dropped out. Klimovsky had felt uneasy about directing a musical, and had relayed his doubts to Newman. After seeing the eye-popping song and dance numbers in **Tenemos 18 años**, Newman decided that the multi-talented Franco was the right man for the job.

**Tabarín** was an important film for Franco. Co-funded by the Spanish film body CIFESA, it was his entry into the professional film world, and a move that might help his chances with future projects. As usual he pepped up the script with some of his own ideas, revamping the staid, stuffy original, trying to make it more fluid and fun. He looked to the American musical for inspiration, its zippy dialogue, its invention and constant movement. Instead of filming with a fixed camera, in the traditional way, he opted for plenty of pure motion. In **Tabarín** the camera glides and moves with gusto. The first half features plenty of snappy editing, which suits the rags to riches story. The second half is more of a tour de force, with lavish dolly and tracking shots following the sequined singer as she delivers the goods. The colours are sumptuous and hypnotic, and the finale grand, gaudy and delirious. Most Franco films pick up when they hit the nightclub, the stripclub and the musical cabaret. He likes eye-balling girls, especially when they're singing, stripping and rollicking around ... almost every Franco film has at least one jaundiced but juicy club scene, where jaded patrons experience some noodle busting onstage scenario. He throws himself wholeheartedly into these sections and often they're the best bits in his films.

While making **Tabarín** Franco became friendly with its star, Mikaela, and it was through her that he met Soledad Miranda, who is generally regarded as his greatest discovery. She was an Andalucian beauty, fragile, enchanting and full of life—one of a lively mob of gypsies and half gypsies who lived in Mikaela's house, where Franco was a frequent visitor. After featuring in **Tabarín**, her second film, Miranda appeared in a number of Spanish productions, in which, as Franco puts it, "they (Spanish cinema) tried to

◄ (Facing page) Morpho abducts buxom babe, **The Awful Dr Orlof**

▼ Spanish poster, **Tenemos 18 años** (1959)

turn her into the usual idiot, into a doll."

While making **El conde Drácula**(1969) several years later, he had an opportunity to cast in Spain and managed to save her from becoming just another lifeless cinematic icon.

After **Tabarín**, Franco kept up the musical theme. His next outing, **Vampiresas 1930** (Vamps of 1930), was another Spanish style homage to classic Hollywood musicals. This time around the brew was even wilder. The finale was goofy, big band and black face. The male stars are foxed up in evening dresses, smeared with dark make-up, blowing big band riffs on sax, trumpet and trombone. Female players are turned out in tails and cheap wigs, made up like old time minstrels and 'coon show' stars. It was a gob- smacking show-stopper that made the audience blink in disbelief at its daft audacity.

The opening of the film, too, was soaked with this tainted bravura. Mikaela decked out in a weird bat outfit, hams it up with some other kooky cohorts in a parody of Hollywood movie-making that's a direct homage to **Singing in the Rain**. The whole of the film is shot through with these affectionate nudges or jokey references—what Franco calls "a little wink at the audience."

Looking at Franco's early films—the musicals, the highbrow shorts and the quirky entertainments, they all seem a long way from the ice cold dementia of **The Awful Dr. Orlof**. In **Orlof**, when someone looks at you, it's dangerous. The polished Doc spends most of his time in the shadows sizing up luscious strip-teasers and singers. Any gal that attracts his gaze could end up in his dungeon of doom, drained of blood—fodder for his next vile experiment. Looks can kill in **The Awful Dr. Orlof**, and with this film Franco stepped boldly into uncharted terrain.

**Orlof** was the first Spanish horror movie. It was a change of pace for Franco and a breakthrough for the stolid Spanish film industry. The catalyst for this innovation, believe it or not, was the blockbusting success of the British Hammer horror film. Back then, Hammer caused a worldwide sensation, bringing fangs, blood and a bit of sin back into fashion. There were queues around the block to see Hammer's **Dracula** in London, and the film had the same effect on the Continent and in the U.S.A. As a rabid film fan Franco was familiar with the range of horror—his producer Serge Newman wasn't. So, when they were in Nice shooting **Vampiresas 1930**, Franco took the unsuspecting Serge to see **The Brides of Dracula** and the Spanish horror film was born.

Franco liked Hammer's superb technical proficiency, but he found the English approach a trifle distant, not involved in a love affair with the subject matter. He preferred to get inside the baroque and bizarre horror universe, rather than just coolly recording it. So he threw all his energies into **Orlof**, upping the ante and making a film that swirled to the backbeat of the irrational.

Horror has always been a nifty, acceptable way of handling the erotic. Even the most stuffy English horror films have the occasional saucy barmaid or knicker- flashing Can-Can dancer. By getting into horror, Franco increased the erotic potential of his films. His earlier films featured eroticism in what the continentals call 'the third degree'. With **Orlof** he moved up the ladder, testing the limits of what was acceptable.

Some film-makers are drawn to sexy, erotic scenarios. Franco says that when he watches a film, any film, he doesn't like it if it's sexually ambiguous. It appears dishonest to him if there's any doubt surrounding the sexual shenanigans or motives, and he finds it disconcerting that sex is played down in Hollywood films. The attitude in Europe is different. As Billy Wilder said, "What Americans call dirty, Europeans call lusty." Franco endorses this peculiarly European approach. He talks about watching Hollywood films with Fernán Gómez ... afterwards both of them agonised: "Did Robert Mitchum screw Ida Lupino, or not?" Clearly they both took the whole thing very seriously.

This philosophy applies to all Franco films. If there's the slightest inkling of sex, he's in there wholeheartedly. When there's a night club scene, the dancers don't just go through the motions, there's always some kinky, voyeuristic buzz in the air.

**Orlof** was Franco's first sojourn into this uncharted sexual terrain. He would return to it again and again. This willingness to immerse himself in the fetid, alluring arena of sex is something his critics hold against him—they forget it takes a certain amount of bravery to venture into dark, unfathomed waters, to create these strange disillusioned fables where the romantic and the perverse intermingle with twisted glee.

The eroticism of **Orlof** may seem mild by todays standards, but two versions of it were released at the time. The complete, uncut version was premiered at the Midi Minuit in Paris, where it received a unanimous thumbs up from the French horror brigade. As Franco says, "This was the perfect place for it and nobody in the audience was shocked." The trimmed version was shown in more censorship orientated countries such as Spain, England and the U.S.A. Franco had to snip out a couple of scenes for this edition of the film, "because if I hadn't they'd kill me, push me out of Spain or something." Even in the early 1960's it was clearly too much for some people to handle.

**Orlof** was shot just 10 miles outside Madrid, but to Franco it was a first taste of freedom. Inside the Spanish film industry at that time there were an unsettling number of restrictions, a veritable rule book of things you could or could not do. For this reason most Spanish film-makers tended to stick with the same old tedious topics, turning out brain numbing literary based epics that focused on the tired legacy of Spain's past. In short, anything cozy. By the end of the 1950's this approach had produced a breed of film-makers who were stuck in a rut. The industry had become isolated, and was beginning to feed off itself. Sure, a few film-makers kicked against the bureaucratic pricks, but on the whole it was easier to play the game. Inside a system like this it was almost impossible to be optimistic and enthusiastic about the whole wider possibilities of cinema.

Despite these restrictions, Franco was constitutionally drawn to innovation. His love for cinema could not be contained. He wanted to forge a style that went beyond the petty say-so of the power-hungry money men. This was one of the factors that pulled him towards the erotic. The other was his compulsion towards voyeurism and the sins of the flesh. In the end, like Buñuel, he was forced to jettison the shackles of Spain and take his camera and his compulsions elsewhere. **Orlof** was the beginning of this process, a movie that, shown without cuts, would have invoked the wrath of the Spanish censor. He'd tasted freedom—after that there was no going back.

By anybody's standards **Orlof** was a success, so producer Serge Newman asked Franco to do a sequel. Unfortunately, this took a few grey years to materialise. The original had been so low budget, and the French company that co-produced it so small, that only a few copies of the film were run off from the negative. Leo Lax had taken up the world rights to **Orlof**, but because there were so few prints of this grisly gem available it took over two years for it to turn a profit. It's part of the curse of low budget filmmaking, a curse that was to follow Franco throughout the rest of his career. Even when he

delivered the goods and nudged film fans into uproar, the whole penny-ante aspect of the business seemed to work against him.

**Orlof** was Franco's first feature to be shown outside Spain. The distributors suggested he modify his christian name to make it more acceptable outside his native country. On the advice of director and actor Robert Hossein he shortened it from Jesús to Jess and became Jess Franco, which is his legitimate name as a director.

Unfortunately it's not the only one he uses. Franco's career is infernally dotted with pseudonyms and name changes. When he began making films outside Spain he was forced to use an assortment of *noms de plume*. Filming in Europe can be a complicated business, with all sorts of red tape. For example, if you direct a French film you get heavily taxed if you aren't a French national—Franco got around this by having his French producer register himself as Clifford Brown. This meant that the producer could pick up the royalties for him and, more importantly, Franco was free to direct under the name Clifford Brown.[2]

Over the years Franco has used a heap of other pseudonyms: Jeff Franco, Jess Frank, James P. Johnson, Franco Manera, Frank Hollman, Roland Marceignac, James Gardner, Dan Simon, Dave Tough, Charles Christian, A.M. Frank, David Khune Jr, Jeff Manner, James Lee Johnson and Pablo Villa. Some of them are used for specific countries. For example, Jess Frank and Frank Hollman appear on his German productions & co-productions, Franco Manera on his Italian films. This tangled web of pseudonyms is something that's developed over thirty years in the low budget film biz.

With an arm-long list of fake identities to his credit, Franco looks like a guy who is trying to stay one step ahead of the law. It has helped fuel the myth that he's a cinematic madman on a deranged film kick. But if you look beyond the ever rolling list of changing names another story becomes visible, and that's the one we're here to tell.

A key figure in understanding the whole strange tale is Orson Welles. In some ways Franco and Welles are kindred spirits. Both of them had large appetites—for good food, wine, literature, cinema and art. They were both cinematic badboys, guys who went their own way regardless of the consequences. Each has been true to his own nature. In the final analysis they are both flawed geniuses, men who are godlike and infantile at the same time.

en EASTMANCOLOR

MIKAELA
YVES
MASSARD
JUAN
RIQUELME
ANTONIO
GARISA
DANIELLE GODET
MAURICIO de LA PEÑA
con la colaboración especial de
JULIO RISCAL
GUADALUPE M. SAMPEDRO
ALFREDO
MAYO

PRODUCCION :
CIFESA PRODUCCION
HISPAMER FILMS

La
**REINA**
DEL TABARIN

DIRECTOR
*Jesús Franco*
Productor ejecutivo
SERGIO NEWMAN

FERNANDO
FERNAN GOMEZ
JEAN SERVAIS · LAURA GRANADOS
(Y LA COLABORACION DE
MARIE VINCENT
ANTONIO PRIETO)
RIFIFI
EN LA
CIUDAD
CON
ROBERT MANUEL · LUIS MARIN
DINA LOY · AGUSTIN GONZALEZ

Orson Welles has always had a special place in the hearts of Continental cineastes. Unable to raise money in the U.S., he was forced to move to Spain in the early 1960's and it was there that he filmed many of his most personal projects— **Mr. Arkadin**, **Don Quixote** and the unfinished **Treasure Island**.

In 1963, Welles was looking for some competent technicians and kindred spirits for his next project **Chimes at Midnight**. His assistant, Juan Cobos, had known Franco for years and put his name forward. Franco was subsequently hired to direct the second unit photography on the film and became firm friends with the great director.[3]

That, at least, is the official version. Another story, frequently referred to in interviews with Franco, perhaps tells more about the relationship between the two men, as well as underlining Franco's rebel status in the Spanish industry at the time. According to this version, Welles had seen Franco's **La muerte silba un blues** (Death Whistles a Blues) in Paris. He remembered the film, and suggested Franco as a possible member of his team. Welles' producers were pretty perturbed by this off-the-wall suggestion—even then Franco's reputation was considered rock bottom. In order to scotch what looked like a nightmare collaboration, the Spanish producers dug out **Rififí en la ciudad** (Rififi in the City; 1963) and screened it for Welles. They thought the film was so bad it would cure him of his strange notion. But they were gloriously wrong.

**Rififí** turned out to be a restless, fast moving homage to Welles' œuvre—like **The Lady from Shanghai** it had lots of action, odd angles and frantic dolly work. Technically it was just what he was looking for. The film had verve and sophistication plus the right amount of tongue in cheek *homage* to whet the big man's appetite. He insisted that Franco get the job

Whatever the facts, Welles made a deep and lasting impression on Franco. Throughout his career, he has repeatedly doffed his cap to the films of this larger than life American. Some of his humble sex flicks from the early seventies, such as **Le journal intime d'une nymphomane** (Sinner; 1972), have the same structure as **Citizen Kane**. Others, like **Camino solitario** (The Lonely Path; 1983), are ghostly homages to classic Welles films like **The Lady from Shanghai** and **Mr. Arkadin**. These tributes aren't permeated with deep hidden meanings, they're convenient hooks to hang the film on. They're also Franco's strange way of expressing his love.

Most film critics would blanch at the idea that there's any similarity between a talent as big as

Welles and a fast film hack like Franco. Yet it's true. Both shared the same overpowering love of cinema, the same lust for life. Each was flawed and all too human. Welles never made the films he could have, he got screwed by the studios and by his own genius myth. Like Franco, his own nature was also part of the problem, something that got in the way.

Myths swirl around Franco. One of the main ones is the idea that his films got progressively better until **Necronomicon** (1967). This is presumed to be his biggest budget, his most impressive work. The films that came after that are generally thought to be disastrous, sex filled romps with only occasional flashes of brilliance.

It's a simplistic view that barely does justice to his restless desire to keep filming, or to the myriad factors that influenced his rolling trajectory. The Franco story has a healthy unfettered dynamism that's hard to grasp in one potted theory. The best way to approach it is to outline the salient features, then stand back and hope to make sense of this cinematic riddle. Theory and speculation can be dry and arid. By the time the words hit the page the contradictions have evaporated. Inside the Franco tale contradictions are everything. It's better to keep them raw and undigested, they add life to the narrative.

Simple explanations always overlook the tenacity of the man. Without gutsy perseverance he never would have completed as many films as he did. There have been times when it seemed that his career was destined for limbo. Against odds that would have gazumped a lesser man he triumphed and returned to the fray. The three year wait for funds to make an **Orlof** sequel was particularly gruelling. With a successful film doing the rounds you might think it would be easy to finance a follow up. Unfortunately this wasn't the case, and when the money did materialise it was paltry and the whole production was fraught with problems.

Tortured by all sorts of difficulties it's hardly surprising that **El secreto del Dr. Orloff** (Dr. Orloff's Monster; 1964) is an uneven film, but when it's good it approaches the sublime. Despite its flaws, Spanish critic Carlos Aguilar touts it as containing some of the finest sequences in the whole of Spanish cinema. High praise indeed for the film-maker with the lowest rep in the world. In its best moments **El secreto** certainly has a kind of spooky greatness. The pre-credit sequence is especially eerie. The evil Orloff's head is filled with accusing images from the past—the brother he's turned into a zombie ... the face of his adulterous wife. Each

◀ (Facing page) The Welles' inspired **Rififi in the City** (1963)

▼ Orson Welles, **Chimes at Midnight** (1965)

of them haunts him. Other audacious scenes include the Orloff opium pipe sequence, another opportunity for hazy, potent images. The best scene in the film has the lonely, messed up zombie hanging around the cemetery, gazing down at his wife's grave, bereft but dehumanised. In true Franco style the film cuts from this City of the Dead to a smoky nightclub, where Perla Cristal delivers a sultry paean to lost love.

A marvel of the macabre and the sensual, although dogged by tribulations, **El secreto** still had a few flashes of uninhibited genius.

Franco didn't hang around waiting for the money to materialise for this second **Orloff** vehicle. He kept busy, got out there and hustled, making four films himself as well as acting in Fernán Gómez's **El extraño viaje**. After delivering the first **Orlof** he turned his sights towards the thriller front, filming one of his most vivacious vehicles, the jauntily titled Death Whistles the Blues (**La muerte silba un blues**; 1962), the film that had impressed Orson Welles in Paris. Busting with hot'n'intimate nightclub numbers, it's grade 'A' Franco, brimming over with seduction and action. Seduction in the shape of sexy chanteuses—nightclub vixens replete with winning hairdos and off the shoulder dresses, who sing torch songs to a backdrop of gutbucket jazz. The film is filled with these breathy numbers. The rest is fast flowing action, all captured in wide angle and shot in an offbeat manner that's a lighthearted salute to Orson Welles' incredible **Touch of Evil**.

Like all Franco films it was made quickly, so it would look different and spontaneous. It's a unique approach to film-making. Sometimes it works, sometimes it doesn't. **La muerte silba un blues** is one of the few Franco's where everything gels. Perhaps it's the abundance of nightclub numbers that makes it a winner. Franco films always pick up when they enter this territory, something about the languorous atmosphere of a smoke-filled club strikes a chord with him. Almost all of his films have at least one cabaret scene, one sequence of lingering but legal voyeurism. The acts are invariably kooky, but always sensual. At its most extreme you'll have a gal tweak her way along a spider's web to make love to a mannequin. At its simplest she'll wiggle around in fishnet stockings and corset, warbling some snazzy number while an appreciative patron mumbles "that song sure looks good."

In American films, the nightclub number is usually a backdrop to the action. Not so with Franco. It's the main event, so he focuses linger-

ingly on it and gives it his own anarchic twist. Sometimes it's cheeky, a black stockinged charmer wiggling her spotlighted bottom with naughty aplomb. In lesser hands it would be cheap and dull. But Franco makes it look like the most important event in the world. Perhaps for him it is.

You could search the world for wigglers and warblers like the gals you see in Franco's films. He cites French stripper Rita Renoir as an influence on his unusual nightclub sequences—she was one of the stars of the Crazy Horse Saloon, the legendary French nightclub where Russ Meyer shot part of **Europe in the Raw** (1965) and **Mondo Topless** (1966). Renoir was great, but even at her wildest she never touched the cracked humour or the unhealthy fascination of Franco's creations. These hot, club scenes are one of the reasons for watching his films, they give you something that you'll just never experience any other way.

Inside Franco's nightclubs the cheesy jazz combo is supreme, it provides the backbeat that the action hinges on. His musical sensibility is deliciously askew, like the visuals it oozes a twisted familiarity. The performers move, the audience sits transfixed and incredulous, their eyeballs gripped by the strange, sexy scene, their brains tingled by the peculiar goofy mix. You could write it all off as sex filled and voyeuristic, but there's always the persistent throb of puckish humour to pull you in another direction.

His next couple of films after **La muerte silba un blues** had their moments, but overall they were fairly routine. If they are important, it's because they were the first films he made with Daniel White, the man who would provide the music for many of the 150 or so subsequent films that Franco was to make.

White is one of the unsung geniuses of soundtrack music. Nobody turns out tunes with the same sleepy, lascivious qualities that he does. Over the years he's become a staple ingredient in the Franco canon, and as Franco moved deeper into uncharted erotic waters, White's music followed, endlessly echoing his lingering sensibilities. Although born in Yorkshire, White has the air of a sophisticated Scottish gentleman. He could have been a major figure in the soundtrack stakes, but like most Franco collaborators he chose to avoid the ratrace, enjoy life and cut down on the wear and tear of the mainstream. It's a familiar story and one that appears with stunning regularity when you look at the colleagues and associates of this maverick Spaniard.

**Death Whistles a** ▼
**Blues** (1962)

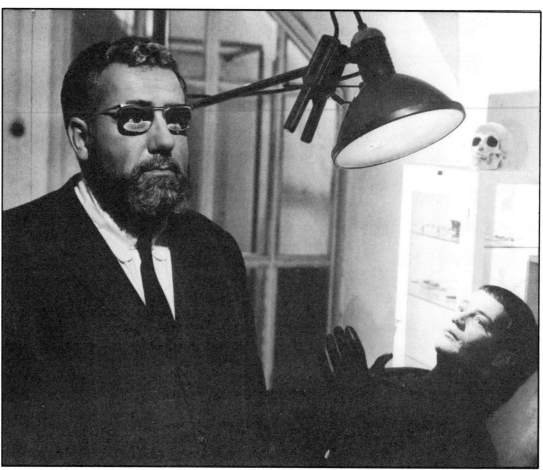

You could describe the people who work with Franco as misfits, but that misses an important point. They're all cultured, charming and intelligent. They choose to work with him because he offers things that money can't buy ... unpredictability, spontaneity, a chance to do things their own way. For White this meant he wasted less time making career moves, trying to impress people for whom he had no respect. What's more, life in the bargain basement was interesting and fun. His collaborations with Franco took him outside the studio. He played small roles in some of the films, and he enjoyed the intimate hepped-up feeling of being part of the team. White talks fondly of the great days of movie making with Franco. The films may be low rent, naughty rubbish by some people's standards, but for White they still exude the essence of cinema. When he made these films with Jess there was a crew of only 5 or 6 people. Everyone mucked in. Franco came up with ideas on the spot. The whole team buzzed with his enthusiasm for getting something off-kilter onto celluloid.

With Franco there are no rules. It's like being back at the birth of the motion picture industry, when some crazy guys grabbed a camera, hired a few actors, and accidentally turned out some-

thing raw and fabulous. All of the people who've worked with him echo this sentiment. Howard Vernon maintains that it's "unthinkable that Franco would not have been a film-maker ... he was born with a camera in his hands." White agrees, and producer Karl-Heinz Mannchen says "Jess Franco *is* cinema."

These sentiments describe Franco's intent when he makes a film—which is not always reflected in what finally turns up on screen. Making a film is different from writing a book, or even composing music. With film you take real things, fiddle around with them and hope to make something new, mythic and fantastic. Like the bearded Alchemists of old, film-makers like Franco want to take base metal and transform it into something precious and shiny. White's account of the glorious days of working with Franco prompts this impression ... flashing lights, crazy experiments, the glee and intensity of creation. On the one hand you think these guys are out to lunch. On the other you wonder ... maybe they're right. Maybe they know something I don't. Something important, something strange but profound.

Franco is a catalyst. His infernal love for cinema inspires his collaborators like an infectious disease. The films he turns out are almost mere side effects. It's impossible to meet him and not be smitten by this cinema bug. He's a small and surprisingly nimble man, but with a powerhouse of a brain. Dangerously intelligent, tenacious, and a lively conversationalist, the complete opposite of the bumblers, half wits and goons he often plays on film. His eyes are large, embedded in deep sockets. They seem bigger than normal. It's as if they were made to see more, or that seeing is one of the all important things. At first you think he's all eyes, all brain and that everything is channelled into these organs. Then when he begins to speak you realise that's not true. As Howard Vernon says, he's just a "terribly intelligent guy" searching for things to sustain his interest.

When he talks about his own films he gets agitated. They hardly ever turn out the way he planned, he's nearly always dissatisfied with them. Maybe this is why he keeps reworking the same ideas. But get him onto the subject of films he's enjoyed and his knowledge is incredible, his analysis thoughtful, meticulous and profound. The same is true about music, especially jazz. He has a photographic memory and can dig into the storeroom of his mind to quote from reviews of his films, sections from books, comics and a host of other sources. The eidetic memory is merely the icing on the cake, even without it he'd still be formidable and fun.

Knowledge, enthusiasm, action. These words sum up Franco's approach. As a young man he wrote intensely and passionately about cinema in the Spanish magazine *Film Ideal* that he founded with three other film fans. In the late fifties he championed directors like Robert Siodmak, Joseph Lewis, Phil Karlson, John Brahm, Raoul Walsh, John Ford and Douglas Sirk. Franco and his friends were regarded as deluded idiots for rating these guns-for-hire above serious film-makers like Antonioni and Vittorio de Sica.

Time has caught up with Franco. Nowadays most film buffs get dewy eyed when they talk about Sirk and Siodmak. Back in the fifties they were thought of differently, they were regarded as competent, workmanlike directors—'craftsmen with nothing to say'. Chaps who made melodramas, thrillers and westerns. In some ways Franco has tried to emulate them, even though this has forced him to sink to the cinematic depths. The men he championed made 'B' features, his are even cheaper—they're not C's or D's ... they're Z's. Why does a highbrow guy dive into the lowbrow end of the business? When it's a man like Franco you can be sure that

the answer is intricate, and twisted. He's following the same route as his idols, but in his own hellbent way.

Perhaps his penchant for the erotic is the deciding factor. Throughout the 1960's and 70's this certainly was the case. As his films went deeper into the labyrinth of sex, they also showed a similar fascination with the big 'D'—death. In consequence, the budgets shrank as the investigation became dark and dangerous.

One of his finest sojourns into this dodgy area was 1965's **Miss Muerte (The Diabolical Dr. Z)**. In this deranged classic, the killer was a compelling nightclub performer, a shapely gal with long poisonous finger nails, her mind reprogrammed by the diabolical Irma Zimmer. Transformed into an amoral hellcat, she begins her mission of doom, seeking out top notch scientists with machine-like precision; her derailed aim is to seduce and destroy. It was a stunning reworking of the **Orloff** chestnut. This time around the zombie-like killer wasn't a disfigured misfit, but an alluring and lively vixen.

**Miss Muerte** was Franco's third variation on the sex and surgery theme, and over the years there'd be many more. Some cheap, some nasty, some downright silly. **Miss Muerte** was one of the best. Perhaps it was the script by Buñuel regular Jean-Claude Carrière? Perhaps it was less dogged by money troubles than the earlier, and similar, **El secreto del Dr. Orloff**? Who knows. In the final analysis there's plenty of pure Franco in there, and the visuals are peppered with his unmistakable trademark: it's packed with women. In most Franco films they are the hub on which the action spins, **Miss Muerte** is no exception. There's Estella Blain as the death dealing babe with a neat line in fashionable spider caps, plus the evil Irma, whose scientific genius knows no bounds. Even the background is filled with an endless supply of

▲ Nightclubbing, **Rififi in the City** photonovel

◄ Orloff returns, **El secreto del Dr. Orloff** (1964)

The Labyrinth of Sex

91

MISS MUERTE

MABEL KARR
ESTELLA BLAIN
FERNANDO MONTES

GUY MAIRESSE • MARCELO ARROITA • HOWARD VERNON • LUCIA PRADO
DIRECTOR
**JESUS FRANCO** HESPERIA (Madrid) - SPEVA - CINE ALLIANCE (París)
UNA COPRODUCCION

Spider Girl woos ▲
mannequin during nightclub
number. **Miss Muerte**

women. When the action hits the nightclub
there's girls, girls, girls and instead of the usual
male dominated combo, there's a couple of
girls. One plays muted, sleazy trumpet, while
the other comps suggestively on piano.

Evil-minded Irma wields a weird contraption.
A machine created for good and evil that she har-
nesses for her own vile ends. Metallic, clunky and
menacing it could only have been dreamed up by
a mind like Franco's. Originally he envisioned a
crablike creation. Working with his own special
effects team from Madrid this evolved into a
bizarre spiderlike device. The whole thing was
pieced together cheaply, designed and supervised by Franco—and it worked a treat. It was
simple, yet managed to suggest all sorts of scientific skullduggery. The manipulation of the
contraption from outside the frame lent an eerie
and disturbing effect. Compared with the special
effects budgets for today's horror films, on **Miss
Muerte** they worked with peanuts. Like many
Franco films it shows what you can do with little

or no money—all you need is good ideas, determination and a dash of brilliance.

To stretch the pennies, Franco had to make
the best of the resources he had at hand. This
often meant getting people to do any number of
jobs, even things they were untrained for.
Music maestro Daniel White, for example, was
wheeled in not just to do the soundtrack, he also
had a hefty part as the stiff-upper-lipped sidekick to the police inspector—played by Franco
himself! White's score for **Miss Muerte** was
audacious and avant-garde in places, velvet
smooth in others. A lone trumpet during a
surgery scene adds a disconcertingly sexy ambience to the whole proceeding.

As with many Franco films, **Miss Muerte** is
filled with all sorts of nudges, references and
jokes that point a knowing finger to the world
of comics and cinema. The first line in the film
is a cheeky wink aimed at the discerning film
buff. The phone rings, Irma Zimmer answers.
The message is from Bresson: "A condemned
man has escaped!"

All of Franco's films are dotted with these
playful allusions. They tantalise but offer no
real information. Some keep popping up again
and again. Names like Lorna, Linda, Al Pereira,
Radek ... all gleaned from obscure thrillers and
other half-forgotten, once popular movies. In
fact there's so many of them they're like a maze.
A maze that illustrates his astonishing memory.
If you were to note down all the references
you'd be wiped out, physically depleted. You'd
also know very little more about the man and
why he makes his offbeat films.

Quirkiness is one of the hallmarks of the low
budget film. Because there's less money
involved everything has to be done faster.
There's also a little more freedom. Freedom to
be outrageous, plus freedom to take chances
and make mistakes. In a really big budget flick
every element in the script is double checked.
Producers can give it a thumbs up or thumbs
down. More money involved means more planning and more processing. This irons out any
idiosyncratic elements. Moneymen don't like the
unpredictable, it can be bad for their investment.

The phrase 'low budget' doesn't really capture
the essence of Franco's approach, his method
has more velocity, it's more of an an on-the-hoof
approach to filmmaking. He gets an idea, works
out a few pages of script, then gets down to
filming. It's fast, spontaneous and pulled along
by the ideas that his supercharged brain throws
up. If Franco has a problem, it's this. He has too

many ideas. In Hollywood, film folk snort all sorts of class 'A' substances, but Franco doesn't need drugs to get his imagination going. If anything, he needs them to calm it down!

It's not easy to illustrate his out-of-control creativity. Ideas multiply like a disease with Franco. He'll take one theme and twist it into countless permutations, each one different from the last. One of his favourites is the zombie motif, originally taken from the 1939 film **The Dark Eyes of London**. He used it in his first horror film, **The Awful Dr. Orlof**—four years later, in **Miss Muerte**, he snazzily reworked the same theme. His next film, **Attack of the Robots (Cartas boca arriba**; 1966), had a veritable army of snappily dressed zombie men. Grey suited chaps with shades, programmed for assassination. This could have been one of his most adventurous thrillers but the production was dogged by money problems. Colour sequences were planned but these ended up junked, victims of erratic finance. The film suffered, and the end product was more pedestrian than it should have been, given the talents of Franco and co-writer Jean-Claude Carrière.

After **Attack of the Robots** Franco made his last French/Spanish co-production **Residencia para espías (Golden Horn**; 1966). In five years he'd turned out nine films—some great, some good, some real non starters—most of them co-funded by the French company Eurociné, a low budget operation that he would work for again during the 1970's and 80's. By 1966 it was clear he'd have to find new sources of finance if he wanted to keep filming and pumping out the product. While working on **Golden Horn** he hooked up with Karl-Heinz Mannchen, who would later help to produce Franco's most famous film, **Necronomicon**(1967). Mannchen also worked with German producer Artur Brauner, who financed some of Franco's daringly titled early seventies' sex flicks, including **Vampyros Lesbos** (1970) and **Sie Tötete in Ekstase (Mrs. Hyde**; 1970).

**Golden Horn** was Franco's last black & white film. His next, **Lucky, el intrépido (Lucky, the Inscrutable**; 1967), was a transitional film, his entry into colour-filled European co-produc-

◀ Decision time for Eddie Constantine, **Attack of the Robots** (1966)

tions. This time around the money came from Spain, Italy and Germany. This doesn't mean the budget was substantially bigger—it merely meant they'd found another donor, an extra source for that vital cash injection. The Italian connection was particularly useful because if they used an Italian composer for the film they wouldn't have to pay a cent. Franco selected the talented Bruno Nicolai to provide the all important music track—a quality score for zero cash.

**Lucky** was a fast'n'furious feast of pure hokum, Franco's first attempt to make a film that zipped around like a comic strip. Others have tried, but Franco is the only low budget director to have really succeeded. **Lucky** is unique, it's not a pastiche, it's not a homage. It's a comic strip on film. Even today it still seems super modern. Made on a shoe string, the film is every bit as zany as Robert Altman's **Popeye** or Warren Beatty's megabuck **Dick Tracy**.

Franco is renowned as a fast worker, he can make a film in a week. But no matter how fast he zooms and dollys, there are always money problems. He's forced to either can the film, hustle for some more funding, or sell another project. The low budgets inevitably lead to complications. After **Lucky**, his next project was **Necronomicon** (1967), one of the few films for which he had a reasonable budget. Yet even with this one, there were problems. Maybe looking at its chequered production history will give some idea of the ups and down of the low budget ballgame.

After Franco came up with the idea for **Necronomicon** he visited Karl-Heinz Mannchen with an eight page script. Mannchen contacted his friend Adrian Hoven, an ex matinee idol now better known as the producer of the infamous shocker **Mark of the Devil** (1969), who lined up some moneymen to finance the film.

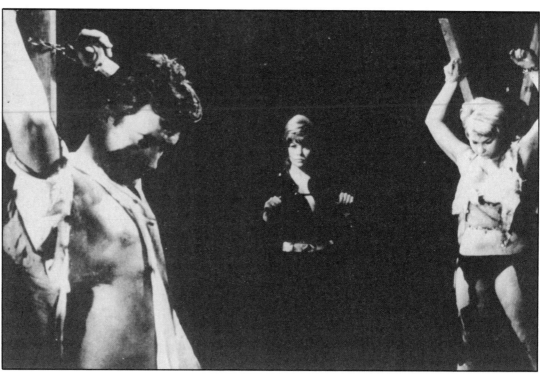

Mannchen had enough cash for a few days shooting so Franco went off to Lisbon to begin work. After a few days Hoven arrived in town, but his financial contact in Germany had pulled out of the deal. They were eight to ten days into shooting, almost out of money, and getting desperate. Hoven had another idea. This one was a long shot. He had a capricious friend, very rich, who would maybe like to back a movie. Hoven called him long distance but kept it short as their money was evaporating fast. He invited the millionaire to the set in Lisbon, a generous gesture which might save the day. Franco and Mannchen both O.K.'d this idea because they'd pay for the air fare later, when they had money. The millionaire, Caminecci, accepted the free ticket and, although very skeptical about the whole affair, visited the set. As he watched the filming he became enthralled by the female lead, luscious Janine Reynaud.

This saved the day as well as subtly changing the film. Caminecci took over the financial reins, arranging for the clothes and the music. After shooting in Lisbon they went to Berlin to finish the movie. Caminecci paid for everything. By this stage Franco, Mannchen and Hoven were out of cash, and when the film was completed he gave them some money, and said 'The film's mine". Caminecci worked on the cutting of the film, and produced his own version, which he promoted in the U.S.A. Without his publicity, the film would never have been as big. Hoven, Franco and Mannchen didn't have Caminecci's

resources—it was Caminecci who arranged a special screening for **Necronomicon** at the Berlin Film Festival, without which Fritz Lang would never have seen it, and it might never have become heralded as an erotic masterpiece.

Retitled as **Succubus** for the English speaking market, **Necronomicon** caused a nationwide stir when it was first released in America. Men's magazines like *Duke* and *Debonair* had a field day exploiting this hot slice of movie erotica ... 'a film that makes **I Am Curious, Yellow** look like a Walt Disney production.' It had all the hallmarks of a dangerous, decadent European film: S & M nightclub scenes, beautiful women who kiss and kill for lust, spooky dream sequences, strange word games that end in death, mad hedonistic parties, lesbianism and mannequin terror. By American standards it was an amoral sleighride that blurred the boundaries between fiction and reality, perversion and playfulness. Was it art or was it pornography?

**Necronomicon** had just the right amount of gloss, abstraction and delirium to confuse the censors. Back then, almost anything European with a hint of skin and sin did big business in the U.S.A. and England. **Necronomicon** slipped onto the market at just the right time and, despite the low budget, it looked sumptuous, colour-filled and Continental. It was pitched at the audience who'd been wowed by **La dolce vita** and **Boccaccio '70**, and the trailers and promotional material emphasised the daring and sophisticated naughtiness of the film. The men's magazines took a different approach, like Caminecci they focussed on 'the wanton sex siren, Janine Reynaud'. Janine was 37 when Necronomicon was made, and only appeared in a few more films before she retired. Exquisite, glamourous and deadly, she was made for the central role of the succubus, Lorna.

In real life, Reynaud was married to Michel Lemoine, a talented and unusual looking actor who went on to direct the brutal but subversive **Seven Women for Satan** (1974). He had a small part in **Necronomicon**, but during the production stayed firmly in the background; he knew his wife was having an affair with the millionaire Caminecci, but kept quiet because it was good for business.

Like **Lucky, the Inscrutable, Necronomicon** didn't have a traditional plot. Whereas **Lucky** hopped, skipped and jumped from absurdity to cheeky absurdity, **Necronomicon** merely slipped further into misty abstraction, a dreamlike acid haze where sex and death raised their ugly heads. Reviewers were quick to note that the film was not a 'a nudie or a plot movie'. Some found it meandering ... 'an unappetising froth of surrealistic dream iconography'. Almost all of Franco's films have this wayward quality, it's partly to do with the way he works. On **Necronomicon** he had virtually no script, he made it up as he went along. Every morning he'd come down to breakfast with a page of dialogue and action that he'd written the night before, and get actor Jack Taylor to translate it from Spanish into English. Even his first film, **Tenemos 18 años**, followed this improvisational blueprint and, as his budgets became smaller, more and more things had to be made up on the run.

Film has a form all its own. Unlike literature, it doesn't need to be linear or logical. Does Franco experiment with this potential, or does he merely fool around with it, hoping everything will work out alright in the end? This is one of the 64,000 dollar questions, and one that in true Franco style deserves two answers. When it works, he was experimenting. When it doesn't, he was bored and screwing around.

Despite production problems, **Necronomicon** turned out to be Franco's biggest budget film so far. It would be twenty years before he would have a similar amount, when he made **Faceless** for René Château in 1988—in between these two titles he would direct another 140 films. Generally, when you describe a film as having a big or substantial budget this means there is enough money to cover everything—clothes, food, travel and all the other incidentals. No matter how big the budget was by

Franco standards, **Necronomicon** was still a cheapie. Karl Lagerfeld may have supplied outfits for Janine Reynaud, but Caminecci's money didn't stretch much further and everyone else had to supply their own costumes—which accounts for the high fashion/weirdo look of the film, and lends it a retrospective charm.

Having completed two effervescent, comic strip type films in a row, it seemed that Franco was on a roll. Perhaps it was the freedom of leaving Spain behind. He had always felt confined there, felt someone peering over his shoulder checking the things he was doing. Franco talks of the **Necronomicon** period as a breakthrough—"a chance to make cinema inside another system". In Spain the film was regarded as pornography, perhaps this indicates what he means.

To make **Lucky** and **Necronomicon**, Franco had found new producers and formed new partnerships. Like most people he's always more buoyant at the beginning of a relationship. His film career has gone through several phases like this ... he hooks up with someone new, they work together, perhaps become friends. The partnership splits up after a number of films when "they know each other very well, and lose respect for each other". Each phase has a different style, but the basic ideas are always the same. Franco has a few favourite themes he keeps returning to, but they come out looking different, partly because of the input of the producer. Each one has his own pool of workers, actors and technicians. This gives the films they do together a different surface gloss, yet underneath this shiny exterior beats a heartful of twisted Franco. A look at his next two films for Adrian Hoven's Aquila company should illustrate this point.

**Bésame, monstruo (Kiss Me Monster)** and **Sadisterotica** (both 1968) were produced quickly to cash in on the success of **Necronomicon**. Both starred Janine Reynaud, and several of the other **Necronomicon** stalwarts such as Michel Lemoine and producer Adrian Hoven. Although the budgets were slightly smaller, the uninhibited drive was pretty much the same, they followed the same care-free tack, the same make-it-up-as-you-go-along directive. This approach goes way back with Franco. His first film, **Tenemos 18 años** skated along this knotty curve. **Tenemos** also had two girls in the lead roles, an unusual phenomenon for 1959, and the sort of thing that was hyped as original in films like **Thelma and Louise** thirty years later.

Franco loves this two-women-together scenario. **Bésame, monstruo** and **Sadisterotica** are

▼ Necronomicon

# Bésame, monstruo

**ROSSANA YANNY · JANINE REYNAUD · ADRIAN HOVEN · ANA CASARES**

films where the girls have a field-day. The guys are one dimensional, the women are sexy chameleons, fun filled, intelligent and ahead of the game. **Bésame, monstruo** is a sixties' spy spoof that takes this idea to its logical conclusion, the two girls, played by Janine Reynaud and Rosanna Yanni, effortlessly avoiding the killer machinations of a group of klutzy males. For them it's as easy to sidestep a killer as it is to slip into a new skimpy sixties' outfit.

**Sadisterotica** has a similar two girl plot. This time, Reynaud and Yanni play frisky private investigators. Reynaud skulks around in a neat bat outfit, solving crimes and leaving an imprint of her full red lips as a suitable memento. Her enemy is a psychotic artist with a weird penchant for photographing girls. His beastly sidekick, Morpho, grabs them and chokes them, while he goes crazy with his snapper. It's a return to familiar Franco terrain, it's **Orlof** revisited. Only this time the setting isn't Gothic nor the motivations dark and perverse. Despite its menacing title, **Sadisterotica** is lightly ghoulish. It's a giddy comic strip filled with impudent humour. Producer Adrian Hoven plays the bad-ass artist Radek. Decked up with an evil goatee and sinister eye patch, he hangs out in strip clubs, puffing furiously and recklessly eye-balling the local red-light babes. Franco also appears in a cameo, an effeminate art-hound, a bloated inept buffoon. Twenty minutes into the film he's dispatched by Hoven, and grovels whimperingly before he dies. It's a typically twisted Franco in-joke. The producer plays a kill-crazy goon, the director a total bean brain. One skewers the other with psychotic abandon.

There's something frothy about these two Franco films. They're light, gaseous affairs, and it's hard to resist their carefree effusion. They rework his favourite themes with love and aplomb. The style is kitsch and sixties, the gags nifty and seemingly never ending. Each of them moves at a jaunty pace, throwing you off guard, making you forget their similarities.

**Sadisterotica** was Franco's last production for Adrian Hoven. After this, he moved on to work for the infamous Harry Alan Towers. Towers is the sort of wildman that only cinema seems able to produce. He's a real-life Mr. Arkadin, a mystery man reputedly connected with an assortment of major scandals, including the Profumo affair. Samuel Z. Arkoff has described Towers as "the blandest guy I ever met". Others call him a lovable rogue. Klaus Kinski, always a good man with a quip, adds to the Towers legend, observing that

"Harry spends half his time in jail, and the other half making films." The Harry Alan Towers' myth could fill a book, or fuel a series like **Dallas** or **Dynasty**. He's one of those men who love the strange brand of fame that movie making can bring. And when the legend becomes bigger than the man, I guess you have to run with the legend. Especially when it makes better copy than the films he's made.

In Franco terms, Towers looked like the big time. His productions seemed more expensive, and they had stars, so in that sense it looked like a step up the ladder. For the first time in his career Franco could work with headliners like Christopher Lee, Herbert Lom, George Sanders and Jack Palance. But this was the late sixties, and many of these men were on their way down or in a career trough. There's always been a kind of phony ring to the films Franco made for Harry Alan Towers. The roster of former high flyers is unsettling, cheapskate and depressing. If Franco has any talent, it's a talent for creating wacky, oddball worlds, places where anything can happen. When you enter his realm you leave behind the familiar. Famous wrinkled stars carry too much weight, they're too well-known, too commonplace for the crazy cinematic dreams of Franco.

Of the nine films he made for Harry Alan Towers, only three stand out from the crowd. **Eugenie ... The Story of her Journey into Perversion** (1970), **The Girl from Rio** (1968), and **Venus in Furs** (1969).

▲ Drinking with class, Jack Taylor in **Necronomicon** (1967)

◄ (Facing page) Girls, Gags and Guns, **Kiss Me, Monster** (1968)

◄ Maria Röhm in **Blood of Fu Manchu** (1968)

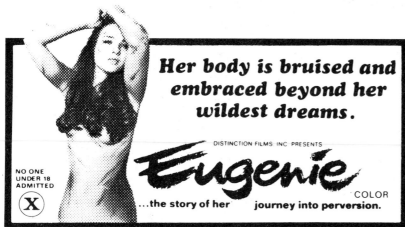

Her body is bruised and embraced beyond her wildest dreams.

DISTINCTION FILMS INC PRESENTS

*Eugenie*

...the story of her    journey into perversion.    COLOR

NO ONE UNDER 18 ADMITTED

X

Eugenie (1970) ▲

Twenty years down the pike, **Eugenie** still packs a punch. The story is like something straight from the works of the Marquis de Sade. A couple, played by Jack Taylor and Towers' wife Maria Röhm, keep drugging a helpless young female. Every night they tie her up for their unspeakable pleasures. Each morning over breakfast they act like nothing has happened. In the evening they begin again ...

**The Girl from Rio** (1968) is another Franco whammer. Like **Eugenie**, it's a departure from the rest of his films with Harry Alan Towers. Made as a follow-up to Lindsay Shonteff's **The Million Eyes of Sumuru**, it was Franco's most sexually overt film to date. Sumuru, a character created by Sax Rohmer, was the female equivalent of his dastardly Fu Manchu, and **Goldfinger** starlet Shirley Eaton was an inspired choice for the role of this power-crazed vixen with plans for world domination. Coy and wholesome when she appeared in British feature films, **The Girl from Rio** showed that there was another side to Shirley. Sumuru leads an army of gun-toting lovelies, crushes men beneath her heels, and is a dab hand at seduction, torture and death. Her world is a pervert's paradise, her female accomplices are like hell-cats from a classy S & M comic strip in their high heels and skintight costumes. Franco's earlier films had lesbian undercurrents, such as cat fights and girl flat-mates, but in **The Girl from Rio** he takes this obsession firmly out of the closet.

Karl-Heinz Mannchen is one of many Franco collaborators who have spotted this predilection for girls together. He was Franco's regular companion, out on the town in Berlin's clubs and cabaret spots. Franco didn't like to stay in at night, he was restless, so every evening they'd seek entertainment, visiting famous German strip clubs and sex shows. They'd see striptease acts featuring lesbian numbers, or pseudo-lesbian numbers, and Karl would ask if Franco wasn't tired of seeing the same stuff over and over again:

"Maybe they'll change the act next time" was Franco's reply—he was happy just looking.

As the sixties became the seventies, censorship loosened. Franco, as always, was at the cutting edge of new developments. Drawn to make erotic films and test the boundaries of what was permissible, his destination was always somewhere 'out there'. Somewhere erotic and uncharted, a place full of women, an erotomaniac's dream. With **The Girl from Rio** he moved deeper into this unknown world. Maybe that's why it was one of his best films for Harry Alan Towers

The film opens with a raunchy sax score from Daniel White. Pure cathouse music. The pretitle sequence is sheer sexual dementia. A wide eyed captive girl. A perspex cage. Foggy gas. She rolls on the floor, her net dress is seethrough. A man gazes, half sneer, half lust. She twists in a drug haze. The naked hero fondles her on the smoke filled floor. Behind an opaque curtain Sumuru looks on, snakelike, with pale green make-up. The drugged damsel rubs her catlike nails across his chest. Sumuru is there. Her boots shine, she poises menacingly. Digging her heel into the man's adam's apple, a smile flickers. Below her the doped-up concubine hovers languorously ...

Overblown, sex crazed and fabulous, it sets the scene for the things that follow. The props Franco uses are simple—coloured lights, smoke, exotic costumes and some see-through plastic.

SOLEDAD MIRANDA - Portada y págs. interiores

High Fashion daze, cover ▲
girl Soledad Miranda

Cheap things that anybody could get hold of. The end result is way-out and bizarre. Some of the evil henchwomen wear scanty outfits, revealing numbers snipped together from sticky black plastic. These cover their bodies like crude brushstrokes, and don't peel off, even during the lesbian seduction scenes. Prisoners are also taped, their mouths fixed by broad, black adhesive material. The whole effect isn't brutal. It's shocking but aesthetic. Like the gags in drawings by bondage artist John Willie. Few other films offer an unfettered taste of kinky material like this. It's comic-strip stuff, but too mysterious to be one dimensional. Back in 1968 it must have had a raw unholy zing—even today it looks outlandish and compulsive.

The final highlight from Franco's Harry Alan Towers' period was **Venus in Furs**. Like the earlier **Necronomicon** it was mercurial, a mood film that slipped easily from solidity towards unreality. The opening sets the shifting scene, outlines the unease and torment of Jimmy, a mixed-up trumpet player (James Darren). "It all

began last year, near Istanbul on the shore of the Black Sea. Or at least I think it did. I tried to remember why I buried my horn, it was like burying my life. But I had to find it and dig it up and keep running. Musicians will understand. A guy without a horn is like, well, a man without words." He finds his trumpet buried in the beach. It's in its case. He takes it out and begins to play. A body is washed up nearby, naked and beautiful, but punctured with knife wounds. The dead girl is Wanda Reed, a girl from his past. The rest of the film slips from Rio to Istanbul and back again, while Jimmy tries to make sense of his memories and the things he's seen. Wanda keeps reappearing, returning to haunt and seduce him. She has come back to destroy her perverted murderers—rich playboys, art dealers and fashion photographers from the jaded jet set who carved her up and killed her during one of their sadomasochistic revels. She bumps them off one by one, making the punishment fit the crime.

This familiar revenge plot turns up in a whole range of Franco films including **Sie Tötete in Extase** (1970) and **Miss Muerte** (1965). **Venus in Furs** is different. It's more fragmented and hallucinatory. Like John Boorman's **Point Blank** it gets inside the mind of a half dead or dying man, following his elliptical, meandering thought processes and his sweaty unease. It's a scenario that suits Franco's anarchistic method of writing and making films. The idea for **Venus in Furs** was suggested to Franco by jazz trumpet player Chet Baker. Chet described his favourite method for improvising solos. He told him—"When you are playing, it's wonderful to close your eyes, begin to improvise and, to pass the time, see your life fragment by fragment, to feel transported to an unreal world ... and when you finish the solo, and two minutes have passed, you look at the faces of the spectators, which are the same as before you closed your eyes—but you've been away and you've come back".

This sums up the diffuse approach of **Venus in Furs**. It could have been a masterpiece, but a few things prick the delicate bubble, break the mood, pulling you back towards mundane reality. Grainy stock footage of the carnival in Rio is one. The explanatory voice-over and the 'Incredible Hulk' style slow motion sequences are others. Perhaps it was the low budget. Franco always had trouble getting the necessary money from Harry Alan Towers. He was the classic wildcat entrepreneur, full of good ideas, but stingy with the finance. Franco says that he has "no conscience". The film crew would arrive in Brazil, geared up and ready to shoot, but there'd be no money. Sooner or later they'd become disenchanted, which would have a detrimental effect on the finished film.

Is Franco a good ideas man whose films are messed up by dodgy producers and the uncertainties of low budget film production? Or does his own wayward personality add to the blips that mess up the final result? The answers to these difficult questions are elusive. **Venus in Furs**, like many of Franco's films, is flawed. In the end the finger of guilt must be pointed at both producer and director. Each of them should share the blame and take responsibility for the highs and lows of the end result

**Venus in Furs** gives you a glimpse of what's great and what's grating about the typical Franco film. Some scenes are shot with quirky precision and painstaking attention to detail, while others are cobbled together cheaply. The inevitable reaction alternates elation with irritation. Elation at sampling something unique and unheralded. Irritation at the slipshod and the mundane.

Franco's collaboration with Harry Alan Towers was bumpy and exciting. Like all directors and producers they had disagreements, money wrangles and other quibbles, yet working for Towers was good for Franco. He had a chance to make international productions, film outside his usual European locations, jet to Rio and Istanbul, and sample strange food and exotic locations. Sometimes the fringe benefits make anything bearable.

Over the years Franco has worked with almost every European low budget producer. His prolific career offers more than just a quick guide to the European scene. It's a *Who's Who*, that namechecks all the major movers and shakers, and most of the other maverick moneymen. Though few are as flamboyant as the larger than life Harry Alan Towers, they're an interesting and diverse group of individuals. Cultured but oddball. Very different from American or English low budget producers. They're European. They don't follow the American showman route of David F. Friedman, or the cheeky car salesman approach of British sexploitation entrepreneurs. They're not flash, brash or innocently garish. The major difference hinges round their sophisticated savoir-faire. To paraphrase Franco—they might make silly films but they are not silly men. Many of them come across like old world diplomats. They surround themselves with original paintings, art objects and the furnishings of the good life. Most of

them are cultured but crusty, they like to do things their own way, in their own time. In this sense they're all misfits, misfits who've found a niche producing bizarre films that satisfy some kooky need and supply enough money for their own expensive tastes.

In 1970 Franco entered a new phase in his career. He stopped making films for Harry Alan Towers and began work on **Sie Tötete in Ekstase**. As usual he ran out of money, so he phoned around for help. He talked to Karl-Heinz Mannchen and asked him to come to Berlin. Together the two of them looked for a backer, and eventually latched onto Artur Brauner, one of the most prolific post-war German producers. They showed Brauner an eight page script. Brauner was a very charming gentleman, and a shrewd businessman. He invited them to dinner and worked out costs on his napkin. No matter how low their budget was, he'd always try to beat them down. He also liked to have a say about the script and the actresses who starred in his films. According to Mannchen, his taste wasn't Grade A, number one.

Franco's zoom laden reputation probably started with the films he turned out for Brauner. Zooming in and out is a cheap, quick method of making films. It saves time and reduces the number of camera set-ups, but makes the end product a trifle irritating. The effects of watching a zoom riddled film can be long lasting. Critics are like elephants, they don't forget easily, and many of them have branded Franco as a zoom hound, someone who uses this brain jarring device repeatedly and without mercy. This isn't the case. He used it a lot when working for

▲ Swinging Sixties skit,
**The Black Cats** (1964),
featuring Soledad

▼ Dennis Price captivated
by **Venus in Furs** (1969)

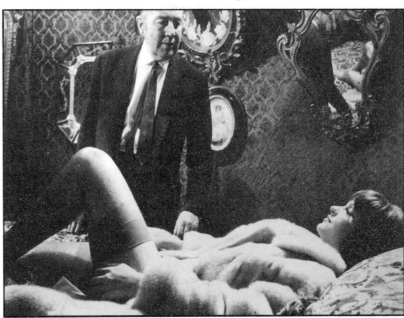

Ewa Strömberg, an ▲
**Heiress Of Dracula**
(1970)

Artur Brauner, and later for Robert de Nesle. After that he abandoned this irritating trait, but the damage had been done.

For a film filled with nudity, strange decor and kitschy muzak **Sie Tötete in Ekstase** is a downbeat, depressing affair. Even the presence of the lovely Soledad Miranda fails to revive the tortured, repetitive plot. The film overflows with death and thwarted desire. Like Irma Zimmer in **Miss Muerte**, Soledad's character is a gal obsessed with vengeance, in this case for the death of her lover, Fred Williams. The way she gets even isn't scientific, it's sadistic, predatory and sexual. She seduces her enemy using feminine wiles, kinky underwear and a range of cheap wigs. Four bureaucrats are involved, three men and one woman. So there's the usual lesbian episode and lots of lobsterlike sex scenes, where one body lies limply on top of another. Franco plays one of the four villains

and Soledad carves him up with laid back venom. She ties him in a chair, circles round him wearing a decadent purple cape and frisky underwear. She runs her knife along his bare chest, drawing blood, and he seems to like it. In the end she finishes him off with a vicious knife-thrust to the groin. The film closes with Soledad driving over a cliff with her dead lover beside her—deprived of sex and genuine affection she embraces annihilation.

**Sie Tötete in Ekstase** is deadly serious. Too serious to be entertaining. You get the feeling that it might be a message film, there's an important but gloomy undercurrent. Like a lot of Franco's work it's morbidly obsessed with oblivion, a fixation that's out of place in a lusty sex film. Death, like impotence, is a topic that's guaranteed to get the average sexploitation fan trembling with pain and annoyance. But Franco keeps returning to this bleak wasteland. The audience recoil, their heads spinning, but Franco pursues his investigations. If the budget was bigger, the producers would curtail his experiments and force him to do something less personal and more commercial. But they don't have the time to get involved. Perhaps this is why Franco prefers the freedom of low budget movie making, it means he can do what he pleases, and concentrate on the off-beat ideas that interest him.

**Vampyros Lesbos** (1970) is a great exploitation title. Like **Sie Tötete in Ekstase** it featured the exceptional Soledad Miranda, whom Franco had first met ten years earlier when he was filming **la reina del Tabarín**. Her first major role for him was in **El conde Drácula** (**Count Dracula**; 1969), starring opposite Christopher Lee. The normally reticent Lee waxed poetic about the sheer chemistry of this naturally poised beauty. During filming they had to retake the neck biting scene over two dozen times, and even after twenty or thirty takes he still felt goosebumps and shivered with natural electricity during every take. She had the X ingredient, that indefinable quality that could have made her a star.

She made eight films with Franco and died tragically, shortly after finishing **The Devil Came from Akasava** in 1970. Her husband, a pilot, was driving their convertible which collided with another car, crushing her side of the vehicle. She was taken to hospital, badly injured, and died after days of agony. Soledad's death was shocking and unexpected, a real blow for everyone who knew her. Producer Artur Brauner was upset by the news, but the effects on Franco were strange and long lasting. He was haunted by her memory. He dreamt about her. Karl-Heinz Mannchen remembers changing their shooting location because of Franco's dreams. He said she had come to see him, and that they had to find another location. There was no alternative but to move.

Perhaps the suddenness of her death sparked something inside Franco. It's always unsettling when someone special meets a grisly, premature end. Soledad's demise left a nebulous void. The emptiness was filled by the arrival of Lina Romay, who, according to Franco was "a little bit of a re-incarnation of Soledad Miranda." Romay arrived in Franco's life in "a strange manner" when they were shooting in Madeira. For many people, and Franco is one of them, it's a truly magical island, one of those places where eerie things happen on a daily basis. It has its own magnetism. The landscape provokes extreme reactions and overblown sentiments.

Some people visit it and become reborn, find themselves and stay there for the rest of their lives. Others can't wait to get out. To Franco, it seemed that Lina was a projection of Soledad. She moved like her; it was uncanny, almost as if she were trying to live up to the image of Soledad, trying to fill the black hole left by her death. Franco says that the legacy of Soledad lived on through Romay, but over time Lina's real personality began to surface. When they were making **Celestine, bonne à tout faire** (**Celestine**) in 1974 it finally happened, and "she unconsciously became another actress."

The Franco story is full of these odd repetitions. Lina Romay slips into the Franco landscape to become a lusty re-incarnation of Soledad. Franco mainstay Howard Vernon, who played the awful Dr. Orlof, was succeeded in the 1980's by Antonio Mayans, who stepped into Vernon's shoes, appearing in sixty four Franco films to date. Over time Mayans has matured as an actor, and in some films he projects a granite psychosis that's almost an homage to Howard Vernon

Inside Franco's films there are even more echoes and repetitions. It's not just the names of the characters and the recurring themes that he's drawn towards, even ideas that flopped dismally get revamped and re-used. If they didn't work properly first time around, that doesn't stop him, he'll keep trying until they do. **Sex Charade** (1970) is one example. It was pieced together using left-overs from other projects. Like most low budget men, Franco doesn't like to waste precious footage, he's a master at assembling snippets and pieces, then adding new sequences, creating

▼ Lina Romay, **The Bare Breasted Countess** (1973)

another saleable item. Few other film-makers have his rapacious capacity, his gift for stitching together movies from a mixture of old and new footage. It's one of the reasons he's made so many. Putting together a film from what he has in storage is also useful in other ways. Franco has plenty of unfinished projects, films he's started to make and then run out of money. Re-using what he has in the can makes solid sense. With another film in distribution there's more possibility of finding some cash to finish one of his uncompleted projects. The over-riding priority for Franco is to keep filming. Making films is his life. It's something he must do, no matter what.

**Sex Charade** was a cyclical film, a series of stories designed to be shown continuously. The audience could walk in at any point, sit down and follow the on-screen action easily. A good idea, but the end product didn't live up to expectations, it was a low key sexploitation romp that didn't go anywhere. Franco wasn't satisfied with the results so he decided to test drive it again in **El sexo está loco** (Sex is Crazy; 1980). This time he refined the formula, smoothing out the bumps by drawing on the irrational, sliding structure of Buñuel's **Phantom of Liberty**. Buñuel's film has the kind of narrative form that an anarchist like Franco would obviously be attracted to ... it flowed along like a river fed by a thousand tiny tributaries. He was fascinated by the way the camera abandoned one person then followed another, then another.

**The Devil Came from ▶ Akasava** (1970)

It was playful, and neatly avoided the pitfalls of routine narrative.

Is Franco a cinematic anarchist? That's a difficult question to answer simply. His penchant for the erotic immediately places him outside the mainstream, indicating that he works to a different set of rules, moves to a different beat. When he worked for Artur Brauner, his films often went too far for the old man's taste. Brauner was an elderly, respectable businessman—he didn't like it when the sex scenes got weird, wacky and intense. So even inside the sexploitation business Franco didn't follow the rules. His erotic tendencies tested the limits of the acceptable, as he followed his urge to film the unthinkable.

Franco's last few films for Brauner were pretty hit and miss. **Jungfrauen Report** (Virgin Report; 1970) was a strange, mondoesque sex education film, while **El muerto hace las maletas (Death Packs his Bags)**, made the same year, was a lifeless descent into Edgar Wallace territory.

Wallace was a Franco favourite. He loved his twisted thrillers and found inspiration in film adaptations like **The Dark Eyes of London** (1939), a film filled with spooky organ music, cold-hearted villains called Dr. Orloff, blind organ grinders, clunking policemen, duped monsters and sadistic, pulpy horror.

The Edgar Wallace stories were very popular on the Continent, so popular that films based on them popped up at regular intervals over a long period that began in the early 1920's, peaked in the 1960's and finally petered out during the mid seventies. The Edgar Wallace name was good for business—on Continental promotion material for the films it was a guarantee of public interest. Franco's **The Devil Came from Akasava** (1970) came at the tail-end of the cycle and, although it was promoted as an Edgar Wallace vehicle, it was actually based on a story by his son, Bryan Edgar Wallace. Earlier Franco films, such as **The Awful Dr. Orlof** and **El secreto del Dr. Orloff**, used Edgar Wallace material successfully as a launching pad for their garish fables. With **El muerto hace las maletas** the cycle had reached rock bottom.

His final films for Brauner, **Der Doctor Mabuse** (1970) and **X-312 Flight to Hell** (1971), were horror thrillers with very little to recommend them. It was obvious that the relationship was drawing to its inevitable conclusion, so Franco hooked up with a new producer, Robert de Nesle. His budgets for de Nesle were even smaller than the low budgets he'd had with Brauner, and the films became even weirder.

**Immoral Tales**

Robert de Nesle was a respectable producer from a solidly bourgeois background. He moved into the sexploitation business but never told his wife the real nature of the films he made. It was his little secret. Like many producers he felt duty bound to check out the charm of his starlets. He auditioned them himself and got them to peel off to make sure they had no unsightly stretch marks, scars or other undeclared blemishes. He clearly took the whole job very seriously.

Franco's first film for de Nesle's French company, Comptoir Français du Film(CFF), was the relatively unremarkable **Robinson und Seine Wilden Sklavinnen (The Sexy Darlings**; 1971). After this the whole mix became weirder, wilder and more unpredictable. Many of the films he directed for de Nesle were shot in a couple of weeks in Portugal, with composer Daniel White providing assistance. As always, Franco's films depended on finding atmospheric but cheap locations that would add the necessary flavour and suggest the proper emotions. The most cost-effective method of hunting for them was to hire a taxi and drive up and down the coastline looking for somewhere unusual that hadn't been over filmed ... architecturally interesting surroundings that resonated with the ideas bubbling inside Franco's brain.

Necessity and desperation added the extra impetus. He picked out places that might not have looked suitable to the untrained eye. When he was filming, the camera would select details—bizarre shapes, interesting angles.

When they were pieced together they created a mood, an atmosphere that wasn't typical of the location at all. The skill lay in selecting all the little bits, then assembling them into some crazy whole. **Les exploits érotiques de Maciste dans l'Atlantide** (Maciste's Sexy Adventures in Atlantis; 1973) is a good example. On a rocky stretch of coastline, with a few actors and some of his mates, Franco attempts to do the impossible and turn out a sexy but funny peplum. Peplums are normally costume epics with muscle men in short skirts—unless you're making a series they cost an outrageous amount of money. With a few swathes of rich material, one Elizabethan costume, some platform sandals, a great location and some chums who can deliver their lines without sniggering, Franco manages to concoct a film that has its own goofy reality. That's an achievement in itself.

His best films for Robert de Nesle include **The Erotic Rites of Frankenstein**, **The Demons**, **Sinner** (all 1972), **La Comtesse Perverse** (1973) and **Lorna, L'exorciste** (1974). A mixed bunch to say the least.

**The Erotic Rites of Frankenstein** has got to be one of the strangest horror films of the 1970's, with a plot that takes in Doctor Frankenstein, his daughter, old-time sorcerer Cagliostro, a blind, nubile bird-woman and a whip-wielding monster covered in metallic paint. It's a film that's poised permanently on the edge of delirium, like the Italian adult comics that were an inspiration for so many of the films Franco made for de Nesle.

▼ **The Corpse Packs His Bags** (1970)

Dennis Price, Howard ▶
Vernon during the shooting
of **Dracula vs
Frankenstein** (1972)

Veteran British actor Dennis Price weighs in as Doctor Frankenstein. As the amoral cad in **Kind Hearts and Coronets** (1949), Price had displayed his cool English savoir-faire. **The Erotic Rites** caught him at the end of a career slide; bloated and booze-raddled, he staggered around hazily as Doctor Frankenstein. Howard Vernon, on the other hand, turned in one of his best performances as the wizard Cagliostro. Rising above the drawbacks of a cheap goatee, he managed to deliver half-baked lines with wide-eyed compulsion. No matter how gonzoid the action, Vernon was always believable. As Cagliostro, his plans were over-blown and demented. He controlled Frankenstein's monster, and had the metallic hulk deliver sadistic punishment with sweating gusto. Cagliostro ripped the clothes off his enemies, tied them together in mixed couples and had his shiny man-thing whip them until they fell, exhausted, onto a bed of twelve inch, razor sharp, poisoned spikes. Melissa, the blind bird-woman, was his oracle, hissing out her predictions with erotic fervour. In return, goatee-toting Cagliostro did her the occasional simple favour. He would let her do a crazy bird dance round a captive prisoner. Blind, blood-crazed, she'd circle her prey, clawing rapaciously. When she'd worked herself up to a frenzy she'd descend on the chained victim, savage his neck and end his torture.

Like any real film fan, Franco loves villains. Inside his horror films the good guys are always banal ciphers, chaps who drift through life. The villain is different, he has plans which are grandiose, self-centred and diabolically clever. The inspiration for these villains comes from dark, demonic horror films like **The Mask of Fu Manchu** (1932), where Boris Karloff had sinister soliloquies, deranged plans, and a world view that was beautifully evil. Franco follows this tradition, takes the villain seriously, and updates the model, giving it a more sexual, sadistic twist.

The evil scenes of lust-filled fantasy are the best things in **The Erotic Rites of Frankenstein**. No film could maintain this intensity for 90 minutes, and it would be impossible to do it on a low, low budget. When you're filming quickly you have to move fast, take chances and forget about perfection. The end result of this method of working is that Franco's films tend to oscillate ... inspired, fantastic sections, separated by long, plodding plot development. The realistic bits usually feature the hero. In Franco's films the woman is always dynamic, the hub around which his crazy fantasies spin. The hero, on the other hand, is ordinary, a dullard who merely bolsters up the status quo—he's not passionate, obsessive or driven by high ignoble desires like the villain. He doesn't have fire or conviction, he isn't a crazy dreamer—he just takes life as it comes. When he triumphs over the villain it's by accident. Franco describes these heroes as "incorruptible idiots ... men who are systematically stupid." Is it hard getting actors to play these well meaning plodders? His method is simple. If you ask them to act like idiots they'll pull faces and fall around like Jerry Lewis. So he convinces his actors that these men are wonderful, that they should play their parts with determination and conviction. This effortlessly turns them into cut-out stereotypes.

The heroes and good guys in Franco's films are generally simple folk, guileless and therefore dull; they're stunted bureaucrats, anaemic pen pushers, people who live in a narrow arid world. Deep down Franco's sympathies are with the bad guy, and he injects more of his imagination into the villain's outrageous plans. It offers him the chance to get strange and lusty. So when it comes to filming these scenes his approach is more inventive, his camera set-ups more thought out and meticulous. This adds to the annoying fluctuation of his films. They dip like a steep rollercoaster, moving from feverish intensity to half-baked ordinariness and back again. These undulations can leave your head throbbing and your face feeling like it's been slapped around with a wet fish.

Only a few of his films avoid these irritating troughs, the rest swerve around. Some sequences are great, others look thrown together, and seem jarringly dull compared to the good stuff. This

▲ Surreal sadism from **The Mask of Fu Manchu** (1932)

ultimately gives the impression that Franco is erratic, a film-maker who just doesn't care about the overall result. He argues that these dull sections are "passages", sequences that ease the film from emotional highlight to emotional highlight. If this is true, why are many of them so irritatingly filmed? Part of the reason is the low budget, the rest is down to Franco, the crew and the producers. Many of his collaborators say that Franco loses interest very rapidly. He can't stay in one spot too long. He's not constant, he has a problem focussing attention on things that don't stimulate him. This makes life difficult for the producer, and it's one of the reasons why his films are uneven. On the other hand, when he does focus his attention the results can be incredible and highly enthralling.

His films for Robert de Nesle have their own unique style. Each producer influences the surface sheen of Franco's output—they suggest actors, actresses and a few of the technicians, and somehow this affects the look of the film and its general ambience. But deep down inside there's a ribald grandeur that comes direct from Franco. It's unmistakable. Nobody uses camera angles the way he does. When he was working for Robert de Nesle he experimented like a madman. **Dracula versus Frankenstein** (1971), for instance, is packed with off-kilter shots, the camera constantly zaps from one jazzy angle to another. Unnerving, slightly infuriating and sometimes inspiring, it's like a deranged experiment in cinematic form ... the camera is like a restless probe constantly looking for stimulation. Franco says he's a jazzman who makes

◀ **Dracula vs Frankenstein** (1972)

Sex, surgery and bondage, ▲
staple elements of Mexican
horror

films. Like any jazzer he loves the fresh and new—the inspired; he seeks "the sound of surprise". When he watches a film that's plodding and predictable, he leaves the cinema, an attitude that permeates his films. They're as restless as he is, constantly on the prowl for that inspired moment, that elusive instant when the old rules are shattered and something compelling and unexpected hits the screen.

If anything, there's almost too much movement in **Dracula versus Frankenstein**, too much peppy experimentation. Like many Franco films it's a fractious experience. But if you sift through it, you find heady globs, lumpy traces of the man's impish, disobedient sense of humour. Like the unusual camera angles, it cocks a snook at the normal and acceptable, revelling in the absurd, the sexual and the exotic. One scene in particular is suffused with this irreverent sexotic approach—the nightclub abduction scene. Monsters, strippers, a beauty grabbed by a man-made beast. This was standard fare in 1950's & 60's horror films like **The Head** (1959) and **The**

Extravert floozy becomes ▶
one of **99 Women** (1968)

**Brain That Wouldn't Die** (1960). Mexican Spanish-language horror films also relished the mad scientist aspect, especially when it included buxom women tied up in dark labs. Films like **Santo contra los zombies** (1961) used the scene as bait, featuring it boldly on promotion material as a sure fire draw, compulsive and irresistible to young horror audiences. Beautiful girls, monsters and scientific madmen also feature regularly in Franco horrors like **The Awful Dr. Orlof** (1961). Each outing revitalised this stock idea, but **Dracula versus Frankenstein** was perhaps his most salty excursion into this well trodden area.

The singer is salacious, dolled up in a wild red wig and body hugging dress. She flashes her underwear with carefree vigour. Her French song is cheeky, risqué and brimming with doubles entendres. She sings of bums, thighs, easy sex and olives that might be testicles. She oozes life, wiggles provocatively on the lap of some giggling patron. Her lips are bright red, her charms irresistible. She winks at the audience, her yellow, feather-topped dress a fetishist's delight. She finishes her number, offering them a peek at her pale white, dimpled bum. As she rushes off they burst into uproar. One chap grins manically, barely able to contain himself.

Inside the dressing room, she peels off. High heels, stockings, vivid red garter and tight black corset. As she prepares to relax, the badly stitched-up monster rips back the red curtain and throws her onto his shoulder, hacking his way through the nightclub crowd. Gunshots are useless against this unnatural creation. His eerie outline reflected in a convex mirror, he shuffles off towards the lab. She awakes strapped to a table. Blue thongs bind her, hold her helpless, captive for an indecent experiment. Her make-up is still perfect. Blue mascara, black corset and suspenders. Doctor Frankenstein adjusts the calibrator. She moans in terror as the electricity peaks and hums. It's clinical, sexual and sadistic. Her blood pumps into a science jar, dribbling over a bat that gnashes its teeth and splashes wildly in red, life-giving liquid. The cable burns, up as the charge goes through the jar. The bat transforms into cape-flapping Dracula ...

It's a throwback to those old pulp scenarios, the depraved scenes that artists such as Margaret Brundage painted exquisitely for the covers of horror magazines like *Weird Tales*. Brundage's creations sported diaphanous gossamer gowns. Franco favours a more fetish orientated approach: white thighs encased in black stockings, interrupted by tight suspenders

and topped by bodice enhancing corsets. It's an old fashioned fetishism, something his audience responds to with slack-jawed glee. He returns again and again to this timeless fascination—his most recent horror film, **Faceless**, is full of these corset clad women, even the cold hearted, feline, surgical assistant Brigitte Lahaie sports one on an off-duty romp. Uninfluenced by fashion, Franco's predilections don't change, he simply reworks and reinvents them, increases their intensity, revels in their gaudy delight.

As the seventies came into full swing, Franco went deeper into this fetishistic sexual playground, his films for de Nesle easily surpassing the frisson of most of his Artur Brauner and Harry Alan Towers' films. **Quartier de femmes (Lovers of Devil's Island**; 1972) was Franco's second Women in Prison (WIP) film; his first, **99 Women** (1968), had been less fetish ridden, less overtly sexual. All his WIP epics follow the same model: prison is a dehumanising hellhole, governed by perverts, lesbians and slimeballs. Prisoners are merely numbers, objects to be used and abused by the lowgrades who wield power. The camp commander is always a crop wielding dyke, the prison doctor a spineless impotent dupe. Together they corrupt the prisoners and play cruel sadomasochistic games. Their power is absolute. They take life and answer to no one. The authorities are implicitly in on the game, they don't care what happens to

society's flotsam, all they care about is law, order and the status quo. Life is routine and doomed in a woman's prison. Escape is impossible and ends in futility, death and more gruesome incarceration.

It's a bleak world view. A nasty subject with depressing overtones. What it does offer Franco is the opportunity to tune into a captive community and focus his lens on a veritable sea of women. There's plenty of scope for lesbian frolicking, perverted activity and scenes of torment where scantily clad, caged women writhe around on wooden beds. If there is any pleasure it's quickly followed by pain. **Devil's Island** was more brutal and desolate than **99 Women**, with more outright torture, more lesbian activity and depravity. Like his other films for de Nesle there were also lots of choked close-ups. This was his style during the period. Effective and claustrophic, it added atmosphere to the gruesome monkey business and was useful in covering up the cheap production values.

Franco's other films for de Nesle were a mixed bag ... a children's film, **Un capitan de 15 años** (A 15 Year Old Captain; 1972); a female vampire film, **La Fille de Dracula** (Daughter of Dracula; 1971); sexy comedies like **Celestine, bonne à tout faire (Celestine**; 1974); and strange thrillers, including **Al otro lado del espejo** (The Other Side of the Mirror; 1973), co-scripted by Franco's wife at the time, Nicole

Guettard. This one was a disturbing weirdie that featured another recurring Franco theme—the hanged father. This primal image returns with a vengeance in **Christina, princesse de l'érotisme (Virgin among the Living Dead;** 1971), where the father dangles in a noose and returns to haunt his daughter, talking to her, offering advice and laughing.

It's hard to be around Franco and not be sucked into the world of film-making; anyone who comes within his orbit is inevitably drawn into his crazy cinematic schemes. His wife was no exception to this rule. She was script girl on early works like **Miss Muerte** (1965), and later contributed to the fetid and disturbing **Lorna, l'exorciste** (1974), a film filled with impure heroes and throbbing sexuality.

**Lorna** is like an updated version of **Necronomicon**, with Guy Delorme's family suffering under the seductive spell of Lorna (Pamela

Stanford), who has returned from his past to claim the soul of his daughter, Linda (Lina Romay). The music is plaintive but sensual, binding the audience to the onscreen action as it descends deeper into a tainted world. The film begins with slow, steam laden scenes of lesbian love-making. There's the usual Franco fascination with alluring pubic hair, which he seems determined to turn into an art form. He likes the way it glistens and grows. His camera seeks it out relentlessly, lingering, hovering, and zooming, catching its immodest undulations. In **Lorna** the lesbian activity is slow, painful and disturbing, but fascinating. The first ten or more minutes of the film are spent drowsily capturing Romay and Stanford's oral lesbian fixations. Franco delays the descent into the plot as long as possible, increasing the claustrophobia, working out his compulsions.

**Lorna** isn't a film for the faint hearted. Although in some ways it's one of his best films, in other ways it's guaranteed to get you running to the door for fresh air. The oxygen is mighty thin inside Franco's obsessive world. Guy Delorme is great as the haunted and hunted main man. Pamela Stanford is outstanding as the temptress dressed up in slinky costumes by Paco Rabane. Yet underneath the veneer of sophistication lurk strange desires, psychic fuel for odd occurrences and outrageous events. Describing something as strange can smack of cliché; with Franco words can only go so far in describing the outlandish intensity of the onscreen action. **Lorna, l'exorciste** is a perfect example of this, words like weird and bizarre barely do justice to its unhealthy landscape. In one queasy scene, small crabs crawl out of a horrified Jacqueline Laurent's pudenda. Another scene, missing from most prints, centres around a dildo, blood-licking and witchcraft. Yet these scenes are just the sleazy show stoppers—the entire film is permeated by uneasy delirium. The protagonists act like they've been infected, victims of a psycho-sexual contagious disease.

While **Lorna** was Franco's most over the top and fevered film for de Nesle, some of the others, like **The Demons** and **Sinner** (both 1972), come pretty close to its creative outrage. **The Demons** was one of those 1970's films that used witch-hunting as an excuse for sadistic sexual shenanigans. It was less flat than the earlier **Der Hexentöter von Blackmoor (Night of the Blood Monster;** 1969), which tackled a similar subject. Despite lashings of dungeon scenes and pernicious nipple torture it had some joyous overtones. The demons, or witches, of the title

French film mag asks: 'Would you buy a ticket to Hell with Lorna?' ▼

le reflet de la vie moderne périodique mensuel n° 23 prix : 12 F

EURO CINEMA

Voulez-vous prendre un billet pour l'enfer avec lorna

were lusty catalysts of desire who writhed around with tumescent vigour. Unlike other films inspired by Ken Russell's **The Devils**, these demonic nuns weren't neurotic figures, they were more like unstoppable forces of nature. In contrast, the witchfinders were one-dimensional power brokers, puritans, who in the end were defeated by their own repressions. In another break with most period films, the music in **The Demons** wasn't ambient or mediaeval, it was pure European progressive rock, with plenty of rapid bongo beating, scattershot guitar solos and atonal bowing and bending on the strings. Twenty years on, it adds a kitsch quality to the proceedings, making the film ripe for rediscovery.

Franco returned to this devils-in-a-convent theme later, in **Die Liebesbriefe einer Portugiesischen Nonne** (Love Letters of a Portugese Nun; 1976), which he filmed for Erwin C. Dietrich's Swiss-based Elite Films Company. **Liebesbriefe** was less pagan, more ecumenical than **The Demons**, which is full of intense but short soliloquies, paeans to lust and nature. One nun, overcome by nature's promise, delivers a pent-up breathy speech that's a celebration of fertility and renewal. "I can't help it. Springtime is so lovely. The softness of the air and the country scents stir deep within me. My sleep is troubled and I dream that I'm running naked in the wheatfields with the wind caressing me." Later, a female witchfinder, overpowered by lusty lesbian sensations, asks the eternal question "have you ever made love to a woman?" She lifts up the heavily lined dress of the fresh faced witch, resting her cheek lovingly on the demonic nubile's bottom. She sighs in ecstasy ".. there are some moments in life you can't forget ... they linger in the mind." The witch kisses her, transforming her into a bony skeleton.

**The Demons** is basically another Women in Prison film. There's the same heated bed-writhing, the same fixation on lesbian activity and depraved frolics. Unlike the Women in Prison films, the authorities can't cope. The Mother Superior reels, red faced and turned-on, when she finds a hot-blooded naked nun rolling around in a cloistered bedroom. Overcome by lust, she throws herself off the balcony rather than give in to her amplified desires.

*"Oh Anna, your mouth pressed against my sex makes me excited, what a shame you're so cold. I want to give my body, my feelings, my sex, to my sisters and brothers, those who have only known pain in their lives*

◀ Spanish pressbook for **Sinner** (1972)

*...Today I met a fascinating creature, Maria Toledano. I watched her dance, and she excited me so much, the way she moved, just watching her I came. From the way she looked at me, I could tell right away she likes women. I know I please her. Tomorrow I'll dance for her to excite her. I'll make her feel what I felt, watching the swaying of her beautiful, voluptuous body. I've got to have her, we must possess each other."*

These are a couple of extracts from the intense, feminine voice-over that links the disparate segments of **Sinner**. Filmed shortly after **The Demons**, it's one of Franco's cheapest yet most satisfying lesbian orientated productions. "If there is any message in my films" says Franco, "it's about the distance between people", and **Sinner** is a field trip into seventies' alienation. Most of the linking action takes place in a late night disco, The Lucky Ghost, where girls frug energetically to lumbering progressive discoid rock in crocheted purple mini dresses or lemon yellow numbers ... man made, slightly decadent outfits, offset by necklaces and high heeled slingbacks. It's retro heaven and seventies' hell.

The film tells the story of Linda, a teenage nymphet who is sexually abused by a balding, moustachioed mack-man during a ride on a fairground ferris wheel. The film documents her brief encounters, linked by extracts from her intimate diary. This has Snoopy on the front, is filled with

▼ Two hot nuns, **Love Letters of a Portuguese Nun** (1976)

doodles, and holds Linda's innermost thoughts, telling of her search for love, her vulnerability and her close encounters of the lesbian kind.

The first sequence deals with Linda's revenge on the dweeb that messed up her life. They get rotten drunk together. She takes him to a hotel room. He collapses on the bed. She strips down to her stockings then phones the cops to report a murder. She cuts her own throat, falls on his body, bleeding, and dies moments before the police arrive. They cart off the still sozzled, paunchy guy—her revenge is complete.

The rest of the film is an investigation. The wife of the accused man seeks out people who knew Linda and tries to find out what really happened. She meets the dead girl's friends and lovers who tell her story in flashbacks. One of them reads extracts from the potently frank diary that documents Linda's love affairs, each flashback filmed in roughly the same style, painting a picture of pleasure and, ultimately, alienation. The film starts with a red-light lesbian nightclub act, which more or less sets the scene for the female frolicking that follows. As the film progresses, the lesbian activity increases, becoming longer, more intense and exotic with each passing segment. It climaxes with an extended all-girl photographic romp. Miss Schwartz, Linda's next door neighbour, snaps Linda getting hot'n'heavy with a buxom model.

The kitsch clothes and the prog rock buzz on the soundtrack pull the film sideways, take it out of the sleaze ghetto and elevate it into that grey area that lies somewhere between trash and social commentary. The film is dotted with outrageous fashions—orange plastic zebra-striped dresses, Mondrian sunglasses and other unhinged apparel. It's a minefield of perversely coloured clothing, supplemented by an Iron Butterfly-meets-Vanilla Fudge, grunge soundtrack.

**Sinner** is one of those strange creations you can only find in the bargain basement of cinema. In lesser hands it would have no discernible style, no garish intonations to take it outside the usual cheap sex film limitations. If the film works, it's because it straddles a stack of opposites. On the one hand it's phony and kitsch. On the other it's heartfelt and serious. Like many of Franco's best films it oscillates, refusing to be tied down by categories, forming a riddle that attracts some and repulses others.

Despite its extremely low budget, **Sinner** is one of Franco's most even productions; it doesn't plunge from the heights of heady fantasy to the depths of sloppily lensed realism. Perhaps the hefty percentage of lesbian material kept Franco's

interest bubbling. On the other hand, the film's structure is a series of different stories about Linda, which may have demanded more concentration from Franco, counteracting the usual hiccups that mar his films. Who knows? Whatever the reason, it works and that's all that matters.

Unlike **Sinner**, **La comtesse perverse** (1973) is patchy. When it's good it's wide angled, kinetic and oddball. When it's bad it's merely reasonable. The story is a female-injected variation on the classic 1932 chiller **The Most Dangerous Game**. Here, the untamed but beautiful Alice Arno hunts down Lina Romay with an ornate bow and arrow. Both women are naked. Arno has neatly trimmed pubic hair covered by a baroque pendant. She stalks Romay through the jungle undergrowth to the sound of searing seventies' guitar and frantic bongos. Howard Vernon commands the hunt, and he too stalks the female prey. His outfit is pure Swinging Sixties' bohemian, his black polo neck and neatly buttoned black suit like something he might have worn for his role in **What's New Pussycat?** The film ends with him delivering the line "This is the finest moment of my life!" The woman hunt has been successful.

**La comtesse perverse** is 'out there'. Out in that rarefied region that marks the limits of crazed fantasy. It's played straight, with commitment, which makes it frightening and funny at the same time.

In the mid seventies, Franco hooked up once more with the French company Eurociné. In the early sixties he'd produced sublime low budget thrillers and horror films for this maverick outfit. Now they wanted films with a hefty dollop of S-E-X—films that ran the gamut from lingering eroticism to hardcore.

When you're down there in the depths of low budget film-making, the cheapest subject to turn your camera on is sex. Franco was an ideal director for the subject, and not just because of his erotic bent. As a sex film director he was also daring, he took the subject to its limits. His camera doesn't just record the action it delights in it, floating over the well lit bodies and zooming inexorably towards that hairy, mysterious region the continentals call 'her sex'. No other director shares his wayward compulsion, his insistent need to probe and investigate. When asked why he keeps zooming towards this normally hidden area of female anatomy, he disarmingly admits: "It's the first place my eye looks".

Apart from the genital zoom, Franco has some other sexfilm trademarks. There's the lesbian nightclub scene. With smoky sensual music,

◄ (Facing page) **Sinner** (1972) 'The intimate diary of a nymphomanic'.

almost begs the camera to linger on the languorous curves of her boots, belt and body. This untitled piece of music is a poignant hallmark of Franco's seventies' and eighties' sexfilms, he uses it repeatedly. It crops up again in **Tender and Perverse Emanuelle** (1973), another key Franco film. This one is a twisted tale about a pianist called Emanuelle, who has carved a career playing a classical variation of sexy Daniel White music. The melody returns relentlessly throughout the film, there's even a murder scene where the pianist who plays it gets the chop!

Franco's style for his 1970's Eurociné films was different from his work with Robert de Nesle. There was less low angle gazumping around with the camera; his framing was like a cinemascope version of a Blue Note jazz album cover. In those old Blue Note covers people often had the tops of their heads missing, it looked modern and punchy. Franco used this truncated style a lot during the seventies. He'd pick out interesting details and highlight them inside his scope frame. The result was audacious and also minimised the effects of the small budget, making the films look more dynamic.

**Tender and Perverse Emanuelle** was a pivotal Franco film. Not just because of its obsessive theme, which documented the unhealthy aspects of love and desire. It was also important because it was one of the first films he made with Antonio Mayans. Mayans was to become a mainstay in Franco films, starting off with short cameos and going on to become one his most popular leading men. Over the years his involvement in these films has increased dramatically. In the seventies he was merely an actor, in the early eighties he acted and handled the paperwork, helping out with all sorts of routine production problems, and by the mid eighties he was an irreplaceable part of the Franco team. Without Mayans, Franco would probably have never turned out as many films as he did.

Around the same time that he began making sex films for Eurociné, Franco also became involved with Swiss film man, Erwin C. Dietrich. Dietrich began his chequered career as a scriptwriter with a story that was turned into a highly successful rural drama film. He harboured dreams of becoming a successful actor, but when he saw himself in a screen-test he decided to forget acting and get into film production. His first film deal was a disaster, he was ripped off. As a result, he vowed this would never happen again, and became notoriously canny with money, gaining a reputation as one of the most frugally efficient low budget

meticulous lighting and lots of s-l-o-w female-to-female action. The bodies are lit carefully and there's always a long drawn out tongue touching scene. It's as well shot as any advertisement, even though the subject matter is basically wet dream territory. This red light but gentle female-to-female, tactile sensuality is a Franco favourite. He returns to it a lot. So much so, that you keep thinking the audience and producers during the seventies must have shared his fascination for this brand of eroticism.

José Larraz has pointed out that finding men who photographed well in sex films was almost impossible. Women, he says, were always easier to film, the results were infinitely better. Perhaps Franco found this as well. Lesbian scenes also made sound economic sense. They were cheap to film and they were one of the few sorts of sex scenes that the Spanish, English and American censors allowed. For some reason lesbian frolics were less likely to be snipped out than normal heterosexual romping. So, in some ways, Franco's taste echoed the fixations of the time.

One of his first seventies' films for Eurociné was **The Bare Breasted Countess** (1973), a dreamlike piece that featured Lina Romay as Countess Irina Karlstein. The film opens as she wanders vacantly through a mist shrouded woodland. Her outfit is minimal, black and fetishistic. The music on the soundtrack is classic Daniel White. Slow, soulful and sexy, it film producers. Over the years he made millions through his companies Elite, Avis and Ascot. He turned out sex films with a vengeance, consistently cocking a snook at the high minded attitudes of his Swiss countrymen. Together with Franco he produced a mind wrenching number of Women in Prison (WIP) films, some soft, others squalidly depressing.

Dietrich owned the rights to the infamous **Ilsa** films, **Ilsa, She Wolf of the SS, Ilsa, Harem Keeper of the Oil Sheiks** and **Ilsa, Tigress of Siberia**. These made a stash of money, so it seemed obvious for him to make a WIP film featuring their star, the overtly buxom Dyanne Thorne. Originally the film was to be called **No Man's Land**, but Dietrich decided to cash in on the infamy of Ilsa, and retitle the film **Ilsa, the Wicked Warden** when it was released in North America and Canada. **Ilsa, the Wicked Warden** has its moments. It was one of the few seventies' films where Lina Romay did more than just roll around in an erotic frenzy, displaying her wanton body for the zoom infested camera. In **Wicked Warden** she was a short haired, pugnacious butch dyke, a typical prison product who controlled a stable of long haired women or 'kittens'. In one infamous scene she gets the 'new fish' to lick her 'culo', in another disturbing romp she receives pain and pleasure in the arms of Dyanne Thorne. Thorne sticks pins into Romay's torso, then embraces her, forcing the pointy needles deeper into the young girl's flesh. It was cheap to film, and looked shocking and sadistic on the big screen.

These Dietrich WIP films radiated depraved exoticism—they were good box office material. During the seventies, European countries like Germany and Switzerland were fascinated by the exploits of the Baader-Meinhof gang. Many of their female activists ended up behind bars, and public interest in WIP vehicles was partly due to this, and partly down to the perennial fascination of deviant behaviour. Fifties WIP films merely hinted at the unhealthy atmosphere and the links between sadism, dehumanisation and power. Jonathan Demme's **Caged Heat** (1974) received good reviews, because it boldly showed the horrors of electroshock therapy, a treatment practised in some institutions at that time. Like Demme's **Caged Heat**, Franco's **Ilsa, the Wicked Warden** was based loosely on real events, a fact he used to motivate his actors and actresses. Many of them, like Monica Swinn, say that they appeared in these depraved films for a political reason, and Franco also uses this as an argument. Whatever the reason, **Ilsa, the Wicked Warden** contains Franco's most serious appearance in one of his own films. Normally he prefers to play bumblers or fey misfits, but here he was a straight-faced fighter for freedom and human rights.

Even if these films were made with a serious motive, that didn't stop the on-screen descent into unrelenting depravity. The electroshock therapy, sadism and surgery in **Caged Heat** was mild compared to the gruesome tableaux in **Ilsa, the Wicked Warden**. Ilsa's jail had an assortment of rooms set aside for her sadistic pleasure, some had strung-up, whipped women, others were filled with human flotsam, the disfigured remnants of her indecent experiments. Dyanne Thorne has disowned some of the extreme stuff in the film, saying that she wasn't told the camera was running. Filming improvised scenes filled with outrageous behaviour is a favourite piece of Franco trickery. It's one of his methods for getting sincere performances and pushing the boundaries of what's acceptable. By filming rehearsals he can get actors and actresses to take part in scenes they might object to if they had more time to think about it.

Many of the most chilling scenes in **Wicked Warden** were cheap but highly effective. They show how much mileage Franco can get out of a few props plus a bit of fake blood when he serves them up with psychological menace. In one scene, the warden gets her kicks with a see through bag—she pops it over the head of a prisoner and asphyxiates her, purring contentedly as the female victim gasps in airless helplessness. It's the sort of childish sadism few film-makers would dare to shoot. They'd con-

▼ Two of the **99 Women**

sider it tasteless and untouchable. Franco's less fastidious in this respect, less hemmed in by rules and scruples, a natural born anarchist who is drawn to defy the status quo.

1970's WIP films were pretty much a catalogue of depravity. They had to be like that to compete with hardcore films. In 1974 things loosened up in Europe; hardcore became legal in Germany, which raised the stakes for producers in the sexploitation film business. If they wanted to compete they had to offer something strong and outrageous, and this pushed them towards the WIP film, which they milked for all it was worth. Like them or loathe them, you can't really ignore these sadistic seventies' films. It's unlikely that there'll ever be a series like them again. Many of them were totally brain numbing and stupid, nothing more than badly filmed, dull looking people engaged in never ending scenes of torture and sadism. To be fair to Franco, his WIP films capture something, they have an attitude. This easily differentiates them from most of the rest.

They usually open with a slow pan, a languid tracking shot across a peaceful watery promontory, or lush, dense, jungle undergrowth. The music is sleepy, slightly hypnotic and calming, a far cry from the action that ensues. **Frauengefängis** (1975) for example, offers women tied up on metal beds rigged up for shock treatment, and the switch is pulled with sickening regularity. They piss into pots under the bed, and when the switch is pulled they have no choice but to relieve themselves.

Like most WIP films **Frauengefängis** isn't for the squeamish or the faint hearted, it's for people who like outrage in their films. Nowadays the WIP film has its own devotees, a hardcore group of low budget film fans. When these films were first released they weren't minority fare at all. In Germany, **Frauengefängis** was the third highest grossing film of 1975. It struck some kind of chord with local audiences, and edited versions of the film have been released in many other countries since then.

Almost all of Franco's output for Erwin C. Dietrich has a depressing ring to it. **Liebesbriefe einer Portugiesischen Nonne** (Love Letters of a Portugese Nun; 1976), perhaps the only exception, was another variation on the profitable Women in Prison theme. Although it was set in a convent, it still had 'new fish', deviant inmates and totally corrupt power brokers. In **Liebesbriefe**, authority figures like the Mother Superior and the head priest were double-talking perverts, folks who spouted the word of our Lord while corrupting innocents to get their indecent kicks. William

Berger is superb as the sophisticated but slimy convent priest. He was another in the long line of Franco discoveries, one of the interesting faces that keep cropping up in his films. Like Howard Vernon, Berger is a character who could have been a bigger star, but chose to live his own life. He preferred to take things at his own pace, working with friends on unusual and interesting projects.

**Liebesbriefe** was rife with unholy perversions. Head priest Berger liked coaxing sexual fantasies from the young nuns while hearing their confessions. His reaction to their innocent fantasies was hardly holy or paternal and he often rocked the box with his physical enthusiasm. The Mother Superior was an even viler piece of work who gave her novices to Satan, offering them up to Old Nick for unspeakable debaucheries. Like **Lorna**, **l'exorciste**, **Liebesbriefe** is one of Franco's wildest and most unhealthy films. The fantasy scenes featuring a horned devil are outrageous and rival Benjamin Christensen's silent classic **Witchcraft Through the Ages** (1922) in their queasy sabbatical intensity. All these movies have way-out scenes, but **Liebesbriefe** has a melancholy edge, and a great performance from Berger. It can't be written off as cheap one dimensional sensationalism, there's just too much going on for that.

**Jack the Ripper** (1976) was one of the few interesting film that Franco turned out for Erwin C. Dietrich. Klaus Kinski played the Ripper in this gloomy downbeat tale, an almost shot for shot remake of **The Awful Dr. Orlof** in places, only more gore filled. Kinski was a methodical mad surgeon who used his scalpel with the regularity of a metronome. In his autobiography he described it as 'another piece of shit', a phrase he used to describe almost all of his films.

**Jack the Ripper** is a cold blooded film with a realistic, scientific edge. It lacks the abstract invention that's a hallmark of Franco's best films. Most of his work for Erwin C. Dietrich has a flatness that makes them easy to spot, with few of the curves, blips or probing abstractions you find in his other films. One of the few exceptions is **Das Bildniss des Doriana Gray (Dirty Dracula;** 1975), a film that featured Franco favourite Lina Romay in the lead. Like **Vampyros Lesbos**, **Necronomicon** and **Macumba sexual**(1981), it's an excursion into the land of voyeurism, sexual excess and death, the central concerns around which Franco spins his unhealthy confections. In **Necronomicon** they were handled sixties' style, the sex was implied, the action decadent but swinging. **Vampyros Lesbos** was more daring and reflected the growing mood of sexual libera-

SADOMANIA
(El infierno de la pasión)

◄ (Facing page) Transsexual wardress Ajita Wilson in **Sadomania** (1980)

tion, with more lesbianism and even more uninhibited writhing. Both films featured svelte, lithe and sophisticated female leads in the persons of Janine Reynaud and Soledad Miranda, women who were perfect for sixties' Euro-exploitation films. By the mid seventies public taste had changed, and in order to compete with films like **Deep Throat** (1972) and **The Devil in Miss Jones** (1972), a more earthy brand of European sex film starlet was needed. Lina Romay was an ideal choice. On film she came across as an uninhibited exhibitionist, a gal who embodied the prurient drive at the centre of Franco's sex film concoctions. Together they formed some kind of unholy alliance and complemented each other perfectly. Franco came up with the ideas, she had no qualms about following them through.

Lina Romay's real name is Rosa Maria Almirall. Her film name was borrowed from a singer in mambo king Xavier Cugat's band during the early forties, who also appeared in films such as **Adventure** (1945) by Victor Fleming—Franco chose the name as an intriguing homage to both cinema and mambo. The present day Lina Romay has a ribald on-screen allure that somehow seems at odds with her day to day persona. In reality she is soft spoken, quiet and self effacing, totally different from the earthy erotic roles she plays in films like **The Bare Breasted Countess**. Off screen she dresses like a young mum, and looks healthy and fresh in

stone washed jeans, slip on sandals and lambs wool pullover. On film her clothes are usually minimal, her movements sexual and slightly vacant; she often engages in sexual excess, pleasure that becomes so compulsive it results in orgasm and death for almost all her partners. Franco discovered her when she was 18, and in her own words she was "a simple young girl from Barcelona who got into the film business by accident." She was married to Franco's camera assistant and helped out by doing make-up. Her initial impression of Franco was that "he was odd, very odd", but she was attracted by the allure of the film business, as well as by his working methods.

Franco's way of making films is quite unique. Where other Spanish directors have a crew of thirty, he works with a small gang who all know each other really well, a regular team of eight to ten, which he supplements with a couple of local technicians. It's more informal than the usual European film set-ups. Instead of having a director who barks out orders to an assistant, who then relays them to another assistant, and then another assistant, Franco prefers to get rid of all the unnecessary middlemen. His crews may be small but they are often multi-national; he can have a German soundman, an Italian cameraman, plus French and English actors. This would be a nightmare for most people, making work slow and cumbersome. Not so for Franco. He speaks eight languages and can handle a mixed crew with ease, slipping from German into English or Portugese as the situation demands.

Like many Franco regulars, Lina Romay started off with small roles in his films. Her first appearance was as a gypsy in **The Erotic Rites of Frankenstein**, in a short sequence that is missing from most prints. After that she had bit parts in **Los ojos siniestros del Dr. Orloff** (The Sinister Eyes of Dr. Orloff; 1972), **El misterio del castillo rojo** (Mystery of the Red Castle; 1972), and **Plaisir à trois** (1973). Her first lead role was in **The Bare Breasted Countess** (1973) where she played "a vampire that likes screwing." This was one of the roles that sealed her reputation as a 'Diva of eroticism', featuring long sequences of her rolling around on a wooden bed, licking the bed post and endlessly humping a loglike pillow. In the closing scenes she splashes around in a bath full of blood, and the zoom lens goes into overdrive, restlessly roving towards her pubic area. It's full-throttled voyeurism. Untamed and unashamed, it's the type of motion you associate only with Franco. The camera zooms and moves around the hairy

The many faces of ► Lina Romay

The many faces of ▼ Lina Romay

region, it glides closer, fearlessly, pulls back, hovers for a while, then renews its obsessive slide towards the female 'hot box'.

Franco has declared he's "a pure voyeur ... a voyeur not just of fucking, but of everything. I'm a voyeur of ships crossing the sea, of horses stampeding across the prairie—of everything. To be a director of cinema how could you not be a voyeur? What happens is, I recognise it and 90% of my colleagues don't. What I'm trying to say is that the voyeur in cinema is something passionate and important, but in life they are idiots." **The Bare Breasted Countess** verifies this statement. There are long abstract passages where the camera moons across the cloud covered sky. The music is slow, sensual Daniel White. The atmosphere is ethereal, dreamlike and intense. It points towards some hidden and half baked other dimension, a far cry from the usual realism that dogs European sexploitation.

Other Franco films share this abstract voyeuristic drive, **Jungfrauen Report** (1970), **Tender and Perverse Emanuelle** (1973) and **El siniestro Dr. Orloff** (1982) are just a few of them. Critics remember the pubic zoom and forget about the voyeuristic urge that also haunts many of the other scenes. Perhaps the exhibitionist buzz supplied by girls like Lina Romay has something to do with this. She delivers an erotic frisson that inanimate objects can't supply, with outfits that are often minimal and fetishistic. In **The Bare Breasted Countess** she wore an impudent pout, thigh high black boots, and a broad belt rounded off with a billowing cape. Naked and unashamed, she basked in the gaze of the camera. If Franco is an eager voyeur, she's a willing accomplice in his hedonistic cinematic shuffle. Like many Franco collaborators she's inspired by his enthusiasm for making films, lifted up by his offbeat ideas and thrilled to be a part of the team. Through Franco she's learned about editing and directing. Her name appears on the credits of a couple of eighties' films, where Franco did the camerawork and she helped with the script and coordinated things.

Since 1972 Lina Romay has starred in dozens of Franco films. Some are erotic, some pornographic, others are mainstream, crazy comedies. But above all, her reputation is as an erotic mover; in other words, a gal who'll do wild things for Franco's camera. Her reputation was sealed by photo spreads in English magazines like *Cinema X* and solidified by others in Continental film mags like *Sex Stars System*. In sexploitation films like **Das Bildniss des Doriana Gray (Dirty Dracula)** she delivered the

◀ The many faces of Lina Romay

goods, mingling madness and sexual desperation. **Doriana** had Romay doing what she seems to do best. There were scenes of overt lesbianism plus plenty of uncontrollable passion, passion that results in madness, orgasm and oblivion. **Doriana** is a film of climaxes. Romay squirms in a fever, seducing everyone with her lust-engorged body. As usual she's a bisexual, who kills with her tongue, bringing her lovers to ecstasy and death. In the end her fetid desires are too much for her and she expires, pulling frenziedly on her beaver, her face distorted in gnawing desperation.

The film had a peculiarly over the top performance from Lina. Franco's camera work was equally unsettling, moving from a romantic, hazy, soft focus style through to claustrophobic genital close-ups. The final section is filled with pubic shots. It stretches voyeurism to its very limits, emphasising the daring but depressing drive that's at the root of this natural instinct. **Doriana Gray** is an unsettling film that mixes hardcore elements with an off-the-wall sensibility. It's a style that Franco returned to in eighties' hardcore films like **Phollastia** (1987) and **Una rajita para dos** (1982). Although these later films were more explicit, they lacked the detached but obsessive thrust of **Doriana**.

**Doriana Gray** and **The Bare Breasted Countess** established Lina Romay's reputation. There were few other sexploitation starlets who could match her uninhibited gusto, nothing seemed too wild or wanton for her to deliver. She's one of a small breed of European actresses who don't look wooden and hung-up when they do rude things on film. In this sense she's pretty unique. Over the years Franco has managed to find a respectable handful of women like her. Alice Arno, Anne Libert, Pamela Stanford, Monica Swinn and Kali Hansa—together they form a veritable stable of erotic actresses. Lina is the most daring and long lasting of the bunch. Many of the others dropped out or went their own way. Anne Libert, for example, seemed like an ideal choice for Franco's wilder erotic outings. She was wide eyed and hypnotic as the blue-feathered bird woman in **The Erotic Rites of Frankenstein**, her hair hanging provocatively in a peek-a-boo style like forties' vamp Veronica Lake. In the end she followed the same route as Alice Arno, Pamela Stanford and the rest. Libert didn't want to make explicit erotic films, especially when the producer would add hardcore scenes to them later. So she dyed her pubic hair different colours, thwarting the possibility of salacious inserts.

Over the years, Lina Romay has become one of Franco's main erotic allies, a female counterpart. He dreams up the sexually kooky scenarios, she acts them out for his persistently rolling camera. **Doriana Gray** and **The Bare Breasted Countess** are at the most overt end of the range of saucy sexploitation films he produced during the seventies and eighties. Many of them featured Lina in slow moving, salacious nightclub acts, kinky routines that featured lesbianism, smoky saxophones and a tactile sensuality that implicated the on-screen audience as accessories in voyeurism.

Many of these films were made as European co-productions for Eurociné; further finance was obtained from a variety of sources that included Spanish producers like Triton, Golden Films, J.E. Films, and Portugese outfits such as Estudio 8. By the tail end of the seventies, disillusioned with working for Dietrich, Franco began to diversify, finding his backing among a multitude of these smaller operations. His own stabs at producing films had proved to be messy and disastrous. In 1972 he had formed Manacoa, the company's name taken from a comic that featured a paradisiac town filled entirely with women. Manacoa was an idealistic name, a fantasy. The films he wrote, produced and directed for it (**Los ojos siniestros del Dr. Orloff, Relax Baby, El misterio del castillo rojo** and **Silencio de tumba**) were all pretty low grade and of little interest. His attempts to go it alone ended quickly in failure, so he returned to directing

low budget films for a mixed bag of investors.

The films he turned out from the late seventies onwards ran the gamut, from cannibalism and comedies through to slasher movies, eroticism and hardcore. The subject matter followed the European pattern of emulating commercial hits. For example, when stalk and slash films like **Halloween** and **Friday the 13th** were big news at the box office, they turned out their own home grown variations. Franco's offering in the Euro slash stakes was **Bloody Moon** (1980), which was banned in Britain when it was released on video. In Spain it went out under the title **Colegialas violadas** or 'Raped Schoolgirls', a title that Franco didn't like, picked by the producers because they thought it was more marketable.

**Bloody Moon** was a wacky slasher flick with a disco soundtrack. Despite its topical commercial theme it wasn't a total success, in fact it was less interesting than his low budget sexploitation films. This was also true with the cannibal films, **I cannibali** (1979) and **Sexo cannibal** (**Man Hunter**; 1980). In films like these, more effort has to go into tangible items like special effects, leaving less room for on-the-spot invention. Franco prefers the freedom to improvise, to be able to make things up as he goes along. It suits his creative nature. His best films during the late 1970's and early 80's were those where he followed his own bent: **Das Frauenhaus** (**Blue Rita**; 1977), **La chica de las bragas transparantes** (**Pick-Up Girls**; 1980), **Orgía de ninfómanas** (**Linda**; 1980), **Macumba sexual** (1981), **El siniestro Dr. Orloff**(1982) and **Camino solitario** (The Lonely Path; 1983).

**Blue Rita** was a weird, sex orientated film that was as outlandish as the earlier **Girl from Rio**. The budget was low, but the spirit of invention was high. Like other Franco films, it mixed scenes of supercharged sleazy invention with long, sluggish passages that reeked of boredom and lack of attention. Yet, despite the quibbles, it was still head, hands and feet above usual European sex film fare. The majority of low budget sex films are pretty third rate and uninteresting. Franco is one of the few directors you can rely on to inject something wayward and interesting into them. Despite his faults (and there are plenty of them), I guess that's why film fanatics persevere. When they are dull, his films are deadly and depressing, but when he's firing on all cylinders they're crazy and unstoppable.

**Blue Rita** moves to its own irrational rhythm, sometimes irritating, sometimes inspiring. It typifies Franco's output. Because it's uneven and because it's a sex film it'll never be taken serious-

LADY PORNO

LINA ROMANY EVELYNE SCOTT
JESUS FRANCO OLIVIER MATHOT
RAMON ARDID

Director: TAWER NERO
Producida por TITANIC FILMS
(VERSION EN ESPAÑOL)

PORNOVISION
GEVACOLOR

**Pick Up Girls** (1980)  ▲

Franco's first big feature, **The Awful Dr. Orlof**, seemed to herald the arrival of a major new talent. Critics and fans were ready to reach for the hyperbole. The success of **Necronomicon** a few years later could have solidified his position; Roger Corman was impressed by its saucy, sophisticated charms and recommended Franco to American movieman Samuel Z. Arkoff. Arkoff picked up Franco's **Venus in Furs** for American distribution and Franco was offered an opportunity to work in the States, which he declined. He turned it down because of his "anarchic nature". He couldn't bear "the bureaucratic system" and could never clock in at the office at 8 am. every day. This attitude epitomises Franco, singles him out as someone who follows his own nature, regardless of the consequences. Like the scorpion in Orson Welles' favourite fable, stinging the helpful frog who is carrying him across a stream, he has no other choice.

Franco's attitude is heroic and childish, but you have to admire his ability to do as he pleases—it's impossible not to envy someone who has managed to make a career out of his obsessions. He's filmed weird stuff for nearly forty years, and indulged his off-beat compulsions in a host of ways. He could have been a real contender. He had the potential to be the finest European film-maker of his generation, instead of which he chose to work in the shadows and turn out marginal little films. He wilfully courted obscurity. Like Milton's Lucifer he's an outcast, someone who'd rather create his own world than follow the dictates of others. It's a paradoxical situation, and one that provokes admiration and dismay. At their best, his films inspire a sense of wonder, at their worst, a feeling of exasperation and despair. His restless need to continually create is at the root of this unique situation. It also makes it impossible to judge him too harshly. To describe him as a hack is too simple and unfair, it avoids the good things in his films, and turns something irrational and dynamic into a cheapskate all purpose put-down.

Unlike most film-makers Franco has too many ideas. His imagination is too fertile, a continual torrent of unstoppable invention. As a child he was renowned as a storyteller, someone who could weave gripping tales late into the night. His relatives say he slept with the light on until he was 21.

There's something almost primal about this continual creativity. On the surface Franco is intelligent, highbrow and cultured. Underneath,

ly as Art, which suits him just fine. He'd rather be branded as a strange, marginal film-maker than promoted as a major cinematic talent. Success might bring critical acceptance, but it would also mean less freedom for him. Most people would consider this attitude wilful and childish. Throughout his career Franco has spurned fame, never made the right career moves or capitalised on any of his opportunities. He was too busy making films to suss out where he was going. Making films is a total compulsion for him, in some ways it's a pathological need. His whole career would make an interesting case history for a modern day Krafft-Ebbing.

there's an unstoppable motor, something that even he doesn't understand. That's why he can never be totally dismissed. His potential for surprise is too great; it's this that powers his fascination as a film-maker, attracting interest against the odds.

His sexploitation films from the late 1970's and early 80's are a case in point. The budgets were low, the resources minimal, but some of the films were skin-soaked minor masterpieces. Films like **Pick-Up Girls** (1980) were filled with hairy butts and crazy invention. The film starts with the familiar nightclub scene. The decor is cheap and purple, but Franco manages to make something unreal and cheesy out of it. The action centres around a real life transexual, with large helpings of voyeuristic coupling, and moments of startling invention. There's a slo-mo two girl seduction scene that ends in drunken murder—daring, and quite unlike anything else in cinema. Blurred and libidinous, the hazy pleasure turns into remorse and a quick getaway. **Pick Up Girls** is a sexy thriller set in cheapo clubland, but unlike many other skin-flicks it creates its own reality. You don't have to like this milieu to appreciate the charm or the inventiveness.

The male lead was Antonio Mayans (his screen name is Robert Foster), an eternally youthful veteran of Franco flicks. Mayans is a typical fun loving, Franco cohort. He studied acting in London and, despite a hint of an accent, carries himself like a bona fide British gent, easy-going and unflappable. He admits he doesn't really enjoy filming when there's too much sexy stuff. "It's nothing to do with Jess, it's nothing to do with me. I don't tend to like the sexy scenes. I have to do them, but it's not something I enjoy the most. Therefore if a film has too many sexy scenes, I enjoy it less. I enjoy the crazy scenes. It's something to do with my psyche."

With Franco, Mayans gets to make films that star his own family. His wife and daughter have appeared with him, and he likes the friendly, intimate atmosphere that surrounds film-making. As they progressed through the 1980's, the budgets on Franco's films got even smaller. This made his method of film-making and production even more self reliant and intimate. They couldn't afford expensive locations, special effects or big name stars, but a film like **El siniestro Dr. Orloff** (1982) shows what can be done with a few friends, some film stock and plenty of determination. It's bargain basement filming at its very best.

In the eighties, Franco began to take more control of the camera. He always had an itch to do this. The budgets were so low he couldn't afford to waste footage or lose an opportunity to catch something on film. With Franco behind the camera the producers could maximise their tiny resources—he could pick out details or move in quickly to capture interesting, accidental happenings, unplanned images, and events that could add atmosphere to the finished film. It might be a passing helicopter. It might be a group of flamingos in flight or the expression on an actor's face. His main aim was to try and make the most of everything that was available to them. Franco's earlier films were created on a shoestring. In the eighties the budgets were so low it was almost like making something out of nothing.

There's something inspiring about this type of approach, and not just because the end result will look different. It also hints at unexplored ways of making films, and suggests that anybody can make movies if they have enough talent and determination. In the final analysis Franco has always used this make-it-up-as-you-go-along method, it's a process that he's refined over the years. As the budgets became smaller it simply became easier to spot.

Great jazz players can take familiar tunes and improvise around the basic chords and structure. Sometimes it comes out dull and clichéd, but if the mood is right it can be sheer aural

▲ Franco returns to Orloff one more time, **Experimentos macabros** (1982)

◄ Franco chop socky epic, starring Bruce Lyn!

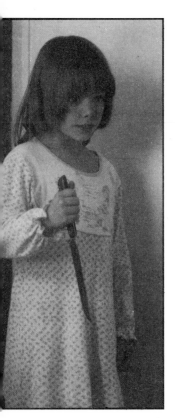

Keeping it in the family ▲
Antonio Mayans'
daughter, Flavia in **Solo
ante el terror** (1983)

**Pick Up Girls** (1980) ▶

inspiration. The same is true of Franco. When he's cooking on all cylinders he's unstoppable, but when he isn't, the end result can be terminally flat and uninspired. Mediocrity is a side effect when you take chances, it's a risk that you can't escape when you improvise on a low budget. There's no money for endless retakes, so if it doesn't work out you have to go with what you have in the can.

This way of working fits in with Franco's restless nature—he can't sit still, he has to be active. Antonio Mayans says Franco gets agitated and uneasy if he isn't making a film. He compares him to the crazy artist in Joyce Cary's *The Horse's Mouth*, who had to keep painting. Whenever he saw a white space or area he could paint on, he'd say "let's go" and then start daubing furiously. Franco himself doesn't agree with this comparison, although other people have noted his compulsion to keep filming. Spanish critic Carlos Aguilar says it's impossible for Franco not to film, he can't help himself. This doesn't mean he has a compulsion to film erotic material, it means he has an unstoppable urge to keep shooting—anything that appeals to his imagination. "If he was here," Aguilar says, "he'd be filming the cars in the streets!"

This drive is one of the reasons Franco is drawn towards the low budget arena and the opportunities it offers for fast and furious film-

making. During the 1970's and 80's his output increased. As the demand for erotic sex films went up, the gap between films became shorter. Much of the finance came from Spanish companies like Golden Films who were eager to cash in on the softening up of censorship that took place after the death of the Spanish dictator, General Franco. Nowadays Spain is one of the most liberal counties in the EEC. Hardcore pornography is freely available on video, there's even a hardcore cable channel. It's not regarded as a problem, and there's no tight-lipped moralising. But Spain didn't leap from repression to freedom in one fell swoop.

After Franco's death the production of softcore comedies increased, censorship became slightly more liberal, and film-makers were allowed to show nipples on screen for the first time. This period was known as *'destape'* (it means 'stripping away') and many of the home-grown Spanish erotic flicks were like the English **Adventures of a Taxi Driver** type films or the German **Schoolgirl Report** series—filled with dopey humour and littered with excuses to show the female breast in all its splendour. These *'destape'* films were a small step forward and, although Spanish film-makers could show nipples on film, they still had to black them out on their advertising and promotion material.

The next stage was the development of the 'S', or slightly more explicit softcore film. Film-makers still weren't allowed to show penetration, but they produced a wide range of sexploitation films for the home market, supplemented by imports. As one of the premier low budget European sexfilm makers, this was a good period for Franco. His erotic films were daring, but they also lingered on the type of action the censor couldn't really object to. Voyeurism, lesbianism and other kinky frolicking were staples inside Franco's sexual universe, and as long as they weren't vulgar or explicit, the censor didn't seem to complain. While he was making **Lilian, la virgen pervertida** in 1983, the Spanish government passed a bill making hardcore films legal in Spain for the first time. Franco quickly shot extra footage on the very day the law was amended, giving **Lilian, la virgen pervertida** the dubious honour of being the first 'official' Spanish hardcore film.

It isn't one of Franco's better sex films. In fact, it's a moderately depressing affair. Unlike **Camino solitario** (The Lonely Path), which was made the same year, the atmosphere is wooden and one-dimensional. **Camino** was a film that got made because of a happy accident. Franco had been kicking the idea around for some time but couldn't get financial backing. Then he had a particularly unbelievable stroke of luck, something that wouldn't be out of place in an Edgar Wallace mystery or in one of his own films. He was offered the winning ticket in a lottery! The result was enough cash to fund his next low budget sex epic.

It was a small, personal film, and seemed to point the way towards the direction he would follow throughout the eighties. As the budgets shrank his team got even tighter, and it seemed that he began to make films for his friends, and for his own amusement. As Antonio Mayans puts it, they became more like "interior jokes". How else to explain things like the sequence in **Frauengefängis** where Franco pretends to fall in slow motion ...

In-jokes and goofy gags. All of Franco's films have this kooky, off the wall approach. They aren't designed for mass market consumption, they're too personal to be truly commercial. "As I shoot I imagine an audience of one, two or three people ... it never occurs to me that I'm making a film for a large audience." So, in a sense, Franco embraces the small scale approach to film production because it allows him the freedom to be quirky. He makes his films with a few like minded folk, people who appreciate his perverse sense of humour, are inspired by his love of cinema, and are sympathetic to his maverick mentality. Samuel Z Arkoff describes Franco as "an odd guy"—for him, all the European erotic film-makers were "odd guys". Like Franco they're individualists, people who are too intelligent to run with the pack. They all have something in common—a need to create their own personal sort of cinema. To do this they have to stay out in the margins. Some are pushed out there, others embrace it. Franco prefers making low budget, fun films—when the budget is large, the film crew is bigger, and he doesn't like having too many technicians hanging around the camera. A small, intimate crew is more fun, more productive, giving him a hands-on-the-camera approach to filmmaking.

There are many reasons why people make films. According to director Sam Fuller—"95% of films are born of frustration, of self-despair, of poverty, of ambition, for survival, for fattening bank accounts. 5% of films, maybe less, are made because a man has an idea, an idea which he must express." Franco makes his films for love and other strange desires. No one really knows why he films the things he does. There's something irrational at the centre of his films, a quality that would be lost in the big budget

shuffle. He prefers to make something small and crazy. Money and critical acclaim are secondary concerns. In some ways he's achieved the impossible, directing over 150 films, and having fun in the process.

This fun aspect became more obvious during the eighties. **Los blues de la calle pop** (Blues from Pop Street; 1983) is a good example. It's a film that few people like, a comic strip detective tale set against the seedy seaside backdrop of Benidorm. The audience may not have understood the film, but everyone involved enjoyed making it—they were in on the joke. Antonio Mayans plays a detective called Philip Malboro, he's on the trail of a villain called Winston. Franco is a piano-player called Sam, who plays three chord blues in a Benidorm bar. Cuddly, wayward and intelligent, he's clean shaven, with the impish charm of Dudley Moore and the weirdo alertness of Spike Milligan—it's a classic cameo that hints at how and why he makes the films he does.

Critics often ignore the humour at the heart of Franco's epics. Perhaps it's too mischievous for their tastes. You can't deny it, his films have a puckish edge, an ironic ambience all of their own. No matter how lowly the subject matter, he still manages to twist things around and give them a gleeful, dangerous zing. It's his style, it's part of his contrary nature. When he went porno in the eighties he stirred things up with his bawdy and lively sense of fun.

The titles of his eighties' outings ring with an earthy nonchalance: Lulu's Arsehole, Sucking in the Rain, A Snatch for Two and Between Cocks There's the Game. Some of his porno films like **Falo Crest** and **Phollastia** (1987) were parodies of U.S. soap operas like *Dynasty* and *Falcon Crest*. Even the unfinished ones, like Crotch Story (**Bragueta story**), had snappy titles; and if the titles were chuckle worthy and daring, the films were often funnier. In **Una rajita para dos** (1982) a sucking couple start commentating on Maradona and Argentina in the middle of the act. While in Lulu's Arsehole, the arsehole of the heroine complains about her owner's erotic abandon. In Franco's porno, ordinary life keeps interrupting the horn-ball action, the mirror image of his mainstream films, where the erotic keeps coming to the surface.

In the eighties the film business really went to hell. Franco was turning out porno films, low budget comedies, mysteries, Women in Prison films, and action thrillers, hinting at the foreign settings by picking out details with his camera, a technique he's refined over the years. The

▼ Antonio Mayans contemplates his next Franco production

OPALO de FUEGO
(MERCADERES DEL SEXO)
CANDY COSTER · NADINE PASCAL · MEL RODRIGO
Director: JESS FRANCO                    EASTMANCOLOR

Weird night club act ▲
with severed head, from
**Two Female Spies
With Flowered Panties**
(1978)

amusements. Outside of his hardcore films the voyeuristic, erotic element began to diminish, there wasn't the demand for it anymore. It still cropped up occasionally—cheeky stuff, but lacking the lingering glory of the early days.

Was Franco losing interest in eroticism or was it just market forces taking their toll? After hardcore, the sexploitation era was over. Franco moved on to newer pastures, partly because of pressure inside the industry and partly because he didn't have the roster of erotic cohorts that he used to have. In the sixties and seventies he had an assortment of interesting faces to choose from. In the eighties this more or less dried up, and Lina Romay & Antonio Mayans became his regular erotic performers. Mayans wasn't made for hardcore, whereas Lina was enthusiastic, the female embodiment of Franco's sexual fantasies. Ajita Wilson was good in the role of Princess Tara Obongo, but it's unlikely that she could have made a career as an erotic headliner. Without her make-up she looked like a gangly basketball star!

Undeterred, Franco kept at it. It seemed like he would go on making small, strange films forever. Then, in 1987, he hooked up with French video mogul René Château. Château was interested in doing a horror film, especially one that starred Euro-vixen Brigitte Lahaie. Franco proposed that he update Franju's **Eyes Without a Face** (1959). The project started small and grew until it became a multi-million dollar, international co-production. It was Franco's biggest budget film ever and featured a host of Franco regulars, minor American stars like Chris Mitchum and old timers like Anton Diffring. Released in 1988 as **Faceless** it proved he could still make a regular film if he really wanted to.

After this triumph, his next couple of films were fairly pedestrian. The eighties was a period of fast and furious filmmaking for Franco, and by the end of the decade he was pretty much broke. Luck was with him however, and he was offered the opportunity to edit Orson Welles' legendary lost film **Don Quixote**. For the first time in years he had a regular income.

The Franco story is indeed a strange tale, you'd be hard pushed to find another to compete with it. It's a story full of paradoxes, perversion and a love for film that has spawned an unholy number of epics. The paradox is—Franco doesn't like his films! He's never really happy with the way they've turned out, yet he still keeps making them. His mad love for film comes through in all of them, sometimes it's continuous, at other times it's sporadic. Despite their flaws, his films are

oriental atmosphere in **Viaje a Bangkok, ataúd incluido** (Trip to Bangkok, Coffin Included; 1985), was provided by by a few minutes of stock footage and supplemented by scenes shot in a local Chinese restaurant.

As the eighties progressed there was less of the voyeurism that had spiced up his earlier films, and when it did crop up it was pretty damn cheesy. **Bangkok, cita con la muerte** (Bangkok, City of Death; 1985) had Lina Romay rolling her well fed bottom, a size 12 boom-boom dancer in a size 9 swim suit. While in **La chica de los labios rojos** (The Girl with the Red Lips; 1986) she was an overtly plump trumpet player who performed topless solos in a jazz dive. Tasteless and grandiose ... it was pure Franco.

**Macumba sexual** (1981) was Franco's last really out-to-lunch film, his last extended trip into delirium: the European sexploitation film was dead, and **Macumba sexual** was one of its last glorious death throes. The film featured the stalky transexual Ajita Wilson as Voodoo witch Princess Tara Obongo, the self styled "Goddess of Unspeakable Lust". She exerts her mysterious power over Lina Romay; with her chocolate coloured dog-men she prowls the beaches and unleashes them when the time is right for some sexual Voodoo ritual. It's hypnotic, trancelike stuff and unfortunately the last full blown erotic film Franco would make. After **Macumba sexual**, Franco's films were divided into two sorts. The hardcore epics and the low budget important. He's tried to film crazy, impossible things and shoot for the moon, experimenting all the way. Franco's story is filled with idealism and roguishness. He's a mixture of Don Quixote and Sancho Panza. In the best bits of his films, his Quixotic love for cinema is pure and untainted, during the worst sections the other side of his nature come to the fore.

Franco's compulsion to keep making films hasn't diminished. While other low budget horror directors of his generation haven't made a film for years, Franco heroically jests that he's going to make 100 more.

Sometimes the odds seem stacked against him. His most recent film, **Jungle of Fear**, remains unreleased, and his reconstruction of **Don Quixote** met with mixed reviews. Yet the lust to film remains as strong as ever. 1995 finds Franco back in Madrid, juggling new film deals with all the ease of a seasoned performer. **Los gazapos** (The Burglars) is one of the current projects. There are plenty of others. No-one knows what he'll come up with next. Which is exactly how it's always been for one of cinema's true mavericks.

### FRANCO FILMOGRAPHY

All Spain (Sp) except where indicated

### DUBBING DIRECTOR

1952    La môme vert-de-gris (Fr)

### ORIGINAL STORY

1965    Misión Lisboa (Sp/It)
1985    L'ange de la mort (Fr/It)

### SCREENPLAY

1954    El coyote/Il coyote
1956    Miedo
        Fulano y Mengano
1958    Luna de verano
1959    Llegaron los franceses
1960    Ama Rosa
1962    La venganza del Zorro/La sombra del Zorro/La Espada del Zorro/Zorro le vengeur/L'ombra di Zorro/Zorro, der schwartze Racher/Zorro, das Geheimnis von Alamos/The Shadow of Zorro
1965    Da 077 intrigo a Lisbona/Misión Lisboa/077 Intrigue a Lisbonne (Sp/It)

### MUSIC

1954    Cómicos

1956    Historias de Madrid
        El expresso de Andalucía
1957    El hombre que viajaba despacito
        El maestro
1958    Un hecho violento/Camp of Violence
1969    Cuadrilátero
1978    Poseída/L'osceno desiderio

### ASSISTANT DIRECTOR

1954    Cómicos
        El coyote
        La justicia del Coyote
        Nosotros dos
        Señora ama
        Felices Pascuas
        Educando a papá
1955    Muerte de un ciclista/Gli egoisti/Death of a Cyclist
1956    Fulano y Mengano
        Viaje de novios
        Historias de Madrid
        Miedo
1957    Los jueves, milagro/Les jeudis miraculeux/Arrivederci dimas/On Thursdays, a Miracle
        El hombre que viajaba despacito

### PRODUCTION ASSISTANT

1959    Solomon and Sheba (Sp/US)
1963    55 Days at Peking (Sp/US)

### PRODUCTION DIRECTOR

1958    Ana dice sí
        Luna de verano

### EXECUTIVE PRODUCER

1987    Biba la banda

### SECOND UNIT DIRECTOR

1965    Campanadas a medianoche/Chimes at Midnight (Sp/US)
1987    Biba la banda

### ACTOR (In films not directed by himself)

1956    Miedo
        Around the World in 80 Days (extra)
1958    Ana dice sí
1964    El extraño viaje/Strange Journey
1976    Razzia sur le plaisir/Une cage dorée/Les filles dans une cage dorée
1987    Esa cosa con plumas/With Feathers

British poster for ▲
**Necronomicon**

Lucky the Inscrutable (Sp/It/Ger)

Necronomicon-Geträumte Sünden/Necronomi-con/Succubus/Delirium (Ger)

1968   Bésame monstruo/Küss mich, Monster/Das Schloss der Gehenkten/Kiss me Monster/Castle of the Doomed (Sp/Ger)

El caso de las dos bellezas/Sadisterotica/Rote Lippen-Sadisterotica/Der Wolf-Horror Pervers/ The Case of the Two Beauties/Two Avenging Angels/Der Wolf/Red Lips (Sp/Ger)

Fu Manchú y el beso de la muerte/Der Todesküss des Dr Fu Manchu/The Blood of Fu Manchu/ Kiss and Kill/Against all Odds/Fu Manchu and the Kiss of Death/Blood of Fu Manchu (Sp/Ger/GB/US)

El castillo de Fu Manchu/The Castle of Fu Manchu/Die Folterkammer des Dr. Fu Manchu/ Il castello di Fu Manchu/Assignment: Istanbul/ The Torture Chamber of Dr Fu Manchu (Sp/GB/Ger/It)

La ciudad sin hombres/Rio 70/Die Sieben Männer der Sumuru/Sumuru, regna di femi-na/Sumuru/The Girl from Rio/ Future Women (Sp/Ger/US/GB)

99 mujeres/99 Frauen/Der heisse Tod/99 donne/99 Women/Prostitutes in Prison/ L'amour dans les prisons des femmes/Les brûlantes/Island of Despair (Sp/Ger/It/GB)

Marquis de Sade: Justine/Justine, le disave-ture della virtu/ De Sade, les infortunes de la virtu/Les deux beautés/Il due sorelle/Justine and Juliet/Marquis de Sade's Justine/Deadly Sanctuary/Dulce Justine (GB/It/Ger)

1969   Black Angel/Venus in Furs/¿Puo una morta revivere per amore?/Venus im Pelz/ Paroxismus(GB/It/Ger/US)

El proceso de las brujas/Der Hexentöter von Blackmoor/Il trono di fuoco/The Bloody Judge/Night of the Blood Monster/Le trone de feu/Il giudice sanguinario/Le bucher aux sor-cières/De sadistiche rechter (Sp/Ger/It/GB)

El conde Drácula/Count Dracula/Il conte Dracula/Nachts, wenn Dracula erwacht/

Les nuits de Dracula/Le Comte Dracula/ Verenhimoinen Dracula/Bram Stoker's Count Dracula (Sp/GB/It/Ger)

De Sade 70/Die Jungfrau und die Peitsche/Les inassouvies/ Eugenie... the Story of Her Journey into Perversion/Philosophy in the Boudoir (GB/Ger)

1970   Las vampiras/Vampiros Lesbos-Die Erbin des Dracula/Heiress of Dracula/Vampyros Lesbos/ Sexualité spéciale/Die Erbin des Dracula/ Heritage of Dracula (Sp/Ger)

Sie Tötete in Ekstase/Crimes dans l'extase/Elle tuait en extase/She Kills in Ecstacy (Ger)

Sex Charade/Le labyrinthe de Sexe(Liech)

El diablo que vino de Akasawa/Una venere senza nome per l'inspectore Forrester/Der Teufel kam aus Akasawa/The Devil Came from Akasava (Sp/Ger)

Eugenie/Eugenie de Sade/Eugenie de Franval (Liech/Ger/Can)

Les cauchemars naissent la nuit/Les yeux de la nuit/Los ojos de la noche/Eyes of the Night (Liech/Be)

El muerto hace las maletas/Der Todesrächer von Soho/Allarme à Scotland Yard: sei omicidi senza assassino/The Avenger/The Corpse Packs his Bags/Death Packs his Bags (Sp/Ger)

La venganza del Dr. Mabuse/Der Mann der sich Mabuse nannte/Dr. M. Schlägt zu/Mabuse 70/Der Doktor Mabuse/El doctor Mabuse (Sp/Ger)

Vuelo al infierno/X-312, Flug Zur Hölle/ Infierno, tuya es la victoria/X-312, Flight to Hell (Sp/Ger)

1971   Jungfrauen Report/Virgin Report/Les vierges et l'amour (Ger)

Robinson und Seine Wilden Sklavinnen/Trois filles nues dan l'île de Robinson/Trois vicieuses sur une île/The Sexy Darlings/L'isola dei plac-ceri proibiti/Robinson and his Tempestuous Slaves/Robinson '71 (Ger/Fr)

Dracula contra Frankenstein/Dracula prisonier de Frankenstein/Dracula contro Franken-stein/Die Nacht der Offenen Särge/ Dracula, Prisoner of Frankenstein/The Screaming Dead/ Satana contra Dr. Exortio (Sp/Fr)

Christina, princesse de l'érotisme/I desideri erotici di Christine/Une vierge chez les morts vivants/Los sueños eróticos de Christine/ Exorcismo per una vergine/Una virgen en casa de los muertos vivientes/Zombi Holocaust/ Le labyrinthe/A comme apocalypse/La nuit des étoiles filantes/Una vergine tra gli zombies/Una vergine tra i morti vivanti/Eine Jungfrau bei den Lebenden Toten/Eine Jungfrau in den Krallen von Zombies/Virgin Among the Living Dead/ Christina chez les morts vivants (Fr/It)

Los amantes de la Isla del Diablo/Quartier de femmes/Violences érotiques dans une prison de femmes/Violenze erotiche in un carcere fem-minele (Sp/Fr)

La fille de Dracula/A filha de Dracula/De vloek van Dracula (Fr)

1972   La maldición de Frankenstein/Les expériences érotiques de Frankenstein/Das Blutgericht der gequalten Frauen/De verdoemnis van Franken-stein/Erotic Rites of Frankenstein/Curse of Frankenstein/Les exploits érotiques de Frank-

enstein (Sp/Fr)

Os demonios/Les démons/Les démons du sexe/
Les enfants du démon/Le domone/Die nonnen
von Clichy/The Demons/The She-Demons/The
Sex Demons/Les novices perverses (Fr/Port)

Le journal intime d'une nymphomane/Diario
íntimo de una ninfómana/Le giornate intime di
una giovane donna/Sinner/Diary of a Nympho-
maniac/Les inassouvies 77 (Fr)

Les ebranlées/La maison du vice/Des filles
pour l'amour/Dolls for Sale

Un capitán de 15 años/Un capitaine de quinze
ans/Un capitani di 15 anni/Een kapitein van 15
jaar (Sp/Fr)

Un silencio de tumba

Los ojos del Dr Orloff/Los ojos siniestros del
Dr.Orloff

El misterio del castillo rojo/El castillo rojo

1973   Al otro lado del espejo/Le miroir obscène/Le
miroir cochon/Le miroir obscène des femmes
obscènes/Outre-Tombe/Inceste/Lo specchio del
piacere/Inside a Dark Mirror/Beyond the Grave
(Sp/Fr)

Plaisir à trois/Les inassouvies 2/How to Seduce
a Virgin (Fr)

Les avaleuses/La comtesse aux seins nus/La
comtesse noire/Un caldo corpo di femmina/
Entfesselte Begierde/Verentahrima Morsian/
The Loves of Irina/Erotikill/Erotikiller/The Bare
Breasted Countess/Female Vampire (Fr/Be)

Maciste contre la reine des amazones/Les
amazones de la luxure/Karzan contro le donne
dal seno nudo/Mädchen die sich lieben lassen/
Yuka/The Lustful Amazons/Wulpse Amazones(Fr)

Les exploits érotiques de Maciste dans
l'Atlantide/Les gloutonnes/Maciste et les glou-
tonnes/Sexes au soleil (Fr)

Sexy Blues/Valse para un asesino/Embrasse-
moi/Blues au clair de lune/Aime-moi, assassin/
Serenade à Barbara/Tango au clair de lune/
Emanuelle Blonde/Kiss me Killer/Kiss Me and
Make Love to Me/Come With Me My Blond
Emanuelle (Fr)

Mais qui donc a violé Linda?/Les nuits bru-
lantes de Linda/La felicità nel peccato/Le plaisir
solitaire/Carresses des chattes/Morbosita/Linda,
la maison de pecheresses/Who Raped Linda?
(Fr/It)

La comtesse perverse/Les croqueuses/La
comtesse Zaroff/Un caldo corpo di femina (Fr)

El último escalofrío/Le chemin solitaire/
Frissons sur la peau/Dernier frisson/Tendre et
perverse Emanuelle/Siccarius-febbre di sesso/
Tender and Perverse Emanuelle/The Last
Thrill/French Emanuelle/The Lonely Path (Fr)

La noche de los asesinos/Im Schatten des
Mörders/Syspiri/Night of the Assassins
Relax Baby/Un Tiro/ En la sien/ A Bullet in the
Head (unfinished)

1974   Les chatouilleuses/Les nonnes en folie (Fr)
Celestine, bonne à toute faire/Infedelmente
vostra Celestina tutto fare/Mädchen für Intime
Stunden/ Celestine, an All Round Maid/
Celestine, Maid at Your Service (Fr)

Les emmerdeuses/Les petites vicieuses/Les
petites vicieuse font les grandes emmerdeuses (Fr)

Lorna, l'exorciste/Les possédées du diable/Les
possédées du démon/Sexy diabolic story (Fr)

L'homme le plus sexy du monde/Le jou-
isseur/Der Sex Playboy/Roland, l'homme
le plus sexy du monde (Fr)

Exorcisme/Exorcisme et messes noires/ Expériences sexuelles au château des jouisseuses/ Le viz-
iose/ Sexorcismes (hardcore version); re-edited
and released in 1979 under the following: El sádico
de Notre-Dame/L'éventreur de Notre Dame/Le
sadique de Notre Dame/ Sadist of Notre
Dame/ Chains and Black Leather/ Demoniac
(Sp/Fr/Be)

1975   La coccolona/Sylvia la baiseuse/Piacere erotici
di una signora bene/Sexy Blues/Lady Porno/
Midnight Party/Porno Pop (Fr)

Shining Sex/La fille au sexe brillant/Alpha/Le
sexe brillant/Porno Dama (Fr/Be)

La suceuse/Les suceuses/Justine, Lady Lujuria/
Julietta '69/Julietta/Juliette/De Sade's Juliette
(Switz)

Frauengefängnis/Penitencier pour femmes/Les
gardiennes du penitencier/Peniteziaro fem-
minile per reali sessuali/Meisjes achter trailies/
Caged Women/BarbedWire Dolls (Switz)

Downtown, Die puppen der Unterwelt/Die
Nackten Puppen der Unterwelt/Les putains de
la ville basse/Les bas-fonds/Schwarze nylons -
wilde Engel/Lèvres rouges et bottes noires/
Heisse Berührungen (Switz)

Das Bildnis der Doriana Gray/Die Marquise de
Sade/Ejaculations/Le portrait de Doriana Gray/
Dirty Dracula (Switz)

Des diamants pour l'enfer/Visa pour mourir/
Prison sado pour femmes/Una secondina in un
carcere feminile/Women Behind Bars/Punition
Cell/The Whip (Switz)

1977   Die Sklavinnen/Die verschleppten/Les flagéll-
ées de la cellule 69 (Switz)

Jack the Ripper–der dirnenmörder von
London/Jack l'eventreur/Erotico profondo/Jack
the Ripper/Sohon Teura Staja (Switz/Ger)

Frauen im Liebeslager/Mujeres en el campo de
concentración del amor/Camp érotique/Camp
d'amour/Camp d'amour pour mercenaires/Die
Unersättliche/Sex Kazerne/Love Camp (Switz)

◄ A ticklish situation from
**Linda** (1980)

Die Liebesbriefe einer Portugiesischen Nonne/
Cartas de amor a una monja portugesa/Lettres
d'amour d'une nonne portugaise/Confessioni
proibiti di una monaca adolescente/Tuhansien
himojen luostari/Love Letters of a Portuguese
Nun (Switz/Ger)

Die Teuflischen Schwestern/Deux soeurs
vicieuses/Ton diable dans mon enfer/Sexy
Sisters/Aberraciones sexuales de una rubia
caliente/Frenesie erotiche de una ninfomane/De
wellustige gezusters/Swedish Nympo Slaves/
Satanic Sisters (Switz)

Der Ruf der Blonden Göttin/Le cri d'amour de
la déese blonde/La déesse nue/La vengeance de
la déesse nue/La revanche de la déesse blonde/
Passions et voluptés vaudoues/Las diosas del
porno/Porno Shock/Love Cry of a Nude
Blonde(Switz)

Greta, Haus ohne Männer/Le penitencier des
femmes perverses/Ilsa, ultimes perversions/
Greta, la tortionnaire/Gretta, la donna bestia/
Greta, huis zonder mannen/Ilsa, the Wicked
Warden/Wanda the Wicked Warden/Greta the
Torturer/Greta the Mad Butcher/Ilsa-Ultimate
Power/Ilsa-Ultimate Perversion (Switz)

Mädchen im Nachtverkehr/Heisse sex im
Nachtverkehr/Wilde Lust (Switz)

Weisse Haut und schwartze Schenkel/Weisse
Haut auf schwarzen Schenkeln (Switz)

Frauen ohne unschuld/Femmes sans pudeur/Il
insaziabili notti di una ninfomane/Het huis der
manzike vrouwen (Switz)

Frauen für Zellen-Block 9/Kamp der blanke
slavinnen/Flucht von der Todesinsel/The
Women of Cell Block Nine/Cellule 9 (Switz)

Das Frauenhaus/Blue Rita/Le cabaret des filles
perverse (Switz)

1978 Elles font tout/Quel certo piacere/Quel certo
sapore (Fr)

Je brûle de partout (Fr)

Cocktail Spécial (Fr)

Opalo de fuego/El opalo negro/Mercaderes del
sexo/Deux espionnes avec un petit slip à fleur/
Espionnes au soleil/Two Female Spies with
Flowered Panties (Sp/Fr)

Sinfonia erótica/Symphonie érotique (Sp/Port)

1979 Une fille pour les cannibales/I cannibali/
Mondo Cannibale, teil 3/Mangeurs d'hom-
mes/La déesse blonde/La déese cannibale/Les
cannibales/Die blonde Göttin/Barbarian
Goddess/Cannibals/White Cannibal Queen/La
dea cannibale (Fr/It)

Las chicas de Copacabana/Las muchachas de
Copacobana/Les filles de Copacabana (Sp/Fr)

1980 El sexo está loco

Eugenie, historia de una perversión/Erotismo/
Lolita am Schedeweg/De Sade 2000

Sexo cannibal/Chasseur de l'enfer-Hell
Hunter/Chasseurs d'hommes/Jungfrauunter
Kannibalen/Il cacciatore di uomini/The
Man Hunter/Mandingo Manhunter/Devil
Hunter (Sp/Fr/Ger)

La chica de las bragas transparente/Pick-Up
Girls

Brigitte Lahaie dispatches ▲
another victim in
**Faceless** (1988)

Sadomanía/Sadomanía, el infierno de la passión/ Sadomania, Hölle der Lust/L'enfer du plaisir/Hell Hole Women/Prisoners of the Flesh (Sp/Ger)

Orgia de ninfómanas/Die nackten Superhexen von Rio Amore/Linda, de stoeipoes/Linda/The Naked Super-Witches of the Rio Amore/ Captive Women (Sp/Ger)

Die Säge des Todes/Colegialas violadas/Lune de sang/Profonde tenebre/Bloody Moon (Ger)

1981 Aberraciones sexuales de una mujer casada

El lago de las virgenes/ La isla de las vergenes

La noche de los sexos abiertos

El hotel de los ligues

La tumba de los muertos vivientes/L'abîme des morts vivants/Le tresor des morts vivants

Macumba sexual

1982 Gemidos de placer/Pleasure of Death

Historia sexual de 0/Sexual story of 0

Botas negras, látigo de cuero

Las orgías inconfesables de Emanuelle/ Emanuelle's Last Orgy/Emanuelle Exposed

El siniestro Dr.Orloff/Experimentos macabros

Las casa de las mujeres perdidas/Perversíon en la isla perdida

Mil sexos tiene la noche

Confesiones íntimas de una exhibicionista

Una rajita para dos

La mansion de los muertos vivientes

1983 El tesoro de la diosa blanca/Les diamants du Kilimanjaro/Diamonds of Kilimanjaro

Camino solitario

Sangre en mis zapatos

Sola ante el terror/Los monstruos de Fiske Manor

Los blues de la calle pop/Aventuras de Felipe Malboro, volumen 8

Furia en el trópico/Mujeres acorraladas/Orgasmo perverso

Lilian, la virgen pervertida

Las chicas del tanga

El hundimiento de la casa Usher/Los crímenes de Usher/Nevrose/Revenge in the House of Usher/Neurosis/Fall of the House of Usher/Die Rache des Hauses Usher (Sp/Fr)

Barrio chino/Barrio porno

Scarlet/Escarlate la traviesa y su prima la condesa/El abuelo, la condesa y Escarlata la traviesa

1984 La sombra del judoka contra el Dr. Wong

En busca del dragón dorado

¿Cuánto cobra un espía?

Juego sucio en Casablanca

Bahía Blanca

Voces de muerte

Tundra y el templo del sol/Les amazones du temple d'or/Golden Temple Amazons

El asesino llevaba medias negras

Un pito para tres (co-dir, Lina Romay)

1985 Las últimas de Filipinas

Bangkok, cita con la muerte

Viaje a Bangkok ataúd incluido

La esclava blanca

El ojete de Lulú (co-dir, Lina Romay)

El chupete de Lulú (co-dir, Lina Romay)

Entre pitos ande el juego (co-dir, Lina Romay)

1986 Esclavas del crimen

La chica de los labios rojos

Las chuponas (co-dir, Lina Romay)

Para las nenas, leche calentita (co-dir, Lina Romay)

El mirón y la exhibicionista (co-dir, Lina Romay)

1987 Falo Crest/Caprices sados pour salopes du plaisir

Phollastia/Fellations sauvages

Operación cocaína/Les fleurs du mal/Dark Mission/Dark Mission-Flowers of Evil/The Columbian Connection (Sp/Fr)

1988 Les predateurs de la nuit/Los depredadores de la noche/I predatori della notte/I violentatori della notte/Faceless (Fr)

1989 La bahía Esmeralda/La baie Emeraude/ Esmeralda Bay/Karibian Kapinalliset (Sp/Fr)

La chute des aigles/Una canción para Berlin (Fr)

1990 Downtown Heat/La punta de las viboras/ Vipers(Sp/Fr)

1992 Don Quijote (reconstruction of Orson Welles'

original footage ; Sp)

1994 **Jungle of Fear** (Sp/US)

Special thanks to Marc Morris and Carlos Aguilar for their help with the filmography

[1] The multi-talented Fernando Fernán Gómez was born in Lima(Peru) on the 28th of August 1921. He began his career as a theatrical actor and then, in 1943, moved on to become a popular actor in comedy films. He began directing serious films in the fifties, and one of his most important films, **El extraño viaje** (The Strange Voyage; 1964) featured Jess Franco in a leading role. Despite his popularity as an actor, Fernán Gómez'z films weren't taken seriously—he had to wait twenty years for critical acclaim and serious dramatic parts. His big break came in 1973, with **El espiritu de la colmena (The Spirit of the Beehive)**. After this he won many awards, and is now very highly thought of as a novelist, director and playwright. He lives with actress Emma Cohen and writes regularly for the newspapers *El pais* and *ABC*.

[2] See Appendix for more on pseudonyms.

[3] Franco's name doesn't appear on the credits for **Chimes at Midnight**. During filming, Welles ran out of money. Franco phoned up his friend Harry Saltzman, producer of the Bond movies, and told him about the project. Saltzman said he was interested but would need to see a print before he'd invest. Franco sent him a rough-cut of the film without Welles' approval. Saltzman looked at the rough-cut and agreed to put up some money. When Welles heard about this he hit the roof and literally went for Franco's throat. Because of this Franco's name didn't appear on the finished film—even though it might never have been finished without Saltzman's money and Franco's duplicity.

▲ Soledad Miranda in **The Devil Came From Akasava** (1970)

# LA VAMPIRE NUE

UM FILM DE JEAN ROLLIM • PRODUCTION FILMS A.B.C

# Back to the Beach

## THE FILMS OF **JEAN ROLLIN**

### Part One *The Far Country*

- L'idéal a moi: c'est un songe
Creux; mon horizon—l'imprévu—
Et le mal du pays me ronge...
Du pays que je n'ai pas vu.

(My ideal: is a hollow dream;
My horizon—the unforeseen—
And my homesickness is extreme...
For a land I've never seen.)

From *Paria* by Tristan Corbière

The lights go down and the opening credits roll. 'Le viol du vampire', they announce: 'A melodrama in two parts'. Like all good melodramas, it begins with a story. Two young men and a girl listen while an old man tells them about the four vampire sisters.

"Listen...listen to me..." he intones. His voice is dry, cracked. His accent thick and foreign sounding. "Listen and obey!"

A hand caresses a naked breast.

Someone in the cinema laughs out loud. Someone else tells them to shut up. More voices. More comments.

Suddenly the door to the auditorium flies open. Light floods in, drowning the black and white images on the screen. There's a whiff of something acrid. Tear gas.

From the street outside come loud voices. The sound of an angry crowd. Strange slogans fill the air; half political, half poetical.

"After tomorrow comes tomorrow!" someone shouts.

"Opium is the religion of the people!" another voice responds.

Then the noise of Police sirens and the clatter of stones deflected off shields.

On the screen the old man is warning the villagers: "He has set the vampires free! He has broken the cross and let loose the evil!"

1968 was a Year of Revolutions. In Paris, in May, the revolution took to the street in the most violent protests that Europe had seen for 120 years. By the end of the month the city was in the grip of a general strike.

Jean Rollin's feature, **Le viol du vampire**, was one of only two new films that opened that week in Paris. Audiences flocked to see it. The spirit of insurrection was in the air. People were looking for something new and startling. They certainly found it in **Le viol du vampire**.

In the guise of a 'horror' film a series of apparently unconnected images was being shown: women drinking from a huge jar of blood, a game of skittles played by a blind woman, a vampire queen emerging from the sea, a marriage of vampires taking place in the old Grand Guignol theatre, two lovers being sealed inside a coffin.... and so on, up to the final image of the hero, cradling his lover's body in his arms in the deserted Place de la Bastille, and reciting from ancient pulp author Gaston Leroux. To cap it all, the film was laced with splashes of nudity, ridiculous dialogue that seemed to be made up as the actors spoke,

◀ (Facing page) Original poster for **The Nude Vampire** (1969)

▼ Girl and candelabra from **Le viol du vampire** (1968)

Le viol du vampire ▶
(1968) provoked a strong
reaction in many viewers

and had a cast who were killed off at the end of the first half hour and then came back to life for the final fifty minute play-out.

Not sure whether to laugh, scream, or ask for their money back, the crowd howled out their disapproval. And it wasn't just vocal: shoes, fruit and empty cans all found their way towards the screen. It was, as the French say, 'un succès de scandale'. And before three weeks were out, more than forty five thousand people had been to join in the riot.

The film was Jean Rollin's professional debut. While the strikes had been fomenting in Paris, he had been off in the countryside with a small team of wild-eyed and enthusiastic collaborators, putting together what the posters announced was 'The First French Vampire Film!' That was just the commercial hyperbole. In fact the film had been made almost by accident, and in a spirit of fun and adventure that was part of the mood of the times. The most Rollin had expected was that it might find an audience amongst the small band of Parisian horror fans. An almost underground group, of which he considered himself a member. Many of its leading lights were in the film. Hopefully, they had enough friends to fill a small cinema. There was no way he could have predicted such a dramatic opening for his small, surreal masterpiece.

All the newspapers sent reviewers to see the film. They all hated it. The effects on Rollin's subsequent career were long lasting. He became known as the man who had made the 'incomprehensible' **Le viol du vampire**—and he became labelled as a horror-film maker, something he had never wanted to be. The events of May '68 cast a long shadow, and it was many years before sympathetic viewers began to latch on to what Rollin was really trying to do. Although the French are great cinema goers, they don't really like to be provoked too much. Any film-maker who dares to be different is in

for a rough ride. Like Jean-Pierre Mocky, who dabbles in all sorts of genres, Rollin is known as a marginal; someone who probably has his audience, but is really more of a nuisance than he's worth. Which is a shame, because his films do have something special to offer, something that people could respond to....if they were given the opportunity to see the films.

For many years, Jean Rollin was an almost underground name. He was widely written about in fanzines and in books on the history of the horror film, but very often the information was partisan or inaccurate. Usually just repeating the same half truths and prejudices. Very few people who wrote about him had actually seen any of his films. Now, a new audience is rediscovering this unique film-maker. Once again, as they did in France twenty years ago, people are asking—who is Jean Rollin? and: why does he make his films the way he does? To answer the second question properly, you have to know some of the answers to the first .

Jean Rollin was born on the 3rd of November, 1938 in the middle-class Paris suburb of Neuilly-sur-Seine. It was an artistic family. His father was an actor and theatre director, under the name of Claude Martin, and his younger brother, Olivier, also became an actor and then a painter. Georges Bataille, author of the surreal *Story of an Eye* was a close friend of his mother. Years later Rollin would remember the bedtime stories that Bataille told him, about 'Monsieur le Curé', a wolf dressed in the robes of a priest.

He was always a lover of the fantastic—in painting, in books, in cinema. The first film he remembers seeing was Abel Gance's **Capitaine Fracasse** (1942), with its incredible storm sequence. Coming out of the film he told his mother that he wanted to do that; to be the orchestrater of storms, a creator of images. In other words, to be a film-maker. Nothing else was important after that and, like so many other film-struck kids, he began to see his whole life through a view finder.

Later, just to be a part of the film-making process, Rollin would work at odd jobs as an extra on films being shot in Paris.[1] And all the time he was going to see films, devouring them hungrily. Even years later he would be able to describe in detail favourite sequences from Fritz Lang's **Moonfleet** or Mario Bava's **Black Sunday**; sequences that he would later refer to in his own films whenever he had the chance. But he was also busy creating his own personal mythology.

As a child on holiday with his family at Dieppe, he wandered by chance onto a deserted section of the beach. In the shadow of the high cliffs, old fortifications left over from the war had tumbled into the sand and long lines of barnacle encrusted poles stretched out into the sea. There was something fascinating, sad, and at the same time stimulating about the scene. As he stood there, perhaps rehearsing in his head some lines he had just discovered from Tristan Corbière, Verlaine's favourite 'poète maudit', he promised himself that when he made his first film he would make it here, on this eerie seascape with the sound of the gulls wheeling overhead.

The first steps towards realising his dreams came during his National Service in the Army, when he learned the rudiments of editing, working on recruitment films. Discharged in 1955, at the age of seventeen, he secured a job with the Paris-based animation company Saturne.[2]

He made his first film in 1958, at the age of twenty. It was a twelve minute, black and white short called **Les amours jaunes** (The Yellow Loves), inspired by a Tristan Corbière poem. Perhaps Rollin was attracted by Corbière's peculiar reputation, with its stories of 'tranvestitism and brothels', perhaps it was Corbière's troubled relationship with his father—the famous author of *Negrier* and other sea-based adventures—or maybe it was his short and doomed life, tragic love affair and 'outsider' status in French literary life. Whatever the reasons, Corbière's influence was profound and lasting. Huysmans said of Corbière : 'It was scarcely French...but then, out of this jungle of comical conceits and smirking witticisms there would suddenly rise a sharp cry of pain, like the sound of a violoncello string breaking'—remarkably similar to the way Rollin's films have been received by critics over the years.

Rollin 'borrowed' an ancient 35mm camera from the newsreel company he was working for at the time and, with a small group of friends, would set off early every Sunday morning to Dieppe. There, under the shadow of the cliffs, he began to fulfil his schoolboy dreams. The camera—a Maurigraphe—was incredibly heavy, noisy and complicated—but it cranked out crisp, professional looking black and white images. These were combined with a voice-over reading of a section of Corbière's poem, and some drawings by Fabien Loris, an actor and singer who had worked with Prévert and Carné.[3]

The following year Rollin went to work for SCA, again as assistant editor, and then the year after that as an editor at a TV station, working on newsreels and documentaries. In 1961 he

began his next black and white short, the ambitious, surreal **Ciel de cuivre** (Copper Sky). Only twenty minutes of the film were shot.

During these years, Rollin was still attempting to break into the industry, applying for jobs as assistant director, writing and submitting scripts and generally getting himself known. He met both Buñuel and Franju and worked with a theatre company, devising sets and costumes for a production called *Une leçon d'histoire*. Then, in 1962, came his first experience of working on a full length feature. **Un cheval pour deux** (A Horse For Two) was directed by the famous comic actor Jean-Marc Thibault. Jean Rollin was employed as assistant director. He admits that it was not a happy experience, and it was probably this event that hardened his resolve to continue as before—financing and helming his own productions.

The professional contacts he had made were to help him with his next project, which was to be a feature based on his own script called **L'itinéraire marin** (The Sailors' Journey). This was the first film from his own production company, ABC, financed by his own savings, his brother Olivier and anyone else he could persuade to part with a few francs. In the main roles he cast Gaston Modot, who had been in Buñuel's **L'age d'or**, and René-Jacques Chauffard, collaborator of the award winning novelist and screenwriter Marguerite Duras.

Chauffard liked the story, but felt that the dialogue could be improved. With Rollin's agreement he showed it to Duras who found it interesting and agreed to rework it with help from another writer, Gérard Jarlot. Shooting began early in 1963, with a week in Dieppe followed by three weeks in Bretagne. Almost an hour of footage was in the can before the money ran out. Although listed in French production catalogues the film was never completed, and with the subsequent death of Modot the project ground to a halt.

At this time, in the early 1960's, a new, young French cinema was just beginning to emerge, based around the magazine *Cahiers du cinéma*

Many of Jean Rollin's ▲
early films have the same
collage-like structure of his
favourite painter, Clovis
Trouille

and its star writers, Chabrol, Goddard, Truffaut. It was a violent reaction against the old styles, in particular that of Marcel Carné. In films like **Le quai des brumes**, **Les portes de la nuit** and **Les enfants du paradis**, Carné, together with the writer Jacques Prévert, had created a particularly French form of cinema that someone aptly described as 'poetic realism'. Rollin's sympathies lay with Carné and Prévert and not the so called 'new wave,' and **L'itinéraire marin** is a bittersweet tale that's pure Prévert. The film, as so often with Rollin's work, ends on the beach at Dieppe as two would-be sailors stand, facing the rolling waves, dreaming of the never-to-be past. The casting, with Gaston Modot who had played Fil de Soie, the mysterious blind beggar in **Les enfants du paradis**, is also a nod to the old school, as was the involvement of Fabien Loris in Rollin's first film **Les amours jaunes**.

A key moment in **Les enfants du paradis** comes when one of the characters, Baptiste, says: "Dreams and life—it's the same thing; or else it's not worth living." This kind of doomed romanticism is a common element in nearly all Rollin's films. Many of his early stories feature intense, haunted young men so like the Baptiste of **Les enfants**. To the new wave this poetic realist touch had come to seem distinctly drippy and old-fashioned, as had the declamatory style of the acting and poetic speeches that are another of the features of Rollin's early films. By the late sixties, when he began to include these alongside exploitation elements—sex, horror, explicit violence—the mixture

became even more anachronistic, giving his films a strange flavour that French viewers in particular found unsettling.

During the early sixties, Rollin was politically active, associating with a variety of fringe groups. Through these contacts he came to the notice of a Spanish anarchist cell, who were looking for someone to produce a short documentary film to help the anti-Franco resistance movement. Limited funding was provided and a small team set off for Madrid to begin shooting. The political situation in Spain was extremely tense at the time and, unknown to Rollin and his friends, Frédéric Rossif was also in the area gathering footage for his film **Mourir à Madrid (To Die in Madrid)**.

The military police got wind of what was going on and set off in search of Rossif. They ended up on the trail of Rollin. A tense ten days ensued, with the small group often only a few hours away from being discovered. But eventually they made it safely back to Paris, where the footage was edited down into the half hour **Vivre en Espagne** (To Live in Spain), which was shown widely at conferences and at political meetings.

During this time Rollin was still working full time as an editor for TV. In 1964 he began work for Actualités Françaises, a newsreel company, as sound editor. It was a job he kept for four years, until the success of **Le viol du vampire**, in 1968, led him into full time filmmaking. He had also begun to write at this time and was part of a group of avant-garde intellectuals, young and old, who centred around the Paris-based publisher Eric Losfeld.[4]

Losfeld, who was later to achieve notoriety with *Barbarella*, had catholic tastes, being the original publisher of both Ionesco and Emmanuelle Arsan.[5] At the Saturday afternoon salons in Losfeld's offices in the rue du Cherche Midi, the young Rollin met critics, writers and filmmakers such as Ado Kyrou, Jacques Sternberg and Isidore Isou. Losfeld became interested in the young film-maker and agreed to publish his first novel, *Les Pays Loins* (The Far Country), under his Terrain Vague imprint. The book was never, finally, published but it provided the title and inspiration for Rollin's next short film which was completed in 1965.

Filmed in the ancient Paris suburb of Belleville, **Les pays loins** tells the Kafkaesque story of a man lost in a parallel universe in which everything was subtly changed. He spends the film trying to find his way back—or to discover his own identity. This was a theme that Rollin would return to many times over the years in a variety

▲ From *Saga of Xam* (1967)

of forms. Perhaps it expressed his own uncertain feelings about trying to make it in the world of cinema at the time. Less specifically, the mood of being an outsider, of nostalgic longing for something on the margin of comprehensibility, is a constant element in his films and books.

During 1966 Rollin was a frequent visitor to a large, ramshackle flat shared by a group of young artists who were just beginning to feel the influence of the hippy movement filtering through from the States and from England. Among them were Nicolas Devil and Philippe Druillet. One of the frequent topics of conversation was the emerging art form of comics, just starting to shake free from the rigidity of the post-war years and the politically dubious superhero figures of the American models. From Italy had come the 'fumetti neri' with characters like Diabolik and Kriminal and the *bande dessinée*,[6] thanks largely to Eric Losfeld and *Barbarella*, was laying the groundwork for a whole new appreciation of the political and revolutionary aspects of the medium.

Rollin was struck by the designs being done by Nicolas Devil and took some of them to Losfeld, who immediately suggested that they collaborate on a strip that Le Terrain Vague would publish. The result was *Saga of Xam*, which appeared in book form in 1967. Its unique style[7] and its strong sexual content gave it a huge impact. *Saga of Xam* broke most of the rules of the traditional comic strip and, even in those revolutionary times, it was a little too far out for many readers. In fact the whole scene soon became too far out for Rollin. Unable to keep up with the real life psychedelic experiments of Devil and co, he abandoned the story, leaving it for Devil and Druillet to complete by themselves.

Rollin has always been attracted by strong pulp images. They form the basis of much of his work. When they happen to include unintentionally surreal elements they become even more appealing. The comics provided one source of inspiration, the serials of Feuillade and his American counterparts another. Running parallel to them in Rollin's affections were the garish but wonderful covers of the cheap, popular paperbacks that had flourished in France in the first decades of the twentieth century. As a child, Rollin had haunted the second-hand shops and street markets of Paris, searching out these crumbling treasures.

One of the authors he discovered in this way was Gaston Leroux. Although known for *The Phantom of the Opera* and the series of stories featuring the detective Rouletabille, Rollin discovered that the prolific Leroux had also written dozens of genre pieces in his own unique style.[8] He became an avid collector of these books, with titles such as *The Queen of the Sabbath* and *The Bleeding Doll*, and eventually produced the first full-length study of this popular but often overlooked writer.

*Aujourd'hui Gaston Leroux* (Today, Gaston Leroux), published in Losfeld's magazine *Midi-Minuit Fantastique*, linked both aspects of Rollin's life at this time—the literary and the cinematic. At the end of the final article in the series, he included an extract from an unfilmed screenplay written in 1961 and credited to 'Michel Gentil'. This marked the first appearance of a pseudonym (actually a variation of his real name—Jean Michel Rollin le Gentil) that he would later use for the series of sex films that began with 1973's **Jeune filles impudiques** (Shameless Young Girls).

Although serious about his writing, Rollin was still in love with cinema and with the idea

▼ Gaston Leroux's *La poupée sanglante* was an influence on Rollin's film, **La vampire nue** (1969)

of being a director. He hadn't forgotten that storm that had so inspired him at the age of five. Everything he had achieved so far was only to push him further in the direction of realising that first over-riding ambition.

He was still submitting scripts, still talking to anyone who would listen, and in this way he met a Belgian producer and writer, Jean-Paul Torök, to talk about a script that he had prepared called **Le dernier vampire** (The Last Vampire). Torök introduced him to an associate of his called Samuel S. Selsky, an American who had been living in Paris since the late forties.

Selsky was an amazing character, with a life story that would have provided the subject matter for several novels. Originally trained as a geologist and mining engineer, he had led several

Rivers of blood revive the ▼ cast of **Le viol du vampire** (1968)

expeditions to far flung corners of the globe, being at one point captured by a group of head-hunters. After the war he ended up in Paris as an administrator for UNESCO, working under Julian Huxley. Always an adventurous spirit, Selsky used the severance pay he got from leaving UNESCO to buy a small art cinema in Paris and was soon running a chain of picture houses. A chance meeting with an old army buddy led to an offer to be European producer for the popular American TV series *You Asked For It!* After seven years Selsky realised that pictures were in his blood. Using his unique position and many contacts, he set himself up as an importer of American films for sale to French TV and cinema chains.

He was immediately struck on his first meeting with the young Jean Rollin, not only by his enthusiasm, but also by the originality and sound commercial sense of his ideas. **Le dernier vampire** was a still-born project, but Selsky was interested in getting involved in production and was keen to look at anything else that Rollin might bring him. The chance came soon through another contact of Rollin's.

The distributor Jean Lavie had just acquired the rights to an old American B film directed by the prolific Sam Newfield (his 1943 epic **Dead Men Walk**), which was to be released under the French title of **Le vampire, creature du diable**. Unfortunately the film was too short—just over an hour. Lavie knew that he would have to find at least another 30 minutes of film to make up a complete 'programme' that he could sell to exhibitors.

Rollin went to Selsky again. This time with the idea of making a short film to go out on release with **Le vampire...** It would have to be a horror film and Rollin had already come up with the title **Le viol du vampire**. He also had the idea that it would consist of a collage of images, drawn from the vast range of influences that he had carried with him up to that point: the frenetic, pulp poetry of Gaston Leroux, the sexy comic book images of *Xam*, the bitter romanticism of Tristan Corbière, the political surrealism of Buñuel and Franju and the poetic realism of Jacques Prévert. What he didn't have at that point was a script. That seemed only a minor problem at the time and, as Selsky recalls, it was only a matter of weeks from that second meeting until the small crew that Rollin had assembled were shooting the first feet of film.[9]

They were a disparate bunch, united only in their enthusiasm for the project and by their complete lack of experience. Even the electrician was a novice. Shooting began in a place called

Claysoullis where there was an old abandoned château due to be pulled down in three month's time. The cast and crew were staying nearby, in a hotel that was so cold it was impossible to sleep at night. However Selsky's long experience on *You Asked For It!* and Rollin's inexhaustible energy and ability to improvise proved invaluable. Nothing was taken for granted. An old car was purchased to carry the equipment; it also became the carriage of the Vampire Queen. When a dolly shot was needed, Selsky recalled a sequence he had supervised some years before in the ruins of Pompeii, when a wheelbarrow had been used for just such a purpose.

Rollin soon learned that what had looked good on paper, when he was constructing his scenario, often turned out to be unachievable given the limited means at his disposal. The script was gradually altered and finally changed out of all recognition. Rollin avers that over 50% of the final film was totally improvised on the spot. His cast were not actors but friends; mostly artists, writers and even a female psychiatrist.[10] In spite of their lack of experience each

of them had something they could offer to the final product. They threw themselves into it with a vengeance, in some cases risking serious injury in impromptu stunt work.

Finally the footage was edited down into as coherent a form as possible and it ran for almost 45 minutes. Total cost had been 100,000 francs (about £10,000). When he viewed the film Selsky, with his sharp producer's mentality, was impressed above all by how cheaply it had been done. A shame to throw it all away as a second feature, he told Rollin; why not shoot another 45 minutes and then we can release it as a feature in its own right?

Only one problem—all of the cast had been killed off at the end of **Viol du vampire**. Rollin's solution was surreal and simple. He would make what they had already shot Part One of a serial and begin Part Two with the resurrection of the cast, in classic cliff-hanger style. And so shooting began again, this time on **Les femmes vampires** (The Vampire Women).

With the finished film in the can, it only remained to convince an exhibitor to buy it. Here

Sam Selsky's talents came to the fore. At UNESCO they had said of him: "Sam Selsky loves to solve problems; if there weren't any he would create one in order to be able to solve it." Well, he certainly had one major problem with **Viol...** Everyone who saw it—including those involved in its making—declared it to be totally incomprehensible.

Selsky had contacts with the Boublil brothers who ran the chain of cinemas Midi-Minuit-Scarlett-Ciné-Vog St Lazare-Le Styx which specialised in horror pictures. He arranged a showing for them and, aware that they must be kept from trying to understand the film, he kept up an endless dialogue with them as it ran its course; pointing out bits of special effects, telling them various stories, and was quiet only for the sex scenes—which needed no explanation. When one or other of the brothers complained that he couldn't understand what was going on, Selsky would apologise and say that they had missed a key scene because he had been talking. He would then carry on talking, explaining to them the bit they had missed and saying that it would all become clear later.

Since the film had been presented to the censor in the form of two shorts—which were not so rigidly controlled at the time—the sex scenes were passed largely without any cuts. This turned out to be both a blessing and a curse—for the film and for Rollin's subsequent career.

The accident of the film's release at the height of the events of May '68, when there were few new films in the cinemas, meant that all the critics came to see **Viol....**Their scandalised reaction hit the pages of the Paris dailies like dispatches from a battle front. Jean Rollin awoke the next morning to find himself just about the most hated man in Paris. Even Le General de Gaulle was viewed more kindly by comparison. *Le Figaro* wrote that the film had been made by a team of drunks who had escaped from a lunatic asylum. Even those critics who specialised in horror pictures were outraged. *Midi-Minuit Fantastique* hated it. Losfeld, out of loyalty to his friend, would not publish a bad review, and so the film passed without mention in the most influential genre publication in France. Or almost. A reader, Francis Giraudet, saw the film in Bordeaux and sent in a letter full of praise for its surrealist spirit. He wrote that, watching the film, he was 'transported on the wings of a magnificent black and white bird'. Losfeld published the letter in its entirety and so, in a roundabout sort of way, **Le viol du vampire** did get one good review.

The only other publication to view the film kindly was a Belgian fanzine called *Rantanplan*. Rollin, touched by the review, wrote to the magazine. The author of the article, Jio Berk, was an artist and designer who had been active in the underground film scene in Belgium for several

**Le viol du vampire** ▶
(1968)

years. Through Berk, Rollin got to know Jean-Pierre Bouyxou, who had written fascinating studies of the science fiction and horror film, and a whole host of other fringe artists and writers such as Roland Lethem and Rafaël Marongiu, all of whom shared his devotion to the surreal fringes of popular culture. Rollin's films have always been more appreciated in Belgium and his influence can be seen not only in experimental works like Lethem's **Le vampire de la cinémathèque** (Vampire of the Cinema; 1971), but also in more mainstream films like Jean-Louis Van Belle's **Le sadique aux dents rouges** (The Sadist With Red Teeth; 1970).

Jio Berk came to work for Rollin as costume and set designer on his next film **La vampire nue**, and Bouyxou has co-written several scripts with him as well as acting small parts in many of them. Later, when Bouyxou managed to put together his own film—the low budget sex flick **Amours collectives** in 1976—Rollin returned the compliment by supervising the filming and playing the part of 'Mike Gentle, the Vampire'!

The volume and vehemence of the reaction to **Viol...** came as a surprise to Rollin. Of course he could not have predicted the circumstances that led to it, but it set a standard against which his future work was judged. People were either violently for or against him. There was no middle ground; he was either a charlatan or a genius. Pretty soon he came to realise that French critics—particularly the specialist ones—had so many preconceptions as to what constituted an acceptable horror film that he would be for ever damned in their eyes as long as he continued to work in that field. Yet, ironically, it was the *succès de scandale* of **Le viol du vampire** that has had Rollin pegged forever as a maker of 'sexy vampire' films.

He has said himself that he does not make horror films for their own sake. The form allows him the freedom to do things that would not be acceptable in a more rationally based form of cinema. He wrote, in *Midi-Minuit Fantastique*, that 'the fantastique is the opposite of the supernatural.' What he wants is to introduce fantastic elements into the everyday world, to push the normal until it becomes super-normal. The key to this is the creation of an atmosphere in which anything could happen—and frequently does. His films are based around images and sequences of images, not around the logical, point-by-point exposition of a screenplay. The genesis of many of his films is a particular place that catches his attention or a specific image. Other images then follow, and often the screen-play is an exercise in linking the pictures that come almost ready formed to his mind.

Which is not to say, as others often have, that the stories in his films are unimportant. They are essential elements in helping to create a mood, giving strength to the introduction of the outré elements that move the plot on to its next stage. Without the narrative, the images would lack focus. In **Le frisson des vampires**, for example, there is a scene where the vampire, Dominique, emerges at midnight from inside a grandfather clock. The scene has narrative and dramatic sense, and is a startling image in itself; but if the film had consisted of nothing but such moments, the emotional impact of them would be lost. It's the poetry inherent in these scenes that Rollin wants to cultivate, not the shock value of them. His ideal is to find images that are strong enough in themselves to need no final rational explanation. To him, the need to explain takes away the power of the images.

▼ **Le viol du vampire** (1968)

With this idea in mind, his next film, **La vampire nue** (**The Nude Vampire**; 1969), was based around the idea of 'mystery'. Each sequence was to heighten the mystery and lead it forward to the next sequence. Any explanation that had to be given was to be held off until the very last possible moment.

The newsreel company for which Rollin had been working up to this point had recently closed. He was now forced to decide whether to look for another similar job or to devote himself full time to feature film production. The relative success of **Viol...** made it easier to raise money for the next film and, considering the options, Rollin was fairly sure where his future lay. However, he realised that the idea of mounting another film like **Viol...**, with its improvised, serial-like structure, would be commercial suicide and so he was forced to make certain changes. For one thing the film would be shot in colour. This was not as expensive then as it would be now and many exploitation filmmakers were using the inexpensive Eastmancolour process at the time. He would also be using professional actors.

Rollin's inexperience worked against him and the film ended up going over budget. More unfortunate was the fact that it was not particularly well received on its original release. It was picked up for export, however, and was eventually released in the UK in 1973. [11]

The story of **La vampire nue** involves a bizarre suicide cult, a mysterious man known only as The Master, weird experiments with phials of coloured blood, and a dimensional gap into another world. Jio Berk designed the fabulous costumes and the visual style was drawn from pulp comics and old paperback covers. **La vampire nue** is one of Rollin's most enjoyable films and a great leap forward, technically, from **Le viol du vampire**. It also remains remarkably true to its original conception as a film around the idea of mystery, of enigma. Even the ending, when an explanation is given for all the mysterious events, is successfully undercut. The film suddenly takes off into science fiction territory and, as Rollin said later, leaves the way open for a second part to begin just as the first one ends.

André Samarcq, who had helped to sell the film abroad, was in touch with a producer called Monique Natan. [12] Samarcq mentioned Rollin to her and showed her **La vampire nue**. She liked the film and agreed to meet the young director. Preliminary discussions went well. That weekend Rollin produced a treatment for

◄ The Master and his
acolytes, **La vampire
nue** (1969)
◄ (Facing page)
Hooded creatures stalk
**The Nude Vampire**

another vampire film and over the course of the following weeks the two of them worked on the dialogue together.

The resulting film, **Le frisson des vampires** (1970), was Rollin's most assured and commercial film to date. Again it was made very cheaply and quickly. But, through judicious use of lighting and colour effects, the film transcends its limitations, going almost to the point of parody in its manipulation of the traditional horror elements—castle, graveyards, vampires, virgin bride and so on.

Many elements stand out in the film and, with each viewing, become more important than any notion of plot development. First of all the castle, in which much of the action is set, becomes itself a character in the film. Shots of its massive, lowering bulk, brightly lit by coloured spotlights, are repeated throughout the film as it watches and waits, while the farce-like action unrolls beneath. The organic nature of the building is underlined in a sequence where the castle library seems to come alive, hurling books at the unfortunate husband who has come to save his wife from a fate worse than death—eternal life as a vampire!

Then there are the weird assortment of characters who inhabit the place. Dominique, the sexually ambiguous vampire, who appears from chimneys and out of grandfather clocks; the two effete, hippy châtelains who preside over events;

and the two lost orphan girls, one dark one fair, whose mysterious presence is never explained but who may well be orchestrating it all.

Finally, there is the music. Rollin's sound editor Jean-Philippe Delamarre, suggested that he use rock music and introduced him to a group called Acanthus. They were school kids and their total experience consisted of a few youth club dates and lots of wood-shedding. This lack of gloss and their status as enthusiastic amateurs was very attractive to Rollin. He showed them the film and they played him pieces they already had that they felt would be suitable. They specialised in a sort of free-form progressive rock, replete with crashing guitar chords and odd, lyrical snatches of flute and organ. Some of the track, the credit sequence for example, was completely improvised. The results were amazingly successful—but Acanthus, unfortunately, were not; they broke up soon after the film was released.

**Le frisson des vampires** was a small hit in France and was again bought for export.[13] When the film was dubbed, English accents were given to the strange hippy châtelains, in an attempt to bestow a sense of class onto their meandering speeches. The dialogue, which the actors had written themselves, was full of pretentious theorising and pompous nonsense, quite in keeping with the spirit of parody of the whole film but very difficult to convey in translation. It's unfor-

▼ **The Nude Vampire**

Dominique rises from the ▶
grave, **Le frisson des
vampires** (1970)
(Facing Page) English ▶
poster for **Le frisson
des vampires**

the unity of the two "pillars" of film, the sound
and the picture, and present them in divergence
one from the other.' Debord's solution was even
more extreme. His 1951 film **Hurlements en
faveur de Sade** (Howls for de Sade), consisted
of long sections of an entirely black screen, with
no sound, and shorter sections of white screen
with various unseen speakers intoning lines in a
monotone. The final twenty or so minutes were
entirely black and silent. Few audiences stayed
the course.

Monique Natan was pleased with the way
**Frisson** had performed commercially and was
keen to make another film with Rollin. She came
up with the title Docteur Vampire, and the project was announced with Sandra Julien from
**Frisson** as star. But, before any work was done
on the script, Mme Natan died in a car crash and
the project was abandoned. [15]

The following year, in 1971, Sam Selsky
approached Rollin with the idea of another collaboration. Once more it would have to be
quick—a condition of the finance was that shooting would have to begin immediately—but the
budget would be a little bit more than for **Viol**.

Rollin began to think about possible stories and,
as he did so, he had a sudden vision of a piano
being played in an empty graveyard. He began to
imagine the sound that it would make, out in the
open—at night; he saw his friend Louise Dhour
playing the piano; he saw a candelabra with flick-
ering candles; and he saw two young girls—
perhaps the two from **Frisson**?—listening as the
music played. As the image faded in his mind it
dissolved into a shot of the two girls alone, but
now dressed in clown costumes, and driving fran-
tically in a car along a lonely country road....

tunate that this aspect of his films has so often led
to accusations that Rollin is a bad director. Even
in France they say that the dialogue and the visuals go in different directions. When that effect is
amplified by indifferent dubbing the result is
often disastrous. Several of Rollin's films have
lengthy silent passages, and even these are sometimes given dialogue and sound effects in the
export versions.

Rollin admits that he would do things differently today. In later films, such as **Les
démoniaques**, with its self-consciously expressionist style of acting, he managed to integrate
some of these more jarringly non-naturalistic
effects into the structure of the film. But with
**Frisson** he was still largely feeling his way. His
background and his sensibilities were from the
more experimental or avant garde areas of film-
making. At this point he was still learning how to
adapt these ideas into a commercial framework.
It's the struggle between the various elements that
make the films so fascinating, but it also makes
them seem awkward and strange to many viewers—particularly horror fans—who expect
something more conventional.

With his anarchist/surrealist sympathies still
intact Rollin was making films under the shadow of people like Isidore Isou, whom he had met
years before at Losfeld's offices, and the Situationist Guy Debord.[14] Isou's *'cinema discrepant'*
proposes just such a discrepancy between sound
and vision as Rollin's film offers, aiming to 'break

The vampire's servants ▶
**Le frisson des
vampires**

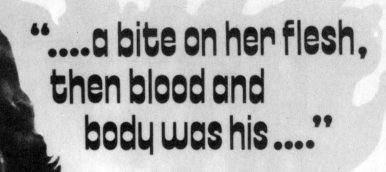

"....a bite on her flesh, then blood and body was his ...."

# Sex and the Vampire

X

Starring
**SANDRA JULIEN**
**NICOLE NANCEL**
**MICHEL DELAHAYE**
EASTMANCOLOR

EfC

As a young boy Rollin had gone off to scout camp. He remembered the stories that the scoutmaster had told them over the campfire at night, and how impressed he had been to discover that the stories were all made up as the man told them. He decided now to try that with a film script, to sit down at the typewriter, tell himself a story and see what happened.

He began with two young girls, in clown costumes, on the run in a stolen car and gradually, page by page, incident by incident he wrote his script, adding another idea as soon as the one he was working on became played out. It was a refinement of the technique he had used in **Viol** and **La vampire nue**, combined with a sort of automatic writing, and with luck he hoped to reach the point at which explanations ceased to be needed. If the story moved with enough pace, if the situations he created were strong enough, then no audience would require them to make 'sense' in any conventional way.

Of course it didn't quite work out like that; but one of the results of this method of composition—with Rollin telling the story to himself—was that for much of the script's length there was no dialogue at all. In fact the first word is spoken 40 minutes into the film.

In the course of a normal production such an idiosyncrasy would be ironed out in the various stages that come between first draft and commencement of shooting. But here speed was of the essence. Rollin had only ten days before shooting was due to begin under the working title of **Vierges et vampires** (Virgins and Vampires). Selsky was not keen on the title and offered a prize to anyone who could come up with a better one. No-one was surprised when Sam declared himself the winner with the title **Requiem pour un vampire** (**Requiem for a Vampire**).

**Requiem** has very little sex in it; only one short scene which is cut from most release prints. This was shot at the express wish of the financiers of the film who made no other demands on him. That year at Cannes an announcement went up that there was to be a screening of a short section from Rollin's latest vampire film—'Now shooting somewhere in France!'

And of course it was the five minute sex sequence that was shown.

The film was bought for the US by the notorious Harry Novak, a former plugger for Walt Disney and a veteran of the exploitation industry. On hearing that his beloved—and prizewinning—title had been changed to **Caged Virgins**, Selsky growled that he was going to kill someone; on reflection he mellowed, musing that "Americans probably don't know what requiem means anyway."

Le frisson des vampires had been a move by Jean Rollin towards a more commercial form of cinema, while still being an attempt to integrate some of his more personal concerns. **Requiem** was a consolidation of the experiment. It works both as a straight horror film and an exploration of personal mythology. For the first time Rollin's ideas and his ability to visualise them were coming together. The simple story tells of two girls on the run from a reform school and how they end up in the clutches of the 'Last Vampire.' He's a sad and weary sort of monster—more pathetic than terrifying—and he's looking for two virgins through whom to propagate his race.....

Lots of themes that had been floating about in Rollin's mind came to fruition in **Requiem**. The two girls—Marie and Michèle—or at least versions of them, pop up in many of his later films. Runaways, lonely castles, figures dressed in clown costumes, ill-fated love affairs and humanistic vampires. All these would later become familiar features of the Rollin landscape.

The man responsible for selling both **Requiem** and **Frisson** for export was another veteran of the industry, Lionel Wallmann.[16] During the early 1970's many French producers were casting envious glances over the waters to the US, where films like **Deep Throat** were creating a porno boom that was making fortunes from very low investments. On the domestic market the practice had come in—apparently originating in Marseilles—of adding short hardcore sequences to erotic films to cash in on the interest generated by the porn boom. Wallmann approached Rollin with the brief to make a film that would go as far as was then legally possible in France, with the understanding that it would contain scenes that would allow the 'insertion' of hardcore footage should the opportunity arise at some later date.

The result was a low budget sex film with horror overtones—**Tout le monde il en a deux** (Everyone Has Two of Them)—that Rollin directed in 1973 under his old Michel Gentil pseudonym. The film, described by critic Jean-Marie Sabatier as 'avant garde hardcore', tells the story of Malvina (Joëlle Cœur), the high priestess of the "sect of lovers of fresh flesh" and how two girls, Sophie and Valerie, fall into her hands.

The film was later rereleased, with added hardcore scenes, as **Bacchanales sexuelles**. It did well at the box office, with over 320,000 viewers in France, and later that year Wallmann expressed interest in doing something with a larger budget. Rollin began to work on the

'The Last Vampire,' **Requiem pour un vampire**

script of **Les diablesses** (Devil Women), which later became **Les démoniaques (Demoniacs)**.

Although it was to be a horror film with sexual elements, Rollin wanted to inject into it some of the spirit of the old adventure films he had loved as a child, the swashbuckling pirate films of Raoul Walsh and Michael Curtiz, such as **Blackbeard the Pirate** and **The Sea Hawk**.

He planned a credit sequence for the film drawn straight out of old Hollywood; a large book would be opened and, to the strains of evocative music, a voice would read the scene-setting opening words as the heavy vellum pages were turned by an invisible hand. Although he did later use such a beginning for **Fascination** in 1980, it proved to be impractical for **Les démoniaques**. Instead, there is a shot of a burning ship and a voice over introduces each of the characters, describing them in wonderfully over-the-top style, as their faces appear framed against the fiery background.

Rollin had written a script, one he was very pleased with, and initial casting had started, when Wallmann fixed up a co-production deal with General Films. They were a Belgian company, and the deal meant that 50% of the film had to be shot there and a Belgian actress used as one of the two leads. This would entail extensive rewrites. To add to his problems, Rollin had already suffered one setback when a French actress cast in a leading role had suddenly pulled out. She had been warned not to work with him. The word in the business was that Rollin was using his young actresses as prostitutes, to raise finance for his films, and she was afraid to go out on location with him.

There were some advantages to the co-production deal, however. For one thing it meant slightly more money, and working in Belgium, where Rollin had many friends, would allow him to use

avia.films et L'ONF. WALLMANN PRESENTENT

**tout le monde il en a 2**

un film de **MICHEL GENTIL**

interdit au moins de 18 ans

Shipwreckers and their ▶
victims, **Les démoniaques**
(1974)

his contacts there, including Jio Berk the talented artist who had worked with him on **La vampire nue**. In fact there is a scene in **Les démoniaques**, set in a tavern, where everyone present is a friend—it's a kind of Rollin family portrait.

Just as the film had been planned as a sort of adventure story, so it turned out to be in the actual shooting. The location for the beach scenes that comprise much of the final film was on the island of Chausey, near Granville on the Normandy coast.[17] Bleak and desolate, the place is inhabited only by a small community of crab fishers, whose meagre catch was about all the cast and crew had to live on for two weeks. To add to their troubles they had chosen to arrive just as the weather was turning. For several days high seas cut them off from all contact with the mainland. Finally, as they set off for Belgium to complete location shooting, Rollin was forced to rewrite much of the film on the way as the planned locations were unavailable.

Yet, in spite of all production problems, **Les démoniaques** is one of Rollin's strongest and strangest films. Even the gaucheness and inexperience of the two actresses cast in the lead roles—two girls who fall into the hands of a gang of vicious shipwreckers—works to the film's advantage. They emerge as even more innocent and naïve than might have been possible with more seasoned performers. Which

makes their eventual fate and violent revenge all the more effective.

One of the film's trump cards is the presence of Joëlle Cœur as Tina. She was a painter whom Rollin had first met in 1972 when a mutual friend had suggested her for a part in **Jeunes filles impudiques**, the first sex film that he had made under the pseudonym of Michel Gentil. She had subsequently appeared in **Tout le monde** the following year. Her role in **Les démoniaques**, as the insatiable and sadistic Tina, leader of the band of ship wreckers, is one of Rollin most disturbing creations. The scene where she masturbates on the beach as her gang torture two survivors from their latest shipwreck, reaching orgasm as their screams fill the air, is not an easy one to forget.[18]

The film is shot in a deliberately expressionist style, drawn from old silent films that Rollin had seen and loved as a boy. In films like Murnau's **Nosferatu** and Joe May's **Indian Tomb**, gesture, archetype and symbol are used to express emotional states of mind. Characterisation and psycho- logical depth take second place. This use of expressionist style places **Les démoniaques** slightly apart from the main body of Rollin's other films, but is one of the reasons that it works so well.

In all his early films, characters deliver their dialogue in a non-naturalistic, artificial way that sometimes seems at odds with the rest of the action. One of the characteristics of expressionist style was this very artificiality, with broad and slow gestures used to amplify the emotions. The American, John Rico, who plays Tina's lover in the film, is particular well adapted to the style. The scenes in the tavern, where he seems to see the ghosts of the two dead girls, are particularly pure examples of expressionist acting. For him nothing exists but the terrors of his haunted mind. The whole sequence, with its mocking bursts of jaunty accordion music and the strange black angel with burning eyes, is an expression of the terrors within him and, like much of the film, has no external, dramatic logic.

The title of the film, too, with its echo of a quote from Leopold Ziegler, is a nod to the German cinema of the 1920's:

*'German man is the supreme example of demoniac man. Demoniac indeed seems the abyss which cannot be filled, the yearning which cannot be assuaged, the thirst which cannot be slaked.'*

**Les démoniaques** was released in 1974, just as the invasion of porn was sweeping into French cinemas. There were mutterings from many parts of the industry, and from the press, about the moral implications of this tide of filth. Rollin found himself caught up in the controversy when he saw a letter containing the comments of the Board of Control who had certificated **Les démoniaques**. Far from merely deciding the age classification of the film, the committee—which consisted of film-makers as well as bureaucrats—had seen fit to pass judgment on the film itself, describing it as being 'of a complete stupidity'. Rollin was outraged. Even more so by the fact that he knew some of the board members personally.[19]

He wrote a letter to the trade papers about the incident, and was soon in contact with a small group of directors and producers who had started a campaign to defend the rights of low budget film-makers against the moral majority, as represented by the press and the official censors. The driving force behind the campaign was José Bénazéraf, whose energy, fiery wit and fierce intelligence greatly impressed Rollin. Bénazéraf had seen and liked **Les démoniaques** and he suggested that Rollin use an actress he knew, Mylène d'Antes. Sure enough, she later played one of the lead roles in **Phantasmes** (1975). This is the only one of the many porno films he has made that Rollin signed with his own name. An act of faith that was largely due to the impression

made on him by Bénazéraf. He felt it necessary to make a stand at the time, to deny that there was any shame in making sex films—even if they were little more than an economic necessity.[20]

At about this point, Rollin's career had reached an impasse. In a short time, and with only a handful of films to his name, he had managed to create his own genre within the French film industry. There was now a recognisable Rollin style. Specialist critics and fans of horror films used to refer to them as 'Rollinades'. And there were even 'Rollinades' directed by other hands—**The Horrible Sexy Vampire**, for example, and **The Curse of the Vampyr**. Jean-Marie Sabatier identified them as 'cheap films, full of the cliches of horror cinema and sprinkled with amateur eroticism....elegantly made popular cinema, art for the masses.'

There's a lot of difference between someone like Rollin, who brings a genuine sense of mys-

▼ They sold their souls to the Devil, **Les démoniaques** (1973)

tery and joy to familiar forms of cinema, and films that use clichés and archetypes in a tired and uninspired way. Unfortunately, the term 'Rollinade' was created more as an insult than in praise. Fans and critics alike would throw up their hands in despair at each new assault on their sense of what constituted acceptable horror 'style'.

Rollin knew he was being ghettoised, but was also aware that the chances of breaking out of that ghetto were decreasing rapidly. He had already made two pseudonymous sex films and was realistic enough to see that this was a direction many other low budget film-makers would be forced to take in the years to come. He decided to take a risk and make a film that would go completely against the grain of his work to date.

For some time he had been thinking of the challenge of coming up with a film that was based entirely around a mood and a place. All of his films had been infused with both, but always diluted by commercial requirements. Now he decided to go 100% for it. All he needed was an idea that was strong enough to be the jumping off point for his imagination. He found it quite by accident.

One day he was out driving with Jean-Jacques Renon, who had been director of photography on **La vampire nue** and **Frisson**, scouting for locations. It was late in the afternoon when they reached Amiens and passed by a large cemetery. Rollin has always found old cemeteries fascinating places. Not for morbid reasons. He is

Rollin moved into the ▼
porn getto with
**Phantasmes** (1975)

attracted by the visual qualities they offer—the stone statues and crosses and the wild undergrowth that weaves around them—and the special atmosphere this creates.

They stopped the car and decided to investigate. As they walked around night began to fall, and they decided it was time to retrace their steps. But they couldn't find the way out. For twenty minutes they searched and they found the spirit of the place beginning to affect them. At one point they almost believed they would never get out—or at least might have to spend the night there.

Suddenly the thought came to Rollin that here were the seeds of a story. Two people lost in a place, trying to find their way out and only becoming even more lost.

Naturally it was a difficult project to find backers for. There was no real horror in it—no vampires—and no sex. But eventually, with the help of Sam Selsky and with a large chunk of his own cash, Rollin began work on **La rose de fer** (**The Crystal Rose**; 1973).

If finding the money had been a problem, actually making the film was even more of one. On paper it had looked cheap—only one location and two actors. However the location wasn't in Paris and so the whole crew had to stay in a hotel, which pretty soon escalated costs sky high. Rollin also had a lot of trouble with the male lead. Fortunately, Sam Selsky was on hand with all his considerable diplomatic skills. Although he did finish the film, the actor, Hugues Quester, demanded that his name be taken off the poster. [21]

Rollin decided to present the finished film in person at the 2nd Convention of Cinéma Fantastique that April in Paris. The place was packed with French horror fans and he knew, from past experience, that he was not going to get an easy ride. But, patiently, he explained to them the genesis of the film and how he had tried to do something different, which he hoped they would receive in the right spirit.

The film had hardly begun before the walkouts commenced. Pretty soon it was obvious that he had a disaster on his hands. The subsequent reports in the French trade and specialist press delighted in retelling the whole affair at Rollin's expense. *Cinématographe* recounted how both he and his film had been roundly booed by the audience, in a way that the writer had never seen a director booed before. So much so, in fact, that for the next few days whenever Rollin was spotted he was given wide berth and the comments and catcalls repeated.

▲ Françoise Pascal in **La rose de fer** (1973)

*L'Écran Fantastique* took the usual route, describing him as a sex-film maker who uses horror as a pretext 'to double the numbers of his victims, the spectators.' In particular, they noted how the dialogue had given much cause for general hilarity.

Rollin was devastated. The film was now unlikely to find any distributor willing to take a chance on it. All the money he had made on his earlier films was invested in **La rose de fer**. Now he had probably lost that too. Eventually the film was picked up by an art-house distributor, but failed to find an audience amongst the devotees of the *'cinéma d'auteurs'*, while its status as a film permissible to anyone over 13 made it anathema to the horror crowd.

For the next few years Rollin was unable to find backers for any of his personal projects. It had always been a problem raising the money for a horror film in France. Low budget films of any sort—and particularly those without recognisable stars or artistic prestige—had little or no box office potential. Now the problem was com-

pounded by the arrival of porno. Suddenly it was no longer possible to guarantee a release by merely adding a dash of sex to the mixture. The public wanted the whole thing, undiluted. Naturally the distributors were not slow to give it to them. Soon all of the small cinemas and chains that had specialised in horror films and low budget features went over to an exclusive diet of wall-to-wall sex.

During this period Rollin worked extensively within the sex film industry. From 1973 to 1978 he made 12 films—all done very cheaply and none of them under his own name (apart from **Phantasmes**). He worked most often under the pseudonym of Michel Gentil, but also used the shared monickers of Robert Xavier and Michel Gand. Of course, it was an open secret who the real director of these films was, and the trade press were not slow to dig the knife in. Even in cases where the prints were shown without credits they didn't hesitate to name Rollin, using the occasion as an excuse to wipe out his earlier

achievements. *Écran*, in reviewing **Hard penetrations**, even went as far as blaming Rollin for the whole wave of French porno; saying that it was his 'half dozen turds a year' that had led to the present situation, killing what was left of indigenous French cinema. Had it not all been so savage and ill-informed, Rollin might perhaps have appreciated the irony.

Few of these films were released outside France. Only **Phantasmes**, made it to the UK in 1978 under the title of **Once Upon a Virgin**. Reduced from its original 88 to a mere 49 minutes, it was dumped onto the fading softcore circuit as a programme filler.

Rollin had tried, unsuccessfully, with **Phantasmes** to make a film that appealed to both markets, combining horror with sex. It contains elements familiar from his earlier work—even a delirious beach-scene—but the low budget, and the problems of using a mostly non-professional cast, weakened the film's ambitions. In future, Rollin would keep the two sides of his career quite separate.

In exactly the same way that writers like Alex Trocchi and William Burroughs had written pseudonymous sex books for publishers like Olympia, Rollin has paid his rent by working as a hired hand on a wide variety of projects. For the Paris based company Eurociné, he worked as technical director on a Spanish co-production called **El lago de los muertos vivientos (Zombies' Lake)** in 1980. Even by the low standards of Eurociné the film was ultra cheap. At one point technical problems meant that the camera was running slowly, making the filmed action appear speeded up. There was no possibility of getting it fixed and time was precious, so Rollin had to teach the cast to act in slow motion to compensate. Such is life in the underbelly of the commercial cinema. Rollin also shot a fifteen minute zombie sequence that turned up in Eurociné's rerelease of Jess Franco's **Virgin Among the Living Dead**. And as late as 1990 he directed another Spanish sequence for Eurociné—**Chasing Barbara**—that was to be added to yet another ancient Franco film for a planned release as a 'new' film.

Occasionally, as with the later **Les trottoirs de Bangkok** (1984), or **Perdues dans New York** (1989), the hack work can be a launching point for something interesting. But more often than not it's a millstone around his neck, confirming all the worst prejudices about his lack of technical ability and poor direction of actors. For many years **Zombies' Lake** was the only 'Rollin' film widely available on video outside France. That it's a total disaster is impossible to deny,

and it did nothing at all for his reputation. His attempts to play down his involvement with it only served to encourage those determined to stick the knife in.

At the end of 1975 a young producer, Jean-Marc Ghanassia, who had seen and admired several of Rollin's earlier films—including **La rose de fer**—approached him with the idea of working together. He only had a small budget, but was sympathetic to Rollin's ideas and was prepared, if the film was done cheaply enough, to let him have his freedom. It seemed like a dream come true. Rollin worked hard on the script for what became **Lèvres de sang** (Lips of Blood) and very soon realised that it was the strongest story he had come up with. It combined all of his previous concerns—memory, time, deprivation of love,—wrapped up in a solidly commercial story, with more than enough space to drop in many personal references, including even a clip from **Frisson**.[22]

(Facing page) Philip Caza's original poster for **Lips of Blood** (1976) was banned by the French censor

HET MEER DER LEVENDE DODEN
ZOMBIE'S LAKE
LE LAC DES MORTS VIVANTS
Un film de/Een film van J.A. LAZER
met/avec Howard Vernon / Pierre Escourrou / Annouchka
Met medewerking van
avec la participation de      Jean Rollin
coproduction Eurociné/J.E. Films

**Back to the Beach**

155

**Lèvres de sang** (1976) ▶
(Facing Page) Sex Star ▶
Brigitte Lahaie in **The
Grapes of Death** (1978)

In the film, Frédéric is at a launch party for a new brand of perfume called Nordia (the name of Lionel Wallmann's production company). He recognises a castle on the advertising poster as somewhere he dimly recalls from his childhood. It suddenly becomes very important for him to discover where the place is and why it seems so significant. At every step he's thwarted by false information and dead end leads. But always a mysterious girl dressed in white appears to lead him on to the next stage of his quest. Eventually he finds the castle and discovers the secret that his family have been trying to keep from him.

Four weeks were set aside for the actual filming, and Rollin had a well worked-out shooting script, when one of the backers suddenly pulled out. There was only a week to go before filming was due to start. They were presented with the choice of either cancelling the film or shooting in three weeks what had been planned for four.

Desperate to make an attempt on what he realised was his best script to date, Rollin spent a frantic week eliminating scenes and writing new ones to compensate. As a result the final

film is, by Rollin's own admission, a little unbalanced. Much of the development of the plot is revealed in voice over and dialogue. The final scenes take place on the beach at Dieppe, and Rollin had to fight tooth and nail with the film's backers to be allowed to shoot there.

In fact that last scene almost led to the end of his career. The producer had hired an expensive coffin, in which the hero and the mysterious woman he had been pursuing would float out to sea. The waves were fiercer than had been expected and soon it was obvious that the empty coffin was being pulled out into deep water. When Rollin dived in to rescue it a particularly vicious wave brought the coffin crashing down on his head, knocking him unconscious. He was only saved at the last minute by his lead actor, Jean-Lou Philippe, who dived into the waves to rescue him.

When the film was released in 1976, at the height of the porn invasion of French cinemas, it flopped miserably. It was not even classed as an 18 release and so the horror fans shunned it along with everybody else. In order to recoup some of the investors' cash Rollin allowed the out-takes and alternative scenes to be used for a porno called **Suce-moi, Vampire** (Suck Me, Vampire). Unfortunately this film has sometimes been described as an 'alternative version' of **Lèvres de sang**, although Rollin is adamant that he didn't make it. The irony of the situation is that **Suce-moi, Vampire** was a considerable hit in Paris sex cinemas.

The following year Rollin met a producer, Claude Guedj, who was interested in making a movie that would combine the zombie film

**Immoral Tales**

and the popular disaster film; **The Poseidon Adventure**, **Towering Inferno**, **Airport** and so on had all recently been big international hits.

Rollin and his producers analysed the disaster films they had seen, and worked out a basic archetype: all of them consisted, essentially, of a group of people trying to get from point A to point B and being beset by a variety of difficulties on the way. It was a very simple formula and seemed to give them a wide choice of subject matter. Rollin came up with two story ideas. Both would entail some kind of ecological catastrophe that was turning people into zombies—but 'conscious' zombies, whose tragedy was that they were aware all the time of what was happening to them. And it would be either wine or tobacco, polluted by a new form of chemical pesticide, that would spark the disaster off.

The producers decided that wine was the thing—although in France poisoned tobacco would have been just as much of a disaster—and Rollin set off to write his script, together with his old collaborator, Jean-Pierre Bouyxou. He was to be given a slightly larger than normal budget, but with the disadvantage that the producers would have more control over the final outcome of the film. This was something new to Rollin. Throughout the script stage, and even during the filming, there was producer interference. Constant additions were made to the script as one or other of the financiers found something in their favourite disaster film that they wanted included.

**Les raisins de la mort** (The Grapes of Death; 1978), as the film was called, was probably the first French gore film. It was certainly the first to include the sort of special effects that were familiar from American films such as **Carrie** and **The Omen**. Most of these effects were provided by an Italian company, as there were no French specialists capable of doing them. However, due to the extreme weather conditions at the time the film was shot—in deepest winter—many of the effects just didn't work. In the end a friend of Rollin's from Brussels, Rafaël Marongiu, ended up providing some of the most satisfying trick shots, in particular a scene of a pitchfork piercing a woman's body.

The film is Rollin's most straightforwardly commercial piece, and was well received by horror fans. It was also shown at specialist festivals and had a good general release. However, as so often with his films, it was not widely seen in Paris. Although it received an unusually large number of reviews in the daily papers—most of them were negative.

Rollin made some money from **Les raisins de la mort.** Together with a young would-be producer, Joel de Lara, he decided to mount a low budget sex film which, over the course of their discussions, became a horror film with sex— pretty much the usual formula for the films Rollin had made his name on. Funding was minimal, and the schedule only allowed for 12 days of shooting. In normal commercial terms an impossibility, but Rollin had always been a fast worker. He planned each shot and sequence in his head to facilitate editing and worked out a script that would require only a minimum number of locations and could be made with a very small cast.

The starting point for **Fascination** (1979)[23] was Jean Lorrain's story *Un verre de sang*, and the image Rollin had was of a group of upper class women, dressed in the costumes of the late nineteenth century bourgeoisie, drinking blood in a clammy abattoir. From this starting point the script grew to include a gang of wandering criminals, an unlikely love-story and a strange, female blood-cult based in a remote château. The project had great potential. There were several effective gore-scenes, enough sex to satisfy the adult audience and it starred Brigitte Lahaie, a former porn-star who was now making the

grade as a straight actress. **Fascination** looked set to consolidate Rollin's success with **Les raisins de la mort** and secure his position in a more mainstream branch of cinema.

Most importantly, the producers had managed to sell the film to UGC, one of the biggest French distributors. It was set to open at twelve screens around Paris—an unheard of prominence for a Rollin film. He was lucky to get his films into three or four cinemas.

All the publicity material was prepared, twelve release prints were struck—in itself a costly move—and then, eight days before the opening, disaster. One of the directors of UGC, who had an old score to settle with the producer's representative, decided to get his revenge by cancelling the bookings. Overnight, it seemed, **Fascination** went from being a film everyone was going to see to a film no-one could see—even if they wanted to.

Eventually a friend of Rollin's, Jacques Orth,[24] pulled strings to get the film into a handful of small Paris cinemas. Unfortunately it was too late. The reviews **Fascination** got in the press were no use since the film had been taken off by the time people read them. This is particularly sad, as for once even the specialist critics had good things to say. In desperation Rollin

Rollin was disappointed with its limited release. It confirmed his opinion that French horror movies would never get the attention they deserved. So when, in 1982, he was offered the chance of working on another thriller he decided to give it a try. **Les échappées** might not have been a total success but Rollin was keen to explore other areas of filmmaking. Taking risks appealed to the anarchist in him.

The producer and distributor André Samarcq, whose company Les Distributors Associés had handled both **Viol** and **La vampire nue**, had recently spent his honeymoon in Bangkok. He had brought back a couple of hours of 8mm footage, which he thought could be used as the basis of a film. Rollin watched the footage and soon realised that the idea was a non-starter. The shots of tourist sights, hotel swimming pools and Bangkok streets were not even usable as stock-shots for exteriors. Still, there was the possibility of making a film, so Rollin pretended to be very enthusiastic about the idea. Through his contacts, Samarcq arranged a very prestigious release in some big Paris cinemas that all had gaps in their programming schedules. The disadvantage being that the film would have to be written and shot in record time to be ready for the planned release date.

Rollin came up with a title—**Les trottoirs de Bangkok** (The Sidewalks of Bangkok)—and suggested a spy melodrama. Then he began to work on the script, bringing in some ideas from the old serials he loved and using locations he already had in mind—the docks at Le Havre, a railway shunting yard and so on. Two days later the ten page script was ready.

Rollin knew that he had to have an Asian girl as one of the leads and he auditioned all the actresses he could find. His first choice dropped out just as shooting was about to begin. Time was short, so he left for Le Havre with the crew while Lionel Wallmann stayed behind in Paris to finish the casting. The first day passed and Wallmann didn't appear. By mid-day on the second day Rollin was desperate. He realised that if he didn't find a leading lady at once he would have to abandon the film and somehow explain to the producers why he had wasted their precious time and money.

Then, far off on the other end of the quay, he saw Wallmann's car approaching and his hopes were raised. But as the car came closer he saw that there was only one person in it. His heart sank. The car stopped and Wallmann got out. As he did so, the passenger door also opened and out stepped the tiny, waif like figure of

Yoko—the lead actress Wallmann had discovered for **Les trottoirs de Bangkok**. Yoko was so small that when seated in Wallmann's big Mercedes her head was below the level of the dashboard.

Rollin remembered that he had met Yoko very briefly the previous year, but was not aware that she had any acting experience.[27] Nervously, he welcomed her onto the set and began to explain the scene they were about to shoot. She had read the script in the car on the way down and was all ready to go. The first shot called for her to climb down a perilous rope-ladder attached to the side of a ship and jump into the icy water... which was made even less attractive by the fact that it was full of jellyfish. After only a few minutes preparation, and with hardly a second's hesitation, she was clambering down the ladder as though she had been doing it all her life.

Rollin was amazed. He realised that he had discovered a natural actress. **Les trottoirs de**

◀ (Facing page) Françoise Blanchard as **The Living Dead Girl** (1982)

**Bangkok** demonstrates one thing above all others—that little Yoko was destined to be a star. Astonishingly, for a project set up in fifteen days from scratch, the film went on to be one of Rollin's biggest successes.

Later, a critic was to write that Jean Rollin had made two good films in his career—**Le viol du vampire** and **Les trottoirs de Bangkok**—and that in many ways they were the same film. Each has the same quality of improvisation, the same playfully pretentious dialogue and wilful script development, as well as the same cliffhanger structure reminiscent of the old serials. It's almost, Rollin admits, as though you could have a card every ten minutes or so saying 'To be continued....'

At this point it seemed as though Rollin's career was going into reverse. Nearly 20 years on from **Le viol de vampire** he was back to doing improvised film-making, working with a small cast of friends and non-professionals, turning out a surreal melodrama in double quick time. That the film was a success is some compensation, but the main reason Rollin survives these ups and downs is that to him film-making remains an adventure. He loves turning vague notions and fantasies into actual images and sequences. That's one of the reasons he films so fast—he wants to catch the idea while it's still fresh and not work it over until it becomes stale and lifeless.

It's also one of the reasons why he takes on projects that perhaps other film-makers wouldn't risk. He enjoys the challenge, the feeling of creating something new that might produce unexpected results.

Amongst the cast of **La morte vivante** was Dominique Treillou, who had worked as Rollin's assistant on a number of other projects. Treillou lived in a flat in the Latin Quarter of Paris and one of his neighbours was a writer and musician, Gérard Dôle, who had published two collections of stories—*The New Adventures of Harry Dickson.* The original Harry Dickson stories had been written by Jean Ray, a Belgian fantasy writer whom many critics now rank alongside Poe and Lovecraft.[28]

Together with Marie Paule Vadunthin, Dôle had also written the panels for an illustrated book based on the character of Harry Dickson that had been put together by the photographer and designer Jean-Michel Nicollet. Previewed on the 'hip' TV show *Apostrophes*, the book had been quite a success and there was a lot of talk about turning it into a film. A smart idea, as the illustrations had been conceived in the form of lobby cards from an imaginary B-movie.

Dôle and Vadunthin wrote a treatment called **La griffe d'Horus** (The Claw of Horus) and began to hawk it round the studios. They soon discovered that neither Jean Ray nor Harry Dickson were flavour of the month with film companies. Although revered by lovers of the bizarre and with a huge cult following across Europe, the stories of Jean Ray were considered to be unfilmable. Furthermore, the rights to the Harry Dickson stories were owned, so he claimed, by Anatole Dauman of Argos Films. He had bought them years before for a planned version to be directed by Alain Resnais, starring Dirk Bogarde as '*le Sherlock Holmes américain*'. Some scenes had been shot back in the early 1960's, and there had later been a vague suggestion that Borowczyk was interested in the project, but to date no film had appeared.

Gérard Dôle tried hard to find backers for the film, and even talked to one of Spielberg's assistants who was passing through Paris. The man was intrigued by the idea but the project foundered on the impossibility of translating the concept of '*fantastique*' into American terms.

"So it's a horror story?"

"No.....Not exactly"

"A thriller?"

"No....Not really."

"So what is it?"

"Well....it's—*'le fantastique'.*"

Gérard Dôle was aware of Jean Rollin and had seen many of his early films. When Treillou introduced them, Dôle said to Rollin: "If anyone can film Harry Dickson, it's you!"

In the mid-eighties the *Arsène Lupin*[29] TV series was very successful in France. Taking this as their model, Rollin and Dôle adapted **La griffe d'Horus** as a series of 25 minute TV segments. They took it round the studios, but no-one was interested. Eventually, one cold October day, they decided that enough was enough. They would shame the TV companies into action by shooting a dummy pilot for the series and letting them see what could be done with a good idea and no money.

One Sunday the cast and minuscule crew (Rollin and Dominique Treillou) gathered by the Seine, which was serving as the Thames that day, to shoot the first sections of the pilot. Again, as with **Le viol du vampire** and **Les trottoirs de Bangkok**, it was a group of friends, enthusiasts and non-professionals. Although their professional worth in other spheres was considerable—Jean-Michel Nicollet, for example, was to play Harry Dickson, Gérard Dôle the part of a London bobby and the famous photographer Robert Doisneau had offered to take the publicity stills.

Shooting, on video tape, took a day and the footage was edited down in another day to 22 minutes, roughly the length of one episode of *Arsène Lupin*. As photographs taken on set that day show, the film is full of the bizarre, anachronistic and almost comical touches that mark out the Harry Dickson originals. Gérard Dôle says that everyone working on the project knew that they didn't have the means to do anything but sketch out their intentions, so they decided to make a virtue out of the cheapness of it all. To make something in the style of the notorious **Plan 9 From Outer Space** or **Horror of Spider Island**.

Sadly, the completed sketch of **La griffe d'Horus** did no more to impress the TV companies than the original script had. It became just one in a long series of disappointments that the 1980's brought to Rollin. The low budget industry in France had collapsed years before. What would have been a small film was now made for TV. And pretty soon Rollin came to discover that he was effectively blacklisted by the main TV companies in France. In any case, horror or fantasy projects didn't interest them. Those were things they preferred to leave to the Americans. It was for these reasons as much as for any that Rollin began to turn his attention to the writing of books rather than screenplays. He was tired of having to tailor his ideas to fit a low, low budget. On the page, his imagination could soar. If he wanted, he could set one scene

in Tibet and the next in a crowded Paris street, without having to worry about special effects and retakes.

His first novel, *Une Petite Fille Magique* (The Magic Child), was published in 1988. The company that released it, Les Cahiers du Shibboleth, was run by the same Francis Giraudet who, all those years before, had written the letter in praise of **Le viol du vampire** in *Midi-Minuit Fantastique*. An example of the kind of loyalty that Rollin inspires in those who believe in him.

Like many of his films, *Une Petite Fille Magique* has the atmosphere of a strange fairy tale. It concerns the adventures of two young girls, Marie and Michèle (the names are familiar from **Requiem pour un vampire** and **Les échappées**), who meet in an empty house in the middle of a wood. There is the vague impression of someone having just left the house; perhaps a young woman with a younger daughter....? Perhaps even Marie and Michèle themselves...? Although the events of that night are not dramatic in the conventional sense, Marie is marked by them in such a way that it makes a return to her previous life impossible. Later, she meets the 'little magic girl' of the title who leads her to the beach, just before dawn, where she has a revelation that helps her make sense of the loss of her friend Michèle.

One of the features of the book is the absence of any male characters. It's a totally female world. And yet, throughout, the presence of Jean Rollin, of the author, is very strong; commenting directly on the action, retelling the story for us and, at several points, addressing the girls directly—even though they can't hear him, of course: "Marie, Marie, little girl lost in the woods, if only you knew how I love you, Marie."

▼ Super detective Harry Dickson, from **La griffe d'Horus** (1990)

This relationship between the author and his characters is taken a stage further in Rollin's next book *Les Demoiselles de L'Étrange* (The Sisters of Mystery), published in 1990 by Filipacchi, the big, Paris-based publishing house.

In this exotic adventure story, the two heroines, Estelle and Edwige, are rescued from an institution by the strange, mystical figure of "The Master". As he sends them off on a series of increasingly hair-raising adventures, combating all manner of physical and spiritual evils, The Master travels with them, telepathically, seeing through their eyes, talking to them and warning them of impending disasters. The story is a fantastic trip through the worlds of Rollin's literary heroes—Gaston Leroux and Jean Ray. Strange mediaeval demons haunt the streets of Paris; mythical monsters such as the Medusa are brought back to life. There are many cinematic references, not only to the old serials but also to Rollin's own films.

His next book, *L'Enfer Privé* (Private Hell), published in 1991, has a more traditional thriller plot, partly influenced by the 1932 film **The Most Dangerous Game**. It features two women, but this time as opposing lead characters. In a story planned originally as a film to star Yoko and Brigitte Lahaie, Rollin has a sophisticated

and cruel Parisienne (obviously Lahaie!) discover a young Asiatic girl—a refugee—living wild on the beach. She takes her in, but plans to use her as human prey in the expensive entertainments she lays on for rich businessmen.

*Les Deux Orphelines Vampires* (Little Orphan Vampires), published in 1993 by the mass market imprint Fleuve Noir,[30] is Rollin's most commercial book so far. Again the main characters are two young women. To the world they appear as harmless blind girls, but when night falls their sight returns and they wander the streets of Paris in a joyous search for blood and sensation. The story is simple and gripping, and Rollin's very black sense of humour runs right through it.

His next film project gave him the opportunity to use some of the ideas that he had been developing through his novels.

In 1985, Rollin was approached by Jacques Nahum, who was the producer of the successful TV series *Arsène Lupin*. He needed some footage of New York for a TV film he was putting together. Knowing Rollin's no-nonsense approach to filming and his ability to improvise his way out of disaster, Nahum asked him if he would be prepared to travel to the States with a film crew. Rollin agreed, hoping he could shoot some extra footage that might later be worked into a film of his own—although he had no script: only a title **Perdues dans New York** (Lost in New York).

The resulting one hour film is a perfect example of how Rollin works. Pascal Martinet has written that Rollin practices a *'cinema référentiel'*, using influences not only from other film-makers, but also from his own work. Sequences that he has used in one film will be continued and refined in later works.

Just before he started editing the footage shot for **Perdues dans New York**, Rollin was called in to shoot some scenes for **Emmanuelle 6**. The previous year, his agent had heard through the grapevine that Alain Siritsky, the film's producer, was trying to turn the series into a more action/adventure type of product. Something along the lines of **Romancing the Stone** or the Indiana Jones films, with elements from the old serials and melodramas. Siritsky was looking for a writer familiar with the territory, and Rollin seemed to fit the bill.

He submitted a script, and the film began shooting in Venezuela under the direction of Bruno Zincone. With about an hour's worth of usable footage in the can, the production ran

The title of Rollin's 1993 ▶ book was a reference to a very well known, much filmed, French melodrama from the 19th century ▼

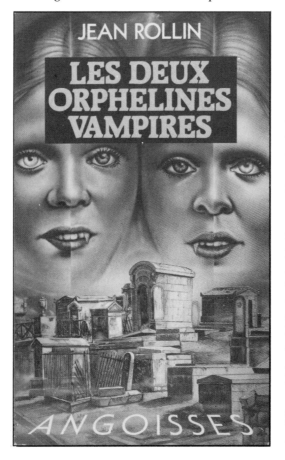

**Immoral Tales**

into trouble. Zincone was called off to another project and Siritsky was left with a pile of film that made no sense at all. Only the more dramatic exterior and location scenes had been filmed. None of the bits in between that made sense of it had been shot.

Rollin constructed a framing story to knit the footage together. Emmanuelle, having been found wandering in the Venezuelan jungle with no memories of her former life, is brought to a strange château, where an unconventional doctor uses shock techniques to bring back her memory. The film contains some typical Rollin touches. The theme of lost identity and memory painfully regained runs throughout his films and books, as does the idea of using fetish objects and images to bring the past alive. The doctor, played by an actor who looks remarkably like Rollin himself, says to Emmanuelle at one point: "Your memories are like rusty muscles. They need to move. To be provoked. To be challenged."

Late one day on location, as the crew were ready to call it a day, Rollin had an idea for a sequence using the talents of one of the extras—a black actress, Melissa, who worked the clubs as a snake dancer. Fortunately she had her snake with her. The shot was set up in double quick time as the light faded. There was no music. The actress had to improvise everything. It was a classic one take situation and it worked so well that Rollin later restaged the scene the following year for **Perdues dans New York**, using the same actress—this time without her snake.

Almost everyone who has been important to Rollin over the years is involved in one way or another with **Perdues.** Much of the action takes place by the sea, and the main protagonists are two young girls—once again Marie and Michèle. They meet by chance in a country churchyard, and the discovery of a magic wooden idol takes them on a voyage through time and space, bringing them, fifty years later, back to the familiar beach at Dieppe where Rollin's career had first started. The two girls discover a cave beneath the cliffs, they enter and the narrator—Rollin himself—tells us that there is only one way in and no way out.

In many ways the film is as an examination of the idea of exoticism and the strength of dreams. An early sequence traces the history of the two girls through Rollin's own films and through a series of static images taken from old book covers and illustrations from the turn of the century, often exotic jungle scenes and adventure stories. The black priestess from **Emmanuelle 6** dances on the beach. She becomes a stone idol that one of the girls finds and which they use to release the power of their imagination to take them on their voyage of discovery—to New York, to Rome, and finally into the secret cave. Throughout the film there are references to an end, to finality: "magic only works once," says Michèle, now an old lady, as she throws away the wooden idol. "Perhaps a new magic girl will come to take us away on a new voyage of discovery."

That journey, when it comes, will be the final one..... death?

Rollin has hinted that **Perdues dans New York** is something of a testament to his film-making period. If **Le viol du vampire** was a statement of intent, then **Perdues** can be seen as an index of all the themes he has worked on; above all the themes of time and memory. Writing is now the most important part of his working life. **Perdues** may well stand as a final salute to his twenty five year struggle to find a place of his own inside the commercial film world.

As a sort of coda to **Perdues**, Rollin made one film in 1993—**La femme dangereuse/Killing Car**. Originally the film was to be released under the name of Michel Gentil. However, as he worked on the script, Rollin realised that he could weave some of his more personal themes into it. The story was very simple. A mysterious woman dressed in black murders a succession of apparently unconnected individuals, leaving a toy car at each killing as a sort of signature.

The basic idea is drawn closely from William Irish's novel *The Bride Wore Black*. Not surprisingly Rollin isn't really interested in the plot, and he uses it to make his most self-referential film to date.

**Killing Car** is a series of set pieces, each of them drawn in some way from Rollin's earlier films. The opening scene is set in a breakers' yard, with a cast of characters who might well have strayed in from **Les échappées**. For the second killing, the assassin hides inside a grandfather clock—as in **Frisson**—and kills with a scythe, in a scene drawn from **Fascination**. Outtakes from **Perdues dans New York** introduce the next couple of slayings, followed by scenes in a sleazy, oriental-style nightclub that could have come straight out of **Les trottoirs de Bangkok**. The last two murders feature actors who have played a large part in Rollin's career—Jean-Pierre Bouyxou and Jean-Lou Philippe.

Rollin himself plays the mysterious woman's lover. We see him at the very end of the film, his head swathed in bandages that cover his eyes. She embraces him as he sits behind the wheel of an old American car, [31] like the one driven by the vampire queen in **Le viol**. She tells him: "Now the last one is dead. Your suffering is over." Then she kills him .

What it all means is anyone's guess. Maybe Rollin is having a playful dig at his career, symbolically killing off his own back catalogue.

Such a series of private references probably sounds self-conscious and sterile but, as we've shown, it's a system Rollin has always used to construct his films. The source of the images he presents lies deep inside him. They emerge through an unconscious process of selection. Often he's not really aware of any connections until shooting has finished. This is particularly true of **Killing Car**, which was made very quickly with little time for reflection. The final shot of the film has the heroine, now sunk into a catatonic state, walking slowly across a huge empty field. It was only when the final editing had been done that Rollin realised the shot was almost identical, in framing and content, to a key scene from his first feature **Le viol du vampire**.

Self-referential—certainly; but sterile—never. The raw material out of which Rollin constructs his films always has a solid, emotional core. In this final shot the heroine sings a little song to herself as she walks slowly into camera:
   "*...Il y a longtemps que je t'aime*
   *Jamais je ne t'oublirai*"
   (I've loved you such a long time
   I never will forget)
This kind of slow burning emotional intensity is at the heart of his films, even the quickest and cheapest of them.

**Part Two - *Themes and Variations***

*"And now the adventure can begin...So what happens next?"*

Emmanuelle, from **Emmanuelle 6**

Jean Rollin has described his first full length film, **Le viol du vampire**, as a kind of trailer for the rest of his career. It's interesting to speculate on what would have happened if his earlier film, **L'itinéraire marin**, had been completed. It's a much more traditional piece and, with the involvement of Marguerite Duras as co-writer and actors like Gaston Modot and Chauffard, much more prestigious than the ultra low budget **Viol**. It's highly probable that his career would have been very different from the way it eventually turned out. The early 1960's was the

time of the *'nouvelle vague'*, when young men with cameras were making their mark. Rollin could never have become another François Truffaut—but perhaps he might have been another Jacques Rivette...?

**Le viol du vampire** caused a great fuss at the time of its release. Now, in the context of Rollin's subsequent films, it makes much more sense. All of the themes and obsessions that he would work on and elaborate over the next 25 years were already there, in embryo.

Asked about these scenes and characters who pop up in film after film, Rollin merely shrugs and says he doesn't know why they come to him. He tries to avoid them but they are always there: "Perhaps a psychologist could tell you." Yet, because of their place within his personal mythology, the images he uses are actually very

▲ Jean Rollin wrote the original script for **Emmanuelle 6** (1987)

**Back to the Beach**

LES DISTRIBUTEURS ASSOCIES Films Modernes Films ABC

présentent

LE FRISSON des VAMPIRES

un film de Jean Rollin
EASTMANCOLOR

specific and richly resonant. In each film they acquire—or reveal—new levels of meaning, rather like a pearl being built up layer by layer over a grain of sand.

Take, for example, the shots from **Viol** featuring a game of skittles. First of all we see a blind girl attempting to roll the skittles down, and then an apparently unconnected shot of skittles on the beach, falling as the waves wash over them. In Rollin's iconography this image of skittles connects directly with the rows of wooden stakes stretching out to sea from the beach at Dieppe where so many scenes of his films are set. He links this also with the standing stones scattered about the Breton countryside which make that such an attractive landscape for him, leading finally to the images of crosses and tall tombstones that are also key motifs. So much so that he made a whole film, *La rose de fer*, to explore this fascination with stone and statues.

The problem for many viewers is that they are always trying to work out what these images 'symbolise' and who these characters 'really' are. Actually they don't symbolise anything. In the same way that Jess Franco uses series characters—Orloff, Radek, Al Pereira—in many of his films and says that they are now a part of his life—"old friends"—so Rollin gives us little glimpses, with each of his films, of the people and places who figure in his own universe.

What Rollin does in films is actually closer to what novelists do. Taking scenes and images from his childhood—memories of holidays spent by the sea, feelings of adolescent confusion, fear of loss, he has built them up, scene by scene, in each subsequent film until they have assumed almost mythic proportions. And what Rollin shows, as all artists do, is that this well of images we carry around inside us is almost

bottomless and constantly renews itself. If we look hard and deep enough the spring need never run dry.

Many critics assume that stories are unimportant to Rollin. That they are just hooks on which to hang these images. Too often this view is not based on viewing the films but from seeing isolated stills. David Hogan, for example, in *Dark Romance*, mentions Rollin's 'visually dense approach,' and claims it is achieved 'at the expense of genuine substance....His images are as provocative as those in a glossy men's magazine, and about as thoughtful.'

This completely misrepresents the way in which the films are constructed. They contain startling images—more, perhaps, in the early than later films—but they work through the movement of these images, through montage. What Rollin does he does through the use of imagery *and* narrative to create an atmosphere of mystery. The problem for many viewers is that although the outward trappings of his films are those of the horror movie, their narrative style is like an old serial. As Jean-Marie Sabatier noted: 'his sources are Feuillade and Gasnier and not Whale and Fisher. His heroines have more to do with Pearl White than with Barbara Steele.' For example, there's an incident in **Trottoirs** where two rival agents are tied to a railway track in the path of an advancing train. They are rescued in the nick of time by their dog, Rudy, in a scene straight out of one of the old cliffhangers.

And just as the serials never ended, so Rollin freely admits that the endings of his own films are often flawed. They don't really resolve, they just fade out. Figures who appear in one film return in another. With each reappearance, these clowns, tragic runaways and sad vampires are slightly different but always essentially the same. They are like wandering spirits, who incarnate themselves anew in each subsequent film

In interviews, Rollin has said—almost apologetically—that he is not a horror film maker. This just happens to be the type of cinema that most closely parallels his own preoccupation with eerie images and atmosphere. He uses horror settings as a convenient stage on which to place his own dramas. The familiar trappings then draw us into his world, just as many of the characters in his films journey from the banal into the strange. For example, the runaway girls in **Requiem**, the honeymooning couple in **Frisson**, the journey to the lost castle of **Lèvres de sang** and the trip to the graveyard in **La rose de fer**.

Skittles on the beach ▼
from **Le viol du vampire** (1968)

At the end of their journey, Rollin's characters are often forced to confront things that are difficult to live with. So much so that they will either try to deny them (the man in **Viol** who keeps saying that there are no such things as vampires) or be misled by others (the many false leads in **Vampire nue** and the obstacles put in the path of Frédéric in **Lèvres de sang**). Finally they have no choice. The real curse in so many of Rollin's films is not the curse of the undead, but the curse of memory regained. The girls in **Viol** lose themselves in dreams of being vampires and Frédéric in **Lèvres** has lost his whole childhood until a chance encounter brings it flooding back. So what happens if you try to live without your memories, without the past? The answer, in **La nuit des traquées**, is a form of living death, that leaves the sufferers helpless prey to the grey forces of repression and dismal order—"the dead wood of love rotting under the skulls of those who live without love", as Prévert describes it in **Les enfants du paradis**.

If **Viol** is a trailer, then **Perdues dans New York** is a sort of index to everything Rollin has done. Here we see how far the themes and images outlined in **Viol** have been refined and mutated over the years. In particular it shows how the far the two female characters, who feature in nearly all his films, have come.

It's in **Viol** that the two girls first appear. During a brief shot in the second half we see them playing an invisible piano, side by side, like two elfin twins. In the following film, **La vampire nue**, they have a more important role as the servants/sexual playthings of Radamante who eventually turn against him. In **Frisson** they are the guardians of the castle and in **Requiem** they come centre stage as the two 'virgins for the vampire'. In each subsequent film Rollin adds more detail to their roles, making them less like twins and more like two halves of the same personality—like de Sade's Justine and Juliette. Eventually, as in **Perdues dans New York**, one cannot live without the other, making the dualism even more explicit. In his last book to date, *Les Deux Orphelines Vampires*, Rollin takes the adventure of Marie and Michèle about as far as it can go. Hounded by a vengeful mob, the two vampire orphans take refuge in a cemetery. With nowhere else to run, they lift up the iron trapdoor on an old tomb and leap into the darkness.

The way that Rollin uses these figures and weaves them into his work is not unique but, for a film-maker working in the genres he does, it's very rare. The hostile reaction towards him, from film fans and critics, is often a result of

▲ **La femme dangereuse** (1993)

their failure to recognise exactly what he's doing. Why, they ask, can't he make films like other people? If he's going to make horror films he should make 'classic' ones—like Hammer films.

In 1973 the critic Jean-Marie Sabatier wrote a piece in the horror magazine *Vampirella* called 'In Defence of the Rollinade'. His sympathetic critique outlined all of Rollin's faults and strengths.

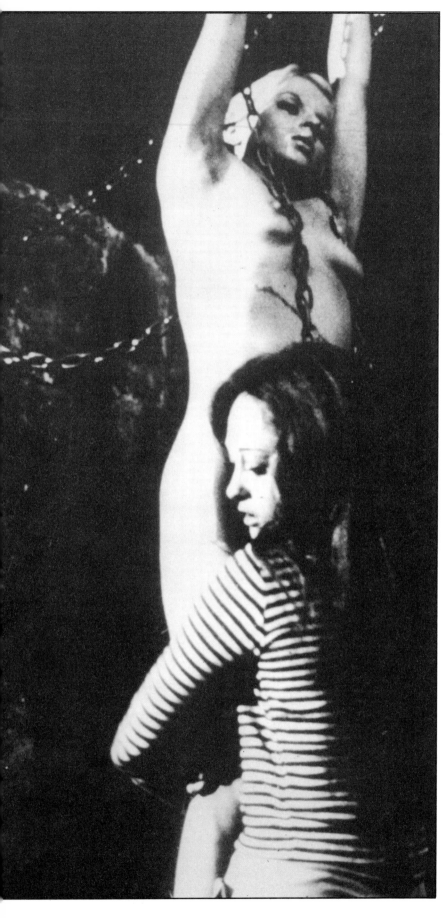

Considering that the best—and most typical—films were still to come it's a remarkably astute analysis. He begins by defining the 'Rollinade'—cheap films full of the cliches of horror cinema, sprinkled with the trappings of pornography—and then goes on to point out that Rollin's strengths were, in fact, those very weaknesses that the sneering put-down 'Rollinade' was meant to underline. They were his trademarks. With only a handful of films to his name he had already created a genre of his own. And he had done it from within the most unsympathetic arena imaginable—the low budget horror film.

It's a mistake to think that the horror audience is an open-minded one. In fact they are even more closed in their perceptions of what makes a good film than the mainstream audience who consume whatever is laid before them. Horror fans have fixed ideas of what they want. Rollin has dared to be different, and in doing so he's laid his heart on the line. His films are probably the most personal testament that any film-maker has ever produced. Personal not just because he weaves them out of his own fantasies and fears. They are even more unique in the sense that he has created his very own sub-genre of the fantastic. And that's why they call them 'Rollinades'.

In the mainstream commercial cinema, someone like Jean Rollin would never be able to make the kinds of films he wants to. Now that the low budget industry has collapsed, opportunities are even thinner on the ground. The B-film world used to be seen as a place where greater freedom could be gained than by working on big budget productions. This was probably true in the days of the Hollywood studio system. There the producer's only requirements would be a good title, some exploitable angle in the story (horror, sex, crime), and a budget so low it would be impossible not to recoup costs. Against this kind of background film-makers like Val Lewton, Edgar Ulmer and Anthony Mann were able to fashion some highly personal and poetic little films out of the raw material they were given.

Now, as Rollin admits sadly, with costs so high and returns so low, everyone is much more cautious. Without the backing of TV very few films get made in France today, and for a director like himself, who is on the blacklist of at least one big TV chain, work of any sort is in short supply.

Whether a viewer responds kindly to the films of Jean Rollin is very much a matter of personal taste, perhaps more so than with most film-makers. What finally has to be asked is whether

Jean Rollin is a film-maker who should be taken seriously.

The question is difficult to answer for one important, and superficially devastating, reason. First of all you have to decide whether Rollin is actually a film-maker at all.

To put that point into a proper context it's necessary to define what a film-maker is. Whether it's simply a question of being a technician, or if other factors are just as important. If, for example, Steven Spielberg is your model—then, no—Jean Rollin is no film-maker. His films are not mass market fantasies. They're too wistful and abstract for that. Neither is he, like Joseph H. Lewis, a skilled artisan who can take any B-movie project and turn it into something robust and personal. Nor can he, like Hitchcock, sublimate his secret fears through montage and skillful direction of actors into something loved by cinema fans as well as critics.

Rollin is not any of these things. The awkwardness of his hired hand projects show that he's uneasy and uninterested in making anything that doesn't reflect his romantic obsessions. If the project can't be transformed into the shape he feels comfortable with, then he's a barely competent technician at best.

And Rollin isn't interested in being just a technician. He's not a nuts and bolts man. This explains his quick way of working, his one shot style. He gets bored having to repeat things too many times. He enjoys the spontaneity, the chance discoveries that come from improvisation. That's why he no longer works from a pre-prepared shooting script.

LES TROTTOIRS DE BANGKOK

So Jean Rollin is not a film-maker; or, at least, not in the sense in which we've chosen to define one. But you have to go beyond a technical appraisal to discover the true worth of Jean Rollin. He may not be a film-maker in the conventional sense—so what? The film schools are churning out competent technicians by the yard. Rollin is something much rarer and more cherishable. He's a weaver of dreams. Like Parsifal, returning to the barren kingdom with the secret of the Sangreal, he has the power to move us all with his out-of-step romanticism and wistful idealism.

As a kid of seventeen Rollin came to England. One day he found himself, as you might expect, by the sea—in Bexhill, of all places. He met a girl there and he kissed her goodbye on the beach. "And I have never forgotten her," he says now. Of course he hasn't; she's there in almost all his films. At their best they are expressions of just that sort of moment, when our lives seem to belong to us. When we feel the enormity of all the possibilities that stretch out before us.

There are many ways of measuring success, but the one the world chooses most often is material wealth. Those who spend their life chasing dreams are usually seen as fools and rarely as heroes. But as Jacques Prévert said, in a quote Rollin puts at the beginning of *Les Demoiselles de l'Etrange* :

'There is nothing sadder than an idiot, but nothing more beautiful than a fool.'

"The things I do for Art." ▲
Jean-Lou Philippe in
**Lèvres de sang**

### ROLLIN FILMOGRAPHY

All France (Fr), unless otherwise indicated.

1958    **Les amours jaunes** (short)
1961    **Ciel de cuivre** (short)
1963    **L'itinéraire marin** (unfinished)
1964    **Vivre en Espagne** (documentary)
1965    **Les pays loins** (short)
1968    **Le viol du vampire: La reine des vampires**
1969    **La vampire nue/The Nude Vampire/Das Lustschloss der grausamen Frauen**
1970    **Le frisson des vampires/Sex and the Vampire/ Terror of the Vampires/Sexualterror der entfesselten Vampire**
1972    **Requiem pour un vampire/Vierges et vampires/ Caged Virgins/Crazed Virgins**
1973    **La rose de fer/La nuit du cimetière/The Crystal Rose**
1974    **Les démoniaques/ Demoniacs** (Fr/Be)
1975    **Phantasmes/ Phantasmes pornographiques/ Once Upon a Virgin/ The Seduction of Amy**
1976    **Lèvres de sang**
1978    **Les raisins de la mort/Pesticide/Foltermühle der gefangenen Frauen**
1979    **Fascination**
1980    **La nuit des traquées/ Filles traquées**
1981    **Les échappées/Les paumées du petit matin/ Fugue mineure/A couteaux tirés/Les meutrières/Die Entkommenen**
1983    **La morte vivante/The Living Dead Girl** (Fr/It)
1984    **Les trottoirs de Bangkok/Bangkok interdit/Killstreet**
1989    **Perdues dans New York** (short)
1990    **La griffe d'Horus.** (video short)

1993    **La femme dangereuse/Killing Car**
1995    **Les deux orphelines vampires**

### PSEUDONYMOUS FILMS

1973    **Jeunes filles impudiques** (Michel Gentil)
1974    **Tout le monde il en a deux/Bacchanales sexuelles** (Michel Gentil)
1975    **Douces pénétrations/La romancière lubrique/ Introductions / Gode Story** (Michel Gentil)
        **Hard Penetration** (Michel Gentil)
1976    **Vibrations sensuelles/Vibrations sexuelles** (Michel Gentil)
        **La Comtesse Ixe/Sueurs chaudes** (Michel Gentil)
1977    **Saute moi dessus** (Michel Gentil)
        **Lèvres entrouvertes/Monique, lèvres entrouvertes pour sexe chaud** (Michel Gentil)
        **Positions Danoises** (Michel Gentil)
1978    **Petites pensionnaires impudiques** (Michel Gentil)
1980    **Pénétrations vicieuses**
        **Le lac des morts vivants/El lago de los muertos vivientes/Zombies' Lake**(Sp/Fr)
        Rollin was asked to help out on this film by Eurociné, who were its French co-producers. He says that he was actually off on holiday when the phone call came—he even had his bags packed! He only read the script on his way to shoot the first set-up and admits that he really had no idea what it was about until he was half way through the shooting. To reassure the Spanish co-producers, a Spanish pseudonym—J.A. Lazer—was used on the film. According to Tim Lucas, Rollin also shot the zombie inserts used by Eurociné in Franco's **Christina, princesse de L'érotisme** when they rereleased the film as **Virgin Among the Living Dead**.
1985    **Ne prends pas les poulets pour des pigeons** (Michel Gentil)
        Rollin claims that this police comedy was actually written and directed by its star Jean-Claude Benhamou. The film was co-produced by Lionel Wallmann's Nordia Films.
1990    **Chasing Barbara**. A 20 minute sequence shot in Spain for Eurociné with music by Daniel White; to be combined with old footage shot by Franco to make a 'new' Eurociné release. None of the participants knew the title of the original film or of the intended result. A classic piece of Eurosoup.

### ALSO

1962    **Un cheval pour deux** (dir. Jean-Marc Thibault) ; Rollin Assistant Director
1987    **Emmanuelle 6** (Bruno Zincone) Rollin wrote the script and directed some additional scenes when the production ran into trouble.

1989    **Cabinet particulier**. Rollin wrote the script of this episode in the TV series **Drôles d'histoires**. It was directed by Philippe Gallardi

## WRITINGS

*Aujourd'hui Gaston Leroux*. A series that ran in *Midi Minuit Fantastique* numbers 23 and 24
*Les pays loins*
*Une petite fille magique*
*Les demoiselles de l'étrange*
*Enfer privé*
*Dialogues sans fin*
*Les deux orphelines vampires*. Fleuve Noir are publishing this book as a serial in five parts:
Part 2—*Anissa*; Part 3—*Les voyageuses*;
Part 4—*Les pillardes*; Part 5—*Les incendiares*
*Bestialité*

## FILM PROJECTS

**Une statue de chair**
**Les demoiselles de l'étrange**
**La louve sanglante**

---

[1] In this way he worked on Jean Delannoy's **Notre Dame de Paris** and George Lampin's **Crime and Punishment**, starring the great Jean Gabin

[2] He worked as a general assistant and editor, leaving the following year to train at the big CTM processing laboratories, eventually working for two years with Joseph Tzipine as assistant editor on musical soundtracks.

[3] He made the first recording of Prévert's song *Les Feuilles Mortes* which, translated into English by Johnny Mercer, became the famous ballad *Autumn Leaves*.

[4] See Appendix for more on Losfeld and *Midi-Minuit Fantastique*

[5] See Appendix.

[6] The Italian comic strips were called *fumetti*—it means 'puffs of smoke,' because of the speech bubbles that the characters talk in. *Fumetti neri*—or 'black' *fumetti* were the adult strips. *Bande dessinée* means 'drawn strips'. Losfeld's books were big hardbacks—rather like today's Graphic Novels.

[7] Rollin himself drew the panels and wrote the script, some of which was so small and complex that a special magnifying glass was given out with the early editions to enable readers to make it out! In keeping with the wild spirit of the project, all the plates became lost in a fire after the first edition had been published and *Saga of Xam* is now of legendary scarcity in its

original form. Rollin's association with the artists of the new wave of *bande dessinée* continued, and Druillet was to design the posters for three of his features (**Le viol du vampire**, **La vampire nue** and **Le frisson des vampires**) while Philip Caza contributed several startling images for the publicity material of his later **Lèvres de sang**. Druillet also pops up in the cast of **Viol** as a mad peasant and in **Requiem pour un vampire** he plays one of the vampire's sex-crazed slaves.

[8] See Appendix for more on Leroux

[9] To raise the money for the project, Selsky called in favours from all the American ex-pats that he knew in Paris. He promised them roles in the film if they stumped up enough cash. The old man, whose story begins the film, was a doctor. His French was far from perfect, but he got by. Others were given non-speaking parts. The man who plays the deformed idiot in the film was also an American chum of Selsky's. All he had to do was grunt and look menacing.

[10] Jaqueline Siegers, who plays the Vampire Queen. She had also been involved in the creation of *Saga of Xam,* and was a psychiatric nurse at the hospital where Druillet worked for a time.

[11] In a cut and dubbed form as **The Nude Vampire**. It played for a few weeks at the Classic in Great Windmill Street in a double bill with Ernst Hofbauer's **Swinging Wives**, receiving a few good reviews. David McGillivray, in the *Monthly Film Bulletin*, described the film as 'more hallucinatory than erotic' and noted the 'bizarre extravagance' of the costume design; had he known how cheaply all this extravagance had been achieved he might have been even more impressed.

[12] She was the widow of Emile Natan, whose company, Les Films Modernes, had been in business since the late forties, producing films like **Manèges** (1949) and **Michel Strogoff** (1956). Madame Natan had taken over the company on her husband's death and was keen on producing a film herself. She didn't want to do a costume drama or anything too expensive, but something contemporary, something to appeal to the young, film-hungry French audience. With this in mind, she had met many of the more prestigious auteurs of the ex-new wave—Truffaut, Chabrol and so on—but had fallen out with all of them. Her only success so far had been with Alain Jessua's **Jeu de massacre** (**Comic Strip Hero**; 1967)

[13] Shorn of some 18 minutes, it was released in the UK as **Sex and the Vampire**. It played for nearly a year at the Jacey, Leicester Square, on a double bill with Torgny Wickman's **Diary of a Half Virgin**, before doing the rounds of the provincial flea pits. 'Quite sexy. Great curiosity value' commented *Time Out*, while James White wrote in the MFB of its 'excellent visual qualities' and 'inadequate narrative'; pretty quickly a pattern was emerging for critical responses to Rollin's work.

**Back to the Beach**

[14] Apparently, Debord's favourite film was **Les enfants du paradis**, and he completely identified himself with the play-writing, psychopathic thief Lacenaire.

[15] Sandra Julien went on to fame of a sort with her next film, Max Pécas's **Je suis une nymphomane**. She visited London with Pécas to promote the film, which actually opened in the UK before **Sex and the Vampire**. For a while it looked as though she might be a contender, but then the curse of hard-core hit the French film industry. Many actresses who had appeared in 'erotic' films but were unwilling to move into the harder areas suddenly found work in short supply. She made a few more films, including two in Japan—**The Insatiable** (1971) and **The Erotomaniac Daimyo** (1972)—and then faded into obscurity.

[16] He had become involved in the film business quite by chance. One day in 1953 he was spotted playing ping pong in a small hotel on the Côte d'Azur and was asked if he could teach the game to Danny Kaye for a scene in a film being shot there. Soon afterwards he moved to Italy and used his connections to get the part of the young Robinson Crusoe in an Italian film. Various odd-jobs in the business followed and then, in 1960, his first production credit—a low budget erotic comedy **Maîtresse de vacance**, directed by Pierre Unia. Over the years Wallmann has made a wide variety of films—comedies, sex films and art films including, in 1969, **Le jardin des Esperides,** directed by Rollin's sometime collaborator Jacques Robiolles (he played one of the leads in **Frisson**) which is set in the same old château as **La vampire nue.**

[17] Bénazéraf had earlier shot two of his films there—**Le désirable et le sublime** and **Frustration**

[18] Not an easy one to see either—the scene seems to be cut out of all release prints.

[19] One of them was the producer Vera Belmont whose Stephan Films company had produced many pictures, including **The Torture Garden** and **The Lover** with Stacey Keach and the uninhibited Valérie Kaprisky. Meeting Belmont on the street very soon after, Rollin took her to task for the comments. "Oh," she said, "I wasn't on the committee that day."

[20] Rollin was particularly incensed by an article from critic André Halimi in the listings magazine *Pariscope*. Called 'The little cowards of porno,' it pointed the finger at all those French directors who were making sex films under pseudonyms during the brief hardcore boom of the mid seventies.

[21] He's credited on the poster as Pierre Dupont

[22] In the film, Frédéric enters a cinema. The film being shown there is **Le frisson des vampires**. As he watches the opening shots, a mysterious woman appears and leads him out of the cinema and into the nearby Montmartre cemetery. The cinema in which this scene takes place was called Le Mexico. It was one of the last surviving cinemas that was still showing horror movies, when so many of the other small cinemas had gone over to porn. The poignancy of the scene is underlined by the fact that it was shot on the very last day of Le Mexico's existence. The next week it reopened....as a porno cinema. The building is still there, on the corner of Avenue Rachel and Boulevard de Clichy. It now shows an exclusive diet of sex videos.

[23] The title is a reference to a sex-mag that was edited by Jean-Pierre Bouyxou

[24] The sex-film maker Jack Regis, who had also written the script for Rollin's first pseudonymous sex film **Jeunes filles impudiques** (1972).

[25] Curiously, **Certain Fury**, an American film from 1985, bears several strong resemblances to **Les échappées**. Its story of two girls on the run who end up in the hands of a gang of cynical drug dealers is very similar, and the ending is almost identical. But, of course, being a Hollywood film, both girls survive. In Rollin's films, love always leads to tragedy.

[26] And had also been in Tinto Brass's **Salon Kitty** and **Caligula**.

[27] In fact she had already starred in a couple of sex films: **Le fruit défendu** and **Une fille dans la peau** for video sex king Marc Dorcel.

[28] See Appendix for more on Jean Ray and Harry Dickson.

[29] He's a sort of gentlemanly supercriminal—a bit like Raffles.

[30] They publish the Star Trek books in France.

[31] In fact it's a tinny old Edsel—the car no Americans wanted in the first place!

(Facing Page) **Trottoirs** ▶
**de Bangkok**

▲ Bizarre dream sequence from José Larraz's **Visita del vicio**

▼ British poster for **Le sexe qui parle**

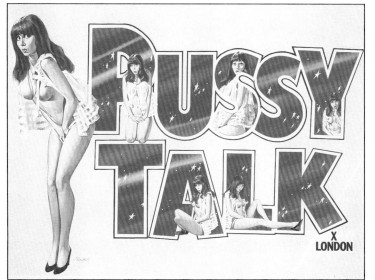

▼ Sandra Julien in **Night Pleasures**

# LAS HIJAS de DRACULA

MARIANNE MORRIS
ANULKA
MURRAY BROWN
Director: JOSEPH LARRAZ
COLOR

CLASIFICADA "S"

# Symptoms

## THE FILMS OF **JOSÉ LARRAZ**

'Last night I dreamed they had returned. They were here again, just like in other dreams, but this time it was more confused. I have a feeling that something is about to happen, something final in which I will be involved.....'

Helen Ramsey (Angela Pleasance) is writing in her diary at the beginning of José Ramón Larraz's enigmatic horror film, **Symptoms** (1974). These few lines typify the undercurrent of unease that permeates all the atmospheric horror films directed by Spanish born Larraz. **Symptoms** is a haunting, original film; Jack Nicholson raved about it when it was screened at the Cannes film festival, and critic Dave Pirie called it 'mesmerising' and 'really impressive', but it's never received the word of mouth reputation it deserves. For twenty years the film has languished in the vaults and, like many of Larraz's films, it's ripe for rediscovery and reappraisal.

What makes **Symptoms** different from other British based horror films is its bona fide air of mystery. The sort of quality you expect to find in English horror stories by the likes of E. F. Benson, Arthur Machen and M. R. James. In **Symptoms** everything seems to hold a secret, the large rustic house, the woods, the river and even the people. The mystery is not in the plot,

◀ (Facing page) Spanish poster for **Vampyres**
◀ José Larraz during his Paris days

this is actually quite obvious from the start, it's in the odd and unsettling nuances that are never resolved.

The English approach to the horror film is more or less typified by Hammer—well made films, but they tended to concentrate on logical stories and narrative realism. Inside a Hammer film the old dictum 'what you see is what you get' applies through and through. Everything is explained. There's no mystery, no doubt, and above all there's nothing irrational lurking beneath the surface. Although **Symptoms** was made using British technicians and actors, it doesn't look like any other English horror film, and the catalyst that made the difference was José Larraz. Larraz had received no formal cinematic training, he more or less learned the ropes by making films. Before **Symptoms** he'd directed three other low budget films; **Whirlpool** (aka **She Died with Her Boots On**; 1969), **Deviation** (1971) and **Scream and Die** (aka **The House That Vanished;** 1973), that had brought a new sensibility to the English horror film. Before entering the business Larraz had worked as a comic strip artist and a photographer, both of which had an important influence on the way he made films.

Born in Barcelona in 1929, Larraz moved to England, via Paris, in the late sixties. He's a self confessed anglophile. "I am neurotic, like any good Latin," he's says, "and for me England is a big pill of Valium. I feel very relaxed when I am here." One of the things he likes most about England is the wooded countryside, with its atmosphere of dank mystery. If he was a native these sentiments would sound jingoistic and clichéd, but being an immigrant he's free from these constraints, making his infatuation sound disarming and refreshingly enthusiastic.

When it boils down to it, few native born film-makers have been really inspired by the English landscape, all of the films that have

◀ Larraz in Spain

**Whirpool** (1969) ▲

used it evocatively have been made by people who were in some way outsiders. From Powell and Pressburger's **Canterbury Tale** (1944) to Jorge Grau's **The Living Dead at the Manchester Morgue** (1974), it's always the immigrant or the prodigal son who's been moved by the countryside, with its connotations of Albion and Mystical but Merrie England.

Larraz's films are filled with shots of eerie, inspiring sunsets, woods and neo-Gothic buildings. His England is a place with a life of its own. It's not Arcadian like Michael Powell's **Canterbury Tale**, or apocalyptic like Jorge Grau's **The Living Dead at The Manchester Morgue**. It has elements of both. In Larraz's films the architecture and scenery are often more important than any of the main characters. He makes these elements a vital part of his films and shoots them in an inventive number of ways. It's a different style of filmmaking, one that's inspired by Larraz's continuing fascination with the beauty of England, as well as the inevitable constraints of a low budget.

Creating moods by filming woods, rivers and quaint buildings may be easier than handling actors, but it still requires a certain eye and a knowledge about what you're trying to achieve. The way Larraz frames and lights things is quite unique. it's a legacy of his background in comics, a period of his life that started off in Barcelona, after he dropped out of University. His father had died, money was tight, but there were also political reasons for his decision. As Larraz puts it, "My father wore red"—his family were left wing. This made University life difficult, because if he mentioned Marx or Engels in an essay the police would come to his family home and ask questions.

After working in Barcelona drawing comics for two or three years, he got married. With his new wife he moved to Paris to find work. It was 1952, seven years since the end of the war. Paris was battle scarred and filled with Spanish republican refugees. Larraz had a tremendous amount of good luck there. He entered a competition hosted by the prestigious King Features syndicate, which he won, and became a highly paid comic strip artist. Comics have always been treated more seriously in France than in England and the U.S.A., and Larraz's reputation was high during the fifties and sixties.

Over the years, many film-makers have looked to comics for inspiration. Larraz is unusual, because he's moved from comics to film. His films aren't constructed like comics but, because of his background, the way he frames his shots is different. The angles he chooses aren't predictable. The differences are subtle but crucial. His camera positions are more idiosyncratic, which means that his films have their own kind of rhythm, they don't follow a familiar pattern. The angles are always slightly higher or lower and the way he lights his shots also adds to the unusual atmosphere. Producer Brian Smedley-Aston has astutely described it as "a freewheeling style, which might be a bit rough round the edges, but there is a joie de vivre and elan."

During the 15 years he lived in Paris, Larraz switched from producing comic strips to working as a professional photographer. He'd been interested in taking pictures since he was a teenager and had learned the rudiments of the trade while he was living in Spain. One of his first girlfriends was the daughter of a photographer. They would meet in her father's darkroom; "We were very innocent, and this was the only way to feel the ass of this girl at that time." He worked as a fashion photographer for four years, snapping beautiful girls for the covers of *Vogue* and French fashion plates like *Femmes d'aujourd'hui*. As a top fashion photographer he was skilled at handling lighting, creating a mood and getting the right expressions from his models, attributes that would come in handy when he switched to filmmaking.

Life as a fashion photographer was good. In fact it was almost too good. Surrounded by beautiful girls, temptation was too much for Larraz. All the other photographers were homosexuals. It was "like being at a banquet filled with lots of dishes that you'd like to eat and you're the only one that's hungry ... you get indigestion." In the end he had to hang up his camera and return to comic strips, or forget he had a family.

Some of Larraz's best work for the magazines *Creepy* and *Eerie* were his jungle strips. Animals are a big part of his life. His workroom is festooned with the heads and horns of wild beasts, and over the years he's had a number of feral friends, including a pet leopard. Jungle films such as the **Tarzan** series were a big influence on him during his formative years. They were exotic and erotic—**Tarzan and his Mate** (1934), for example, had plenty of pre Hays Code nudity and featured Maureen O'Sullivan in skimpy costumes and silk stocking in a jungle setting. Larraz has a suitcase full of stills from this inspired epic, snitched from Barcelona cinemas during the war-time blackout. Later on, when he lived in England, he became firm friends with O'Sullivan and she often invited him to dinner. "If somebody had told me when I was a kid that Jane, the mate of Tarzan, would cook chicken for me in her Chelsea flat I would have collapsed," he chuckles amiably.

At heart Larraz is a passionate film fan. For him "the important thing is to shoot, because for me my life is celluloid," a need he shares with other low budget European sexploitation directors, such as Rollin and Franco. His first step towards making films came about by accident. The producer of **A Fistful of Dollars** was one of his friends, and Larraz was asked to play a scout in the film when one of the actors became sick. Through this connection he got to know the Italian producer Remo Ovedaine. This proved to be a lucky break, as Larraz's Belgian publisher had made lots of money from a children's comic and was thinking about investing some of it in film production. Other backers soon appeared. Softcore sex films were big business at the time and they thought it would be fun to do one of those. Larraz wrote a simple story containing loads of sex. They had some money and a story, all they needed was a capable producer to organise things and market the finished product. Through Larraz's Italian friend they eventually hooked up with the Danish based Sam Lomberg. The film, **Whirlpool**, was released in 1969.

When he began making the film, all Larraz had to go on was his enthusiasm, his talent as an artist and photographer, and the experience he picked up along the way. "I was never in a film studio, I never had any training.....more than going to the cinema every day of my life. I knew nothing about technique, particularly. The only thing that helped me out was that in Brussels I became friends with a projectionist at the Film Theatre. He helped me because he had a moviola, I could get films and study them." Legendary director Josef von Sternberg also encouraged him to get into movie making, which boosted Larraz's confidence. Von Sternberg told Larraz that when he made **The Blue Angel**, with Marlene Dietrich, he had had no money—just determination to finish the film. Everyone helped out, Marlene cooked food for the crew, and they all worked together like a family.

Although Larraz wasn't familiar with many of the technical aspects of film production, and gleefully admits that he didn't even know what a clapperboard was, he still knew what he wanted. On **Whirlpool** he worked closely with the lighting technicians and the cameraman, explaining the mood he wanted to create, then working out the lighting set-ups, framing the shots himself, and leaving the rest in their capable hands. It's a method that he has used for each of the 26 films he has made since. Larraz is a great admirer of film technicians and lighting men, for him they're the unsung heroes of film production. He always collaborates closely with them, which is no doubt the reason why his films look better than the majority of low budget epics. Some members of his crew are astonished that he takes as much care as he does to make the film look good. They're more used to working with directors who simply want to bang the film out and get on to the next one.

**Whirlpool** was begun in Barcelona, the exteriors were shot in London, and the film was dubbed in Rome. The budget was minuscule— a mere £20,000 ... later on they sold the American rights for $100,000. **Whirlpool** capitalised on the sex angle in a number of ways. With Lomberg as producer they had the film registered in Denmark, which made it more 'risqué' to English audiences. The film also starred the luscious Vivian Neves, one of the Swinging Sixties' most famous models. As the first woman to appear topless in the *Sunday Times* she was practically a household name. Contrary to popular opinion, Larraz didn't meet Neves when he worked as a photographer, he met her while they were holding auditions for **Whirlpool**. In true Hollywood style, Neves was the last model they looked at.

"She looked appalling because of the way she'd been made-up." Larraz made her wash off the make up. "Then we made her up again and she was very beautiful. She was very photogenic, like Carol Baker or Lee Remick, and the body was very, very beautiful."

▼ Larraz on set of **El mirón** (1977)

Neves was a major selling point for **Whirlpool**, she oozed sex appeal. In real life she was "quite randy". While they were filming in Barcelona she asked Larraz to get some batteries for "a massage machine"—she had a lover but, as Larraz genially puts it: "The boy who was in the film was her human vibrator, but she needed much more than him....probably he couldn't afford such intensive work."

Although **Whirlpool** made a tidy profit, Larraz had some regrets. "It was a lousy start for my career. I was labelled as a cheap, sex movie director forever afterward....People misunderstand the expression cheap film," he says, "they think it means rubbish. For me it means a film that doesn't cost too much." The budget may have been low, but the film was made with affection and some care for detail. Like **Scream and Die** (1973), which he made a few years later, **Whirlpool** was a sex thriller set loosely in the photographic industry. The plot revolved around a pornographic photographer and his aunt, a murderous pair on the lookout for yet another victim. All of Larraz's horror films, including **Symptoms**, feature this fascination with intense claustrophobic relationships that lead to dark deeds.

After making **Whirlpool**, Larraz wanted to make a totally English film, one that had English technicians, money and actors. Originally he planned to shoot the film in Belgium. Shooting in England was more expensive, but worked out better in the long run because they could take advantage of the Eady

Levy, a government subsidy. The resulting film, **Symptoms**, was a minor masterpiece, and featured Donald Pleasance's daughter, Angela, in her finest film role. French writer and critic Maurice Bessy thought the film was so good he nominated it as the British entry for the Cannes festival. Larraz wasn't too happy about promoting **Symptoms** at Cannes because it was a low budget film, and would be at a disadvantage when compared with glossy big budget productions.

When he arrived at the festival these fears proved to be the least of his worries. Some disgruntled British directors, led by Michael Winner, had condemned the film. They wanted Ken Russell's **Mahler** to be screened instead. As Larraz saw it, the main bone of contention seemed to be his dago impertinence—"What was a bloody Spaniard doing making films in Britain?" Cannes was pretty unbearable for him that year because everyone wanted to get in on the act. His fellow countrymen were outraged because he'd left Spain to make films in Britain, the French were miffed for the same reason, it seemed that everyone had an axe to grind over the film's nomination.

Despite being selected for Cannes it took two years for the film to be screened in Britain, and it sank without trace after a few months. Occasionally it turns up on late night television. The Cannes fracas cast a shadow over Larraz's next two or three films, which were just as impressive as **Symptoms** but never received the critical attention they deserved.

However, the film was good for Larraz in that it marked the beginning of a partnership with producer Brian Smedley-Aston. Smedley-Aston was a well connected man. His father, E.M. Smedley-Aston, had worked on numerous British black and white thrillers. He himself went on to edit the cult classic **Blue Sunshine** in the 1970s, and produced sex films like **Let's Get Laid** (1977), which was directed by Trevor Wrenn (cameraman on several Larraz goodies, such as **Symptoms** and **Scream and Die**), and starred sex starlet Fiona Richmond.

The films Larraz made in England were similar in some ways to other English sexploitation films from the time, particularly those made by Pete Walker. Walker is generally regarded as the best of the British sexploitation directors, distinguished from the rest by the fact that his films had an edge. They had an atmosphere of 'suburban menace', an important quality for film critics, as so few British sexploitation films had any atmosphere at all. Larraz's films were

UNA PRODUCCION **JOSE FRADE**

**Alfredo Landa**

EN

**Polvos Mágicos**

CON
VINCENZO CROCITTI · CARMEN VILLANI
JOSE M. CAFARELL · CARMEN DE LIRIO
ELISA MONTES · MARIA VICO · EDUARDO FAJARDO
EASTMANCOLOR   DIRECTOR **J.R. LARRAZ**

**Immoral Tales**

more menacing than Walker's, they were made with more care and had an aura of danger that was virtually relentless.

For some reason, the only book devoted to the history of the British sex film, David McGillivray's *Doing Rude Things*, ignores Larraz's contribution to the 1970's sex cycle. This is partly because Larraz wasn't just a sexploitation film director, and partly because his films were marketed as thrillers or horror films. Sex is important in many of Larraz's films. He's doesn't back away from the subject in the British way, his approach to the topic is more European, more open and unashamed. When British directors handled sex they did so in an uncomfortable manner, their films are full of awkward fumblings and embarrassment. Larraz's attitude was more whole hearted. As a consequence, most of the horror films he shot in Britain have as much nudity and monkey business in them as any of the sex films from the period. The main difference being that Larraz handled the sex material better, the sexual element was always more intense and believable.

One of the reasons for this was Larraz's way of working. He spent more time on these scenes. Home grown directors rushed though them, but Larraz took care to make sure that the actors and actresses looked plausible during the sex scenes, which inevitably made them seem daring by British standards. In Larraz's films, sex is always tied up with other emotions, it's deep, and often tainted with violence and intensity. While British directors did their best to ignore the subject, Larraz used sex as a vital ingredient in films like **Scream and Die** (1973) and **Vampyres** (1974). In these films sex wasn't used as a simple crowd pleaser, it was used to add depth to the mystery and to the implicit atmosphere of danger.

It's useful to look at this eroticism, because it's at the heart of the unique ambience that pervades Larraz's horror films. **Whirlpool**, his first film, had less sex than those he turned out later in the seventies, yet the fascination with dangerous relationships is already there. It's something that haunts all his horror films. Sex in a Larraz film is never idyllic, it seems linked to some dark undercurrent. When he photographs the countryside he uses the same approach, hinting that something unknown lurks beneath the surface. Nature, sex and everything else are simply part of the jigsaw. Each tiny detail is well shot, and when they're all pieced together the effect is a mood of enigmatic danger. The sex scenes are important because their heightened emotions make this quality easier to spot.

▲ Prepare to meet **The Edge of the Axe** (1988)

The dialogue in **Symptoms** was short, cryptic, and punctuated with almost oppressive silences, silences that made the film seem intricate and abstruse. The pauses performed the same function as the lingering shots of moody woods, rivers, landscapes and buildings. They added to the mounting air of inexplicable jeopardy. It's a technique that Larraz has refined and reworked over the years: in **Vampyres** it was daring and obvious while in **La visita del vicio** (**Violation of the Bitch**; 1978) it was subtle in the finest sense of the word.

**Symptoms** is Larraz's most ambiguous film. Although the plot is simple—(an unhinged woman invites a female friend to her country retreat, the odd job man discovers the corpse of her previous guest in the river, leading to more murder and the woman's complete breakdown)—the film is a sombre and complex affair that implicates everybody and everything. As the story progresses, the tension builds, the questions mount and the line between fantasy and reality becomes blurred. Everyone appears tainted, touched by some unknown aura that is not dissipated by the violent finale. This special quality is due in some degree to the excellent acting. **Symptoms** featured great understated performances by Peter Vaughan, Lorna Heilbron and Angela Pleasance. The supporting cast were also good and Larraz managed to make even the bespectacled Mike Grady deliver the goods.

Many of these actors are often type cast, including Grady—**Symptoms** showed how a little bit of care and a dollop of genuine mystery can easily break the stranglehold of familiarity. Grady's other roles in British sex comedies were pretty one dimensional, from **Carry on Loving** (1970), **I'm Not Feeling Myself Tonight** (1975)

through to **Spanish Fly** (1975). In **Symptoms** he was less of a caricature. Larraz managed to get something from Grady that other directors hadn't, and the same goes for the rest of the cast. If you compare Peter Vaughan's performance in **Symptoms** with his work in the TV ghost story **A Warning to the Curious**, you'll find this holds true. In **Symptoms**, he's enigmatic as Brady the odd job man, exuding a look that's predatory but hunted, indicating that even a menacing 'heavy' can be someone's quarry. **Symptoms** is filled with these sorts of nuances, they keep the audience guessing, suggesting all sorts of possibilities. On **Symptoms**, Larraz had a fine group of professionals—unfortunately it would be several years before he had as good a team again. For most of his subsequent films the budget didn't stretch far enough and the cast were often a mixture of regulars and non-professionals. When he began making Spanish comedy films in the late seventies and early eighties he had a hard working, experienced team, but until then he had to make the best of the low budget limitations.

**Symptoms** should have established Larraz's reputation, but it didn't. He was pushed towards making films with a higher quotient of sex and blood. This presented him with a dilemma. He's not really interested in shooting films that are filled with people humping, simple bare assed on-screen sex is not his style. "I'm not really interested in sex and things like this," he says with concern; "I've never seen a porno film. I find them stupid and in bad taste, and also porno is not reality. I never liked to see close-ups of penises and pussies and things. I don't think it is erotic, it is like religion. I'm not a believer."

Larraz prefers to make films that are equivocal and disturbing. So, when he's forced to include sexy scenes, he tries to make them add something tangible and dangerous to the flavour of the film. **Symptoms** had a little bit of implied lesbianism in it, but it was more intellectual than physical. As Larraz says "Homosexuality is often associated with intensity and passion. The way you approach horror, terror and the mysterious, you are attracted by an ambiguous situation, shadows and things like this. Normally 90% of crimes are linked with sexual problems, jealous husband or love problem. So that's why it's difficult to make a film like this that doesn't have something of that kind. Normally something like sex triggers the action. When you have no money, the only guarantee for the box office is sex. How can I make a film like **The Spy Who Came in from**

the **Cold** with inexperienced actors and no money? So you have to put something like this in instead."

All of Larraz's early films follow the same understated approach to sex as **Symptoms**, in fact the only one that ups the ante on this front is **Scream and Die** (1973). His first three films— **Whirlpool**, **Deviation** and **Emma, puertos oscuras** are evocative, unsettling horror outings. The sexual dimension is there, but not with the same intensity as in **Vampyres** or **Scream and Die**. These two films aren't really typical of Larraz's output. He tries to give equal weight to all the pieces in the puzzle. Too much sex in a film destroys the delicate tension he prefers, interrupting the feeling that things are slipping towards something cathartic and unknown.

**Scream and Die** was a Spanish/English co-production. All the mysterious, atmospheric shots were filmed in England, the rest was shot in Barcelona. It was a transitional film for Larraz, it solidified his links with the British low budget film industry, making it possible for him to do his first completely English film, **Symptoms**. The credits for **Scream and Die** implied that it was a British film through and through. Sex film director Derek Ford, for example, was given a screenplay credit even though he had nothing to do with it. This played down the Spanish angle, making it easier to get distribution in England, also increasing the likelihood of American companies picking it up for the U.S. market.

The producers of **Scream and Die** wanted a fairly hefty quotient of sex in the film, and

◄ (Facing page) **The National Mummy** (1981)

▼ Angela Pleasance in **Symptoms** (1974)

though this wasn't exactly to Larraz's taste he didn't back away from the subject. He's aware of the off-beat sexual things that people do; "That's why lesbianism and homosexuality for me isn't of the other world. I approach the subject with ingenuity. For me two men or two women in a bed is no more a scandal than a man and a woman." Although most of the sex in **Scream and Die** was pretty damn lurid it was handled in a curiously humane way. The first sex scene took place in a typical Larraz location—an eerie house in the country; weird sex, and murder spiced up with a dash of voyeurism.

The voyeurism was supplied by two trespassers, who witness the whole sick affair while hiding in the shadows. They see an odd couple, the man keeps his leather gloves on, while his girlfriend peels off down to her panties, straddles him, then lifts his gloved hands onto her ample breasts. They share a cigarette. She plays along with his 'strange whims and fancies', his gloves, his introspection and his misanthropy. Despite which, he stabs her in a cold blooded frenzy. It was unwholesome material and Larraz approached it head on, turning out scenes that were tender and highly perverse. It was a real 'in your face' approach to the topic, made all the more potent by a lack of moralising. Larraz's non judgmental stance is obvious in the film, judgment is a one sided affair and just not his style.

The kinky murder that kicks off **Scream and Die** is a puzzle that's solved at the film's climax. The effeminate killer is locked into an intense, incestuous relationship with his mature aunt, played by Maggie Walker. In one unforgettable scene, the two screwed up relatives get hot'n'heavy on a king-size bed. The episode has all the hallmarks of the forbidden, which makes it impossible to avoid looking at the unnatural display. As they embrace violently on the bed the aunt's face is flushed, her skin is saggy and white. The naked couple make love urgently, in a frenzy that's as revolting as it's unmistakably passionate.

**Scream and Die** was Larraz's most explicit sojourn into sordid sexual depths. His later film **La muerte incierta** (1977) also has an incest theme, but shot in the restrained, ambiguous manner he prefers. Here the plot centres around a planter who lives with his son in a remote part of India, and has an affair with a native girl who kills herself when he returns to England and remarries. After the wedding the planter becomes seized with a superstitious fear. The girl has cursed him, he feels her presence and imagines she is stalking him in the body of a

▲ **Vampyres** (1974)
◄ (Facing page) **Black Candles** (1981)

tiger. Shortly after this presentiment, his wife and son become attracted to one another. Larraz isn't fascinated by incest, he's more interested in intense emotions, and incest is a claustrophobic breeding ground for violent, unstoppable feelings that must erupt somewhere down the line.

Larraz's horror films have similar preoccupations. Pent-up emotions and buried secrets help build up the tension, leading to a blood soaked coda or finale. His 1974 film **Vampyres** was slightly different in that there were several crescendos rather than just one. **Vampyres** is a great film but it's not his favourite, he prefers the moody and complex **Symptoms**. **Symptoms** is too sombre to be a real crowd pleaser, and in the final analysis **Vampyres** is easily his most commercial film.

These days it's regarded by many people as one of the great English horror films, yet reviews at the time were mixed. Cincinnati critic Tim Lucas rated it as 'a generally poor horror film... poorly acted... extremely gruesome and lacking the thickly delicious atmosphere of **The Vampire Lovers** and the dynamism of **Count Yorga, Vampire**'. In the cold light of the nineties, it's easier to appreciate its merits—and there are plenty of them. **Vampyres** is one of the few really evocative British horror films. The heavyweight *Aurum Horror Film Encyclopaedia* describes the female vampires as 'simultaneously objects of terror and intoxicatingly desirable ....sex and other bloodthirsty activities are depicted with exuberant explicitness achieving a hallucinatory eroticism...which genuinely succeeds in conveying the ambiguities of *amour fou*—of loving and being loved to death'.

If **Vampyres** is flawed, it's due to the restrictions of the low budget. Shot in three weeks for £40,000, the result has a few small but important glitches. The plot is a little mundane in places, vampires thumbing rides and a camping couple in a caravan are the most obvious examples. Another minor irritation was Murray Brown (Ted), a cut-price, paunchy leading man with badly conditioned hair, as the overweight love interest. It's hard to accept the idea of a buxom vampire being trapped in a lust binge with this chunky gazebo.

Murray Brown was certainly wooden in comparison to the two blood sucking femme fatales played by Anulka (Miriam) and Marianne Morris (Fran). Morris had appeared in a couple of minor British sex comedies, **The Love Box** (1972) and **The Over Amorous Artist** (1974), a far cry from the visual ingenuity of **Vampyres**. In **The Love Box** she was a bored, tea sipping wife, in **Vampyres** she was a volatile predator, fascinating and unpredictable. Her facial expression during the bloodletting scenes is incredible, it's practically a symphony of intoxication. The same holds true for Anulka. Together they made a dangerously desirable pair.

Larraz coaxed heady performances from the two of them, and the atmospheric framing and lighting did the rest. **Vampyres** was a real team effort. The crew were like "a mad family, enthusiastic about the work they were doing" says Larraz, who worked closely with cameraman

Zora, la Vampira ▶

Harry Waxman and make-up man Colin Arthur to develop **Vampyres'** uniquely eerie mood. Waxman was an old pro who'd worked on a host of classic English films including Basil Deardon's **Sapphire** (1959), **The Day the Earth Caught Fire** (1961), **She** (1965), **Wonderwall** (1968) and **The Wickerman** (1973). He was a consummate professional and helped Larraz capture the mood he needed to lift the film into the realms of chilling fantasy.

By English standards, **Vampyres** was raunchy and intense, proving too much for the taste of the English censor who snipped nearly three high octane minutes of uninhibited sex and garish bloodletting. The pre-credit sequence was cut down to a mere seven seconds. In the uncut version the vampire girls were blasted into bloody oblivion by a barrage of bullets, while the camera moved in on their naked bodies. Potent stuff indeed, even by today's gore-filled standards. The sex scenes between Fran the vampire and chunky Ted were also highly charged in the uncut version, pushing the film deeper into that twilight region that lies somewhere between horror and a testosterone-soaked wet dream. Even without the extra scenes **Vampyres** is like an erotic nightmare, heightened, compulsive and more than a shade terrifying.

The British censor gave the film an 'X' certificate, demanding that all bloodsucking scenes be trimmed. He was taken aback by the film's violent eroticism, the potent brew of passion mixed with gouts of blood was thought to be too excessive and explosive for public consumption. Larraz's **Vampyres** were an urgent lot, they weren't content to simply slurp blood from the jugular veins of their victims. They slashed them with long knives and fed rapaciously, they were like pack animals who kill in a frenzy of hunger and bloodlust. In Tim Greaves' excellent booklet on **Vampyres**, Larraz says he "imagined them like two panthers, two wild animals... I imagine my vampires turn almost to cannibalism, to eat somebody, to take the blood from anywhere, no matter if it is on the arm or on the balls! Anywhere! I can't imagine anyone coming to suck my blood gently. It would be... very quick, with urgency... urgency because the sun rises. Urgency for the kill, urgency for the blood, because it's what they need. And that is why my film is so brutal."

These sentiments were lost on the censor. Larraz explained his ideas to him, but the film was still cut. One of the most ecstatically frenzied scenes in the film was reduced by nearly

**Immoral Tales**

▲ Vampyres

half a minute. This was where the two girls stab the half naked Rupert, played by Larraz regular Karl Lanchbury. The murder is quick and gory. The girls claw at him, drawing blood from his neck, arms and back, they lap it up in animalistic ecstasy, intoxicated by the feast of lifegiving liquid. The sequence where the two vampires suck Ted's blood had to be shortened because of its lesbianism, and the girls' violent and salacious enjoyment of their nourishment. The two girls suck from a gaping wound in Ted's arm, then they kiss sexually, licking the crimson fluid from each others faces and lips. While Ted lies dazed and weakened they roll around engaging in oral sex. Vampire films have always been about sex and blood, yet few have approached the theme with Larraz's gusto.

The scene where the vampires attack the caravaning couple, John and Harriet was particularly shocking. In the full version, John (Brian Deacon) is slashed across the throat as he attempts to escape in his car, blood squirts across the windscreen as he tries to break free from the hungry duo. There's blood everywhere, resistance is useless, the girls pummel him, Fran grips him from behind while Miriam laps up the red liquid that's streaming down his

chest and stomach. Although John's murder was brutal his wife Harriet's end was even more gruesome. Ten chilling seconds were excised from the English release. Miriam grabs the victim's arms, pushing her onto her knees as the venomous Fran runs forward with her knife poised for the *coup de grace*. She delivers the death blow, eyes wide, focusing intently on the pinioned woman.

The complete version of **Vampyres** is available on video in Europe and has all the material that was chopped from the English release. This version also contains a slightly stronger lesbians-in-the bath sequence, illustrating the difference in attitude to these things on the Continent.

**Vampyres** was the last film Larraz made in England, opportunities were beginning to dry up, so he turned towards Spain for work. He had more contacts there, and ended up directing one film a year for local release. His first was the comedy **La fin de la inocencia** (1976), "a fairy tale about sex", that tackled the problems a young girl faces when she becomes a woman in a country riddled with sexual taboos. It was made six months after the death of General Franco and, although he was gone, the system of censorship lingered on. In Spain at that time film producers were still wary about going too far, they didn't really know which way the wind might blow. A type of self censorship existed, no one was willing to take too many chances, so **Fin de la inocencia** had less bite to its allegory because of this.

Larraz's next film was more heavyweight. **El mirón** (The Voyeur; 1977) was a well crafted, sombre drama influenced by Michael Powell's **Peeping Tom**, and is one of the few films Larraz is pleased with. **Symptoms** and the television series **Goya** are the others. Larraz isn't happy about the low budget sex and horror films he's directed, he had to make too many compromises. Compromises over the script, the actors and the end result. **El mirón** was very visual, there was little dialogue, everything was suggested by looks and gestures. Alexandra Bastedo was excellent as the wife who complies with her husbands voyeuristic inclinations. The film ends with the couple at an important turning point, she's about to reluctantly give in to his strange desires. She smiles in complicity, but there's a tear in her eye, because she knows they are entering uncertain waters.

**El mirón** was one of the few films Larraz has made where he could choose the subject, film it the way he wanted to, and have enough money for excellent actors and a good crew. The film was "serious...serious in terms of 'I made what I wanted'," says Larraz. "It was a story I was

UNA PRODUCCION DE PROMOCIONES AURA S.A.

Un hombre tiene un irresistible deseo:

Ver a su mujer con otros....
¿Por qué?
¿Cómo satisface su obsesión?

**EL MIRON**
(LE VOYEUR)

**HECTOR ALTERIO · ALEXANDRA BASTEDO · AURORA BAUTISTA**
Guión y Dirección J.R. LARRAZ

**The Voyeur** (1977) ▶

interested in myself. A psychiatrist told me about it. I'm not interested in being a voyeur. I'm interested in voyeurism because I think that seeing is a fantastic gift of nature. I like to see everything, put my nose everywhere. Cinema is very voyeuristic because it's in the dark. You have the keyhole which is the screen. I am very interested in people who have this aberration, even though I think the word aberration is very stupid. Nothing for me is an aberration. The world is natural because it exists.

"The film was about the problem of a typical bourgeois, educated, who lives with his mother in a flat in Madrid. He's conservative, with the idea to get married to what society calls 'a decent girl', and suddenly he discovers that he's a voyeur. For him it is a terrible situation, it's against his beliefs and principles. He becomes neurotic. That's the story. It's a problematic of a person who discovers that and he can't get rid of it. It's based on a true story, of an Englishman who was a rich tourist, and this man saw a shoeshiner looking at the knickers and legs of his wife. At the hotel later he said to his wife 'Did you see that dirty old man looking at your legs?' She said 'Oh, I was embarassed, but what could I do?' He noticed something that night—he became more excited than other nights. Next night he'd start again with the same conversation, and that conversation became a leitmotif. Every night he became obsessed with that idea. The moment he can't talk about this he can't get an erection. That is authentic. Then he arrived at the point where he need to see the shoeshiner in bed with his wife, and what happens is it finishes his marriage, his own life. It destroys him. In sex, if you start to be inclined towards something, after going ten degrees you have to go more and more and more."

The next film after **El mirón** was the Spanish-Italian co-production **La muerte incierta** (Uncertain Death; 1977). This was "a kind of a horror movie shot in India" and featured a few tigers. "One of the tigers killed a man a week after we stopped shooting," relates Larraz. "The newspapers said it was my fault because I teach the tiger to be vicious with a dummy."

During the late seventies and eighties he had a good relationship with Spanish producer José Frade. Larraz still continued to live in England, leaving Tunbridge Wells once a year to make a film overseas. "With Frade it was a love affair. He gave me 6 or 7 films to make. It was me who stop," says Larraz. Although Frade is virtually unknown outside Spain he's one of the most important Spanish producers. His company is large and produces popular comedies as well as the more serious, 'message' films that the Spanish

seem to like. Larraz directed both crazy comedies and horror films for Frade, including two blockbusters that made millions in Spain, **Polvos magicos** (1979) and **The National Mummy** (1981). Larraz also wrote the scripts for both of these outings.

**Polvos magicos** was a horror comedy that opened with Tiny Tim singing *Tiptoe Through the Tulips* and featured talking skulls in buckets; **The National Mummy** was an even stranger slice of hokum. "It was made after General Franco died and Franco looked like a Mummy. My idea was a horror film where Franco returns like a Mummy and comes to power, my idea was that they come from Egypt with a Mummy who's short. The archeologist plays Franco's fascist anthem and the Mummy comes to life. **The National Mummy** had real actors, very good theatrical actors. In Spain they like crazy comedies, but in these films I always despise the stupidity of the story. I always try to use mood and atmosphere and different light and give them a little bit more quality. Because if you see these films, you'll see a bit of care. I know I am a lousy director, and my films are worth nothing, but I never had the opportunity to make something grander."

Larraz is a bit vague about many of his films, like Jess Franco he's a little embarrassed about

them, unhappy about the way they've turned out. He's too close to them, too aware of their faults to be pleased with their minor triumphs. He feels it's practically impossible to make a good film the way he has to because of the restrictions of the budget. "When I'm writing a script for a film that I'm going to make that's a low, low budget, I can't make a good script. It's impossible. It's possible if I'm free to do a subject that's very personal, very cheap and very personal. Maybe a story that's very intimate. But the producers don't want that. So when you have a low budget film, there are two things. The low budget and the producer wants something commercial. So this means sex and people in bed."

Over the years Larraz has made a wide variety of films—comedies, horrors, sexy thrillers and psychological dramas— but critics prefer to write about him as a low budget sex and horror director. He's unhappy about this. As an exploitation film director he doesn't have much choice about the subject matter. In fact the only topic he refuses to film is horror with religious overtones. Once he had a Spanish producer who suggested that he make a film about vampires but dealing with religion, "something like **Jesus Christ— Super Vampire**. Well, that was my idea and he loved it. I withdrew because my mother was very religious and I have a kind of respect for

these things. I don't like to hurt people and if you're dealing with these things you will hurt many millions. That's why I don't like to make a film and put a joke in about the Pope, Buddha or Mohammed. It's a problem of my skin, as we say in Spain. I'm not a religious person, but I am a poetical person and for me religion has a poetical angle. For me Jesus Christ and Che Guevarra is the same thing, they both died for an ideal."

One of Larraz's most unusual and satisfying films was a bizarre sex flick called **La visita del vicio** (**The Violation of the Bitch**; 1978). He made this with practically no money, no professional actors and with only a few weeks for shooting. Slammed by critic Alan Jones as a 'a pathetic porno paella... with a sadomasochistic threesome', **La visita del vicio** is a slow moving, tense film with an amoral twist at the end. The dream sequences, featuring a large, carved horse with a girl planted inside, are particularly inspired, while other scenes featuring a naked man on horseback have a disturbing, Freudian edge. Larraz had used the idea of a life-size model horse with cutaways earlier, in one of his strips for *Creepy*, and producer José Frade had one built for the film. It was the most expensive item in the whole production.

Before shooting began, Frade took Larraz aside. He was worried because there wasn't a single professional actor in the whole film. To compensate for this Larraz used a minimum of dialogue. "It was really like an album of pictures. Just beautiful frames," says Larraz. "For everybody it was the first film, except for the

**The National Mummy** ▼
(1981)

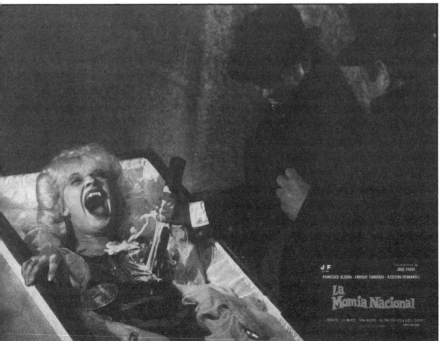

beautiful black horse, he was a horse that played in many westerns. Robert Mitchum ride that horse, Yul Brinner ride that horse. The actor told me he could ride the horse, but he couldn't. He'd jump on the horse and say 'José, my balls, my balls! Get me a cushion, José'. So the stuntman had to ride the horse. I remember one day I was cross with the actor and I said the only professional here is the horse."

Against the odds, Larraz made something out of practically nothing. **La visita del vicio** had an atmosphere, an eerie ambience that's different from any other European sexploitation film. Although each frame is practically flooded with light, the film has a dark psychological dimension, a feeling of tension and unpredictability. In short, the qualities that Larraz puts into all his sex and horror films.

Larraz isn't happy talking about **La visita del vicio**, yet compared to his next film, a female spy spoof called **The Golden Lady** (1979), it was an undisputed masterpiece. **The Golden Lady** "was one of the worst films I've ever been involved with," winces Larraz. "The script was written by some pretty boy who couldn't write a letter home to his mother!" The only film he hates talking about even more is **Los ritos sexuales del diablo** ( **Black Candles**; 1981).

"I don't like that film. That film made a lot of money. I'm very interested in sabbatical things and witches. To do a good film about this you need a lot of money and good actors and actresses, and you don't go so far with the sex. No one in that film could act. So what do you do with them? You put them in bed and have them jump on each other."

**Los ritos sexuales del diablo** was Larraz's last sexploitation film. Because of the success of **Polvos magicos** (1979) and **The National Mummy** (1981) he became known as a comedy director—"That's all anybody thought I could direct from that point on." He still managed to squeeze in a few horror films during the eighties, starting with **Estigma** (1981), a patchy, slow moving film influenced by **Carrie** and **The Fury**. Nicely shot, and with a few interesting scenes, but overall a disappointment. For most of this period Larraz received backing from a fruit exporter, or "Philistine moneymen" as he refers to his backers. They wanted a sure return on their investment, so Larraz's next two horror films, shot under the pseudonym Joseph Braunstein, were gory, direct-to-video Spanish-American co-productions. The first, **Descanse en piezas** (**Rest in Pieces**; 1987) starring Dorothy Malone, featured plenty of gore-filled nightmare scenes; the next, **Filo de hacha (Edge of the Axe)**, was just as bloody. After this Larraz decided he'd had enough of blood and dismemberment, his next film would be a return to suspense and mystery.

In 1989 he teamed up once more with producer-editor Brian Smedley-Aston. The resulting film, **Deadly Manor**, although not as groundbreaking as **Vampyres**, was "quite a nice film". The cast were all unknowns picked up from the New York area where the movie was set. It was a modest affair, and unlike most slasher films it was a moody piece with an eerie atmosphere. The idea for the film came from one of Larraz's friends, whose wife was killed in a car crash. After her death the husband kept the smashed-up car in his garden, more than a just a battered monument to his grief—the husband would often spend hours inside the wreck playing songs they'd heard together on the day of the accident. A similarly strange situation crops up in **Deadly Manor**, when the teenagers uncover a car, coffins and bodies behind the walls of an old dark house.

Completed in 1990, **Deadly Manor** has still to receive a general release. Larraz is quite pleased with the film, but disappointed with the special effects and make-up. They didn't have enough money to make the deranged female owner of the house look convincing, and the latex make-up on her face was quite appalling. It was hard work making the meagre resources stretch, but Larraz continued undaunted.

His most serious work to date has been the television series **Goya**, based on the life of the famous painter. **Goya** was produced by the Spanish director Narcisco Ibañez Serrador, who hired Larraz because he needed someone who could give the production a dark, sombre mood. He'd seen Larraz's atmospheric horror films and decided that José was the right man for the job. Unfortunately, the series ended up dubbed with bland mid-atlantic accents, which more or less ruined the delicate atmosphere of the production and detracted from its impact.

**Sevilla Connection** (1992) is Larraz's last film to have a general release. It was another comedy vehicle, featuring two klutzy coppers in an assortment of embarrassing situations. It would be sad if this was the final film from this talented director. Larraz is one of the few film-makers living in Britain who has a feel for the uncanny. Against the odds he's tried to make films that have a patina of class, an edge of mystery that separates them from the pack. If you're interested in watching or making low budget horror

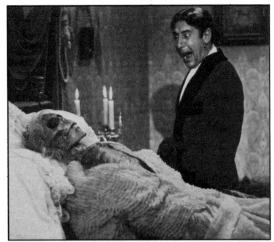

◄ **Polvos magicos** (1979)

films his output is essential viewing because it shows what's possible when you don't have much money. When all you have is talent, and the determination to make something personal rather than just low grade, run of the mill exploitation.

**LARRAZ FILMOGRAPHY**

1969    **Whirlpool/She Died With Her Boots On/ L'enfer de l'érotisme** (GB/Den)

1971    **Deviation** (GB)

1973    **Scream and Die/Psycho Sex Fiend/The House That Vanished** (GB)
       **Emma, puertas oscuras** (Sp)

1974    **Symptoms/The Blood Virgin** (GB)
       **Vampyres/Daughters of Dracula/Vampyres— Daughters of Darkness/The Vampyre Orgy/ Ossessione carnale/Las hijas de Dracula** (GB)

1976    **Fin de la inocencia** (Sp)

1977    **El mirón** (Sp)
       **Luto riguroso** (Sp)
       **Muerte incierta** (Sp/It)

1978    **Visita del vicio/Violation of the Bitch** (Sp)

1979    **Ocasión** (Sp)
       **Golden Lady** (GB)
       **Polvos mágicos** (Sp)

1980    **Malizia erotica/And Give Us Our Daily Sex/El periscopo** (Sp/It)

1981    **Las alumnas de Madame Olga/Sex Academy/ Madame Olga's Pupils** (Sp)
       **Estigma** (Sp/It)
       **La momia nacional** (Sp)
       **Los ritos sexuales del diablo/Black Candles/ Naked Dreams** (Sp)

1982    **Juan la loca...de vez en cuando** (Sp)

1987    **Descanse en piezas/Rest in Pieces** (Sp)

1988    **Filo del hacha/Edge of the Axe** (Sp/US)
       **Goya** (Sp) TV series

1990    **Deadly Manor/Savage Lust** (Sp/US)

1992    **Sevilla Connection** (Sp)

produit
et **PAR JOSÉ BÉNAZÉRAF**
réalisé

*Cover Girls*

# The Cry of the Flesh

## THE FILMS OF JOSÉ BÉNAZÉRAF

"Life is a paradox," says José Bénazéraf cheerfully. Sitting in his beautiful apartment in one of the plushest suburbs of Paris, surrounded by all the trappings of the good life, he looks content. It's hard to believe that this patrician gentleman, who has made over 70 films, is still largely unknown outside France, a marginal, an outsider. He's crusty but sophisticated, and a far cry from the popular notion of a lurid sex-film maker.

Bénazéraf is now 72. His career began in the early sixties with sexy thrillers that established his reputation as a man to watch. Once upon a time he was the darling of the critics, his name a trade mark for provocative and classy cinema. The *New York Herald Tribune* said he was 'as important as Godard and Resnais.' And Henri Langlois, founder of the famous Cinémathèque, announced that 'his films are like rivers carrying stones that are absolute gems.'

But that was then, and now he's pretty much forgotten. His downfall came fast and can be traced to that period in the mid-seventies when censorship loosened, giving him the freedom to do exactly what he wanted, which meant a move deeper into the taboo territory of eroticism. Bénazéraf is a cultured rebel, an irreverent enemy of conformity. Throughout his career he's continually cocked a snook at conventional values. "One image I find very erotic," he says, "a nude girl with a marriage veil on her head, who is caressing herself or caressing some guy's prick. I find that very provocative at the level of the social concept because it overturns everything...chastity, virginity, all of the fortresses."

As the sex in Bénazéraf's films became harder, his reputation dwindled. Even one of his most sympathetic admirers, Paul-Hervé Mathis, commented: 'It is a little saddening to see one of the very great film-makers relentlessly churning out whatever comes to hand'. Yet no matter how explicit his films became they were more than just cheapskate porno movies. They had attitude and class. Rare qualities in that area of the film world and probably due to the total control that he insists on.

With **L'éternité pour nous** (**Sin On the Beach**) in 1961, Bénazéraf became one of the very first Europeans to write, produce and direct his own films. But even then he wasn't entirely free from the sort of petty interference that so exasperates him. The distributor found the title "too literary" and suggested **Le cri de la chair** (The Cry of the Flesh). Bénazéraf said, "Well, if you want...but why not **My Grandfather's Bollocks** !"

During the 1970's, the State refused to allow any advertising for sex films. No photos outside the cinemas, no pictures on the posters. Only the title to attract paying punters. This led to a preponderance of leadenly obvious film names. Bénazéraf retaliated by poking fun at the censor with the outrageous jokiness of his titles. They ran the gamut, from the direct **Baise moi partout** (Fuck me all over), through the sublime: **Antiquaire à la chatte trempée** (Antique Dealer with a Wet Pussy), to the ridiculous: **Je te suce, tu me suce, il nous......**(I Suck You, You Suck me, He....).

In 1974, Bénazéraf said that he made films: "Because it gives me fun, enormous fun..... and to fight against the bannings, the censors, that's not bad too....The day when it starts to bore me, I promise you I'll stop....Never for a second do I take the cinema seriously. It's not a serious enterprise."

Unfortunately, in a country like France where they *do* take their cinema very seriously, Bénazéraf's non-stop provocation finally became just too much to bear. From being 'The Antonioni of Pigalle' and judged on the same terms as Fellini and Minelli, he became just another misguided hack. 'It has to be asked', wrote the high-brow film mag *Positif*, 'if the interests of the viewers of such films is really proportional to the efforts of Bénazéraf to take the genre out of its sub-cultural ghetto. One cannot answer this question in a very optimistic fashion.'

Bénazéraf was born in 1922 in Casablanca, which made him even from birth a sort of outsider in French society. He studied Political Science and was a pilot during the war, flying missions over Germany from a base in England. After the war he began to deal in industrial cotton. Using the money he made, together with his Air Force pension, he set up his own production company, Les Films d'Univers (later Les Films du Chesne). His first release was a musical comedy, **Les lavandières du Portugal** (1958), about a stunt to launch a new washing machine.

Bénazéraf's first cinematic loves were the German expressionist classics of the 1920's and the Russians such as Eisenstein and Vertov. This led him to hire a French veteran director of silents—Kirsanoff—to direct this first picture. Unfortunately the old man died during the shooting of the film and Bénazéraf tells how his body had to be locked in his office for three days because the police didn't want to come and take

◀ (Facing page) A favourite of the new wave, **Cover Girls** (1963)

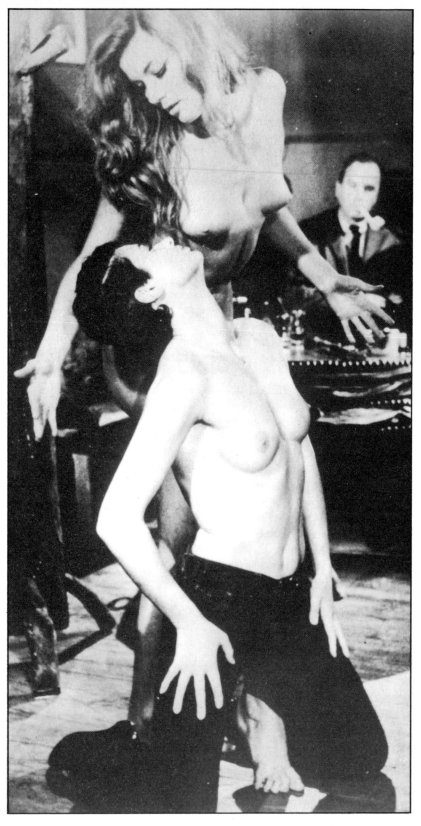

Hot dance sequence from ▲
**Sexus** (1964)

written himself about a young German girl who falls in love with a prisoner of war .

Two more productions followed—**Un martien à Paris** in 1960 and **La fête espagnole** in 1961—before Bénazéraf finally decided to direct for himself from a script he had co-written with Yves Denaux. The film was **L'éternité pour nous** (**Sin on the Beach**; 1961), and it was shot in twelve days for a ridiculously low budget. Now the film can be seen as a sort of classic of the genre, largely created by its own success, of films set by the beach, illuminated by the bright summer sun and with a plot that allows lots of female flesh to be put on display. In other words, **L'éternité pour nous** is the first real French—or European—piece of softcore porn. Like all Bénazéraf's films, its aim is to show the subversive nature of the erotic. How sexual desire breaks down the rational, conforming shells we try to construct around ourselves. For Bénazéraf eroticism is revolutionary. "In bourgeois society eroticism is a form of anarchy." The structure of his films show this, with their tense, claustrophobic scenarios that suddenly explode into sexual life. His purpose is always to provoke this reaction in the viewer. As Paul-Hervé Mathis writes: 'His films exist to give you a hard-on. The praise depends upon the size.'

The success of **L'éternité** launched Bénazéraf on a series of films that mixed sex, action and politics into an explosive brew. So explosive that he was never far from trouble with the French censor. "Intellectually, cinematically and sexually inferior" is how he described them. Small wonder that they took their revenge on him.

Other directors, such as Max Pécas, were able to get away with eroticism because they were less provocative. Bénazéraf was a thorn in the side of the censor and became a sort of whipping boy, which turned out to be good for business. He enjoyed the notoriety, the rebel status. Soon his name became a byword for the dangerous and the erotic. This reputation lingered on well into the 1970's. Years later he was able to bring out an anthology of clips cut from his earlier films and sell it as the latest word in sexual freedom. In fact, many of his later films—from the mid-70's on—consisted of little more than re-edited highlights strung together.

Still, in 1961 he had it all before him and his next film, following the model of **L'éternité**, was another sexually charged thriller.

**Le concerto de la peur**, released in 1962, is a story of drug smuggling, gangsters and kidnapping. The film had a lot of action and a little sex, coupled with a great soundtrack from Chet

it away at the weekend. Incidents like this helped put the seal on his already well developed contempt for bureaucracy and petty officials.

When he'd completed the film Bénazéraf travelled to the States, returning a year later with enough cash to produce his second feature, **La fille de Hambourg** (1959). This was a story he'd

Baker. It was bought for US release by Bob Cresse and released as **Night of Lust**, with added scenes filmed by R. Lee Frost.[1]

The success of the film in the States led to Bénazéraf's next project, **Paris erotika (Paris, Oh, La La!**; 1963). Originally called **24 heures d'un Américain à Paris**, the film features the roly-poly Dick Randall as an American businessman adrift in Paris. The camera follows him as he samples the delights of the capital's bars and strip-clubs. It's a hymn to the delights of the flesh, and a celebration of Pigalle and Montmartre, the famous Crazy Horse saloon and the Folies Pigalle.

The films was shot quickly, in only six days, with the sound track of cheesy music from Louis Guy, and Bénazéraf's own voice-over, added during the editing.

Seen today, **Paris erotika** has a nostalgic appeal that was certainly never intended. The area in which it was made has now passed into history and the sex sold there today exhibits all the "vulgarity and stupidity" of which Bénazéraf declared himself the enemy. "Pornography and eroticism can only survive if they are transcended by lyricism", Bénazéraf said in 1975. "It has to be a song of love." And **Paris erotika** is certainly that. Its appeal lies in its unashamed and almost documentary-like view of an enclosed world where sex is a show and the onlookers are willing participants. Paul-Hervé Mathis describes its intended audience as 'Sexual obsessives', but then goes on to say that the term is not meant as a put-down—that sexual obsession can be a healthy thing: 'Perhaps it's even an indication of a heightened, sharpened sensibility'.

This quality was easier to detect in Bénazéraf's next film, **Cover Girls** (1963), which received the accolade of a full two page review in the film buff's bible, *Cahiers du cinéma*. The critics dragged out their superlatives for this 'meditation on love, life and cinema'. Now Bénazéraf was being compared with Vincente Minnelli in his ability to visualise the internal dream world of the artist.

**Cover Girls** is a supremely claustrophobic film. The editing reinforces this mood with subtle, almost subliminal cuts joining long sequences into a continuous flow of action.

For his next two films, **La nuit la plus longue** (The Longest Night; 1964) and **L'enfer sur la plage** (Hell on the Beach; 1965), Bénazéraf returned to the B-thriller style of **L'éternité....** Both films were successful, and both featured the expected Bénazéraf mix of action, pretty girls and bare flesh that had already become his trade mark. But another, slightly more worrying, trait was also in evidence. As *Cahiers du*

▲ Michel Lemoine and Sylvia Sorrente **Sin on the Beach** (1961)

*cinéma* noted, it was impossible to make any sense of the stories. Daylight shots appeared in the middle of sequences filmed at night; the dialogue often seemed unrelated to the action; establishing shots were done away with; long scenes filmed in a single take replaced any conventional montage. The wilfulness that had always been present now took centre stage. But still there was a power and a presence there and a determination to film, come what may. Even without a story, without dialogue and with no idea of where he was going Bénazéraf loaded his camera and began to shoot. 'With all the stubbornness and dignity of an angler in the middle of the desert.'

At the end of **L'enfer sur la plage**, Bénazéraf gives his own view: "Don't be deceived by appearances. Nothing happened by accident. Everything has been worked out, planned, premeditated....," he says, as the camera moves through a darkened apartment.

At this point in the mid sixties, Bénazéraf was gaining quite a reputation amongst the public and the more radical critics. But it was his next film, **Joe Caligula** (1966), that really made his name. The film was banned, not because of sex or nudity—although it has both—but on account of the violence with which it tells the story of the title character's attempt to rise to the top of the Paris underworld.

The scene where a gang member lacerates a woman's back with a knife was wildly over the top for its day. But Bénazéraf defended it, say-

The censor killed it, ▲
**Joe Caligula** (1966)

ing that "if Stroheim, Fritz Lang and Bergman have the right to deal with violence and shock. Why not me?"

Unfortunately, the censors didn't agree. The film was refused a certificate for two years, only seeing the light of day toward the end of 1968, clipped of nearly half an hour of its more excessive moments. By then, following in the wake of Arthur Penn's **Bonnie and Clyde**, the effect it might have had had been dissipated and the film sank into obscurity.

In the meantime Bénazéraf had made three more films, **Les premières lueurs de l'aube** (The First Light of Dawn; 1966), a German co-production, **Un épais manteau de sang (The Subject is Sex**; 1967) and **Flesh and Fantasy** (1967). The last one was again made for Bob Cresse's Olympic International Films.

Both **Lueurs...** and **The Subject is Sex** are thrillers in the good old Bénazéraf tradition, with moody night club scenes, twitchy, nervous anti-heroes and always lots of female flesh. **Lueurs...** also shows Bénazéraf's poetic side, with its slow depiction of the coming of a grey dawn over the Hamburg docks as its wayward hero waits to die.

**The Subject is Sex** was one of the first of Bénazéraf's films to be shown outside the familiar Midi-Minuit-Styx circuit.[2] From the very first frame the audience was confused. Hardly surprising. The prologue to the film is a bizarre strip-tease performed by Kacia Bartel, which finishes with the voice over comment: "That's just for my own pleasure. Now we talk about serious things, because it seems that we have to talk about serious things."

For the next couple of years, following the banning of **Joe Caligula**, Bénazéraf was in a sort of wilderness.[3] In 1969 he came back with a

bang. **Le désirable et le sublime** (The Desirable and the Sublime) and **Frustration (Frustrated Woman)**, which followed in 1970, are two of his strongest films. Both take place in enclosed situations with a small cast of characters, and both are exposés of the sexual undercurrents in middle class life.

In **Le désirable**, a typically bourgeois doctor and his wife are visited by a stranger. The three of them dine together while watching TV coverage of an election. Over the course of the meal they lay bare their own political philosophies and inadequacies. The film then becomes very bizarre as the stranger seduces the doctor's wife and opens up a whole parcel of weird sexual fantasies. Another girl appears—or is imagined—various games with a whip ensue and things get steamy, until finally the doctor pushes his wife off a cliff for the sea to swallow her up. The film was controversial, more for its political than for its sexual content, and was heavily cut in many parts of France.

**Frustration** is a continuation of some of the themes of **Le désirable**. Again it's set in a claustrophobic location—an ancient manor house in the country—and again there's a trio at the centre of it. Once more it's a doctor (played by Michel Lemoine, who also wrote much of the dialogue) and his wife, Agnes, who share the house with the wife's sister, Adelaide (Janine Reynaud). Adelaide is in love with her sister, but sublimates her feelings with fantasies of being married to Michel. Her dream life begins to take over from reality. Early in the film we see her walking along a corridor and opening door after door—and in each room she sees her sister and Michel making love. She tells her sister that Michel has a mistress, who she describes in loving detail—including a strange, dreamlike meeting in a cafe, with Edith Piaf's song *Milord* on the soundtrack.

A young German couple arrive at the house by chance; their car has broken down, and Adelaide invites them to stay. In a horrifying dream sequence she imagines Michel making love to the girl and then having her tortured. While Michel is out looking after a sick patient, Adelaide at last imagines herself making love to her sister. Then she takes a knife, that actually looks more like a crucifix, and stands over her sister's bed with it. When Michel gets back he finds that Adelaide has killed herself.

As in Buñuel's masterly **Belle de jour**, which it resembles in some ways, there is no easy distinction made between reality and fantasy in **Frustration**. Largely, our point of view is that of

**Immoral Tales**

Adelaide. Consequently it's her uncertain, neurotic and dangerous world that the film expresses, always with the possibility of violence lingering just beyond the edge of the frame. As Bénazéraf explains, Adelaide's suicide is a turning in on herself of all the violence and frustration she projects onto the world around her

**Frustration** was Bénazéraf's last "soft hard" film. It was released in 1971, just as the sex film boom was beginning in France. By 1974 it was in full swing, and suddenly he found himself able to film and show things that would have been impossible in the 1960's. Films like **Adolescence pervertie** and **La soubrette perverse**[4] soon gave way to **Les gouines**, the first real hardcore Bénazéraf, in 1975. The film starred Beatrice Harnois and Claudine Beccarie, both important stars of the French porno wave. It was a typically wry Bénazérafien look at bourgeois morals, in which a lawyer divorces his wife and marries his best friend's daughter in order to avoid a charge of rape that would ruin him socially.

However, in spite of Bénazéraf's uniquely personal style of editing and the sharp political points he injected into the screenplay, the need to add hardcore scenes only served to reduce the narrative to a series of cliches, clogging up the action like dance sequences tacked onto a melodrama. He soon came to realise that the audience for hardcore films was not really interested in stories. They paid their money for one thing—to see screwing, in close up, on screen. And worst of all, the actors and actresses who formed the stock company of most porn films of the time were not really actors at all, in the traditional sense.

In 1976 the French Government introduced the so-called 'X-law', a series of fiscal measures aimed at containing the burgeoning porno business within acceptable limits. The social and market perceptions of what a sex film was changed very rapidly. No longer was there the option of showing one's product in the prestigious Champs Élysées, for example. Small, licensed, 'specialist' cinemas sprang up, mostly fleapits with all the allure of a three day old cheese sandwich. The days of **Emmanuelle** and **Immoral Tales**, sex films with class, were over. The notion of producing quality hardcore was pretty soon a thing of the past.

Bénazéraf admits that this period, from 1976 to 1981, was an absolute nadir for him. He survived largely by re-editing old films (**Sequences interdites**) into compendiums as he had done earlier with **Bacchanales 69**, or by rereleasing old films with new titles and added hardcore scenes

(**Une garce en chaleur, Un diner très special**). His products of this period show a wilful abandoning of all the things that had once made him special. **Bordell SS**, for example, with rising star Brigitte Lahaie, exhibits all the worst signs of the rushed job. Here even Bénazéraf's eccentric editing style looks like the work of an amateur. As *Positif* magazine commented, this period marked the 'end of the "political" Bénazéraf' as well as the end of the Bénazéraf 'style.'

By the beginning of the 1980's his reputation in France was at an all time low. He made a living making and selling films abroad—mostly in Germany, Italy, Spain and, above all, the US. But he accepted that he was well and truly ghettoised. TV, such an important source of finance for film-makers, refused to talk to him. If they wanted sex films they could buy them at bargain rates from the vaults of companies like Alpha France. And if he went to them with a different sort of film they wouldn't take him seriously. His reputation as a sex-film maker excluded him from being considered as anything else.

▼ Girls just wanna have fun, **Les deux gouines** (1975)

Bénazéraf's earlier outspokenness against the mediocrity of French cinema and its official guardians now came back to haunt him. He had dug his own grave as far as they were concerned. The sex film business was a business still, but it now had little to do with cinema. From the early eighties, much of the product was shot cheaply on video and sold as cassettes, or shown in the video-booths of Pigalle and Clichy. It was not a situation that interested Bénazéraf, but he had no chance of moving out of it. Pécas, who had dabbled in hardcore in the 1970's, now returned to the sexy and violent thrillers that had first made his name, but for Bénazéraf there was no going back.

Abandoning all notion of moving into the quality arena, with cherished projects such as his **Trotsky**, he bit the bullet and began to make quick, cheap hardcore films for the export market. Over a hundred of them from 1983 to 1989. Although he signed them with his customary signature there were probably few who cared—or even knew who he was.

For a man who claims that he never took cinema seriously it may seem to some like a due reward, but an industry that can't find a place for someone with Bénazéraf's talents will always be the poorer for it. Perhaps, like so many others in the commercial underground, he is just too intelligent, too self-willed and too much of a maverick to be able to deal with the money men, accountants and petty bureaucrats

**The Infamous House ▶ of Madame X** (1974)

on anything but his own terms. And those terms are always—No Compromise.

## INTERVIEW WITH **JOSE BÉNAZÉRAF**

▶*How did you get involved in making films?*

Fantasy. Complete fantasy. I had no idea that I was going to make movies. French movies made me sick. You know, that was the time of Jean Delannoy and all those shitty old fashioned directors. Brigitte Bardot and all that stuff. Entirely conventional and boring. I was crazy about German movies. But German movies of 1933-34. Around the time of **The Blue Angel**. All those guys who left Germany for America because they were Jews. To me they were just so great. Their films were like a cry of desperation. But I hated those damn *'frenchy'* movies—full of bourgeois satisfaction. Even when Delannoy made **Notre Dame de Paris** with Lollobrigida, it was shit. I hated all that. And I also liked the American film noir—with John Garfield, for example, whom nobody remembers today. They only remember Bogart who was the worst of them. You had Cagney, George Raft...people of the streets who knew how to love, how to die. They were fantastic. That was my taste.

And then one day someone I knew came to me and suggested a musical comedy. I told them that my musical horizons were Monteverdi and Bach—so forget about that. But I asked them how much they wanted and they said 2 million francs—that's old francs, about 20 or 30 thousand francs today—and I said OK. Then, later, I was in Milan and I thought well, what can I do with this damn piece of paper? So I went to some distributors and told them about the film—**Les lavandières du Portugal**—and they really liked it! So I made two or three movies like that and I made a whole lot of money. Completely by accident.

▶*As a producer?*

Yeah, strictly as a producer. And then I lost it all with **La fille de Hambourg**. It was a complete disaster. And so I said "Stop! José, if you want to make movies you are going to have to direct them yourself, produce them yourself and then, if they're bad you've only got yourself to blame." So I started to direct movies as a *'boutade'*—you know what that is? The word is important.

▶*A whim?*

Yes, OK. So I started making movies as a whim. I liked pretty girls—which is a male reaction, but completely simple and elementary. So I started making movies with pretty girls in them. And, making movies with pretty girls, I found I put some erotic scenes in because it was quite ...exciting, let's use the word. But every step of it was completely by accident. I mean, the books I liked were not the books of erotic writers, my music was not the music of erotic movie makers—I was completely unaware of all that. I had some success with soft movies, but eventually I had to go down into the world of those cheap arseholes—sex film writers and directors who were all completely useless, talentless bastards. They couldn't even serve behind a bar. They had no class, no style, no culture. They put no sophistication into fuck movies and so they committed a kind of auto-suicide. Until video came along. And now they add up how much penetration you have on the cassette, how much sodo, how much S & M—how many minutes of each, and they list that all on the cassette. And so they establish a product. Now the poor girl has to be fucked 22 times every ten minutes by three men and they put all that into the advertising. And I had to go into this world, which was definitely not my world.

Then, from 1983 to 1989 I made almost a hundred movies for an American video company called Caballero. I wanted to shoot in America—in Louisiana and Florida, places I love. But they said, no, José, you'll have trouble with the unions. Make your films in Europe. So I made movies in Spain, Germany, Scandinavia. Sometimes two movies in a week. It was fun and they paid well. But we were always completely unprepared. I had co-producers just to arrange the actors and for a place to shoot. Then we'd arrive in a group in, say, Ibiza. I'd ask my Spanish co-producers to find a nice villa and a private beach—very important. And we'd turn up with six, seven, eight gorgeous girls and maybe two or three guys. You can't avoid a few men in these things sometimes! And I would have no idea what we were going to shoot the next day. I'd just make up some funny story...put a little drama into it. And always a lot of irony and a kind of detachment. And anyway, my movies seem to have had some sort of class. I don't know if many French producers were selling porno to America at that time. So I did that for about eight years. Meanwhile in France I made two or three soft movies which were shown on the TV without any interest. I just wanted the French to remember that I still existed, that was all.

▲ Bénazéraf goes down big at the Midi Minuit cinema, Paris
(Photo: Paul-Hervé Mathis)

▶ *Your importance in the French industry is, historically, quite considerable. And yet you've never had the kind of notice that perhaps you should have. Do you feel bitter about that?*

It's a good question. I don't know anyone who would be indifferent in that situation. Having a reputation makes it easier to do certain things. But for years my attitude was very snobbish and very condescending. When TV called I'd say "No, I'm too busy". I didn't want to get involved in some shitty TV thing. So I had an attitude—very *'refus'* (stubborn) But, if you want to go further, of course I would like to have had the recognition. It makes things easier if you want to do something more important and need money from the government or from a co-producer or a TV station. A couple of months ago I went to Canal Plus, with a scenario a young guy had given me that I liked, and at the end of the meeting the girl said: "But, Mr. Bénazéraf, who is going to direct this film?" I said, "OK, bye." And I picked up my script and left Canal Plus. I mean, imagine if you're a painter and they ask you—who's going to paint this picture?

▶ *Was that because they didn't know your name?*

Oh, more or less. Or they thought that I was out of the business.

▶ *At one time, in* Cahiers du cinéma, *they compared you with Minnelli. Did you find that funny?*

It was completely crazy. Hysterical. Too much. I thought it was a joke. I still don't know if they were serious or not. 'The opening of **Cover Girls** was like Minnelli because it had a plane in it.' Planes fascinate me so I always try to put one in at the beginning or end of my movies.

But life is a paradox. You never can tell what critics are going to say. I made a little soft movie

that was shown on French TV. **Cynthia's Diary**. It was completely improvised on the spot. I just made shots of a girl walking around with no clothes on or doing her shopping in the little market, swimming in the sea. We went crazy trying to edit it. To make sense of it. because there was no sense to any of it. And it got the most fantastic response. 24% viewing figures. So you never can tell. Life is a paradox.

▶ *How did you team up with Dick Randall in* **Paris, Oh, La La?**

He came to see me one day. He was representing a guy in Los Angeles who was more or less a gangster (Bob Cresse). He wanted to buy a little film of mine called **Concerto de la peur**. To me it was new selling to the Americans. But he paid me cash—10 or 15 thousand dollars. Not a lot of money but it was only a couple of weeks shooting. I made my films quickly even in those days. I asked him if he wanted a contract and he said, "No—why bother?" He had a big success with that film in the States. It was called **Night of Lust** over there. Then he came to me again with another $15,000 and asked if I had another film. And I said, No. I was shooting **Cover Girls**. I was thinking it was my masterpiece. I had a very intellectual touch, you know. Marx, Engels, Freud—they were all in the movie—but only in the dialogue! And he said, "But I have to go back to America with the negative in a week." I said, Are you crazy! In a week?

So I shot Poupée La Rose[5] in 2 days and 2 nights. Literally without stopping. Going through all the cabarets in Paris. Shooting, shooting. And Poupée was fantastic. With the most divine arse. It was crazy. Then I edited it in 2 days and I gave him the negative. One week. It made a lot of money, too. Even in France

it made a fortune. It's always like that. Without any thought or conviction. Like a whim.

▶ *They called you the Antonioni of Pigalle*
That's right.

▶ *But now it's sad to see how sordid it's all become.*
Yes. Even the Champs Élysées these days. It's so sad.

▶ *One of the pioneers of French erotic cinema is Michel Lemoine. You worked with him several times. First of all in* **L'éternité pour nous**........

That was my first movie. It was quite an adventure. I had no CNC authorisation to make that film. No director's card, nothing at all.[6] When I finished it they said you can't put it on. So I said fuck them, and I started showing it in Belgium, in Germany. I even sold it to Japan. For a fortune. The success was so big that they couldn't ignore it and so eventually they gave me a director's card and a Visa to show the movie in France.

▶ *How did the film come about?*

Well, it was the same old story. I was at Cannes and I met a girl. I was lying on the beach reading a book and I saw this girl coming out of the sea. She was quite beautiful. And as she passed me by I said "Are you an actress?" And she said, in a little girl's voice, "No. But I would like to be." "OK—you're going to start next week." And so we started next week. I did everything. Even operated the camera. Michel Lemoine was just someone I knew at the time and I said, "Come on, you're going to make a movie with me. Bring me two girls!" And I didn't even leave Cannes. I went to Agd, where some friends I knew had a house, and we shot the movie there on the beach. It was a fantastic success in Germany. Constantin bought it and it made a fortune. I made it for 200,000 francs.

▶ *What's the story behind* **Joe Caligula?**

It's a very sad story. I made the film with Gérard Blain, who was quite a star of the *nouvelle vague*. It was a story of incest—but intellectual incest—between a man and his sister. I made it in a kind of—in France we say 'extase'—because I believed totally in that movie. I took it very seriously. I invested a lot of money. I shot it in black and white. It was **Bonnie and Clyde**—the same kind of mood, the same kind of tenderness and the same kind of violence. It was **Bonnie and Clyde**—but two years earlier. I showed it to the censors and they said over 18 only. So I said, OK, over 18 only. I

Belgian poster for **Sin on** ▼
the Beach (1961)

had national release and on Wednesday, the day before release, we had 30 or 40 copies across France and they said "No. Completely banned". And I was left with 30 prints of the film and all the costs to pay. And I couldn't export the film or exploit it. It was a disaster. And it's so sad because perhaps it's the best movie I ever made. The only really good one. They said I was making an apology for violence. You know—the old routine. Gratuitous violence.

▶ *Do you think the banning of* **Joe Caligula** *was the revenge of the authorities for your earlier defiance?*

Absolutely. Absolutely. It was revenge. Because of my opposition to all that administration and bureaucracy. So they fucked me and they fucked me well. I didn't want to touch a camera after that. And besides I lost a lot of money. Then, two years later, along came **Bonnie and Clyde**—which was a much bigger film, with prestigious actors and so on. I cut **Joe Caligula** and put a couple of sex scenes in it and got a lamentable release in Midi-Minuit and Scarlett and nobody cared. Two years on it had completely lost its impact. Because everything had got more violent. It's like sex in movies. It's all a fashion. Things change quickly

▶ *After that experience did your films become more bitter—more serious?*

No. On the contrary. I made one political movie, **Le désirable et le sublime**. Which again caused an incredible fuss. To show it I had to rent three theatres and put in all the projection gear myself. I worked day and night without any authority from the police to run a theatre. The film eventually ran for six months. It was quite a success, although nobody talks about it now. I tell you, if you go outside the rules of the big distributors you are lost. Lost. The whole system of exporting and exploiting has to all be just so. Otherwise you become marginalised. But I had to adopt that attitude because nobody wanted that film. It was a completely Trotskyist movie. Anarchistic. Spitting on De Gaulle and all his crew.

▶ *At one time you wanted to make a film about Trotsky?*

Yes. It's my big frustration. My head was full of Trotsky. To me he was the most authentic hero of the Russian revolution. The true hero of Marxism. Perhaps even more than Lenin. And his image has only been used in a dramatic sense, and in a stupid way, by Losey. A fantastic waste of money and energy. So I wrote a scenario. It was a serious movie—about 25 mil-

▲ Joëlle Cœur (centre)
**Black Love** (1973)

lion francs budget. Not very big. But I couldn't find any backing. I found closed doors—and closed minds!

But, you know, I hear this kind of thing from so many directors, and I don't want to sound like a marginal—because I'm not. I make money. I do OK. I can't complain about marginality. I'm not lost in the corner. OK—I make marginal movies—sex movies....

▶ *You once said that eroticism is a form of rebellion.*

Completely. Even though I'm now 70 I feel the same way. It's a rebellion against the contract of marriage, against society, against religion, against the incredible conservatism all around us today. Now AIDS has frightened people so much it's killed all forms of rebellion, except voyeurism—and that's the success of video. Video and masturbation.

▶ *Which is the opposite of revolution.*

(Laughs) Yes! The opposite of revolution.

▶ *Which do you think are your best films?*

3 or 4 of them were not badly done. Out of 50 or 60, just 3 or 4. One was **Le désirable et le sublime**. Beautiful 'image'—besides the political message. And **Cover Girls**. The girl in that film was so beautiful. An explosion of blonde hair with green, oriental shaped eyes. And **Les lesbiennes**. Again a beautiful 'image'. But that's it. Nothing more.

▶ *The two driving forces in your films seem to be sex on the one hand and politics on the other. Which is the most important?*

**Cover Girls (1963)** ▲

Today? Sex! (Laughs) Twenty years ago it was politics. No, but even today sex is the still the most important thing in life. And now I'm sad about all the time I lost in politics, losing a part of my life and spending money on political movies. Yes, sex is the most important thing. But everyone is going to tell you that. It's not an original thought. Especially when you see the disaster of what you were thinking was good in politics. When you see the unsuccessful examples of socialism all over the world. And people like Bush, Reagan, Clinton at the head of the most powerful country in the world. It's got to make you skeptical about politics. So don't waste your time, your brain, your conviction, your energy. Dedicate yourself to life. But this is a very elementary principle.

▶ *How did you find the girls in your films?*

Completely by accident. Even in porno movies I used people who were not professionals. They just did it for the excitement. But always I was looking for some class. It's in the face. I mean, for me the sexiest woman ever was Gene Tierney. She was a big star in the thirties. And Lauren Bacall. They released in me an orgasm of enthusiasm when I was very young. I was not attracted to the sex bombs like Jane Russell or Marilyn Monroe. I was attracted to the classy kinds of women. So I try to find that kind of actress.

▶ *Does Brigitte Lahaie fit that bill ?*

Not for me, no. I made a couple of movies with her. One of them was not bad. And when I say not bad I mean that there was a good *'image'*.

That's the only definition—in that kind of movie—good or bad *'image'*. The vulgarity of the porno cinema makes me mad. I like to make it my way. Classy, or not at all. That's the title of your piece! Classy, or Not At All.

### BÉNAZÉRAF PARTIAL FILMOGRAPHY

All France (Fr) unless otherwise indicated

1961　**L'éternité pour nous/Le cri de la chair/Sin on the Beach**

1962　**Le concerto de la peur/La drogue du vice/Notte érotique/Night of Lust**

1963　**24 heures d'un Americain à Paris/Paris erotika/Paris Oh, La La!/Sexy partie** (Fr/US)
　　　**Cover Girls** (Fr/It; released 1965)

1964　**La nuit la plus longue/L'enfer dans la peau/Sexus**

1965　**L'enfer sur la plage**

1966　**Joe Caligula**
　　　**Les premières lueurs de l'aube/Plaisirs pervers/St Pauli Zwischen Nacht und Morgen** (Fr/Ger)

1967　**Un épais manteau de sang/The Subject is Sex**
　　　**Flesh and Fantasy** (US)

1969　**Le désirable et le sublime**
　　　**Bacchanales 69**

1970　**Triangle**(short)

1971　**Frustration/The Trip to Perversion/Frustrated Woman**

1972　**The French Love**
　　　**Racism** (US)

1973　**Black Love/L'homme qui voulait violer le monde**
　　　**Bacchanales 73**
　　　**Orgie et bacchanale**

1974　**Adolescence pervertie/Adolescenza perversa**
　　　**Le sexe nu/Naked Sex/Un homme se penche sur son destin**
　　　**Le Bordel (1ere Epoch:1900) ou la maison des confidences/The Infamous House of Madame X**
　　　**La soubrette perverse/La soubrette/La suc... perverse**
　　　**Voir Malte et mourir**
　　　**Orgies et voluptés**

1975　**Les deux gouines/Les gouines/Victoire and Isabelle**
　　　**Les incestueuses**
　　　**J.B.1./Porno Technique/Joy**
　　　**La veuve lubrique/La veuve/The Randy Widow**
　　　**Une garce en chaleur (**hardcore version of **Voir Malte et mourir)**
　　　**Les lesbiennes/Une femme plus une femme**
　　　**Sequences interdites** (Compilation of scenes cut from earlier films)

La planque 1/Sex Porno
La planque 2
Sappho et Lesbos
1977 La bonne auberge/Içi, on baise
Un diner très special
Les vices cachés de Miss Aubepine
1978 Anna, les cuisses entr'ouvertes
Baise-moi partout/Attention, je vais jouir
Grimpe-moi dessus et fais-moi mal
Bordell SS/Freudenhaus 42
Ouvre-toi
1979 Hurlements d'extase
Nicole par-dessus par-dessous
1980 Amours d'adolescentes pubères
Brantome 81: vie de dames galantes
Les contes de La Fontaine
Je te suce, tu me suces, il nous...
1982 Patricia, Valerie, Anna et les autres
Anthologie des scènes interdites, érotiques et
pornographiques
1983 Chattes chaudes sur queues brûlantes
Detournement de mineures
Éva la grande suçeuse
La Madonna des pipes
Le Majordome est bien monté
Rita la vicieuse
La star sodomisée
Le viol à bicyclette
1984 Antiquaire à la chatte trempée
Le cul des mille plaisirs
L'espionne s'envoie en l'air
Du foutre plein le cul
Le port aux putes/Whores' Port
Ingrid, Whore of Hamburg
Je mouille aussi par derrière
Je te suce, tu me suce ou la vie d'un bordel de
province
Petits culs à enfiler
Sexologues en chaleur
1985 Adventure in San Fenleu
Erotic Intruders
Gilda la ravageuse
Hot Close Ups
Madame Deborah
Making a Porno Movie
Mrs Winter's Lovers/Confidences pornographi-
ques de Lady Winter
Olinka, Grand Priestess of Love
Revolution
Trashy Tourist
Yacht Orgy
1986 Fantasies of a Married Woman
Hot Patutti
Naughty French Fantasies/House of Ill Repute
Passionate Pupils
Sex Resort

Triple Penetration
Voyage au bout du vice
1987 Saint-Tropez interdit

## AS PRODUCER

1958 **Les lavandières du Portugal**
dir Pierre Gaspard-Huit
1959 **La fille de Hambourg**
dir Yves Allegret; Bénazéraf co-scr
1960 **Un martien à Paris/A Martian in Paris**
dir Jean-Daniel Daninos
1961 **La fête espagnole**
dir Jean-Jacques Vierne; Bénazéraf co-scr
**Le quatrième sexe/ The Fourth Sex**
dir Michel Wichard
1962 **L'accident**
dir Edmond T. Greville
1963 **Mourir d'amour/La mort a les yeux bleus**
dir Dany Fog
1966 **Model's International** (short)
dir Jacques Scandelari; Bénazéraf co-scr
1970 **Les enfants de Caïn**
dir René Jolivet
1974 **Magasin de lingerie/Tout bas** (short)
dir Noël Simsolo

[1] Bob Cresse was a notorious figure of 1960's sexploitation. His Olympic International company, based in Los Angeles, imported foreign films to play on the exploitation circuits as well as making their own low budget versions. R. Lee Frost was the creative side of the partnership. To many people, Cresse came across as a gangster and, in Dave Friedman's words, "a closet Nazi." His most notorious films include **Hot Spur** and **Love Camp Seven**.

[2] Midi-Minuit-Scarlett-Styx were three Paris cinemas that specialised in genre films—horror, sex, Italian westerns etc.

[3] He produced and co-directed one short film during this time with a young French film-maker, Jacques Scandelari, a story called **Model's International**. Scandelari, who had worked as a critic and film publicist, went on to fame and some fortune with his subsequent film **La philosophie dans le boudoir (Beyond Love and Evil;**1969), but eventually he, too, ended up in the seventies porn ghetto, making gay films under the name 'Marvin Merkins'.

[4] Shown in England undubbed and with no subtitles—the onscreen action was not felt to require any verbal explanation.

[5] A famous exotic dancer of the time.

[6] In France, directors have to be licensed by the Centre National du Cinéma.

WALERIAN BOROWCZYK

LES
FILMS

STORIA
DI UN PECCATO
(HISTOIRE D'UN PÉCHÉ)

# A Private Collection

## THE FILMS OF **WALERIAN BOROWCZYK**

In November 1973, the editor of the *New Statesman* wrote a short piece about the 17th London Film Festival, which had just finished. 'What on earth does the British Film Institute think it is up to?' he began. He went on to describe a film that had 'sent even the National Film Theatre's normally unshockable audience shuffling out shamefaced.'

The film was a short section from a work in progress by one of world cinema's most prestigious directors. It was called **La bête** (**The Beast**) and, according to the *New Statesman*, 'featured only two characters—a bear and a woman—who then engaged interminably in sexual intercourse.'

The fallout from this first showing of **The Beast** was profound. Nobody who saw the film was left untouched by it. Hate it or love it, it was impossible to ignore. However, it was almost four years before the general public were given the chance to make up their own minds about it.

The director of this shocking piece of cinema was the Polish born Walerian Borowczyk. And there was nothing in his previous output—a respectable career that stretched back to the late 1940's—to prepare the viewer for this terrible outrage. Or perhaps, if you looked hard enough, there was. For the exotic and the erotic—and the downright weird—had always been a part of Borowczyk's cinematic universe.

He was born in September 1932 in Kwilcz and trained as an artist and illustrator. During the late forties he began to make animated films. These were mostly very short—in some cases only a few seconds. Eventually he teamed up with a fellow poster artist—Jan Lenica—and the films got longer and more complex. He also began combining live action with animation.

Borowczyk has always been attracted to strange and disturbing images, and this was apparent in all his early animations, culminating in his 1958 short **Dom** (The House). This begins like a science fiction film, with strange, flying saucer-like objects swooping low over the roofs of a row of houses. We enter one of the houses and a series of illogical, repetitive rituals commence. These culminate in an image of bizarre horror, when a lump of human hair comes suddenly to life and starts crawling, devouring everything in its path.

Borowczyk grew up in the late thirties and early forties. He saw the rise and fall of the Nazis and the eventual emergence of the Eastern bloc, with its nightmare maze of bureaucracy. But remnants of the past remained, in Warsaw's decaying 19th century splendour. All of these influences came together in his surreal, sophisticated and unique short films.

Images of the concentration camp, the impersonal factories and forced collectivisation of the Soviet system underpin his last great animation, **Jeux des anges** (Angels' Games). This begins on a nightmarish train ride through a red landscape, which takes us right into the heart of a terrible factory. There, in a series of claustrophobic rooms, bizarre operations are being performed. Angels' wings, cut by the teeth of a saw, bleed cold, blue blood. Two headless figures fight and are merged into a lump of limbs and flesh. An armless woman seems to wait for the gift of wings.

It's a strange and unforgettable film. After this it was hardly surprising that the next step was to move into live action features. **Goto, Island of Love** was released in 1968, starring his wife Ligia who had also been in a few of his earlier shorts

The film takes place on a strange island, seemingly isolated from time. The inhabitants all have names that begin with 'G' and there is a sense of futility—of circularity—about the tasks they perform. One of the prisoners, Grozo, falls in love with Glossia, the wife of Goto III, ruler of the island. He contrives to take the place of Goto and have Glossia for himself. She kills herself but, as Grozo lays her body on her bed, she opens her eyes.

Critics at the time pointed out the similarity between Borowczyk's vision of Goto and the

▲ Critical reaction to **The Beast** (1975)

◄ (Facing page) Italian poster for **Story of Sin** (1975)

◄ **Goto, Island of Love** (1968)

**Immoral Tales (1974)** ▲

work of Kafka—particularly his story *The Prison Colony*. But Borowczyk denied any direct influence, explaining that it was simply a way of looking at the world that they both shared.

Borowczyk continued to make both short, live action films as well as animations. In 1971 he directed his second full length feature, **Blanche**. Set in the middle ages, it tells the story of the ill-fated obsessions of a group of men for the innocent heroine of the title.

Although it's a long way from the rampant displays of **The Beast**, **Blanche** deals with the destructive power of sexuality and sexual repression in a way that's common to all Borowczyk's films. The style of them comes from his long training as an animator and painter. He films his characters like puppets, framing them in odd tableaux that seem to concentrate on extraneous details, rather than telling the story in the conventional close ups and establishing shots of mainstream cinema.

This way of using the camera is quite deliberate. Borowczyk's concept for each film is clear in his mind as soon as he starts work on it. He directs from a precise shooting script and chooses very carefully all the objects that feature in the frame, giving the same weight to everything that appears on the screen—whether it's an actor's body or an inanimate object. For this reason he's probably the most genuinely 'painterly' of all directors. And, because he is a painter himself, his use of the camera is very different from glossy art films, where each frame looks like a picture postcard. Borowczyk's films have an attitude and irony; the camera bobs and moves about like a real person.

**Blanche** was widely shown at international festivals and in art-house cinemas and it seemed like the consolidation of a major talent in the making.

**Sirpa Lane flees** ▼
**The Beast (1975)**

In 1973, Borowczyk began work on another short—**Une collection particulière**. This is basically a documentation of a collection of erotica—in fact Borowczyk's own collection. An unseen host guides us through the objects, selecting and commenting as he goes. The film shows Borowczyk's fascination with objects in themselves as well as the love of listing and cataloguing that several of his animations feature. It also acted as a statement of intent for what was to follow—a sort of visual overture.

Originally, both **Une collection particulière** and **The Beast**' were to be part of a five section film called **Contes immoraux (Immoral Tales)**, which was to show aspects of love and desire through five historical periods. When the film was finally shown, in 1974, neither of the two shorts were included. What we got were four stories: **The Tide**—about a young student who persuades his cousin to fellate him while the tide comes in; **Thérèse, the Philosopher**, where a young girl, locked in a room full of erotic objects, masturbates with a cucumber; **Erzebet Bathory**—the story of the so-called Bloody Countess, who tried to preserve her looks by bathing in virgin's blood; and finally **Lucrezia Borgia**, in which the famous poisoner indulges in an incestuous *menage-a-trois* with her father, the Pope, and her brother.

**Immoral Tales** pulled few punches for its time and was widely condemned. After this, the film prizes which Borowczyk had collected regularly since 1957 dried up completely. Some critics tried to laugh it all off as a sort of bad taste joke, but most were outraged, seeing the film as a slide away from art and a move towards grubby pornography .

Needless to say the film was not widely distributed in the UK. It was only several years later, and with a GLC X certificate, that it could be shown at all in London. But the best (or worst) was yet to come.

The full length version of **The Beast** was finally screened at the London Film Festival in 1976, three years after its first tentative appearance there. It caused a scandal in the hallowed ranks of the BFI. The showing had already been sold out weeks before on the strength of rumours percolating over the Channel. There were stories of £1 tickets eventually changing hands for £17.

When New Realm, who had distributed **Immoral Tales**, presented **The Beast** for certification, they had little hope of it being passed uncut. In fact they had already taken two minutes out of the print before submitting it. James Ferman,

ancient Rome in all its minutiae. You can't tear your eyes away from the screen for a second, it's so rich in colour and incident. Again, as with **The Beast**, shared dreams and fantasies constantly invade the plot. In a dream within a dream, Claudia imagines herself clambering inside a wooden structure shaped like a cow. A man wearing a bull's head advances on her from behind. A shot shows the cheeks of her buttocks peeking through a gap. Then we see that the man has a huge bull's pizzle. He takes off the mask and it's Ovid, lecturing to his class.

A strange coda to the film has Claudia waking up in her jeep by the side of the road in contemporary Italy. As she drives on to Paris, a newspaper headline tells us that she was assistant to a famous professor of archeology whose picture is that of Ovid in the film. He was found dead in the excavated ruins of Pompeii.

**Ars amandi** could have been a widely seen and popular film. It might have restored some of Borowczyk's lost reputation. Unfortunately the Italian producers tampered badly with the film after it was shot, faking letters from Borowczyk giving them permission to add hardcore scenes. Although these only occur in a few flashes in the final print, they were probably enough to consolidate the notion that he had taken yet another step down into the basement of porn.

His next few projects were largely still-born but then, in 1985, he was hired by producer Alain Siritsky to make **Emmanuelle 5**. Siritsky described Borowczyk as a sort of renaissance man of the cinema, saying that "...he can do everything: write, lighting, set design, edit and even do the poster."

With **Emmanuelle 5** Borowczyk finally lost any lingering respect that the critics may have held for him. At one time he had been a darling of the international film festival set. Now he opened **Emmanuelle 5** with an ironic scene of the Cannes' audience flocking to a hardcore epic, **Love Express**. There is some doubt as to how much of the final film was actually directed by Borowczyk. He wrote the script but found the star, Monique Gabrielle, difficult to work with and let his assistant, Thierry Bazin, do most of the action scenes. However, his idiosyncratic editing style is much in evidence, with the actual story seeming to take place somewhere else than on the screen. In particular, the extracts from **Love Express**—the film that the fictional Emmanuelle is promoting at Cannes—are pure Borowczyk, full of the anachronistic period detail that he loves. They are also full of extremely explicit and bizarre sexual episodes—

so much so that the UK release print is short by some 12 minutes.

*Variety* described the film as 'an unconscious parody'. But it's obvious to any sympathetic viewer that Borowczyk knew exactly what he was doing. He even included copious references to his earlier films—the egg from **The Streetwalker** puts in a brief appearance, and there is an ironic reference to Walt Disney—going back to Borowczyk's description of **Snow White** as far more 'erotic' than any of his own films due to its "stench of unsatisfied desire".

The **Emmanuelle** series had moved on from the early Sylvia Kristel days. Now the emphasis was more on exoticism than eroticism. The locations move rapidly, from Cannes to Paris, to Las Vegas and the Seychelles, with the non-Borowczyk action scenes filmed in a very straightforward style. Later, they were edited down to a 50 minute pilot for a projected **Emmanuelle** TV series. His true sensibilities come out in the many erotic sequences added onto the basic story line. The section from **Love Express**, together with scenes shot in the Harem of the evil Rajid, who kidnaps Emmanuelle, are the best things in the picture. Lovingly shot and lit, replete with humour and fetishistic touches, they are like extracts from a Nineteenth century novel taken straight from the Private Cabinet of some wizened old libertine.[4]

Borowczyk's last film to date is 1988's **Cérémonie d'amour** (Rites of Love). Based on another story by his friend André Pieyre de Mandiargues, and starring Marina Pierro, the film gives a vivid picture of Borowczyk's adopted home city of Paris. Set almost entirely on the trains and platforms of the Metro, it's the story of the gradual destruction of Hugo (played by the wonderfully inexpressive Mathieu Carrière) by a coolly controlled prostitute, Miriam.

▼ Marina Pierro in **The Art of Love** (1983)

Un film de
WALERIAN BOROWCZYK

CÉRÉMONIE
D'AMOUR

The final scenes of their lovemaking where she puts on a set of vicious, Freddy Krueger-like fingernails and rips his skin to shreds, are as shocking as any Borowczyk has filmed. But more savage is her verbal denial of any love between them, as she coolly demolishes his male illusions about her sexuality.

*Variety* commented on the film's 'underlying misogyny', noting that the production had been an attempt by Borowczyk to 'regain some of his former prestige'. If so, it was an attempt that failed. **Cérémonie d'amour** has never been shown in the UK and, like most of Borowczyk's later films, has virtually disappeared from any form of distribution. It's a sad fate for one of world cinema's most original and consistent visionaries. If there's any sort of consensus on his work it seems to be that he made a few good—even great—films in the sixties and seventies but now he is a marginal and unexceptional film-maker who has irretrievably sullied his art in the muddy waters of pornography.

Borowczyk himself seems unconcerned by the critical indifference surrounding his more recent films. He is currently working on a production with the erotic comic book artist Milo Manara, and there is even talk of a follow up to **The Beast**. Like all true originals he ploughs his own furrow. He'll never be a maker of mass appeal movies, and perhaps it's best that he remains one of those artists people have to work a little bit harder to find. In many ways his films are like the clandestine books, drawings and artefacts of the anonymous 18th and 19th century pornographers that he so often alludes to.

As his friend Robert Benayoun wrote: 'Let us say that his work now belongs to the Museum of the Rare, where it will one day be exhibited. The dates will be merely given for reference.'

## BOROWCZYK FILMOGRAPHY

All France (Fr) unless otherwise indicated

### SHORTS (15 SECONDS - 2 MINUTES) ANIMATION

1947-65  **Strip tease**
**Etendard des jeunes**
**Le magicien**
**La tête**
**La foule**
**Les Stroboscopes: magasins du 19me siècle**
**L'écriture**
**Les bibliothèques**
**Les écoles**
**La Fille sage**
**le musée**
**Le petit poucet**
Title sequence for René Clement's **Les felins**
Title sequence and trailer for Rappeneau's **La vie de château**

### SHORTS (6 - 15 MINUTES)

| | |
|---|---|
| 1946 | **Mois d'août** (live action) |
| 1954 | **Photographies vivantes** (live action) |
| | **Atelier de Fernand Leger** (live action) |
| 1955 | **L'automne** (live action) |
| 1957 | **Il etait une fois** |
| | **Le sentiment récompensé** |
| 1958 | **Dom (La maison)** |
| | **L'école** |
| 1959 | **Les astronautes** |
| 1962 | **le concert** |
| 1963 | **Holy smoke** |
| | **Encyclopédie de grand-maman** |
| | **Renaissance** |
| 1964 | **le jeux des anges** |
| 1965 | **Le dictionnaire de Joachim** |
| 1966 | **Rosalie** (live action) |
| 1967 | **Gavrotte** (live action) |
| | **Dyptique** (live action) |
| 1969 | **Le phonographe** |
| 1973 | **Une collection particulière** |
| 1975 | **Brief von Paris** |
| 1979 | **L'armoire** |

### FEATURES

| | |
|---|---|
| 1962/67 | **Théâtre de Monsieur et Madame Kabal** |
| 1968 | **Goto, l'île d'amour/Goto, Island of Love** |
| 1971 | **Blanche** |
| 1974 | **Contes immoraux/Immoral Tales** |

1975    Dzieje Grzechu/ Histoire d'un péché/ Story of
        a Sin (Pol)
1975    La bête/The Beast/Death's Ecstasy
        La marge/The Margin/The Streetwalker/Eman-
        uelle 77
1977    L'Interno di un convento/Interieur d'un cou
        vent/Behind Convent Walls/Within a Cloister (It)
1979    Les héroïnes du mal/ Trois femmes immorales/
        Three Immoral Women
1980    Lulu (Fr/It/Ger)
1981    Le cas étrange de Dr Jekyll et Miss Osbourne/
        Blood of Dr Jekyll/ Bloodbath of Dr Jekyll/The
        Experiment
1984    Ars amandi/L'art d'aimer/The Art of Love (Fr/It)
1985    Emmanuelle 5
1988    Cérémonie d'amour

## ALSO

Un traitement justifié
The Almanac
Two episodes from the French TV show **La série rose**

earlier in **Une collection particulière**, taken from Borow-czyk's own collection of antique sex toys.

▲ What goes on, **Behind Covent Walls** (1977)

---

[1] Filming of **The Beast** actually began in 1972. Borowczyk was hired by producer Anatole Dauman to shoot a new ending for a film directed by Alain Fleischer called **Les rendez-vous en forêt** (Meetings in the Forest). The Fleischer film was an intensely literary and self-conscious attempt at creating an adult fairy tale. Its main appeal was the gorgeous Catherine Jourdan, who had just made her name as an art-porn star in Alain Robbe-Grillet's film **Eden and After**. Borowczyk was asked to give Fleischer's film some much needed fizz. He constructed the beast for the film, but Fleischer refused to allow the new ending to be shot, going to court to prevent it. Later, Borowczyk remembered an old French legend—*La veritable histoire de la bête de Gevaudin*—that he decided to make a film of, using the creature he had constructed. It was several years before he had the opportunity to re-use the footage in a full length film.

[2] Under the pseudonym Pierre Morion he had written one of the most obscene novels ever set on paper—*L'Anglais décrit dans le château fermé*. The book has never been translated into English and is so extreme it was even banned for more than 25 years in France. De Mandiargues also wrote the book that became the basis of the film **Girl on a Motorcycle**, starring Marianne Faithful.

[3] The film has had a confusing number of titles. The original French title was **Le cas étrange de Dr Jekyll et de Miss Osbourne**. This became **Dr Jekyll et les femmes** and in English **Blood of Dr Jekyll**. But the film has also been known as **Bloodbath of Dr Jekyll** and **The Experiment**.

[4] Both scenes feature extensive use of the erotic artifacts seen

# Playing with Fire

## THE FILMS OF **ALAIN ROBBE-GRILLET**

'The taste of blood, beautiful slaves, the vampires' bite, and so on; it is this second language which will serve as a source of material for the creation of a new form of words, a parallel structure, my own speech.'

Alain Robbe-Grillet made his name as a writer, a great prose stylist of the post Sartre avant-garde. During the 1960's he turned to film along with other writers, such as Marguerite Duras, who used the medium to supplement their investigations into the realm of ideas. The films they made were arty and experimental—what made Robbe-Grillet different is that his films often had a mainstream audience. Three of them were crossover hits ... all three had beautiful girls and a soupçon of sadomasochism. Because of his literary and academic background, Robbe-Grillet would seem to be the most intellectual European sex-film maker. His approach to the subject is certainly cerebral. His films are more self conscious, yet underneath this thick, almost impenetrable veneer, there are similarities, places and points where he connects with other more disreputable film-makers.

Robbe-Grillet was born in Brittany in 1922, the year James Joyce's *Ulysses* was published in France. His family were right-wing and more than a shade oddball. He grew up beside the sea, his early childhood filled with Breton folk tales and nightmares inspired by crashing waves, drowned sailors and whistling winds. During childhood he began to have sadistic fantasies, and in his dreams the Marquis de Sade would come and drag him out of bed. To keep these dreams at bay he would tell himself stories, while his mother sat by the open door reading newspapers. In the autobiographical *Ghosts in the Mirror*, he talks about other early dreamplay. As a young boy he enjoyed playing with two china dolls. 'Bound hand and foot' these two playthings were like young girls and they helped activate the perverse part of his imagination. During his primary school days he had more strange fantasies. 'I cheerfully dreamed of the massacre of my class-mates,' he admits candidly. 'But the ones I considered ugly or didn't like were summarily disposed of, simply to get rid of them, whereas the graceful bodies, with pretty delicate faces enjoyed long drawn out torture sessions tied to the chestnut trees in the playground.'

This obsession with the sadistic killing of women is an important ingredient in Robbe-Grillet's novel *Le Voyeur*, in which he describes the ritual murder of a little girl performed with a stiletto. The killing resembles the sexual act; intense excitement on both sides, the dead girl eventually going to heaven where she becomes her killer's guardian angel, offering him help and solace from beyond the grave. The sado-masochistic crops up in some of his films and novels, not all of them, but his successful films all have this element. In an interview with Jean-Jacques Brochier in the magazine *Littéraire*, the writer-film-maker admitted: 'I am astonished at the way viewers discriminate between my films, between the ones that contain sex and the ones that don't. This discrimination has taken the form of a sanction. I have had two failures, **L'Immortelle** and **The Man Who Lies**, while **Trans-Europ-Express**, **Eden and After** and **Slow Slidings of Pleasure** have been consider-able successes. The same with **Playing with Fire**. Now for me these films are equally erotic, but with some the theme and not the imagery is erotic. Where the theme contains some other sort of mythology—for example the mythology of the resistance hero as in **The Man who Lies**. For I repeat, in the examination that I make in the myths of society there are other things than erotic imagery that interest me. What is remark-able is that the spectator prefers those films in which the mythological games are those of sex.'

Part of the explanation must lie in marketing strategy. **Trans-Europ-Express**, **Playing with Fire** (**Le jeu avec le feu**; 1975), **Eden and After** (**L'eden et après**; 1971) and **Slow Slidings** (**Glissements progressifs du plaisir**; 1974) were all promoted using photographs, posters and actresses that implied an erotic content—they were marketed as art films that had more than a hint of sex. These images are a trifle mislead-ing, promising the viewer excitement and titillation, qualities totally at odds with Robbe-

▲ Art meets artifice **Last Year at Marienbad** (1961)

◄ (Facing page) Sylvia Kristel, Jean-Louis Trintigant, **Playing with Fire** (1975)

◄ Shaken, not stirred, Jean Louis Trintigant in **Trans-Europ-Express** (1966)

Grillet's method of shooting the subject. He always handles the topic with a certain distance—'My films are not erotically stimulating. There is a complete difference between my films and a pornographic film. They aim to excite the audience. I intend to deprive these images of excitement and hope to reveal their banality,' he declares polemically. This is undoubtedly true, but does it make him any less of a pornographer than Bénazéraf or Franco?

In a Robbe-Grillet film, sex is merely part of the game being played. All of his films are intricate games or puzzles that the viewer tries to make sense of. He hopes to engage the spectator on a conscious, rational level. His films are unemotional, there's always a sense of detachment. Unlike his novels, which are experimental but disarmingly easy to read, his films don't have a seductive surface. This would change their overall effect by drawing the viewer emotionally rather than intellectually into the game. By bleaching out the emotional content Robbe-Grillet hopes to investigate how film and the archetypes, icons and myths it uses operate. His aim is to reveal the viewer's part in creating all these fictions, and so free them to invent their own.

Whether or not this sounds like pretentious rubbish is beside the point. What is important is that his films always invoke the concepts of the game and distance—two terms that are important in the world of S&M. In *A Taste for Pain*, Maria Marcus stresses the importance of game-playing and distance in any S&M relationship: it has to be a game otherwise she can't become physically or psychically satisfied. Another factor that's important in S&M is aesthetics—everything has to look exactly right, otherwise the desired effect cannot be achieved. Robbe-Grillet's films have a precision, an attention to detail that's perfectly in keeping with this sensibility, and this is one of the factors that separates him from other film-makers.[1]

This preciseness, or purity, is partly due to his predilections, but it's also inspired by his scientific background. Robbe-Grillet's interest in art began after the Second World War. His early world was strictly scientific—his family were unconcerned about painting, art or literature. He studied biology, maths, physics and chemistry, graduating to become a highly paid agricultural engineer, an authority on diseases of the banana tree. In the early fifties, he gave up this lucrative career to become a writer. His first published novel, *Les Gommes* (The Erasers) came out in 1954, and his reputation was established when the young Roland Barthes wrote a highly influential essay about the book. His next novel, *Le Voyeur*, was awarded the Prix des critiques by Georges Bataille, an event which caused a small scandal. *Les Gommes* was different from Robbe-Grillet's earlier unpublished novels, books such as *Un régicide*, which had been less formal and more surrealistic. *Les Gommes* was his first really modernist novel, and featured what the French call *mise-en-abîme*, a literary term that covers infinite regression, reflexivity and self quotation; in other words—playing games.

This can be better understood by referring again to Robbe-Grillet's scientific background. For him, literature and science aren't as removed from each other as some might think. Both disciplines construct systems and use concepts. Science proceeds by constructing theories to make sense of how and why things work. Theory is always a simplified version of reality, the scientist selects elements or data, draws conclusions and formulates theories. Behind each theory there is always choice. Because of this, some facts, elements and data are considered to be important, and therefore accepted, while others are ignored or discarded. The same applies to the novelist, who works not with facts and theory but with archetypes and myths, using these elements to weave a story—much in the same way that the scientist uses data to create a theory. This notion of selection and construction is at the heart of Robbe-Grillet's literary works. He picks out images, icons and archetypes from all sorts of fiction. He's catholic in his taste and his films use material taken from popular culture (comics, magazines, pulp fiction and film) as well as from high art (literature, painting, history, classical mythology). Robbe-Grillet uses these elements to construct complex narratives, stories that are kaleidoscopic puzzles that the audience has to complete. All his films have missing elements. This means that each film is open to interpretation, and it's this interpretation, or interaction with an audience, that the film is about.

Robbe-Grillet's films deal in 20th century mythologies. One of those mythologies is sex and its sadomasochistic variations. 'I have filled my palace of dreams with young and beautiful girls,' he says, 'from Sade to the illustrations in sex shops and Greek statues. This stuff is the material of our myths. I see in the condemning of this subject, which I have suffered, a good example of puritanism: the unconscious censorship of pleasure which is, without doubt, one of the censorships of the middle classes, whether they describe themselves as radical or not.'

Making films that include sexual images invariably brings a stigma in its wake, yet compared to other low budget film-makers Robbe-Grillet has been lucky. His intellectual credentials and his self-conscious use of this material has meant that

◀ Jean-Louis Trintigant is
**The Man who Lies**
(1968)

Immoral Tales

◀ Art meets exploitation,
**Eden and After** (1971)

his reputation hasn't suffered too much. Most of the books written about the man and his films are academic and tend to avoid judging him too harshly. They play safe, often ignoring the sexual elements altogether by treating the subject formally—as if it didn't really exist.

A key film in solidifying his reputation was **Last Year at Marienbad** (1961), one of the quintessential art films of the sixties and, like all the films Robbe-Grillet has been involved with, as tantalising as it is inexplicable. You can read almost any meaning into it—that's part of its beauty. The film is a suffocating melodramatic puzzle, where the slightest detail seems to be packed with importance. It was directed by Alain Resnais from a shooting script by Robbe-Grillet, Robbe-Grillet's only collaboration to date. He hasn't found another director who could work as faithfully to his shooting script as Resnais did. Resnais added a surface sensuousness to the film, something that you find in Robbe-Grillet's writing but not in his work for the cinema.

Books like *La Maison de rendez-vous* (*The House of Assignation*) are sumptuously readable, and at first glance appear less formal and more obviously accessible than his films. Take, for example, this passage that has more than a few of the features that pop up in his films:

> *Women's flesh in all probability always played a large part in my dreams. Even when awake my mind is constantly assailed by images of it. A girl in a summer dress presents the curved nape of her neck—she is fastening her sandal—her hair thrown half forward to reveal the delicate skin and its pale down. Immediately I see her pressed into granting some favour and my imagination is unleashed. The narrow hobble skirt, slit up to the thighs, which is worn by the smart women of Hong Kong, is suddenly ripped by a violent hand, baring the firm, rounded, smooth gleaming hip and the tender hollow of the small of the back. The leather whip in the window of a Paris saddler, the bare breasts of a dressmaker's dummy, a half clad figure on a poster, an advertisement for suspenders or for a perfume, two moist parted lips, a metal bracelet or a dog's collar impose on me their insistent, provocative decor.*

If **Marienbad** had the surface appeal of Robbe-Grillet's prose, much of the credit for this must go to Alain Resnais' ability as a director. Their collaboration was mutually beneficial, and gave

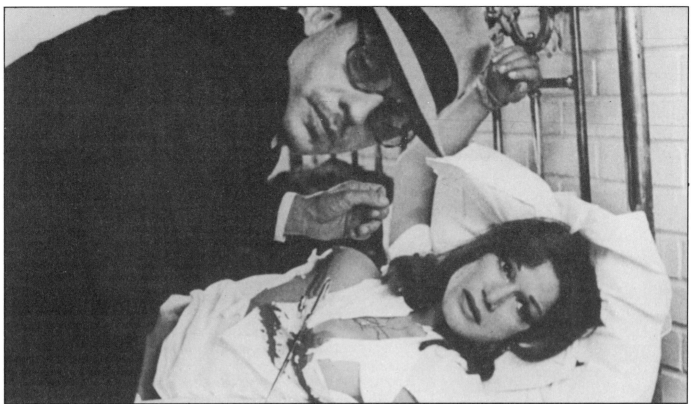

**Glissements progressifs ▲
du plaisir (1974)**

Robbe-Grillet his first practical experience of film-making. His shooting script for **Marienbad** was meticulous, mapping out every shot, image and cut that was to be in the film. One scene, however, had to be dropped from the script. Resnais objected to a short rape scene and this was never filmed. Later on, in **Trans-Europ-Express**, Robbe-Grillet returned to this theme and now the British censor, John Trevelyan, objected to it, wanting the central portion of the film to be severely trimmed. Elias (Jean-Louis Trintignant) has a fairly innocuous rape fantasy with a prostitute—it was quite low key and playfully objective, but the censor found it too much for the time and the film was banned. Today it's screened in the evening on television, described as a comedy thriller, and nobody bats an eyelid. On top of that the British censor has no qualms about passing all of Robbe-Grillet's films without cuts for video release. Time certainly has moved on.

In 1961, during the final stages of **Marienbad**, Robbe-Grillet was approached by a big Japanese film company who thought he was a popular writer. When Robbe-Grillet sent them a script they were taken aback, and asked him to change a large percentage of it. Robbe-Grillet refused, he wanted complete control over the shooting script. His films have always been personal, he makes them for his own amusement, he doesn't tailor them towards a specific audience. So it's hardly

surprising that his films are more successful when they're promoted using sadomasochistic or erotic imagery.

Robbe-Grillet's first film as a director was **L'Immortelle** (1963), which had been written before **Marienbad**. The film was shot in Turkey for business reasons—producer Sammy Halfon had met an entrepreneur who wanted to take his money out of Turkey, the easiest way being to turn it into a few cans of film. Although this was a lucky beginning, there were hiccups to follow. The finished film was stiff compared with **Marienbad**, which very fluid, practically jampacked with slow zooms and tracking shots. Robbe-Grillet's shooting style favours less camera movement, building his films around montage and single shots; the single shot is a 'generating cell' in his films. The problems on **L'Immortelle** didn't arise from the shooting style, they came from the crew. Like any newcomer to film, Robbe-Grillet needed help from his technicians, as Fragola and Smith put it: 'a crew receptive to his vision and able to contribute to it'. The cameraman/cinematographer on **L'Immortelle**, Maurice Barry, gave Robbe-Grillet a hard time. He wanted the film to be more lyrical, and often refused to follow Robbe-Grillet's directions. Cinema, unlike writing, is a collaborative art and this influences the finished product, no matter how formal or experimental the film is.

**L'Immortelle** (The Immortal Woman) was originally to be called **Les chiens** (The Dogs), but was changed because actress Françoise Brion's presence added something to the film that Robbe-Grillet hadn't planned—she was beautiful and mysterious. The film had many similarities with **Last Year at Marienbad**— plenty of stopped frames, actors wearing different clothes during a sequence ... plus the same fascination with repetition and games. The plot consisted of episodes, each episode featuring the same elements in different ways. In the first episode a French teacher, N (Jacques Doniol-Valcroze, *nouvelle vague* director and husband of Françoise Brion) meets a mysterious blonde, L (Françoise Brion), in Istanbul and loses her. He finds her again, she gives him a lift in a Buick, a dog passes and there is a crash— she is killed. After this the same elements occur in different relations to one another. For example there is another dog, another Buick and another crash in which the teacher dies.

Robbe-Grillet's next film, **Trans-Europ-Express** (1966), was an arthouse hit and is one of his favourites. The film's popularity wasn't based on its experimentation, game playing, or intricate construction. It was popular because it was the right film at the right time. By today's standards its sadomasochistic imagery may seem tame, but in 1966 a little bit of bondage went a long way. In

the mid sixties American and British audiences were irresistibly attracted to European semi-erotic art films, movies that had a patina of respectability and a smattering of sex. British sex film maker and distributor Stanley Long declares it was a time when a man would cross town to see a nipple on the big screen. So naked girls in chains must have been a pretty hefty lure for many of these nipple hungry 1960's men.

What did the average cinema goer make of **Trans-Europ-Express**, its multi-layered regressions, and intricate play with images and archetypes? Most probably shrugged their shoulders and wondered—'What does it all mean?' Robbe-Grillet says, 'Nothing exists outside the world of images ... I don't believe a work of art has reference to anything outside itself. In a film there's no reality except that of the film, no time except that of the film ...(it) makes no sense except what the viewer constructs', leaving them floundering even further.

**Trans-Europ-Express** is filled with familiar images and stereotypes plucked from film, pulp literature, advertisements and magazines, all interweaving and overlapping. Jean Louis Trintignant plays himself and also Elias, a character created by Jean (Alain Robbe-Grillet). In one scene the character Elias dreams about the director Jean and wakes up, which poses the question—whose dream or film is it? Finally

**Playing with Fire**

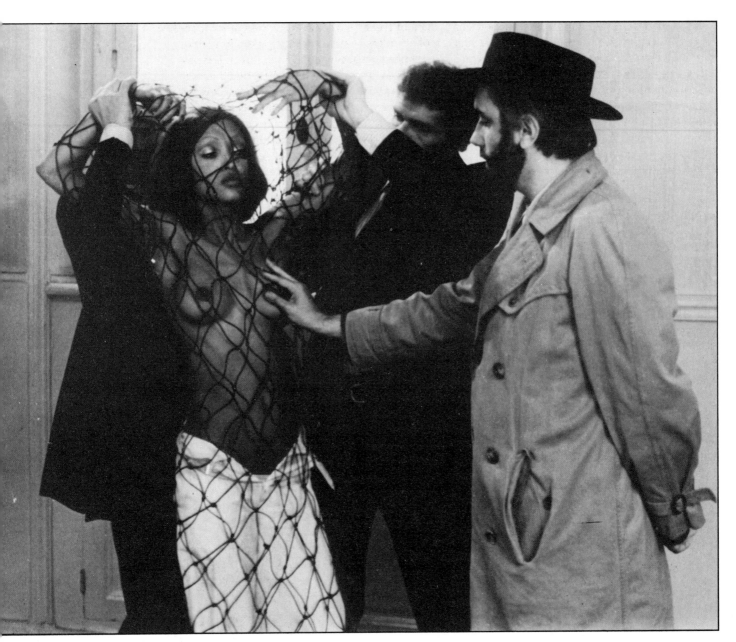

**Playing With Fire** ▲

Elias's sexual obsessions take over the film, distorting Jean's original idea, his obsession ending in death when a policeman lures him to a trap in an S&M nightclub called Eve.

**Trans-Europ-Express** is a compendium of archetypes, all deftly and subtly interconnected. Robbe-Grillet has pointed out that the film has two contradictory impulses, one intellectual the other irrational and sexual. 'The need for order and classification is very much alive in all of us, side by side with the desire for freedom—its opposite ... these two opposing forces within us are in constant interaction both in our conscious mind and in the depths of our unconsciousness.' In **Trans-Europ-Express** Elias's sexual obsessions lead to chaos and death, ending the film and concluding its formalistic preoccupations.

For Robbe-Grillet, playing games with 20th century archetypes and narrative structures has its own purpose. 'The modern world,' he notes, 'finds difficulty in getting rid of the profundities it has inherited from the 19th century, and that influence is still felt in literature and cinema. I am trying to replace the idea of profundity with play.' From anyone else these ideas would sound pretentious and pompous, but somehow Robbe-Grillet manages to make them sound authentic and important. What makes them convincing is his intelligence and the force of his personality; it's easy to go along with what he says and give him the benefit of the doubt. The actress Nathalie Zeiger[2] has remarked on Robbe-Grillet's powers of persuasion; "I considered working for Alain Robbe-Grillet in **Glissements progressifs du** plaisir and **Playing with Fire** as a promotion. He knows how to be nice, amusing and very funny, even if, in **Playing with Fire**, he had me pricked in the arse with a long needle and attacked by a huge dog. The dog wanted to tear off my skirt. Everyone was scared, even the dresser ... except me. I won't make hardcore films ... But he could do it with intelligence, truth and style."

**L'homme qui ment (The Man Who Lies**; 1968) was Robbe-Grillet's fourth film, less controlled, and more improvised than his earlier works. Robbe-Grillet called it 'freedom under surveillance.' After making three films he had realised that everything couldn't be totally controlled, so he decided to include chance occurrences in the film, those improvisations and qualities that bob up naturally during the course of any collective endeavour. This didn't make **The Man Who Lies** chaotic. It was still the usual controlled variation of familiar stories; in this case, tales told about a resistance hero called Boris, played by Jean Louis Trintignant. The stories are set in the 1940's but Trintignant wears fashionable sixties' gear. The film's structure implies that Boris and the Nazis may not be linked, but that they 'coexist independently yet simultaneously in frozen moments of time.' So **The Man Who Lies**, like **Trans-Europ-Express**, is a narrative game that plays around with the 'resistance hero versus the Nazis' scenario. What the viewer is supposed to enjoy is the way these archetypes are shuffled around. The film has no real meaning—like all good tales it's the telling that's important, not what's told.

**The Man Who Lies** was Robbe-Grillet's last black and white film. His producers wanted colour films because they were easier to market. This threw Robbe-Grillet a little. He didn't want to make a film in Eastmancolour because he didn't like the green which tended to make all the other colours look less vibrant. After a trip to Tunisia he changed his mind ... there, on the island of Djerba, he discovered a world where green didn't really exist. The architecture was white and blue and the skies were blue and white—by adding the colour red he could make a film that was painterly, similar to the blobs of vivid colour found in Abstract Expressionism.

Robbe-Grillet's interest in painting was something he kept returning to—**La belle captive** (The Beautiful Prisoner; 1983), for example, was deeply influenced by René Magritte's painting of the same name. The film inspired by his trip to Djerba, **Eden and After**, featured a snazzy nightclub, the Café Eden, which was virtually a homage to the

work of Piet Mondrian. As always with Robbe-Grillet's films, there were other, more lowbrow, influences, most notably a touch of pulpy Sax Rohmer about "the powder of fear" that the mysterious Duchemin offers Violet. The powder unleashes terrifying visions of torture, chains, and murder, as well as the inevitable ingredient of rape. **N a pris les dés (N Took the Dice**; 1971), Robbe-Grillet's next project, was a re-edited version of **Eden and After** made specifically for French television. It's easily his most obscure work and has never been released commercially.

On the other hand, **Glissements progressifs du plaisir (Slow Slidings of Pleasure**; 1974) was his most notorious film. When it was released in France it could only be viewed by people over the age of 18; in Italy, the film was the subject of criminal proceedings, to an extent provoked by the promoter's use of sensationally erotic posters. It was deemed to be obscene, found guilty of violating morals and condemned to be burned in a public place....because it didn't make narrative sense. The judge said that images of women and sadomasochism were acceptable only as long as they fitted into a plot.

**Glissements progressifs** was Robbe-Grillet's most complex, game-playing film to date. Among the many sources of inspiration for the film was Jules Michelet's *La Sorcière* (*The Sorceress*),[3] an apocryphal book that elegantly stated the case for the opposition—the sorceress or woman who was accused of witchcraft.

**Glissements progressifs du plaisir**

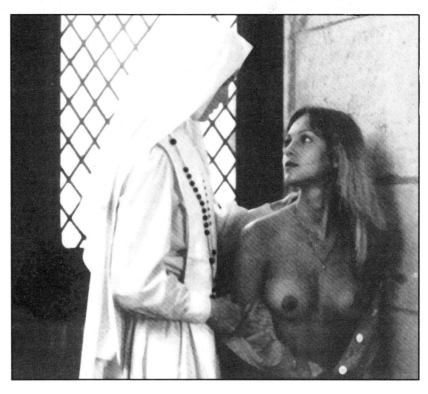

**Eden and After** ▲

Michelet's book gives the witch a dynamic, poetic voice, in striking contrast to the dry, dehumanised language of law and order. It's a dichotomy, a tension that you find in all of Robbe-Grillet's films. Michelet's sorceress represents freedom, nature and the irrational; her judges accuse her because they lack imagination and see her as a threat to order and control.

The language of *The Sorceress* is not logical or linear. It describes in evocative detail a host of disparate events and myths. When they're pieced together they give an impression of an alternative worldview. This impression isn't complete, there are many gaps, but the language is so inspiring that you don't really notice. In the end you realise it would be impossible to describe it any other way.

**Glissements progressifs** was a significant step forward for Robbe-Grillet, it distilled and refined the elements you find in all his other films. The structure of the piece was complex,

filled with allusions to comic books, novels, paintings, videos, films and other 'collective images' plucked from a variety of sources. One of the most insistent themes in the film was foot fetishism, a theme that first appeared in **Last Year at Marienbad**. In **Glissements progressifs** it returns, resurfacing in complex images that hint at eroticism and blood. The film featured the beautiful and innocent looking Anicée Alvina as Alice. Robbe-Grillet's young wife, Catherine, suggested her as a possible lead for the film after seeing her in **Le rempart des Béguines** (1972), Guy Casaril's tastefully kinky version of the famous Françoise Mallet-Joris novel. Her role in **Glissements** was quite intricate. In some scenes she had to look insouciant and erotic, while in others she exuded the ethereal stiffness of that Robbe-Grillet favourite, the mannequin.

The film was viewed by mainstream critics as having too many sadomasochistic images.

Robbe-Grillet was unperturbed by this, for him 'Art is always ahead of the public ... in a real book or a real painting there is always something that resists.' If critics find it distasteful or unacceptable, so much the better, it adds to the uncertainty. In **Glissements progressifs** the images were more ironic than pornographic, yet few critics took this into account. The fact that they were there was more than enough for them. In critical terms it seems that some subjects are strictly taboo and best left alone.

Robbe-Grillet's next film, **Le jeu avec le feu (Playing with Fire**; 1975) is one of his most accessible works to date. Along with **La belle captive** it's one of his few films that has the semblance of a narrative, yet underneath this lurks the same game playing and experimentation. The plot is simple—a wealthy banker hires a detective (Jean Louis Trintignant) to track down his daughter Caroline (Anicée Alvina). In **Playing with Fire** the repetition and circularity that Robbe-Grillet uses in his films is less jarring and formalistic. The scene where the detective finds Caroline in a luxurious brothel (in reality the Paris Opera house) illustrates this change. Earlier films such as **L'immortelle** featured the same elements in successive episodes, each segment reshuffled to produce different permutations. The same device was used in **Playing with Fire**. When the detective moves through the semi-circular lobby he opens each door as he comes across it ... behind each one he finds a different combination of deviant acts, a different set of possible scenarios. But, because time and space aren't as dislocated, these permutations are easier for the viewer to accept. **Playing with Fire** was quite a big crossover hit. This wasn't just because it was more accessible—the film starred Sylvia Kristel, and it was her success in **Emmanuelle** that guaranteed the film's continual pulling power.[4]

Robbe-Grillet turned once again to painting and literature for inspiration in his next film. In 1976 he had written a 'picto-novel', *La Belle Captive*, which reprinted some of Magritte's paintings including *La Belle Captive* itself. His 1983 film of the same name used paintings by both Magritte and Edouard Manet as a launching pad, each painting a 'generating cell' for the film's ideas and narrative. Magritte's *Belle Captive* is a great painting—formal, poetic, mysterious, it hints at all sorts of possibilities. The drawn curtains open onto a beach and sky. In the stony foreground there is an easel and a painting that visually links the world behind the curtain with the vista in the distance. It's an audacious, inspiring work that's a self-conscious reflection on the process of painting, but is also eerie and enigmatic, exuding a strange beauty.

Inspired by the painting, Robbe-Grillet's film consisted of potent fluctuations, movements between reality and irrational fantasy. As in all his films the lines between the two are gossamer thin. In another re-working of Jules Michelet's *The Sorceress*, the catalyst that makes the link possible is a woman. The female lead in the film, Marie-Ange (Gabrielle Lazure), wasn't a witch, she was a vampire who captures the imagination of the male protagonist Walter (Daniel Mesguich) ... she bites his neck, transporting him across the divide that separates mundane reality and erotic fantasy. **La belle captive** is laden with imagery prompted by Magritte's paintings. In one sequence, Marie-Ange mysteriously appears within a picture frame in Walter's room; later on he sees her through the red curtains on the beach, making her a dreamlike creature, an envoy from fantasyland where desire and terror intermingle.

Sound is an important aspect of all Robbe-Grillet's films, and in **La belle captive** it adds to the film's surrealist edge. The skies may be blue and clear, but the soundtrack offers different information, springing to life with ominous thunderclaps. Once again Robbe-Grillet is playing games, thwarting audience expectations, making them work at deciphering the slippery puzzle.

Understanding all the intricate allusions in Robbe-Grillet films isn't essential if you want to appreciate or enjoy them. The average viewer isn't going to pick up on the references to Hegel, paintings, popular literature, Crepax comics and S&M magazines. These references are there, important because they illustrate the way that Robbe-Grillet doesn't differentiate between serious art and popular culture. He may be an

▼ **Glissements progressifs du plaisir**

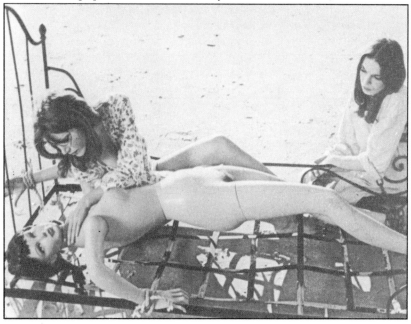

intellectual, but he's not a snob.

This blurring of boundaries is more obvious in some of his lesser known books, texts that emphasise his enduring interest in sex—*Temple aux Miroirs* (1977) *Rêves de Jeunes Filles* (1971) and *The Image (1956)*, a sadomasochistic novel he is alleged to have written with his wife, which was published under the pseudonym Jean de Berg. *The Image* reads like a pastiche of Robbe-Grillet's other books—its main interest lies in the fact that it inspired Radley Metzger's film **The Punishment of Anne** (1975), arguably the best S&M film ever made.

*Temple aux Miroirs* was an elliptical essay about the female castration complex, illustrated with superb photographs by Irina Ionesco. These prints were artistic and provocative, often of very young girls in lingerie and lipstick, and had a dangerous, lingering intensity. Although the girls looked fresh faced and modern, the photo style was partly high fashion and partly *belle époque* pornography. *Rêves de Jeunes Filles* also featured photos of girls, this time well into their teens, by glamour kingpin David Hamilton —the world famous photographer who originated the soft-focus shooting style that became a staple in magazines such as *Penthouse* during the 1970's. Robbe-Grillet must have felt that the collaboration was a success, as they worked together again on *Les Demoiselles d'Hamilton* the following year. Again this was a photo book that

(Facing page) Night-club scene from **Trans-Europ-Express** (1966)
Françoise Brion in **L'imortelle** (1963)

featured David Hamilton's pictures and Robbe-Grillet's words.

Robbe-Grillet's films are difficult because of the way they play around with film form. These experiments with narrative just wouldn't be allowed in a big budget film. As a low budget film-maker he has a certain amount of freedom, he can make the films he likes provided he shoots them quickly and brings them in on time. His method of making films is different from the improvisational style of someone like Jess Franco. Robbe-Grillet knows exactly what he wants before he begins to shoot. His films work on an intellectual level, yet they aren't as far removed from those of other low budget sex and horror film-makers as you might think.

Franco, Rollin and Bénazéraf all make films to please themselves, and fill them with items that run the gamut from high culture to lowbrow entertainment. Each one of them has his own style, his own approach to film-making. What's interesting is the way they feed off the same influences but produce different types of films, works that reflect their own predilections, as well as meeting the needs of the marketplace.

Time has been kind to many of their films and they look better, and are more enjoyable now. Robbe-Grillet believes that 'the political and social significance of art operates over the long term, and that sort of engagement must in a sense be unaware of itself.' So time is important for him too. Perhaps his films will eventually find an appreciative audience, one that can

European sex comic
*Lady Domina*

enjoy their cerebral pleasures, and not be thrown by the self-conscious slipping and slidings of their playful form.

## ROBBE-GRILLET FILMOGRAPHY

All France (Fr) unless otherwise indicated

1963 **L'Immortelle**
1966 **Trans-Europ-Express**
1968 **L'homme qui ment** (Fr/Cz)
1971 **L'éden et après/Eden and After**
     **N a pris les dès** (TV film)
1974 **Glissements progressifs du plaisir**
1975 **Le jeu avec le feu/Playing With Fire**
1983 **La belle captive**
1994 **Un bruit qui rend fou/The Blue Villa** (Fr/Be/Switz)
     Co-dir, Dimitri de Clercq

## PLUS

1961 **L'année dernière à Marienbad/Last Year at Marienbad**
     dir Alain Resnais; written by Alain Robbe-Grillet
1969 **Les gommes** (Fr/Be)
     dir René Micha; based on the book by Alain Robbe-Grillet
1972 **La jalousie** (Ger)
     dir Klaus Kieschner. Made for German TV
1988 **Taxandria** (Fr/Ger/Be)
     dir Raoul Servais; Robbe-Grillet worked on the script of this feature-length animated film.

---

[1] Robbe Grillet's films have received a limited release on video because of this. He prefers people to see them on the big screen because it preserves the aesthetic quality of the images.

[2] Zeiger was a very popular actress in 1970's erotic films. She worked with Michel Lemoine, José Bénazéraf and many others.

[3] The book is best known in the UK and America under the title *Satanism and Witchcraft*.

[4] The film featured a veritable panoply of French erotic film stars from the mid-seventies. Besides Kristel, there was the Italian Agostina Belli, Christine Boisson, Anicée Alvina, Nathalie Zeiger and Jean Rollin favourite Joëlle Cœur.

▲ Spanish press book for **Glissements progressifs du plaisir**
◄ (Facing page) **La belle captive** (1983)

ISABELLE ADJANI       SAM NEILL

# POSSESSION

un film de
## ANDRZEJ ZULAWSKI

et avec HEINZ BENNENT       effets spéciaux CARLO RAMBALDI

images de BRUNO NUYTTEN    musique de ANDRZEJ KORZYNSKI    directeur de production JEAN-JOSÉ RICHER
une co-production franco-allemande OLIANE PRODUCTIONS (PARIS)    MARIANNE PRODUCTIONS (PARIS)    SOMA FILM PRODUKTION GmbH (BERLIN)

# Appendix

In an area as broad as the one we've chosen to look at, it's impossible to deal with everything in depth. The names that follow have been chosen because they're either (a) typical in some way or (b) unique in some way. Almost any one of them would have been worthy of a full chapter. Some might even fill a book.

The surname in capitals is either the most common or the 'official' pseudonym. Names that follow in brackets are the real names. Dates are dates of birth, where available, and death if applicable. References to other entries are given in full caps at their first mention.

Javier AGUIRRE (1935). Spanish director and critic. He was seduced by the cinema very early on and spent most of his time going to see films rather than attending school. At the age of 11 he wrote his first screenplay and by the time he was 13 he was writing reviews of the films he saw. His first reviews were published when he was 15 and he left school to become a film-maker. His first full length film was **España insólita** in 1964—a sort of mondo style documentary. Like several other Spanish directors (KLIMOVSKY, Franco), Aguirre realised very early in his career that he wanted to make films—that was his primary objective. So rather than wait around for years getting together the money for difficult personal projects he jumped straight into the deep waters of the commercial side of the industry, making films in all sorts of genres very quickly. What's unusual about him is that he also continued to work on experimental shorts and soon gained a reputation as one of the most serious practitioners in the field. In 1972 he published *Anticine: Notes Towards a Theory* about this side of his work. His most important genre films include two with Paul NASCHY—**The Hunchback of the Morgue** and **Dracula's Virgin Lovers**, both made in 1972. As the times changed he moved into sex films with the likes of **Carne apaleada** (Beaten Flesh) in 1977, which was the first film to be given the new 'S' certification following the liberalisation of censorship after General Franco's death. The closest parallel to Aguirre's career would be someone like Curtis Harrington in America or Anthony

BALCH in Britain, both of whom straddled the divide between experimental and exploitation film-making.

**ALPHA FRANCE.** The biggest and most influential French distributors of soft and hardcore films. The company was founded in 1970 by Francis Mischkind, using staff from the recently defunct Paris branch of Rank. Mischkind himself had been in the game since the late fifties, having directed his first film—a children's short called **Fric frac au port**—in 1958. In 1966 he began to import subtitled Swedish 'art' films into France, such as **I Am Curious, Yellow, My Sister, My Love** and **Night Games** as well as distributing Radley METZGER's **Thérèse and Isabelle**. Mischkind noticed the broad appeal of these films—not just to the habitués of art houses but also to those looking for something 'harder' than the usual commercial fare. Consequently he began to put out films dubbed into French to make them more accessible to exactly that audience. When the Danes and then the Germans also began to move into more explicit productions, Mischkind was there, buying up their films and selling them into the French market. His involvement was more than that of a mere importer. He was the first in France to involve himself in all aspects of the selling of his films: choosing the distributor, getting the films passed by the censor, designing and executing the publicity campaign and so on. In 1971 he extended his range by getting involved in the production of **Hot and Blue** (**Jeux pour couples infidèles**) for which he also wrote the script. He was also involved in co-production deals with Dave Friedman's EVI company in the States which gave him films like **The Erotic Adventures of Zorro** and **The Long, Swift Sword of Siegfried**. Mischkind and Alpha France were vital parts of the chain that led to an increasing liberalisation of the French screens, however, he was opposed to the X-Law that came into effect in 1976. This licensing of hardcore films and their restriction to a specialist ghetto was what killed off the nascent industry in France—as it later did in Spain. Mischkind has produced films by many of the genre's 'stars' including Claude Mulot/Frédéric LANSAC (**Pussy Talk**), Francis LEROI (**Je suis à prendre**) and Gérard KIKOÏNE (**Parties fines**).

Joe d'AMATO (Aristide Massaccesi; 1936). Has also worked under the pseudonyms of David Hills, Kevin Mancuso, Steven Benson, Peter Newton, Richard Franks, etc. Began his career as a camera assistant and eventually cinematographer during the early 1970's. As always in the Italian exploitation industry, he worked on a wide variety of projects, making his directorial debut, under his real name, on **La morte ha sorriso all'assassino** (Death Smiles on a Murderer; 1973), which he also co-scripted. Following a series of films starring Laura GEMSER, he made probably his best film in 1979—**Blue Holocaust**. He achieved notoriety, of a sort, with his next film, the self-produced **Anthropophagus, the Beast** (1980), which was banned in the UK as a 'video nasty'. He followed that with **Absurd** in 1981 before moving further into softcore sex films with the likes of **Caligula, the Untold Story**, again starring Gemser, and **11 Days, 11 Nights**, 'inspired' by the success of **9 ½ Weeks**. An energetic and opportunistic film-maker, d'Amato has never attracted any mainstream critical interest and for that he is probably crying all the way to the bank.

Alice ARNO (Marie-France Broquet). Franco said she had a "wild talent" and that her pubic hair showed "an astonishing, fascinating beauty." She was brought up in a family of naturists and got into nude modelling very early. Her first film was **Les ponyettes**, a pop music piece starring Sylvie Vartan, in 1967. Since then she has worked with many of the 'names' of adult cinema. She was often used in additional scenes, shot after the film had been completed to 'spice it up'. In this way she appeared in **Liz and Helen**, a late entry in the Edgar Wallace series, directed in 1969 by Riccardo Freda. Her best role is as the naked huntress in Franco's **La comtesse perverse** where she stalks her victims with a bow and arrow. Her sister, Chantal Broquet, is also an actress and the two have appeared together in films.

Anthony BALCH (1938-80) He began in the film business as a production assistant when he was 16, then worked as an editor, before moving on to direct Camay soap commercials for British TV. He moved to France and became a location aide, and then worked on the subtitling of European films (including Robert Bresson's **Pickpocket**) for release in

Britain and America. In 1963 he directed his first avant-garde short, **Towers Open Fire**, with author-friend William Burroughs, and followed it with **Cut Ups**. His taste in films was catholic ... during the 1960's and 70's he programmed two London cinemas, The Times, Baker Street and the Jacey, Piccadilly, reviving old classics like **Un chien andalou**, **Witchcraft Through the Ages** (which had a commentary by Burroughs) and **Freaks** which he double-billed with American & European sexploition movies including **Don't Deliver Us From Evil** and **The Corpse Grinders**. Balch had a nifty way of retitling arty Euro sexploitation, making them more palatable for the home market. In his hands **Le grand cérémonial** became **Weird Weirdo** and **Kapy selan alla—Skin Skin**. Besides programming and distribution, Balch also directed **Secret of Sex** (aka **Bizarre**; 1969), a strange Burroughs-ish sexflick, and the camp comedy **Horror Hospital** (1973). He died from cancer at the age of 42.

Mario **BAVA** (1914-80). Italian director and writer. One of the grand masters of the European horror film. He began as a lighting cameraman in the 1940's and was responsible for much of the final look of many of the films he worked on. Following his salvage job on Riccardo Freda's **I vampiri**, he was able to direct a film under his own name in 1960. **Black Sunday** (**La maschera del demonio**) is now recognised as a classic of the genre, and one of the greatest horror films of the 1960's. Although it might seem quaintly old-fash-

ioned now, the visualisation of such scenes as the reviving of Asa the witch (played by Barbara Steele in her first horror role) gave the British censor much cause for concern and the film was refused a certificate in the UK—a fate that also befell Bava's later **Bay of Blood**. Now with the full length version of his 1972 film **Lisa and the Devil** at last widely available, it's easier to see that Bava's strength was in his mordant, morbid lyricism, rather than in the many shock scenes that most of his films abound in. Directors like Bava, together with Freda and Cottafavi were the commercial new wave of Italian cinema in the 1950's, who broke the back of the then-current vogue for neo-realism that had a stranglehold on the industry. Sex rarely features in any major sense in Bava's films, although in 1969 he made what was widely touted as a 'sex film' under the producership of the ubiquitous Dick Randall (**Four Times That Night**). Bava had a strong influence on Dario Argento and, through him, a direct connection with the florid, sometimes overblown, style of the modern Italian shock-horror film from the likes of Michel Soavi, Lucio Fulci and his own son Lamberto Bava. His death passed almost without note, but now he is beginning to get some of the recognition he always deserved.

Claudine **BECCARIE**. One of the first stars of the French hardcore film. She soon saw the error of her ways and gave up hardcore for 'eroticism' at the end of 1975 when she got married. Her move into respectability was not without its problems: her first 'non-hard' film, the Italian produced **Inhibition** (1976), was classed as 18-only but had hardcore scenes added after classification—much to Beccarie's chagrin. She tried to have the scenes cut out of all the available prints and actually went on hunger strike outside a cinema to publicise her case. She saw hardcore films as "graft", hard work, done only for money not for pleasure—in any sense of the word. She was the 'star' of **Exhibition**, Jean Jean-François Davy's pseudodocumentary hit of 1975. She hated the film, said that it was like being psychoanalysed in public and sued the film-makers. Her sister, Françoise, has also acted under the name of Veronique Visier.

Rick **BIGOTINI** (Richard de Conninck). Actor who has worked with Franco

(Celestine, Julietta '69 etc), production manager, assistant to Duvivier amongst others. First film 1974—hardcore—a sort of erotic version of Rashomon. *Not* a Franco pseudonym, although Franco's **Qui donc a violé Linda?** (Who Raped Linda?) is credited to a Rick de Conninck in some sources.

Sylvia **BOURDON**. Along with Claudine BECCARIE, the biggest home-grown star of French hardcore. Also a writer, her first book was the autobiographical *Love is a Feast*. Like Brigitte LAHAIE, she openly admits to having entered the profession out of an interest in exploring her own sexuality and by virtue of her exhibitionist nature. Also like Lahaie, she gave up the hardcore life when it became routine and "exploitative," in the sense that she was just being asked to endlessly repeat the same actions. Outspoken in her criticism of many of her contemporaries (she described them as allying "sexuality and mediocrity"), she also had little time for most of the directors she worked with. "I don't know if I've met a really intelligent director", she said in 1977. Following Claudine BECCARIE in **Exhibition**—*the* hit of 1975, she starred in **Exhibition 2**, which actually managed to shock even the glibbest commentators with its extreme scenes of S&M torture, and was described by the Commission of Control as 'an incitement to dangerous acts'. Bourdon was known, and widely feared, for her desire to be 'The Wild Girl' of French hardcore. To this end she was the first French actress to agree to have sex with a dog on camera. "Truth obliges me to admit that I was royally paid for this sequence," she wrote. "But I made it with pleasure, because it was the incarnation of one of my fantasies." The credits for Franco's **Sie tötete in Ekstase** were illegally tacked onto the beginning of Bourdon's 1975 film **Sylvia dans l'extase**, which features zoophilia, gerontophilia etc. Sylvia now runs a gallery in Paris that specialises in erotic art.

Jean Pierre **BOUYXOU**. (1946) Actor with Rollin (**Les trottoirs de Bangkok**) and Franco (**Bare Breasted Countess**), assistant to and scriptwriter with Rollin, and writer of respected histories of sci-fi and horror films. Made underground films in his native Belgium and then, in 1976, his first feature, the 'Marxist' hardcore, **Amours collective**, starring the twins Pony and Cathy Castel,

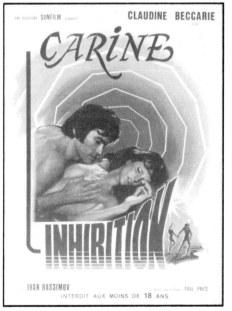

and also Jean Rollin as 'Mike Gentle, the Vampire'! His new book on European hippy movement, *L'Aventure Hippy*, was published in 1992. Rollin's 1979 film **Fascination** takes its title from a magazine edited by Bouyxou. Perhaps his most memorable appearance was in an anonymous super 8mm short made in the 1960s. Dressed as Marie Antoinette he is 'orally pleasured' by famous Situationist author Guy Debord, dressed as a Victorian schoolgirl!

Tinto BRASS (1933). Film and stage director. Studied law in Italy and then moved to Paris for two years. First worked in films as assistant to Rossellini. Directed his first film, **Il disco volante** (The Flying Saucer) in 1960. He became a specialist in classy softcore films with an artistic gloss. His most famous films are **Caligula** (which he disowned, like just about everybody involved in it), **The Key** and **Salon Kitty**. A strident opponent of censorship in all its forms, he recently commented: "I put two balls and a big cock between the legs of the Italian cinema!"

Luis BUNUEL. (1900-1983) Spanish born surrealist. Creator, with Salvador Dali, of two of the first overtly surrealist films—**Le chien andalou** and **L'age d'or**. Later worked in Mexico and finally France. An enormous influence and inspiration to many film-makers from the 1950's onward, and an early advocate, in his films, of the freedom to explore bizarre and deviant behaviour.

Pierre CHEVALIER. (1915) Also known as Peter Knight and Lina Cavalcanti. Veteran director, since 1954, of comedies and thrillers and then, in the 1970's, sex films—largely for EUROCINÉ. His first venture into this area was 1968's **Nathalie—l'amour s'éveille** (Nathalie—The Awakening of Love), the first French version of the popular series of German sex education films that was kicked off by the success of **Helga** in 1967. Not a pseudonym of Franco—this rumour stems from Chevalier's director's credit (not disputed) on **Orloff and the Invisible Man (La vie amoureuse de l'homme invisible;** 1972). He treats his film-making as pretty much a 9 to 5 routine and spends the rest of his time quietly in his Paris flat, where he also writes novels. Workmanlike would be one word to describe his films; uninspired would be another.

▲ Eddie Constantine in **Attack of the Robots** (1966)

Eddie CONSTANTINE (Edward Constantinowsky;1917-1993). Eddie Constantine was born in Los Angeles and followed his wife to France in 1949 to work as a singer. His first film was **La môme vert-de-gris** in 1953, where he starred alongside Howard VERNON. Eddie played the part of Lemmy Caution, the wisecracking toughguy invented by the English writer Peter Cheyney. French film fans were crazy about the American hard-boiled heroes and the time was just right for them to create their very own version. With his dry, humorous delivery, trenchcoat and pork-pie hat, surrounded in a permanent haze of cigarette smoke, Lemmy Caution was their man. Over the next ten or so years Constantine refined the role until the fictional hero and the real life actor were practically indistinguishable. The titles of the films were almost enough: **It's Going to Get Hot, You Dig?; These Dames Like to Mambo** and **Dames Don't Care**. To add a little variety to his style Constantine also played the part of the detective Nick Carter in another series of films. In 1961 Constantine worked with Godard in the film **Seven Deadly Sins** and then, four years later, played Lemmy Caution again in Godard's **Alphaville**—one of the key films of the 1960's. By this time the character had become almost mythic, carrying such a weight of cultural and filmic references that it was obviously time to move on. After a couple of films with Franco—**Attack of the Robots** and **Golden Horn**—Eddie

Constantine worked almost exclusively in Germany with, among others, Fassbinder. In 1991 he played the part of an American General in **Europa**—another film packed full of filmic and cultural references that was almost an homage to the kind of cinematic world Eddie Constantine had helped to create nearly forty years earlier.

Sergio (1926-1990) & Bruno (1931) CORBUCCI. Sergio, the more notable of these two cinematic brothers, began his career as a journalist and assistant director. From the late 1950's he worked on several successful peplums, including **The Last Days of Pompeii** (1959), co-directed with Sergio Leone, and **Goliath versus the Vampire**—which was shown in the UK as an X film—one of the very best (along with Duccio Tessari's **The Titans**) of all peplums. Comedies, thrillers and costume dramas followed, as well as a classic horror with Barbara Steele—**La danza macabra** (1963)—which was finished by Antonio Margheriti. From the mid 1960's Sergio Corbucci made a series of westerns, beginning with **Django** (1966), which are amongst the best of the genre. Bruno's best film is probably **Isabelle, duchesse du diavoli**, a version of the famous comic strip, in which Brigitte Skay is the perfect incarnation of the sexy, spunky heroine.

Jean-François DAVY (1945) Director/ writer. Made his first film at the age of 15 (an 8mm thriller called **Vernay et l'affaire Vanderghen**). Made several 16mm documentary shorts during his military service in Africa and then in 1966 his first full length 35mm film **L'attentat**. **L'attentat** was an ambitious film, but was considered to be uncommercial and was never released. In 1969 he took on a more mainstream project, the crime thriller **Traquenards érotiques** (released in the States as **House of Missing Women**). This time the film was criticised for being too mainstream. In the same year he worked with Michel LEMOINE on the latter's first feature **How Short is the Time For Love (Wie kurz ist die Zeit zum lieben)**. Lemoine returned the compliment by playing a small role in Davy's most ambitious film, the atmospheric horror **Le seuil du vide** (Threshold of the Void; 1971), which also suffered from distribution problems. Following these disappointments, Davy moved into the safer area of sexy comedies with films like **Clockwork Banana (Banane mécanique**; 1972) and **Line Up and Lay Down (Prenez la queue comme tout le monde**; 1973). His breakthrough came with the semi documentary **Exhibition** (1975), starring Claudine BECCARIE. The film was a huge hit and got the whole town talking. He followed it with **Exhibition 2**, which featured scenes of gruesome S&M that made even the staunchest liberals quake. He was also a producer of some of the more interesting hard-core fare (from the likes of Paul Vecchiali and Michel Baudricourt/Caputo). He moved into video in the early eighties. His company, Fil à film, is now one of the largest video labels in France.

Ruggero DEODATO. Italian exploitation director. He began his career at the age of 18 as assistant to the prestigious Roberto Rossellini, later moving into the wonderful world of spaghetti exploitation pix, along with the likes of Sergio CORBUCCI, Antonio Margheriti and Riccardo Freda. Deodato directed his first solo film, a musical with Little Tony, in 1968—**Donne...botte e bersaglieri (Man Only Cries for Love)**—under the pseudonym of Roger Rockerfella(!). From 1969 to 1976 Deodato worked as a publicist, his real directorial breakthrough coming with 1977's **Ultimo mondo cannibale (Last Cannibal World)**, starring Me Me Lay. This laid the

groundwork for 1979's **Cannibal Holocaust**, the *ne plus ultra* of Cannibal movies. The film was famously banned just about everywhere—including Italy—and there are so many different versions of the film now that the chance of ever reconstructing an authentic cut seems remote. Deodato's creation of a truly Sadean universe in **Holocaust** is his most memorable achievement, but he has remained prolific in the variety of genres (thrillers, horror films, fantasy) that the Italian public love, and is an always competent and sometimes inspired film-maker.

Harry DICKSON. In the 1930's, Belgian writer Jean Ray was hired to translate a series of Dutch detective stories into French. He became so bored with the stories that he decided to write new ones instead. The publishers had already paid for the cover illustrations, so he used these for inspiration and wrote stories to fit them featuring his hero 'le Sherlock Holmes américain'. Together with his trusty sidekick, Tom Wills, Dickson investigated a whole host of strange cases all set in a mythic recreation of England as seen through European eyes. Vastly influential and read in most European countries, the Harry Dickson stories are unknown in England and the US. Rollin, Borowczyk and Alain Resnais have all expressed an interest in filming the Dickson stories, so far without success. Jean Ray was born Jean Raymond Marie de Kremer in

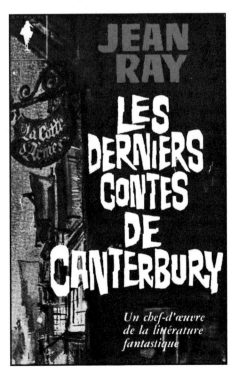

Ghent, Belgium, in 1887 and died in 1964, on the eve of his rediscovery by a mass audience. He worked as a journalist and as a writer of musical comedies before turning out a host of weird tales, full of unique atmosphere and dark humour. His story *La cité de l'indicible peur* was filmed in 1964, by Jean-Pierre MOCKY, as **La grande frousse**. His only novel, *Malpertuis*, was filmed by Harry KUMEL in 1972. Jean Ray's life was as strange and mysterious as his stories. He was believed to be of Native American extraction and to have worked as an ocean-bound bootlegger during the 1920's.

Erwin C. DIETRICH (1930) Swiss writer, producer and (occasionally) director under the pseudonyms of Michael Thomas and Manfred Gregor. Originally he wanted to be an actor and wrote a script for a rustic comedy in which he was to have the lead role (**Der pfarrer von Kirchfeld**; 1955). When he saw his own screen tests he realised that he was not destined to be an actor and became a producer instead. The Austrian co-producers of his first film froze him out and so he decided to go his own way and formed his own company—Urania. He began by producing cozy 'heimat' (homeland) films—full of rural nostalgia and crackerbarrel philosophy—and Swiss dialect films that no-one outside the country could understand. His favourite project—a film about the life of Swiss jazzman 'Hazy' Osterwald—was a flop and Dietrich moved into safer genre areas; first of all thrillers and then sex films. His 1968 film **Guess Who's Coming to Breakfast (Die nichten der Frau Oberst)** was the second most successful film that year in German speaking territories, and soon he had directed a sequel and a whole host of other, hard and soft, concoctions. Titles like **Sex and not Yet Sixteen**, **Champagne for Room 17** and **The Sex Life of the Three Musketeers** give the game away. In 1965 Dietrich increased his empire by buying out the Zurich based company Elite and forming Avis Film, which he later renamed Ascot, based in Berlin. Soon his various activities—directing, producing, importing and distributing, were bringing him in more than 100 million marks a year. In Germany they call him The Pope of Porn. In Switzerland, with their conservative and bourgeois morality, they probably have a less complimentary name for him. During the early 1970's Dietrich moved into the horror area with Franco's **Jack the Ripper** and a whole series of gruesome Women-in-Prison films. In the 1980's he extended his empire even further with big international co-productions, **The Sea Wolves** (1980), **Commando Leopard** (1985) and **Codename: Wild Geese** (1986). Perhaps the best way of looking at Dietrich's activities would be via the title of Kon Ichikawa's 1963 film—**An Actor's Revenge**—or more accurately, a would-be actor's revenge.

EMMANUELLE. The original **Emmanuelle**, based on the book of the same name by actress Emmanuelle Arsan, is the most successful French film of all time and started a whole industry of imitations. The 'official' sequels have now reached number 7, along with a TV series. The copyright to the name Emmanuelle still belongs with Arsan, and consequently the many unofficial derivations all spell the name with one M to avoid legal complications. There have been Black Emanuelles, Yellow Emanuelles, Emanuelles in Prison and in America, Emanuelle as a nun and Emanuelle amongst the cannibals as well as combinations of the above. To complicate matters, Laura GEMSER, the Black Emanuelle (with one M) also appeared with the original Emmanuelle (with two M's), Sylvia KRISTEL, in **Emmanuelle, l'antivierge**, the official sequel to the first film. The film was classified X on its original release—much to the producer's chagrin; a name change to **Emmanuelle 2** lifted the ban! The real Emmanuelle is an actress called Marayat Andriane who was married to a French diplomat. She had a small part in the 1966 Robert Wise film **The Sand Pebbles** and later she directed her own film **Laure** in 1976. Nelly Kaplan's **Nea** (1976) was also based on a book by Emmanuelle Arsan, who is now living happily, and richly, off her royalties.

EUROCINÉ. Paris-based production company. Since the late 1950's they have been producers (and more often co-producers), and distributors of a string of low budget films firmly aimed at the popular end of the market. Horror films, thrillers, sexy comedies and war films are all grist to the mill of this indefatigable production house. As Pierre Charles has pointed out, the true spirit of the 'Midi-Minuitist' of old is incarnated in these cheap and often cheerful little pictures. Many

▲ Typical Euirociné sex thriller set in Paris

of the directors mentioned in this book have worked for Euirociné at one time or another, and the companies' involvement with Jess Franco spans the whole of his career, from **Awful Doctor Orlof** onwards. Euirociné was founded by former street-trader Marius Lesoeur in the mid 1950's and is now run by his son, Daniel. Euirociné are past masters of the art of repackaging old films as new ones. Euirociné films often have great titles that speak volumes about the true nature of the commercial underground: **Sex Life of the Invisible Man**; **Tender and Perverse Emanuelle**; **Special Train for Hitler**; **Girls of the Golden Saloon**. 'Serious' French cinéphile —and many not so serious ones—

hate Euirociné, and the company are notoriously publicity shy. "They never talk to the press," Rollin says; "Guess why!"

FANTÔMAS. A character created by journalists Pierre Souvestre and Marcel Allain in the years before the First World War. He was a sort of amoral, super-villain whose dastardly acts seemed to be performed more often for the pleasure of them than for financial gain. A master of disguise, Fantômas was always one step ahead of the law, in the form of Inspector Juve, and his nemesis, the journalist Jerome Fandor. The first Fantômas book (there were eventual-

▲ Edwige Fenech wakes from a nightmare in **They're Coming to Get You** (1972)

ly 32 of them) was published in 1911 and the series of films based on them began in 1913. Fantômas is more an image than a physical presence and the most startling depiction of him is as a masked man in a tuxedo and top hat, towering over Paris, with an evil look on his face and his right hand clutching a dagger. The surrealists loved Fantômas and wrote poems about him. He was a great influence on later Euro antiheroes, particularly Diabolik and Kriminal.

Edwige FENECH. Actress, born in Bona, Algeria, in 1948. She began her career as a photomodel. Her first film role came in 1966 in **Toutes folles de lui** (Crazy About Him). In the late sixties she appeared in several West German sex farces, like **The Blonde and the Black Pussycat (Alle Katzchen naschen Gern**; 1967) and **Sexy Susan Sins Again (Frau Wirtin hat auch einen Grafen**; 1968). Although her roles were little more than decoration, they did hint at a developing talent for comedy. Fenech's horror debut came as

one of the victims in Mario Bava's **Five Dolls for an August Moon (Cinque bambole per la luna d'agosta**; 1970). After starring in Sergio MARTINO's **Lo strano vizio della signora Wardh** in 1971, Fenech became the girlfriend of his producer brother, the reason she was regularly cast in his many projects. Her uninhibited approach to nudity, gorgeous looks and fine sense of comic timing made her a natural for such saucy romps as **The Naughty Nun (La bella Antonia, prima monaca e poi demonia**; 1972) and **Quel gran pezzo della Ubalda tutta nuda e tutta calda** (Ubalda, All Naked and Warm; 1972). She also made frequent appearances in horror films, too, such as **Erotic Blue (Perche'quelle strane gocce di sangue sul corpo di Jennifer?**; 1972), **They're Coming to Get You (Tutti i colori del buio**; 1972). and **Strip Nude for your Killer (Nude per l'assassino**; 1975). The late seventies saw her creating the roles of La dottoressa (a female doctor), La polizziotta (a policewoman) and L'insegnante (a schoolteacher), all to become staples

of the Italian skinflick comedy canon. An acrimonious split with Luciano Martino did not prevent her working for him again, and her finest hour was in his brother's **Cornetti alla crema** (Custard Croissants) in 1981. Moving slightly upmarket, Edwige began to find herself cast in the films of more critically revered Italian comedy directors, such as Steno, Dino Risi and Pasquale Festa Campanile. In recent years she has made her theatrical debut and has presented many Italian TV shows, as well as launching her own fashion range and setting up a production company with her son, Edwin.

Lucio FULCI. Was an art critic and a medical student before entering the Centro Sperimentale film school in Rome. He worked for years as an assistant director and scriptwriter for several top Italian comedy directors and actors—including Steno and Ugo Tognazzi. **One on Top of the Other**, in 1970, was his first thriller, and one of the first Italian 'gialli'. Fulci calls these films 'mechanical', due to the almost fatalistic way the plot is worked out in them. His subsequent films include **Lizard in a Woman's Skin** (1973), **Murder to the Tune of Seven Black Notes** (1974) and **Zombie Flesh Eaters** (1979). The last film was banned in Britain as a 'video nasty'—a fate that befell several other Fulci films, such as **The Beyond** and **The House by the Cemetery** (both 1981). This notoriety has given him a cult status in the UK and America that he refers to in his 1990 film **Nightmare Concert**, where he plays the part of a horror film director driven mad by exposure to gory movies.

Sergio GARRONE. Has used pseudonyms of Willy S. Regan (or Regent), Richard Jackson and Kennet Freeman. Garrone followed the usual route as assistant director and scriptwriter on a wide variety of product before striking out on his own with the western **Se vuoi vivere...spara**, directed under the pseudonym of Willy S. Regan, in 1968. Several more westerns, a war film and a sexy desert adventure followed, until Garrone entered the horror field with **L'amanti del mostro** and **La mano che nutre la morte**, both apparently shot back-to-back in 1974, with Klaus KINSKI doing his demented nobleman role. A couple of years later, at the height of the 'Nazi Sex' cycle of Italian cinema, Garrone put out **SS Experiment Camp** and **SS Camp 5: Women's Hell**—again both seemingly edited together out of footage shot simultaneously. Sexy thrillers and a couple of dull Women-in-Prison films rounded off Garrone's career. Now, apparently, he is running a restaurant in Rome. His undistinguished but energetic filmography is typical of the generation of Italian exploitation filmmakers who came to prominence in the mid seventies, when the industry was in one of its frequent crises and any bandwagon going had to be leapt on quickly and exploited to the full before catching the next one. Originality is not Garrone's forte, but he puts his films together like pizzas—extra toppings to order and baked to a chewy consistency.

Laura GEMSER (Moira Chen; 1950). Dutch/Indonesian actress. She was discovered by Francis Giacobetti who photographed the famous poster for **Emmanuelle** which showed Sylvia KRISTEL sitting in a big cane chair—an image that helped to sell the film worldwide. He was called in to direct the sequel—**Emmanuelle , l'anti-vierge (Emmanuelle 2)** and got Laura a part

as a sexy masseuse. This led to a long series of films in Italy, where she became a big star during the late 1970's. Many of them, beginning with **Black Emanuelle 2** in 1976, were directed by Joe D'AMATO. Jack Palance, with whom she starred in **Eva nera**, said of her "She has brought something new to sex films".

Guy GIBERT (Jack Guy) Director of **That Girl is a Tramp (Les baiseuses)** the first 'official' (ie—licensed) hardcore film shown in France. Also scriptwriter for EUROCINE (**Special Train for Hitler**). The success of **Les baiseuses** led to a whole slew of similarly titled films (**Les jouisseuses, Les butineuses, Les cavaleuses,Les volupteuses** etc) and to the renaming of other films in an attempt to cash in—for example, Jess Franco's **La comtesse noire** became **Les avaleuses (The Swallowers)**. Later conventions included the '.....en chaleur' (on heat) titling. Thus we had **Autostoppeuses** (hitch-hikers) **en chaleur**, **Chattes** (pussies) **en chaleur**, **Veuves** (widows) **en chaleur** and so on.

Jorge GRAU (1930). Spanish director, writer, actor, playwright and painter. He began as an actor in Barcelona and worked as a scriptwriter for radio before moving to Rome to study in the Centro Sperimentale, the state film school. Back in Spain he worked extensively on Italian co-productions with the likes of Riccardo Freda and Sergio Leone. Like Javier AGUIRRE his career combines the experimental and the commercial. He made two of the best films of the Spanish horror boom—**Legend of Blood Castle** (1972) and **The Living Dead at the Manchester Morgue** (1974). His 1975 film **La trastienda** (The Backside) featured the first full frontal female nudity in Spanish cinema, and in 1978 he made the first version of **Love Letters of a Portuguese Nun**, before Jess Franco. The film featured Lina Romay in one of her rare non-Franco films and also José Larraz as an Inquisitor.

Lucien HUSTAIX (1923-1975). Although he died at just the high point of the French sex wave, Hustaix was already one of its prime movers. He studied law, which gave him a good head for business, and began in films as an extra. He started to shoot documentaries and then moved into production. In 1970 he directed **Edith**—the first step

towards his sex career. Then with **Les caresseuses** and particularly **Les jouisseuses (Unfaithful Wives)** he moved to the top of the ladder. He was particularly adept at selling and marketing his product abroad, tailoring versions of each film for particular countries. His films were unpretentious, low-brow, straightforward and very successful—particularly outside Paris where they weren't so interested in 'art'. His ambition was to make comedies. Lots of people found his films funny for all the wrong reasons.

Just JAECKIN (1940). Photographer and director. His father was Dutch and his mother English and he spent the first five years of his life in England. He trained as a photographer in the army in 1959 during national service. Later he studied architecture and interior design in Paris. He became art director of *Marie Claire* and his photographs appeared in many other glossy fashion magazines—*Harpers Bazaar*, *Vogue*, *Elle* and so on. Later he worked for TV and made advertising films. He really wanted to make a thriller, but the first feature he was offered was **Emmanuelle**. Its astonishing success led to the offer of **The Story of O** the following year and his career was fixed as maker of 'quality' erotic films. Following **Madame Claude** in 1977 he tried to break the mould with **The Last Romantic Lover**, a personal project into which he put a lot of his own money. It was a flop—as was the teenage-oriented **Girls** in 1980. Seeing the writing on the wall, he went back to literary eroticism with **Lady Chatterley's Lover** in 1981, in the process rediscovering Sylvia KRISTEL, star of the original **Emmanuelle**. Just Jaeckin's contribution to world cinema was to help define—or more accurately, popularise—a new form of eroticism: glossy, escapist, and decidedly bourgeois, aimed largely at couples. Previously, sex cinema had been the province of adolescents and dirty old men. That the formula still works is amply demonstrated by the success of the series of films Zalman King has made, beginning with **9½ Weeks** and continuing through **Two Moon Junction**, **Zandalee** and **Lake Consequence**.

Udo KIER (1944) German actor, born in Cologne. He was living in London in the mid sixties when he landed the small role of a gigolo in Mike Sarne's **Road to Saint**

KLAUS KINSKI
ANNABELLA INCONTRERA
SYDNEY CHAPLIN
CHRISTIANE KRUGER

**LIZ & HELEN**
Eastmancolor

**Tropez** in 1967. For the next few years he worked in Austria, Germany, Italy, Greece and France—usually playing 'heavies' in thrillers. It was only really with the two films he made in Italy under the nominal direction of Paul Morrissey—**Flesh For Frankenstein** and **Andy Warhol's Dracula**, both 1973—that he came to the notice of a wider audience. With his wonderfully moody features and almost totally inexpressive acting style, Kier soon became a sort of decadent icon in a whole series of 'arty' sex and/or horror features such as **The Story of O** (1975), **Spermula** (1976), **Hungarian Rhapsody** (1979) and **Bloodbath of Dr Jekyll** (1980).

Klaus KINSKI.(Nikolaus Gunther Naksynski; 1926-1991). Polish born actor. His father was a struggling opera singer who abandoned the family when Klaus was still a child. As his autobiography—*All I Need is Love*—tells, he grew up as a wild, unruly kid of the streets with a tough argumentative streak that never left him. In 1944 he was conscripted into the army and became a prisoner of war for 18 months. It was in the camps that he first discovered his talent for acting, whiling away the long days by entertaining his fellow prisoners. In the confused rubble of post-war Germany he talked his way into a Berlin theatre company led by Boreslav Barlog and was soon getting rave notices. He made his film debut in 1948—**Morituri**—where he was typecast as a Polish immigrant. During the 1950's he became a

popular 'face' in many German films—often playing killers, mad-men or Nazi soldiers. In 1960 he made his first Edgar Wallace film—**Der Racher (The Avenger)** and was soon a regular fixture in the long running series. In 1965 he met up with producer Harry Allan TOWERS for the film **Our Man in Marrakesh**. The Towers' connection led to four films with Jess Franco, including **Jack the Ripper** in 1976. The rest of the 1960s was mostly spent in Italy, where Kinski became a star of many spaghetti westerns, including two masterpieces—**A Bullet for the General** in 1966 and **The Big Silence** in 1968. An important turning point was his 1972 film **Aguirre, Wrath of God**, where he dominates the whole show with a performance that is undoubtedly one of his greatest. The film was a big success, both for its director, Werner Herzog, and for Kinski who suddenly found himself, like Udo KIER, much in demand by Art House directors. Unfortunately, as his fame increased his ability to choose the right part seemed to decrease. Only his role as Karl-Heinz Zimmer in ZULAWSKI's **The Important Thing is to Love** (1974) was really worthy of his talents, and is probably his second most memorable film. During the 1980's Kinski moved to the States and spent the decade making a wide variety of films in which his presence is generally the only memorable feature. He had always wanted to direct himself, and in 1987 he made **Paganini**, a bio-pic based on the life of the crazed violinist. 'Serious' filmgoers love him for **Aguirre** and the other films he made with Herzog, genre fans love him for the Italian westerns and the Franco's; Kinski hated them all. His autobiography, *All I Need is Love*, now withdrawn for legal reasons, is one of the most scabrous put-downs of the film-business ever committed to paper.

Gérard KIKOÏNE.(1946) Writer and director. His father ran a large sound studio in Paris, where he specialised in the dubbing of foreign films for French audiences. Kikoïne began there as an assistant in 1964 and worked on many important films, including, for two years, Abel Gance's **Napoleon**. When his father sold the studio, Kikoïne began to work as a freelance specialist, doing a lot of work for Robert de Nesle's CFF. It was during this period that he worked on several films of Franco's. He would get the films sent on from Spain as black and white workprints,

with a minimal soundtrack and a two page synopsis. Together with Howard Vernon, Kikoïne would 'reconstruct' the films, adding sound, dialogue and music to make, in many cases, something completely new out of them. He began to direct in 1974 with **Weekend Orgy (L'amour à la bouche)** and became known, within the French sex film industry, as a painstaking and original artist who could squeeze a lot out of very little. Later he teamed up with Harry Alan TOWERS, Franco's partner in crime through much of the late sixties, and moved more into the commercial mainstream—where, in fact, he had always wanted to be. 1988's **Edge of Sanity** shows his ability to squeeze much out of a low budget, as well as his trademark use of a multi-layered soundtrack. Such are the vagaries of fame that many people, not recognising his name on the credits, thought it was just another Franco pseudonym.

León KLIMOVSKY (1906) Born in Buenos Aires of Russian parentage. He studied medicine and practised as a dentist for 15 years before becoming involved in cinema. He had an early introduction to the world of film, as his father had worked as a projectionist. He founded Argentina's first film- club in 1929 and wrote film and music criticism as well as presenting the enormously popular radio programme Cinema Diary. He began by making shorts and then, in 1947, his first feature **El jugador**. His second feature, **La guitarra de gardel**, was made in Spain in 1949, and in 1955 he moved there permanently, eventually becoming a citizen. His career has taken in all types of commercial cinema, much like that of Franco who worked as his assistant in the late 1950's. In fact **La reina del Tabarín**, Franco's third film as director, was originally a project for Klimovsky, who was unable to do it for technical reasons. Often made on extremely low budgets and rarely shown outside Spain, unless in badly cut and dubbed versions, there are few films in Klimovsky's long filmography that do justice to his knowledge of and love for cinema. His more important genre films include **Dracula Saga**, **Werewolf versus the Vampire Woman** and **The People Who Own the Dark**. In 1980 he played an irascible Jewish godfather in Manuel Aragon's film **Maravillas**, where, for the promise of an expensive ring, he gets his god-daughter to walk along a rooftop ledge, telling her it will cure her of fear forever.

Sylvia KRISTEL. Born in 1952 in Utrecht in Holland. She had a strict religious upbringing and originally wanted to be an English teacher. Reacting against her background she worked in a bar, as a secretary and even as a petrol pump attendant while trying to make it as a dancer. She started to work as a photographic model in the early 1970's. Her first film was **Because of the Cats** in 1972—based on the book by Nicholas Freeling. In 1973 she won the title of Miss TV Europe and after travelling the world as part of her prize she was discovered by Just JAECKIN for the starring role in **EMMANUELLE**—a part that had been turned down by every eligible French actress. Although she was Dutch, Sylvia Kristel soon came to typify the world's idea of the sexy, liberated French girl. She worked with Alain Robbe-Grillet in **Le jeu avec le feu**, with Jean-Pierre MOCKY in **No Pockets in a Shroud** and with Borowczyk in **The Streetwalker**. Attempts to broaden her

range with parts in **Airport 80** and the Maxwell Smart comedy **The Nude Bomb** never really took off, and she came back to the fold with the starring role in **Lady Chatterley's Lover** in 1981.

Harry KUMEL (1940) Belgian screenwriter, film and theatre director. He began making short films in his early teens and won many awards before moving into TV. His first feature, **Mr Hawarden**(1968), a story of a woman who disguises herself as a man in order to flee a murder charge, was an attempt by Kümel to "unmask reality." The film was dedicated to Josef von Sternberg, whom Kümel had come to know during the last few years of the great director's life. The influence of von Sternberg is even stronger in Kümel's next film **Daughters of Darkness** (1971). This heavily stylised vampire film was also indebted to the Belgian Symbolist artists of the late 19th century, painters like Fernand Knopf and Leon Spilaert. The colour scheme of the film and its hard-edged light-

ing were deliberately chosen to evoke the dry, still and haunted look of the Symbolists. Kümel used the colours of red, white and black (the colours of the Nazi flag) and shot all the exteriors early in the morning or late at night to give the film a sinister and dream-like feel. Kümel was given his biggest ever budget for his next film—**Malpertuis** (1972). The film was based on a novel by Jean RAY, from which Kümel, and his screenwriter Jean Ferry, extracted all the latent surrealism, turning the film into a tour de force of weird imagery and heightened mystery. The film was badly cut by distributors, and Kümel effectively retired from the business, retreating to the safer waters of TV. In 1975 he made a successful TV series called **The Coming of Joachim Stiller**, again based on a famous Belgian fantasy novel. He has also worked for the erotic French TV show **La série rose**. His most recent film, **Eline Vere**, from 1991, is, like **Mr Hawarden**, another pessimistic story of a woman's descent into fantasy and madness.

▼ **Daughters of Darkness** (1971)

Ado KYROU (1923-85). Critic, writer and later film-maker. He wrote the influential *Surréalisme au Cinéma* and was editor of a series, published by Eric Losfeld, that included volumes on Jean Rollin and José Bénazéraf. He directed **Le moine (The Monk)** in 1972 from a script by Buñuel.

Brigitte LAHAIE. (1958) Born in Lille, in northern France, she moved to Paris at the age of 18 and got her first job in the movies through a newspaper advert. She soon became a star of the French hardcore industry of the mid 1970's. Three films with Jean Rollin, **Fascination**, **Les raisins de la mort** and **La nuit des traquées** gave her a taste for straight acting and she retired from the sex industry to learn her craft. On winning one of the star roles in **Joy et Joan** in 1985, she changed her name to Brigitte Simonin to evade her past. Then, coming clean with her autobiography *Moi, la Scandaleuse* in 1987, she reverted to her original name. Small roles in **Diva** and **Henry and June** and starring roles in **L'exécutrice** and **Pour la peau d'un flic** with Alain Delon have made her a bankable asset in France. But she is not afraid of her past, and has worked again, in **Faceless**, with Franco, with whom she made the hardcore **Je brûle de partout** in 1978. Her first novel was published in 1992, and she has also released a pop single and performed a successful one-woman stage show all about her career.

Frédéric LANSAC (Claude Mulot; 1942-86). As Claude Mulot he made a well received low budget horror film—**La rose écorchée (The Blood Rose)**, a version of **Eyes Without a Face**—in 1969. The mad doctor in that film was called Frédéric Lansac, the name later adopted as pseudonym by Mulot when he moved into the hardcore area. His major films include **La sexe qui parle (Pussy Talk)**, **Mes nuits avec Alice, Penelope, Arnold, Maud et Richard (What a Performer)**, **Shocking** and **Échanges de partenaires**. Never entirely happy in hardcore, Mulot returned to directing under his own name and also wrote many scripts, notably for Max Pécas. He died in a swimming accident.

❋

Michel LEMOINE (1933). French. Actor, writer and director. One of the great faces of the commercial underground. Robert Rimmer wrote of his acting style: 'He stares at the ladies so intently that you wonder if he has a glass eye'. He began as a child actor in two films directed by the great Sacha Guitry in the late forties, studied law for a year, and then, after working as an actor on the French stage, was invited to Italy to star in a costume drama called **La vendetta del maschera di fero** in 1961. Over the next half dozen years he worked for some of the top Italian genre directors, including Mario Bava and Antonio Margheriti, as well as starring

in one of Bénazéraf's early films, **Le cri de la chair**, in 1962. He was also hard at work writing scripts and learning the technical aspects of the business. In 1967 he made three films for the German producer Adrian Hoven, including Jess Franco's **Necronomicon**, where he met his wife to be, Janine Reynaud. In 1969, again for Hoven, he wrote and directed his first feature **Wie kurz ist die Zeit zum lieben**. The film was released credited to Pier A. Caminnecci, who had actually financed the production. Starting with **I Am Available (Les désaxées)** in 1972, Michel Lemoine's films came to feature an unashamed eroticism that was combined, in **Les chiennes** the following year, with an eerie sense of the fantastic. His 1975 film **Sept femmes pour un sadique (Seven Women For Satan)**, a version of the Count Zaroff story, was banned by the censor and only released later in a badly cut version. He went on to write, direct and star in a series of always interesting and sometimes outstanding films that exhibited his strong interests in the erotic and the fantastic, and above all an oneiric mix of the two, that makes him in many ways a parallel to Franco. From 1982 to 1987 he worked as a director for ALPHA FRANCE under the name of Michel Leblanc, turning in 12 hardcores, many of them starring the specialist actress Olinka Hardimann (Mary Monroe) and the Italian actor Gabriel Pontello. Several of them were released on video in the UK—**Marilyn, My Love, Swedish Playbirds, Take My Body, White Heat, Forbidden Pleasures, Mobile Home Girls** and **Desert Lovers**.

Francis LEROI (1946). Began with Godardian essays in new wave style in the late sixties (**Pop Game**, **La poupée rouge**) and moved into hardcore during the seventies' boom. Also produced films for Frédéric LANSAC. He directed **Emmanuelle 4** in 1984 and returned to the series with **Emmanuelle 7** in 1993 as well as directing the Emmanuelle TV series.

Gaston LEROUX (1868-1927). French journalist, short story writer and novelist. If Gaston Leroux is known at all, outside France, it is as the author of *The Phantom of the Opera*. However, he was the creator of more than 30 bestselling novels and many equally successful short stories. His closest

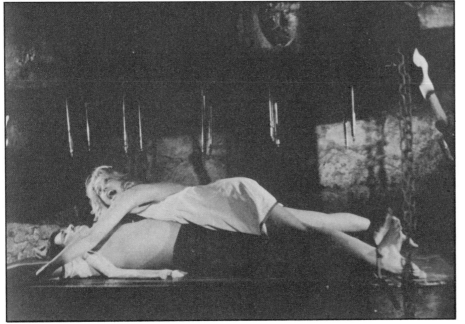

equivalent would probably be Edgar Wallace, and like Wallace his stories have contributed immeasurably to the tone and subject matter of much European popular cinema. Several of his books have been filmed, including his classic 'locked-room' murder yarn **The Mystery of the Yellow Room** (1907) and **The Perfume of the Lady in Black** in 1912, remade in Italy in 1973. Apart from these ingeniously plotted detective books he also wrote many more macabre novels, such as *La Poupée Sanglante* and *La Reine du Sabbat*—which Jean Rollin has been trying to film for years. In the late 1960's Franco and Jean-Claude Carrière wrote a script called **The Man From Guyana**, based around the Chéri-Bibi character who features in five of Leroux's novels. The film, which was to have starred Howard VERNON, Klaus KINSKI and Orson Welles, now belongs to Irwin DIETRICH who's keeping very quiet about it.

Anne LIBERT. The daughter of Jean Libert, half of the 'Paul Kenny' writing team behind the Coplan series of books. She first acted in Vadim's **Le vice et le vertu** and then worked as a model in the States. Her first starring roles were with Jess Franco, most notably in **Erotic Rites of Frankenstein**, where she plays the memorable role of Melissa the Birdwoman. Like Alice ARNO she was brought up as a naturist and had no problems with nude scenes, which got her a lot of work in the early 1970's French cinema where such scenes were *de rigueur* for young actresses. She was dubbed the 'Brigitte Bardot of the sex film'. According to Paul-Hervé Mathis she offered her part in Max Pécas's **Je suis une nymphomane** to Sandra Julien, but worked with Pécas later in **Club privé**. She appeared in a couple of films directed by Claude Lelouch (**Le chat et le souris** and **Le bon et les méchants**, both 1975) and seems now to have retired from the business following a TV series in 1978.

Helga LINE (Helga Lina Stern; 1932). Berlin born actress. Began her career as a dancer and acrobat in circus performances in Portugal and later worked as a model. Moving to Madrid in 1960, she soon became one of the most popular of all genre actresses, appearing in horror films, thrillers, spy films and westerns throughout the 1960's and into the 70's. Her refined, svelte and aristocratic beauty was well used in two of

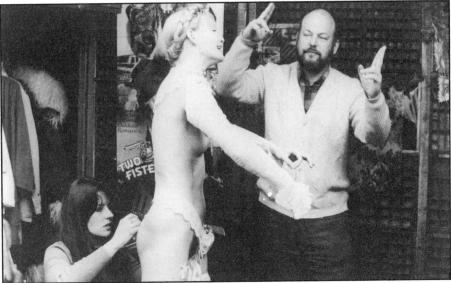

▲ Makavejev measures up in **Sweet Movie** (1973)

Almodóvar's early pictures—**Labyrinth of Passion** (1982) and **Law of Desire**(1986).

Diana LORYS (1940) Spanish. After training as a dancer she appeared in comedies and musicals in Spain in the early 1960's. Following an appearance in Jess Franco's **Gritos en la noche (The Awful Dr Orlof)** in 1961, she became one of the most common faces in Spanish co-productions of the sixties. She acted in westerns, horror films and spy thrillers, including three more films with Franco. Among her more important roles are parts in **Malenka** and **The Blue Eyes of the Broken Doll**, where she plays the sexually insatiable Claude. Franco was amused to note, after her many similar roles, that she had claimed a double was used for her brief topless scene in **Gritos**. Her final roles were in two of the last paella westerns in 1978.

Dusan MAKAVEJEV (1932). Born in the Serbian part of what used to be Yugoslavia, Makavejev became interested in the anarchic possibilities of cinema while a student at Belgrade University. He began by making shorts and between 1953 and 1964 he made a total of 17 short films. Many of them exhibited the iconoclastic attitudes towards authority and the upfront attitude concerning sexual matters that would later become a major feature of his full length films. His first feature, **Covek nije tica**, was released in 1965 but it was with **W.R.—Mysteries of the Organism** in 1971 that his name was made. Ostensibly a doc-

umentary about the life and work of Wilhelm Reich, the radical sex-therapist and political theorist, the film extends into an examination and presentation of all the then current theories and practices of liberation, both political and sexual. The film was revolutionary also in its structure, mixing fiction and documentary in a completely unselfconscious way. The French co-production **Sweet Movie**, in 1973, took things even further and was not widely shown. It was the subject of a court action by its star, Carole Laure, over the way she had been treated. Apart from a brief section in the Dutch compilation film **Wet Dreams**, directed under the name Sam Rotterdam, Makavejev dropped out of sight until 1981, when **Montenegro**, a much more straightforwardly commercial piece, was released to good reviews. Apparently Makavejev was once offered the job of directing **Apocalypse Now**, which he turned down. The mind boggles to think what he might have made of it.

Sergio MARTINO (1938). He began his career in 1963 as an assistant to the likes of Mario BAVA and made his first feature in 1969 (**Mille peccati....nessuna virtu/The Wages of Sin**)—a mondo style documentary. He entered the *gialli* field in 1971 with **Next! (Lo strano vizio della signora Wardh)**, which starred Edwige FENECH, who would go on to become a regular fixture in many of Martino's subsequent films, such as **They're Coming to Get You (Tutti i colori del buio)** and **Excite Me (Il tuo vizio e una stanza chiusa e solo io ne ho la chiave)**, both 1972.

▲ Radley Metzger's stylish **Carmen Baby** (1967)

Martino's best known *gialli*, **Torso** (**I corpi presantano tracce di violenza carnale**), was released the following year, this time with Suzy Kendall in the lead. From the late seventies and throughout the eighties, Martino made films in a wide variety of genres—comedies, cop thrillers and romantic dramas. His most successful films include **Prisoners of the Cannibal God** (**La montagna del dio cannibale**; 1978), **Island of the Fishmen** (**L'isola degli uomini pesce**; 1979) and **Cornetti alla crema** (Custard Croissants; 1981). Recently he has been reunited with Edwige Fenech for an impressive **Twin Peaks** inspired TV series **Delitti privati** (Private Crimes). Sergio Martino's films are unashamedly commercial, but their compulsive vitality and assuredly professional sheen deserve to bring him recognition as a unique figure in the annals of Italian exploitation.

Bruno MATTEI. Italian exploitation director. Has also worked under the names of Vincent Dawn, Jordan B. Matthews and Stefan Oblowski. Widely written off as a talentless hack, his films are even rejected by splatter fans, in spite of their many 'hard gore' sequences. He became involved in the industry in 1951 when his father started up a production company. Mattei has worked as an assistant to Riccardo Freda but is closer to the likes of FULCI, with whom he worked (uncredited) on **Zombi 3**. Mattei is an unashamed exploiter, even cobbling together soundtracks from Goblin records to give his films the gloss of other directors' work (**Zombie Creeping Flesh**;1981). Apart from straight horror, Mattei's filmography includes Nazi-sex films (**Women's Camp 119**; 1976), nunsploitation (**The Other Hell**; 1981) and sex films (**Desire**), as well as Mad-Max ripoffs like **Rats: Night of Terror** (1984). His 1984 release, **Seven Magnificent Gladiators**, teamed Sybil Danning with Mandy Rice Davies in one of her rare film roles. Few have good words to say about Mattei, but his films obviously make money and he is the archetypical Italian exploitation director, always giving the public what they want.

Marisa MELL (Marlies Moitzi; 1939-1992). Austrian born actress who made her name in a string of Italian-Spanish co-productions in the 1960's and 70's. She had an icy but inviting allure that made her the perfect sixties' femme fatale. Her most famous role is probably as Diabolik's girlfriend, Eva, in Mario BAVA's film of the famous Euro comic strip.

Radley METZGER worked as an usher in a cinema after finishing college, then joined the film editor's union. He was called up for the Korean War, and worked for two years as a cutter on air force films. After completing his service he got into the foreign end of film distribution, editing trailers and dubbing European movies for U.S. release. He worked as dubbing editor on Roger VADIM's **And God Created Woman**. In 1960 he started his own company, Audubon Films, turning out his first production, **Dark Odyssey**, in 1961 and releasing **The Alley Cats** (1962) and **The Dirty Girls** (1963). A year later he helped edit Jack Curtis's horror classic **The Flesh Eaters**. While he was in Yugoslavia directing his first colour picture, **Carmen Baby** (1967), he read a review of **I, A Woman**, a film that was causing a stir in Europe. Metzger bought the rights and reedited it for the U.S. market, where it became a great cross-over hit, grossing over $3 million. **I, A Woman** helped open up America for sophisticated European sex-flicks and also helped move U.S. sexploitation away from 'nudies', towards melodrama and action. Metzger's films were classy, aimed at the affluent middle class, and many of them were based on literary works, which made them seem more respectable. His 1969 hit **Camille 2000** was adapted from a work by Alexandre Dumas, and **The Punishment of Anne** (1975) used the S&M novel, *The Image*, as inspiration for its kinky shenanigans. During the mid seventies, Metzger moved into hardcore, directing a series of stylish, ground breaking films under the pseudonym Henry Paris. These included **The Private Afternoons of Pamela Mann** (1974), **Barbara Broadcast** (1975) and an updated version of *Pygmalion*—**The Opening of Misty Beethoven**. Since then he's directed **The Cat and the Canary** (1979) and **The Princess and the Call Girl** (1984). Metzger's films are too elegant to be seedy and David F. Friedman has called him "the only genius working in American exploitation films" and "a man ahead of his time."

**MIDI-MINUIT FANTASTIQUE.** A French film magazine; but so much more. Founded in 1962 by Eric Losfeld, and named after a famous Paris cinema where genre films—peplums, horror films, thrillers and science fiction—were shown. The term 'Midi-Minuitist' became synonymous with a particular kind of sensibility that was drawn to the garish, the mysterious, the peculiar and the downright bad in cinema. Just as their 'serious' colleagues in *Cahiers du cinéma* discovered Sam Fuller, Edgar Ulmer, etc, so the MMF mob championed BAVA, and Michael Powell, created the Barbara Steele cult and pointed the way to a whole new way of looking at cinema. The magazine ceased publication in 1971. There has never been anything like it since. Pierre Philippe's film **Midi Minuit** (1970) is a sort of homage to both mag and cinema. Its story has most of the required elements: two students visiting an isolated country house get drawn into a strange whirlpool of sex, sadism and mystery that ends in a triumph of *amour fou*.

Jean-Pierre **MOCKY** (Jean Mokiejewski; 1929) Actor, writer, director, novelist. A real outsider in the French film industry. He began his career as a child actor, studied law for a year, and then took up acting full time in the late 1940's before moving on to direct with **Les dragueurs** in 1959. Mocky has always dealt with odd and difficult subjects in an often odd and difficult way. His films, which have rarely been shown outside France, include **La grande frousse**—taken from the story by Jean Ray—and **L'ibis rouge**, another version of Fredric Brown's *Screaming Mimi*. Also to add to the list of his achievements (?) is the first 'official' scene of penetration in a French film, in 1973's **L'ombre d'une chance**. Outside France he is probably best known for his brief appearance in Godard's **Prénom Carmen** (1983) where he runs along a corridor shouting "Is there a Frenchman in the house?"—which was also the title of his 1982 feature. Extraordinarily, he was planning a film to star Benny Hill, before the comedian's death put paid to what would have been one of the oddest teams in film history.

Paul **NASCHY** (1934) One of the most important figures of the Spanish horror boom. Under his real name of Jacinto Molina and his other pseudonym David Molva he has written and directed a long series of exploitation films as well as acting in many films as Naschy. Before he started in cinema, Naschy's career followed a bewildering variety of twists and turns. Legend has it that he studied Engineering and Architecture, worked as an illustrator and record cover designer, wrote pulp novels and was a professional weight lifter! He caught the film bug whilst working as an extra on Nick Ray's **King of Kings** in the early 1960's. His first important film was 1967's **La marca del hombre lobo**. The American distributor had already pre-sold it as a Frankenstein film under the name of **Frankenstein's Bloody Terror**, so when he saw that it was actually a werewolf story he added a confused pre-credits sequence that explains (?) how the Frankenstein family had picked up the name Wolfenstein. Naschy wrote the script for the film, which was originally intended to star Lon Chaney Jr. Chaney didn't want to film in Europe, and so the producers suggested Naschy for the role. When the script was presented to the censors, they objected to the

idea of a Spanish werewolf. Naschy changed the nationality of the monster, and became the Polish werewolf, Waldemar Daninsky. He went on to play the character in another twelve films. His best incarnation of Daninsky is in 1970's **Werewolf versus the Vampire Woman**, the film that really kicked off the Spanish horror boom. It's hard to explain Naschy's appeal as an actor. In many ways he's wooden and unconvincing, and his lumbering presence inspires pity rather than terror. Perhaps that's his secret. We feel sympathy for his plight. In many ways he's a sort of lycanthropic James Dean, reaching out his hairy hand for us to grasp onto and tell him everything's alright. In the late 1970's, in the period called 'destape' (stripping off), Naschy's films—like just about everyone else's in Spain—took on a sexy tinge that he seemed even less suited to than he did to horror. Films like **El transexual** and **Madrid al desnudo** were probably the low points of his career. But Paul Naschy is nothing if not a survivor, and he bounced back with a couple of Japanese co-productions (**The Beast and the Magic Sword** and **The Last Kamikaze** in 1983). He directed his last important horror film in 1987—**The Howl of the Devil**, which starred Caroline Munro and Howard **VERNON**. In this one Naschy pretty well exhausted his stable of characters, playing Mr. Hyde, Quasimodo, the Frankenstein

**paul naschy · sara lezana · blanca estrada silvia aguilar · david rocha**
**EL CAMINANTE**
eastmancolor  director jacinto molina  fotografia alejandro ulloa
musica angel arteaga  guion eduarda targioni  jacinto molina
director de produccion enrique jiménez

▲ Max Pécas's **I Am a Nymphomaniac** (1971)

Monster and the Phantom of the Opera. With the industry in one of its low troughs, Naschy hasn't worked for a while, but he shouldn't be written off. As Fu Manchu always says, "The world will hear from me again".

Amando de OSSORIO (1925). Has worked as a journalist and produced radio drama as well as studying painting and photography. Began in films as a writer and assistant director in the 1940's after moving to Madrid. He began by making shorts and industrial documentaries. His first full length feature, **La bandera negra**, was an experimental film that ran into trouble with the censors. He was the first Spanish director to make use of the scope format. In the mid 1960's he made a clutch of paella westerns and then, with **Malenka** in 1968, began to specialise in horror films. He is best known for the four films featuring the undead Knights Templar—**Tombs of the Blind Dead, The Return of the Evil Dead, Night of the Seagulls** and **Ghost Ships of the Blind Dead**. All his films have touches of the surreal and show a real sense of the pictorial unusual in commercial cinema. He

now makes his living as a painter of weird and macabre scenes including many of the ghostly Templars.

Max PÉCAS (1925) A veteran of the business, often mentioned along with Bénazéraf as a pioneer of the sex film industry, which is to overlook their immense differences as film-makers. Pécas began in 1959 with the thriller **From Woman to Woman (Le cercle vicieux)**, but soon moved into the arena of the 'quality' erotic film with **La baie du désir** in 1964 after having worked with Bénazéraf on **L'eternité pour nous** in 1961. He formed his own production company, Les Films du Griffon, in 1963. In **Je suis une nymphomane (Night Pleasures**; 1970), uptight Sandra Julien falls down an empty liftshaft and wakes up in hospital to discover that she has become a sex-crazed nymphet. Thrown out of house and home she moves to Paris, where she is seduced by wicked Janine REYNAUD and smooth Michel LEMOINE. Eventually the Church and the love of a good man bring her back to her senses. Set in luxurious backgrounds: châteaux, the sunny beaches of the south of France and so on, Pécas's films all reinforce the bourgeois values that Bénazéraf questions with every film.

However, he managed to steer clear of hardcore—apart from **Men...I Eat Them (Les mille et une perversions de Felicia)** and **Clockwork Nympho (Luxure)**, both made in 1975. Following the institution of the so-called 'X-law' in France he returned to sexy (softcore) comedies and, in 1984, one of his biggest successes the violent thriller **Brigade des mœurs** (Vice Squad).

Claude PIERSON (1932). French writer-director. He had a role very early on in his career in **L'assommoir**, directed by Gaston Roudes. He entered the business full-time by the conventional route of assistant director, director of shorts and then on to fully fledged features with **Days of Desire (Ils sont nus** later **Elles sont nues)**, a Canadian co-production, in 1966. His most famous film is his 1971 version of **Justine**, starring Alice ARNO. More faithful to the original book than Franco's 1969 film it was banned in France for 18 months and only released finally in a badly cut version. Pierson's intentions—to present an honest view of de Sade—were honourable, but the resulting film fell between too many stools to be an unqualified success. Pierson went on to direct, under the pseudonyms Paul Martin, Andrée Marchand

and Caroline Joyce, a series of hard and soft sex films, often co-written and directed with his French Canadian wife, Huguette Boisvert. Some of them—such as **La marquise porno** (1976), **La fille à la fourrure** (**Porno Zombies**; 1977) and **Perverse Desires** (1984)—continued to show his fascination with the world of the *'fantastique'*.

PSEUDONYMS. Why do so many of the directors of these films use pseudonyms? There are two main reasons, and these subdivide into lots of little ones. The two main ones are (a) personal pride and (b) official reasons. Under (a) are directors like Claude Mulot (Frédéric Lansac), Serge Korber (John Thomas) and Jean-Claude Roy (Patrick Aubin). They either had, or wanted to have, legitimate careers and didn't want their buck-earning duties in the hardcore area to prejudice their chances of mainstream success. To an extent the same thing was true of some actors and actresses. Seems more difficult given the highly visible nature of the evidence against them, but they were probably banking on the fact that no-one important either went to see, or would admit seeing, hardcore films. Under (b) are directors like Jess Franco who needed pseudonyms to be able to work in certain countries that imposed quotas on foreign directors, or levied heavy taxes against imported films. Sometimes the companies he worked for would already have various pseudonyms registered under which a variety of directors would work. This is true of Eurociné, with names like James Gartner and Dan Simon being assigned to several directors, and not always Franco. Other directors, like Rollin, use pseudonyms on projects that they don't feel able to put any personal touch on and don't want to mislead their fans into seeing. It never works, because people always find out. One of the best pseudonyms is Burd Tranbaree, which is an anagram (almost) of the director's real name Claude Bernard-Aubert. Under this name he had been a very respectable post-new wave director in the early sixties, making films about racism and the horrors of war.

Janine REYNAUD (1930) Henri Rode said of her in *Les Stars du Cinema Érotique*: 'You couldn't mistake her for anyone else. What is she? A Circe, a Medusa with emerald eyes, a smouldering mouth, a shock of red hair imbued with a mysterious life.' She began as a model for designer Jean Patou, and in 1967 starred in four films produced in Germany by Adrian Hoven's Aquila Film Enterprises (three of them directed by Jess Franco— **Sadisterotika**, **Necronomicon**, **Küss mich, monster**) where she met her husband-to-be, Michel LEMOINE. The pair worked in several films together over the next ten years, including PÉCAS's **Je suis une nymphomane** (1970) and, in 1971, Bénazéraf's **Frustration** (also co-scripted by Lemoine). Janine Reynaud retired from the business in the mid 1970's and now lives in America.

Pierre B REINHARDT. One of the most prolific of the third wave of French sex-film makers. Still actively at work in the genre, shooting mostly direct to video. His claim to fame is 1982's **Le pensionnat des petites salopes**, the only French hardcore shot in 3D. He has also dabbled in horror with **La revanche des mortes vivantes** in 1986, one of a handful of recent French horror films, that also includes **Devil's Story** (1986) and a couple of films from Norbert Moutier, publisher of *Monster Bis* magazine: **Ogroff/Mad Mutilator**(1982) and **Trepanator** (1990), which featured Jean Rollin as a mad doctor.

Patty SHEPARD (1945) She was born in the USA, in South Carolina, and moved to Spain when she was eighteen. She began to work as a model and appeared in a successful series of TV adverts, which quickly made her a star. Her first film roles were in small parts, beginning with **La ciudad no es para mi** (The City is Not For Me) in 1965. She became a popular fixture in many paella westerns and thrillers from the late 1960's and through into the seventies when the horror boom began. Her most famous role is probably that of the vampiric Countess Wandesa in León Klimovsky's **Werewolf versus The Vampire Woman** in 1970. KLIMOVSKY is convinced that she could easily have become as famous as Barbara Steele, and she certainly has elements of Steele's unearthly presence in many of her horror roles. Unfortunately, again like Barbara Steele, she didn't really approve of the roles she was asked to play and never followed up her initial promise. She went into semi retirement during the 1980's and her last roles to date, in 1987, were again in horror films—including **Rest in Pieces** from José Larraz and Juan Piquer's gruesome **Slugs**.

Pamela STANFORD (Monique Delauney; 1946). In spite of her pseudonym and the English accent she affects on screen, Pamela is as French as ripe camembert. Henri Rode describes her as having 'the charm of a rogue angel', which just about gets it right. Her best role is in Franco's **Lorna, l'exorciste**, where she plays the evil Lorna Green with a conviction and intensity that lifts the film into another dimension. She was a star of Parisian erotic cabaret shows (Theatre des Saints-Innocents) as well as many films, including **Hard Love**, **Special Train for Hitler** and **Paris porno**. Howard VERNON, who worked with her in **Lorna**, said in 1976 that she had "the makings of a fabulous actress."

Monica SWINN (1948). Born in Belgium, she began to act at University in Brussels. Her first films were experimental shorts, including two with Roland Lethem, who also worked with Jean-Pierre BOUYXOU. Through this connection she got a small part in Rollin's Belgian co-production of **Les démoniaques** in 1973. This led to larger parts in several Franco films, including **The Bare-Breasted Countess** (in a torture scene cut from most prints). Her chameleon-like appearance (she seems to look different from one role to the next) assured her a lot of work in the Europrodis/EUROCINÉ area of quick, cheap, sexy, B-films in the 1970's. However, her strong political views ("sex-films don't give people the desire to liberate themselves sexually, because they show sexual freedom as something unreachable") put her on a different plane from many of her contemporaries. Her most memorable role is probably as the terrifying, monocle-wearing, lesbian wardress in Franco's 1975 film **Caged Women**.

Jack TAYLOR. Has had several name changes; he was born as George Brown Randall, but adopted the name Grek Martin for the first stage of his acting career. During the early fifties he appeared in the **Jack Benny Show** with Marilyn Monroe, and also had parts in the TV series **Sheena, Queen of the Jungle** and **Adventures of Captain Grief**. After this he did theatrical work in Mexico, which led to parts in Mexican horror movies such as **Neutron contra Dr. Caronte**(1960).

During his brief stay there he worked with two of Mexico's finest horror directors, Frederico Curiel and Alphonso Corona Blake. He moved to Spain in the early sixties and had a small part in the big budget **Cleopatra** (1963). He changed his name to Jack Taylor and became a supporting actor in films by León KLIMOVSKY, Amando DE OSSORIO, Jess Franco and José Larraz. During the seventies' boom he was a familiar face in European sex-horror movies, including **Dr Jekyll versus the Wolfman** (1971), **Ghost Ships of the Blind Dead** (1974), **The Vengeance of the Mummy** (1973) and **The Night of the Sorcerers** (1974). In 1982 he had a small part in John Milius's **Conan the Barbarian** and during the eighties he appeared in a host of low budget films, including **Serpiente de Mar** (1984), **Panther Squad** (1985) with Sybil Danning, **The Angel of Death** (1986), **Rest in Pieces**, **The Edge of the Axe** and **The Return of the Musketeers** (1989). Taylor is best known for his work with Jess Franco and has appeared in many Franco films, including **Necronomicon** (1967), **Count Dracula, De Sade 70** (both 1969), **Sex Charade** (1970), **The Bare Breasted Countess** (1973), **Der ruf der blonde Göttin** and **Swedish Nympho Slaves** (both 1977).

**Norbert TERRY** (1924). French-American, studied at Columbia University before coming to live in France. A self-confessed fan of Jacques Tati and owner of the rights to *Clochemerle* and *Krapp's Last Tape*, Terry began by making straightforward, if humorous, heterosexual fare, such as a version of the old chestnut *Charley's Aunt*—released in the UK as **The Sexy Dozen** (1969). He imported a gay sex film from the US and was astonished by its success. He then began to make his own gay films (**Hommes entre eux** etc) and then bought a cinema to show them in. Now he produces, writes, directs and distributes his own product. In 1965 he played the part of Kelly in **What's New, Pussycat?**

**John THOMAS** (Serge Korber; 1936). His career began prestigiously enough with highly regarded shorts during the 1960's and in 1973 his **Les feux de la chandeleur** was France's official Cannes entry. He entered the hardcore arena when work dried up in the mid 1970's. His name entered history when his 1975 film **L'essayeuse** was selected as a test case by a combined group of morally outraged citizens who were looking for something 'without any artistic quality or intellectual alibi'. **L'essayeuse** fitted the bill perfectly. An action committee, which included the French Scout Association and even organisations representing the deaf and the blind, went on the attack and the film was condemned to be burned in a public place. The affair marked the end of the 'golden age' of French X films, and Korber pretty soon went back to legitimate productions, suitably chastened.

**Harry Alan TOWERS** Born in London on 19th of October 1920, Harry Alan Towers studied at the Italia Conti stage school before becoming a scriptwriter at the age of 19. He served in the RAF during the Second World War, and when it was over set up his own company, Towers of London and produced radio shows, including a series with Orson Welles. In 1955 he moved to television, producing early TV series including **The Scarlet Pimpernel** and **Dial 999**. In 1961 he was arrested in the US, allegedly for running a call-girl racket, and his address book was confiscated by the police. Undaunted, Towers jumped bail and began to produce films while on the run, skipping from country to country. Many of these were adventure films, written under the name Peter Welbeck. His descent into exploitation and horror began with the **Face of Fu Manchu** (1965) directed by Don Sharp. In 1967 he teamed up with Jess Franco, producing a mixed bag of goodies including **Kiss and Kill** (actually another Fu Manchu film), the superb **Girl from Rio**, **99 Women**, **Venus in Furs**, **Justine**, **Der Hexentoter von Blackmoor**, **El conde Dracula** and **Eugenie**. All the Franco films were produced while Harry was still on the run. Many of them featured his wife, the luscious Maria Röhm. In 1973 he settled in Canada, and during the 1970's he produced more adventure films. In 1981 he gave himself up to the authorities and the charges against him were dropped after he paid a fine of $4,200 for jumping bail. Since then he's turned out more adventure, exploitation and horror films, including **Gor** (1985), **Edge of Sanity** (1989), **Howling IV** (1989) and Robert Englund's version of Gaston LEROUX's *Phantom of the Opera*. He still lives in Canada, and produces most of his films in South Africa. As Jess Franco remarks—"so he can write the script during the long plane flight."

Camille Clovis TROUILLE (1889-1975) French surrealist painter. One of the best kept secrets of twentieth century art. Intensely personal and highly erotic, his paintings are a unique record of the internal life of one man. He was brought up in a conventional middle class family in Amiens, in northern France. He studied for five years at the local School of Fine Arts, acquiring a mastery of all the classical techniques of painting. His early works were all portraits and still life. Then he was conscripted into the army and spent five years at war. The experience changed his life for ever. After the war he started reading Lautréamont, Sade and Rimbaud. He became virulently anti-clerical and anti-militarist. In 1930, his fiercely radical *Remembrance* was shown at an exhibition of revolutionary art. This brought him into contact with the surrealists. Although he remained in touch with them, his love for the old masters of painting and his independent spirit kept him from joining the movement outright. Trouille was never a professional painter. For forty years he worked for a Paris firm that made shop window dummies. This income allowed him the freedom to paint exactly what he wanted, free of the dictates of the art establishment. It wasn't until 1963 that he had his first one man show in Paris. The paintings were so blasphemous and explosive, that entry to the galley was by invitation only. Trouille's paintings are like collages, constructed out of his own obsessions and highly personal memories of the past. One of the constant features of them is his love for cinema. The figure of Nosferatu, rising out of his coffin, the dead Marilyn Monroe, and figures that he recalls from the old pre-war Paris music halls are combined in his paintings in an intense, hallucinatory style. The colours are saturated and the humour is as black as can be. Jean Rollin is a huge admirer of Trouille's work and references to him abound in films like **Requiem for a vampire** and **La vampire nue**. The name of Ken Tynan's 1968 stage extravaganza *Oh! Calcutta!* is derived from a Clovis Trouille painting. In French the title is a slang phrase for "What a lovely arse you've got!"

Roger VADIM (Vladimir Plemiannikof; 1928) Screenwriter, novelist and director. He is now best known as the husband, or lover, of various famous women—Brigitte Bardot, Jane Fonda, Catherine Deneuve etc—an

▲ **Blood and Roses** (1961), Roger Vadim's underrated version of the classic vampire story *Carmilla*

image he has fostered in books and interviews in recent years. A shame, as it puts into the shade his real achievements as a film-maker of some style and originality. He entered the business after the war as a scriptwriter and assistant to the director Marc Allegret. He met the 17 year old Bardot in 1952, after she had failed a screentest for Allegret, and married her soon after, becoming her mentor. She was already well established by the time she starred in Vadim's first film as director—**And God Created Woman** in 1957. Vadim was an inspiration, although not often mentioned, to the burgeoning French 'new wave' of Godard, Truffaut and co. This was more to do with his age and his iconoclastic intentions than with the kind of films he made—although several of them have lasted as well as those of his more illustrious contemporaries. He was always interested in decor and pictorial images as much as in action and character, and for that reason his

best films—**Blood and Roses**, **Barbarella**, **Charlotte**—are like glossy, animated photo albums. He has a strong interest in the fantastic as well as the erotic, which is shown at its best in his section of the compendium film **Tales of Mystery** (1968). Vadim was always slightly ahead of the crowd; his 1962 film **Vice and Virtue** was inspired by the Marquis de Sade, and he filmed **Dangerous Liaisons** in 1960—well before Hollywood's belated rediscovery of the story. Critics always complained that Vadim went in cycles, remaking the same series of films. Lately he's been at it again with a dire US remake of **And God Created Woman** in 1987 with Rebecca de Mornay. As much as PÉCAS or Bénazéraf, Vadim was responsible for the look and style of the French erotic cinema of the 1960's. Ironically the most savage criticism of him came from Bénazéraf who said that "Vadim always films himself: the men in his films are weak, without any drive, with a sluggish attitude to life. There

is always a castle in his films, and a Ferrari. That's his world. He managed to worm his way in there even though he was he was born penniless. He's a snob."

Howard **VERNON** (Mario Lippert). Born 15/7/14 in Baden to an American mother and a Swiss father. He spent his early years in the USA, returning to Europe to finish school. First at Nice then Berne. Initially intended for the hotel trade, he worked in Egypt, then went to live in Zurich where he met Erwin Kaiser who inspired him with the idea of becoming an actor. In 1939 he moved to Paris, where he earned his living as a tap dancer, performing at the famous Casino de Paris and Le Palace, with stars like Josephine Baker. During the war he survived by giving dancing lessons. In 1945 he was employed as an English language broadcaster on programmes intended for the USA. He made his film debut in **Un ami viendra ce soir**, a film about the resistance. Many roles followed. He came to specialise, much to his distaste, in parts as a German officer. In 1947 he played his most famous role as Werner von Ebrenac in **Silence de la mer** by Jean-Pierre Melville. Over the years Howard Vernon has worked with many of the greats of world cinema, including Orson Welles, Rita Hayworth, Errol Flynn, Sacha Guitry, Michael Powell and Eddie Constantine. However, he never really came into his own until he met up with Fritz Lang in 1960 for **Die tausend Augen des Doktor Mabuse**. In 1961 he made his first film with Jess Franco, **Gritos en la noche**, in which he played the part of Dr. Orlof—a role he was to repeat several times over the next 25 years. Later work, with, amongst others, Woody Allen, Godard and Borowczyk has tended to be overshadowed by the enormous number of parts he has played for Franco—more than 35 films to date. Recently Howard Vernon has worked increasingly for younger film-makers, who are attracted to his uniquely expressive face and are not put off by his 'marginal' reputation. A terrific raconteur, highly cultured, and a true film lover, Howard Vernon is undoubtedly one of the treasures of European cinema and deserves to be celebrated.

**Daniel J. WHITE**. Composer. His ancestors were Scottish, and he spent many years of his childhood in West Yorkshire, near the moors. His family moved to Paris, and young Daniel was expected to enter the family textile business. Fortunately for him the company went bust and he was able to pursue his musical interests. During the war he worked as an interpreter with the British army and was nearly killed during the evacuation of Dunkirk. Sitting in his car with the bullets flying around him, he says that he realised then how much of his life he had wasted at silly parties, trying to impress people. He vowed that from then on it would be just himself and his music. After the war he played piano in nightclubs and cabarets and composed his first soundtrack in 1947. He wrote the jingles for many adverts during the 1950's—including spots for Polo and Kit-E-Kat that were shown on British commercial TV. He first worked with Jess Franco on **Le sadique Baron von Klaus** in 1962, and went on to write the music for all of Franco's Eurociné pics as well as working for the likes of Pierre CHEVALIER and León KLIMOVSKY. Daniel White's screen credits number more than 160 titles. He has also made many records under a wide variety of pseudonyms—including comedy records as Emile Doryphore (it means Colorado Beetle in French), rock records as Guy Forlaine and organ music as Virginie Morgane. Like Franco he works very fast, recording 12 tracks for an LP in a day. His favourite composers are Ravel and Debussy and his best tunes combine their French romanticism with a spooky melancholia, very reminiscent of the desolate moors where he was brought up. He loves to compose for the human voice and one of his most effective pieces is the wordless vocal that opens Franco's **Bare-Breasted Countess**, and recurs in several other Franco films. Daniel White has also acted in some Franco films—usually as a police inspector. During Franco's frantic early seventies' period in Portugal, Daniel White worked with him as production assistant and general factotum, effectively becoming his right hand man.

**Ajita WILSON** (1951-1987). Actress. Born in Michigan of an American father and a Brazilian mother. Her first starring role was in **La principessa nuda** in 1975 with Tina Aumont. The film was based on the story of Elizabeth Bagayen, ex consort of Idi Amin, whom he tried to discredit by publishing nude pictures of on the front pages of Ugandan newspapers. Ajita quickly became one of the more exotic stars of European sex cinema, including roles in **Apocalisse sexualis** directed by Carlos Aured, **Gola profonda nera (Black Deep Throat/Queen of Sex)**, **Black Aphrodite** and two films for Franco, **Sadomania** and **Macumba sexual**. She attempted a second career as singer and nightclub performer in Italy. In 1982 she was arrested by police in Florence following a raid on a brothel. After being chased, naked, through the streets she took refuge in a church. Newspapers reported that as she was hustled onto a Rome bound train, wearing only a police jacket, she waved to a crowd of male admirers, telling them: "Ciao, see you soon boys!" She died in Rome in 1987 of a cerebral haemorrhage. Strong rumours persist that she was a transsexual.

**Andrzej ZULAWSKI** (1940). Polish born novelist, screenwriter and director. His father was a famous screenwriter in Poland and sent young Andrzej off to Paris to study film-making in the late 1950's. Returning to Poland, he worked as an assistant to the prestigious Andrzej Wajda (**Kanal, Ashes and Diamonds**). He made his first films as a director in Poland, but it was **L'important c'est d'aimer** (The Important Thing is to Love), made in France in 1974, that first gave him a name. The film still packs a punch today. It's an intense portrait of a group of losers and obsessives and Klaus KINSKI gives one of his best ever performances in it. Zulawski's breakthrough into the international market came with **Possession** in 1980. The film stars Isabelle Adjani, and features her giving birth to a hideous, tentacled monster. Zulawski says "I only want to film stories which have something excessive about them." On account of its excesses, **Possession** was briefly banned in the UK as a 'video nasty'. Although it's his most famous film, he's made much better ones. **L'important c'est d'aimer** and **La femme publique** are two of his best. Zulawski's films are intense, highly theatrical, and often exhausting, as his restless camera chases after the action. Although highly regarded by French critics, his films are not to everyone's taste. *Variety* said that he 'confuses hysteria with style'.

Extra material by Mark Ashworth.

# Comic Book Heroes

## THE EUROPEAN ADULT COMIC

In France, following the end of the second world war, there was a huge hunger for imported, largely American, material—both films and comics. The lack of available product caused by the war led to a glut of imports. Books 'translated from the American' became hot items. So much so that some writers—for example Boris Vian with his 'Vernon Sullivan' books—passed off their own work as translations. The tough, violent style of American films became hugely popular as did their crime and horror comics.

Eventually this lead to a backlash. Boris Vian's book *I'll Spit on Your Graves* was prosecuted for obscenity and in 1949 a law was passed—ostensibly to protect the young—that banned certain types of books and comics and, more importantly, limited the importing of foreign material to a fixed percentage of published work. This had the effect of boosting the production of home-grown material as well as effectively isolating the national industry from the influence of the American strips.

The erotic element in these post war European comics was always subtle. It was not until the end of the 1950's that some of the less popular papers (*Paris-Flirt* for example) began to emphasise these elements in an attempt to attract a readership.

This particular gauntlet was picked up by the publisher of the weekly - later to become quarterly - magazine *V*. Gallet was himself a fan of the fantastic and the erotic and was, most importantly, a friend of many of the comic artists. He allowed them more freedom than they would have found in either

▲ *Kriminal* from Magnus and Bunker

the dailies or the more popular publications. Slipping almost unnoticed past the censor, *V* magazine's quarterly appearance gave it a unique position as a platform for experimentation with new forms and ideas.

*Barbarella*, by Jean-Claude Forest, first appeared in the spring of 1962 and was soon the object of much impassioned debate. Its appearance was timely for a number of reasons. For one thing the comic form was being taken seriously for the first time—not in a critical, proscriptive sense as had happened in US and UK during the fifties. It was being examined as a serious form of artistic expression. Intellectuals were discussing comics—there was a notion of an aesthetic of the form—good and bad were being identified and defined. The Club des Amis de la Bande Dessinée was formed in France in 1962 and the first comic conventions took place in 1965 and 1966 (in Bordighera and Lucca, Italy).

And then again—Barbarella was a woman. Not only that, she was the first really liberated woman to be cast in the role of

heroine in a comic strip. Juliet Jones and Jane may well have been 'liberated' in their own way and according to the codes of the 1940's and -50's, but Barbarella was her own woman. She called the shots. Taking pleasure where she found it and responsibility for her own actions. Most importantly, the moral distance introduced by having the strip set in the faraway vastness of space gave Forest much greater latitude than he would have had with earthbound stories.

The success of *Barbarella* was immense and it soon came to the attention of the Paris-based Belgian publisher Eric Losfeld.

Losfeld was not a fan of the comics, unlike Gallet. But he was interested in pushing against the barriers of taste and saw immense possibilities in the more provocative aspects of *Barbarella* and her ilk. In 1964 he published the first large format collection of the strips. These books were luxurious productions compared to the cheaper publications that had been around before.

▼ Guido Crepax's 1960's classic, *Belinda*

Hardbacks, aimed at an adult audience, and selling for high prices, they were quite a new phenomenon and attracted comment in exactly the way Losfeld had hoped. Perhaps he was too successful in stirring up controversy. *Barbarella* was banned on its first appearance and had to be republished later in a diluted form.

He was not to be deterred and soon *Scarlett Dream*—again appearing first in *V* magazine—followed *Barbarella* into hard covers. Losfeld began to build up an extensive library of titles, selling largely through mail order. Artists from other countries were soon attracted to his stable—from Italy, Guido Crepax with *Valentina* and from Germany, *Phoebe Zeitgeist*. Both titles were extremely daring for their time with a mixture of S&M and eroticism. Young French artists also beat a path to Losfeld's ever open door and he discovered Philippe Druillet—now one of the grand masters of the French bande dessinée—publishing his first book *The Adventures of Lone Sloane* in 1967.

Not to be outdone, some of the old comics hands were also at work, benefiting from the new freedom that the 'adult' label permitted. Foremost among them was Paul Cuvelier who had been publishing since 1946. His *Epoxy* turned out to be Losfeld's most successful title.

However, by the beginning of the seventies the energy had begun to run out of the new medium. Many of the more influential young artists had moved on—Devil, Druillet, Paelaart etc.—to other forms of art. But the influence of Losfeld and co. was immense. Long running publications like *Pilote* began to adapt to the new freedoms and new magazines like *Charlie* picked up the gauntlet. The doors had been opened and things would never be the same again.

Prior to the appearance of the large format, hard cover books of Losfeld came the smaller, pocket sized *fumetti*, originating in Italy. Mostly aimed at a young audience they were hugely popular, with many titles being imported into France and appearing in local editions.

In the winter of 1962 the first *fumetti per adulti* ('for adults') was published. The creation of two Milanese sisters, it told the story of a criminal genius, Diabolik, master of disguise, and the man whose mission it was to track him down—the long suffering Inspector Ginko. Diabolik was a version of

the Fantômas type of character—amoral rather than immoral—but with considerably less of the aristocratic sadism that Allain and Souvestre's hero had shown.

Sex was minimal in the *Diabolik* strips, and eroticism muted, but even so they created a huge new adult audience. Inevitably, many imitators followed. *Kriminal*, from the prolific Magnus and Bunker team, was the first. In his black and yellow skeleton suit and bone-white skull mask, Kriminal presented a much more formidable spectacle than Diabolik. His exploits, too, were much closer to the Fantômas model. His adventures were inspired as much by his endless taste for danger as his need for financial reward, and were run through with a dark and devilish sense of humour.

The term *fumetti neri* ('black') was coined to describe the new-style comic books. Secret agent strips—*Goldrake*, *Goldboy* and *Agente SS10*; crime strips—*Genius* and *Gangster Story*; space strips — *Gesebal* and *Uranella* (a derivative of Barbarella) and even photostrips, like the ultra sadistic *Killing*, were published. Each successive strip pushed the boundaries of what was acceptable; but always within closely observed rules: no genitals or outright nudity, for example.

A precursor of what was, in the seventies, to explode the boundaries of taste in the *fumetti* came with the publication in 1966 of *Isabelle*. Loosely based on the exploits of Angélique, the heroine created in the 1950's by the French writers Serge and Anne Golon, *Isabelle* was the first fumetti in which sex was as important as the story itself. Created by Alessandro Angiolini who had been active in comics since the fifties, *Isabelle* was set in a recognisable but highly fictionalised past. Real characters were featured—Cardinal Richelieu and Vlad Dracul, for example—but the stories also included all the trappings of the old-style Gothic tales of terror; heavy doses of black magic, troupes of wandering gypsies, ruined castles with dank dungeons, swashbuckling sword fights, as well as heavy doses of graphic torture. Their success was immense, and led to a host of imitators.

Renzo Barbieri, publisher of *Isabelle*, led the way with *Jolanda*, which was soon followed by *La corsara nera*, *Ilona la valkira*, *Teodora*, *Saffo* and *Angelica* from a variety of rival publishing houses. One of the most popular of the *Isabelle* derived strips was

*Maghella*, drawn originally by Leone Frollo who is now one of the greats of the Italian erotic comic world. With her enormous breasts, cute pony-tails and permanently wide-eyed expression, Maghella was like a female Candide. All of the above were complete story books in serial form. Slightly different were the erotic fairy story series *Sexy favole* and *Fiabe proibite* which contained several complete stories in the same loosely 'historical' context with a fair smattering of black humour. There were even sexy versions of Snow White (*Biancaneve*) and Little Red Riding Hood (*Cappucetto Rosso*).

At the beginning of the eighties the publishing house Sud-Roma brought out a series of 15 monthly magazines of a slightly larger format than the standard fumetti (16/23 cms) and sold for a higher price—1000 lira. In the same way that Losfeld's *Barbarella* and *Scarlett Dream* albums had changed the face of the French BD, so these titles (*La vedova nera*, *Vampira*, *Pussycat*, etc) bought a new and much harder sexual content into the Italian fumetti. Although not always great in visual terms, the extreme content of the strips gave them a swift and ready market.

Of course the publishers of the old-style pocket fumetti were not to be outdone and they took up the challenge, allowing the artists of their existing series to push things much

▼ Belzeba—daughter of Satan!

▲ Maghella

further. Many of these new strips were contemporary stories, based on current events or news items (*Attualita nera*, *Attualita gialla*, *Attualita proibita*), but the traditional crime, historical and horror elements were also featured.

These strips quickly descended (or evolved, depending on the point of view) into out and out hardcore. Later versions such as *Zora la vampira* and in particular *Lady Domina* went just about as far as it was possible to go with the most astonishing and inventive range of Krafft Ebbing inspired scenes. Isabelle's creator Alessandro Angiolini returned to the fray with *Belzeba: figlia del peccato* (Daughter of Sin).Once more we are back in the world of lascivious priests, huge-bosomed and strangely willing virgins, demonic torturers and decadent noblemen familiar from *Isabelle*; but with one crucial difference. Belzeba has a penis as well as a vagina. Angiolini's draughtsmanship here is of a much higher order than in his earlier work, and the strip is definitely one of the strangest and most extreme of the new-style fumetti; paradoxically perhaps, it is also one of the funniest.

Eventually, by the mid-eighties, there were over a hundred different titles available every fortnight. An astonishing publishing phenomenon.

Few of this later generation of strips were imported into France. Even *Isabelle* herself had been censored there. But in Spain, during the period of total freedom following the death of Franco, there was a new surge of interest in all things formerly forbidden. The local publishing house, Tiburon—using the shark symbol that had been the mark of Edifummeto—began to reprint many of the Italian strips of the eighties, such as *Zora*, *Lady Domina* and Leone Frollo's *Casino* series. There were also home grown strips and a burgeoning 'underground' scene led by magazines like *El vibora*.

In Spain, as in Italy towards the end of the eighties, the adult comic market began to edge closer to the straight porn market, with photographic material and ads for sex toys and videos appearing alongside the strips. Edifummeto in Italy were the first in this market with *Risotissime*, but many others followed suit with titles such as *Shock*, *Drive*, *Flash* and *Zip* appearing. Attempts to publish this type of mixed mag in France has met with little success. In Italy and Spain, however, the two types appear side by side

The influence of the comics on film-makers has been profound in two major ways. Firstly, there have been the various film versions of popular comic series.

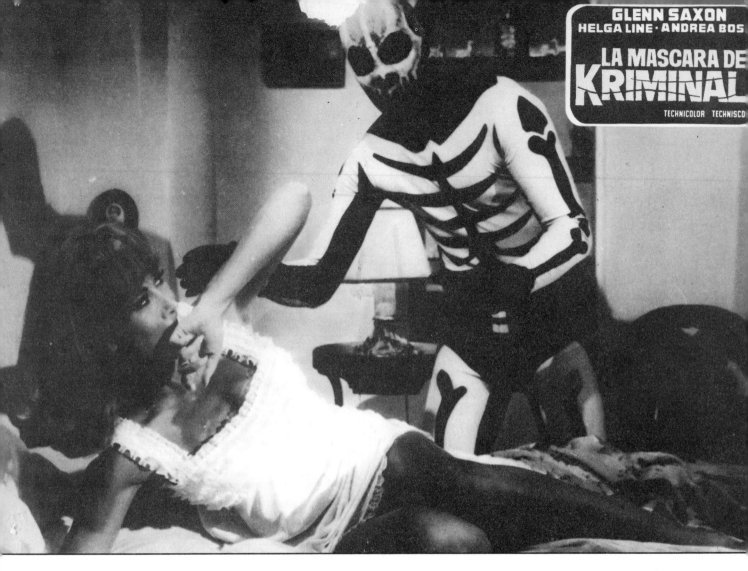

GLENN SAXON
HELGA LINE · ANDREA BOS
LA MASCARA DE
KRIMINAL
TECHNICOLOR TECHNISCO

▲ **Kriminal**

Everyone knows the many versions of *Superman* and *Batman*—appearing as cartoons and TV serials as well as features—but there have been many other films based on European comic characters including **Barbarella**, **Diabolik**, **Kriminal**, **Isabelle**, and **Satanik**. Guido Crepax's Valentina has appeared in a feature film (**Baba Yaga**) as well as an Italian TV series. Then there are the films based around characters who seem as though they ought to have come from comics; these include **Argoman**, **Goldface** and **Mister X**. The comic adaptations have been of variable success, both commercially and artistically, but more profound has been the influence of the style and grammar of comics on a wide range of film-makers.

Several of the directors featured in this book have served stints as writers or artists on strips - Larraz and Rollin have been mentioned earlier. Others, Jess Franco and Alain Robbe-Grillet in particular, have often spoken

of the influence that comics have had on the way they construct their films. Franco's **Lucky the Inscrutable** is a sort of homage to the comic form and is constructed as an imaginary strip based around secret agent Lucky. At various points he addresses the unseen artist who is drawing him and suggests ideas for the progress of the story. **Necronomicon** has a strong affinity with Crepax's work—notably *Valentina*—and in **Los Blues de la calle Pop** Franco attempted to make a film that even looked like a comic strip.

Finally there have been photo-novel versions of many crime and horror films—including **Necronomicon**— which brings the influence full-circle.

During the late seventies and early eighties in France several of the leading lights of the bande dessinée began to work directly in films. Martin Veyron made the sex comedy **L'amour propre** (1985) based on his own strip, and Milo Manara filmed **Le déclic** as well as working with Fellini and Borowczyk. The Belgrade-born Enki Bilal managed to

import his uniquely dark vision, first to Michael Mann's **The Keep** (1983) and the metaphysical thriller **The Name of the Rose,** before directing an adaption of his own strip, the moody **Bunker Palace Hotel** in 1989.

This overt reference to the comic form has allowed many film-makers to escape the demands of a rigid, logical plot development and freed their visual imagination. This has allowed them to tap into a rich and vibrant vein of popular culture where style, movement, glamour and a delight in the possibilities of the amoral are the bare bones of the form, not merely the icing on the cake as with so much 'respectable' cinema.

# Bibliography

## BOOKS

Amour, érotisme et cinéma
Ado Kyrou

Aurum Film Encyclopaedia★
ed Phil Hardy

Borowczyk: Cineaste onirique
Collection La Vue

La censure cinématographique
Philippe J. Maarek

Cine español 1951-1975. ★
A.A. Perez Gomez and J.L.
Martinez Montalban

El cine español—Cine de sub-
generos ★

El cine español en el banquillo

Cinéma érotique ★
ed Jacques Zimmer

Le cinéma fait sa pub
Jacques Zimmer

Il cinema Italiano degli anni 60
Lino Michce

Dark Romance
David J. Hogan

De Mai 68...aux films X
Philippe J. Maarek

Dictionnaire du cinéma
ed Jean Loup Passek

Diva Cinema, 1951-65

Doing Rude Things
David McGillivray

L'écran de l'amour ★
Martine Boyer

Die Edgar Wallace Filme
Florian Pauer

Entre deux censures★
François Jouffa & Tony Crawley

The Erotic Dream Machine
A.N. Fragola & Roch C. Smith

Erotica for the Millions
O. Brusendorf & P. Hennigsen

Erotisme et cinéma
Daniel Serceau

L'érotisme au cinéma
J.M. Lo Duca

Es War Ein Rauschende Ballnacht
Geza von Cziffra

Fant'Italia ★
Guiseppe Lippi & Lorenzo Codelli

Le fantastique au cinéma
Michel Laclos

Germany on Film
Hans Gunther Pflaum

Die Geschichte des Erotischen Film
Bernd Schulz

Ghosts in the Mirror
Alain Robbe-Grillet

Histoire d'X
Yves Rousset Rouard

The International Film Industry
Anthony Slide

José Bénazéraf ★
Paul Hervé Mathis

Love is a Feast
Sylvia Bourdon

Lust und Elend: Das erotische Kino
Karola Gramann etc

Les maledictions du cinéma français
Francis Courtade

Le masochisme au cinéma
Jean Streff

Moi, la scandaleuse
Brigitte Lahaie

900 cinéastes français
ed René Pradel

Original Skin
Gillian Hanson

The Oxford Companion to Film
ed Liz-Anne Bawden

Passion and Defiance
Mira Liehm

Petite histoire de l'érotisme dans
le BD
Henri Filipini

Pioniere und Prominente des
Modernen Sexfilms★
Rolf Thissen/Leo Phelix

Reference Guide to Fantastic Films★
Walt Lee

The Seal of Dracula
Barrie Patterson

Sex vampire de Jean Rollin
Ado Kyrou

Le sexe à l'écran dans les années 80
Gérard Lenne

The Shadow and Its Shadow
Paul Hammond

Spaghetti Westerns
Christopher Frayling

Les stars du cinéma érotique
Henri Rode

Le surréalisme au cinéma★
Ado Kyrou

Les triomphes de la bande dessinée
J.M Lo Duca

The Vampire Cinema
David Pirie

Vampyres
Tim Greaves

Walerian Borowczyk
Valerio Caprara

West German Cinema Since 1945
Richard and Maria Helt

## MAGAZINES AND JOURNALS

Cahiers du cinéma
Cinéma
Cinéma d'aujourd'hui
CinémAction No 59 ★
Continental Film Review
Ciné Choc
Ciné Girl
Ciné Zine Zone ★
Cinema Blue
Cinématographe
Dark Side
Dezine No 4 ★
Dirigido Por
Ecran
Eroscore
El erotism en el ciné
Film Français
Fusion Fantasy No 3 ★
Hollywood Reporter
Image et Son
Midi-Minuit Fantastique ★
Monster Bis
Monthly Film Bulletin
Nostalgie
Positif
Screen International
Psychotronic
Shock Express
Segnocinema
Splatting Image
Star Ciné Video
Sex Stars System
Terror Fantastic
Time Out
Ungawa!
Vampir
Vampirella
Variety
X Films

★ = Essential

# Index

Numbers in bold indicate illustrations. fn refers to footnote. + indicates reference continues over following pages.

## INDEX OF TITLES

## INDEX OF NAMES